PENGUIN BOOKS

Net Worth

David Cruise and Alison Griffiths are writers
whose work has won them four national writing awards. Their acclaimed and bestselling
books include *Fleecing the Lamb* and *Lords of
the Line*.

Cruise and Griffiths live on the Gorge in
Victoria, B.C. with their two daughters.

NET WORTH

Exploding the Myths of Pro Hockey

DAVID CRUISE & ALISON GRIFFITHS

Penguin Books

PENGUIN BOOKS
Published by the Penguin Group
Penguin Books Canada Ltd, 10 Alcorn Avenue, Toronto,
Ontario, Canada M4V 3B2
Penguin Books Ltd, 27 Wrights Lane, London W8 5TZ,
England
Penguin Books USA Inc., 375 Hudson Street, New York,
New York 10014, U.S.A.
Penguin Books Australia Ltd, Ringwood, Victoria, Australia
Penguin Books (NZ) Ltd, 182-190 Wairau Road,
Auckland 10, New Zealand

Penguin Books Ltd, Registered Offices: Harmondsworth,
Middlesex, England

First Published in Viking by Penguin Books Canada
Limited, 1991

Published in Penguin Books, 1992

1 3 5 7 9 10 8 6 4 2

Manufactured in Canada

· Canadian Cataloguing in Publication Data
Cruise, David, 1950-
Net worth: exploding the myth of hockey

Includes bibliographical references and index.
ISBN 0-14-012921-9

1. National Hockey League—History
I. Griffiths, Alison, 1953-   . II. Title.

GV847.8.N3C78 1992   796.962'06   C91-094343-5

Contents

Chapter 1

For the Good of the Game

The Ramada Inn squats in the bleak and busy intersection of Toronto's highways 401 and 400—in the middle of nowhere but on the way to everywhere. It's an ordinary hotel, designed for doing business as quickly as possible and then moving on. Eye-tiring Spanish-style carpet, dark wood and fluorescent lights do not encourage lingering. Conventioneers wearing *"Hello my name is _____, I'm from _____"* tags march purposefully from workshop to seminar, arms laden with material.

The lobby makes a passing attempt at cosiness with a small grouping of chairs stuffed into a dim alcove outside the bar. During an afternoon of steady traffic, no one tarries except a dishevelled salesman whose display case has popped open and disgorged its load of laminate samples. He sinks down wearily, laboriously repacks the case, adjusts his sagging executive socks and, with a practised flick of two fingers, fires a Tums into his mouth.

He's preparing to leave when his head snaps around and he gapes at the front desk. The salesman has spotted a familiar body. From behind, the round head, vaguely blond hair, meaty shoulders, muscular buttocks and thick thighs have changed little in twenty-five years. He cranes his neck for a better angle, then frantically burrows through his case for paper and pen.

Jumping up, he tips over his case, mutters "Shit!" and sprints to the desk. But the figure, like an apparition, has disappeared, and the stolid clerks glance up in surprise at the salesman's rush to the counter. Sheepish, he feigns nonchalance, jams his notebook in his jacket, glances ostentatiously around as if searching for a friend and then wanders back to his scattered bits of laminate.

A waitress in the adjacent cafeteria isn't quite so cool. "Did you see him? Did you see him?" she shrieks to a friend. "Yeah, sure I did. And *I* saw him before you, too," the other woman crows, pointing to a napkin. On it is a loopy signature in green felt pen, bleeding at the edges —*Bobby Hull.*

Oddly, there is no hockey-related promotion here this night. The Golden Jet isn't selling bull semen or endorsing a product. Nor is there a Hall of Fame dinner, a celebrity roast, a testimonial or a charity fundraiser. Yet Hull is followed into the lobby by many of hockey's greatest stars: Gordie Howe, Red Kelly, Johnny Bower, Frank Mahovlich and, most surprising of all, Bobby Orr, who has almost completely divorced himself from the game.

When retired players gather, they're young again. The old-time banter and camaraderie is quickly rekindled in favourite taunts and profane jests. But on this chilly December night in 1990, the atmosphere is muted, almost sombre. The players go through their rituals— laughing, punching shoulders, slapping backs and swearing—but an air of edgy anticipation envelopes them.

Gordie Howe, his narrow, elastic face set in a permanent half-smile, is most at home when in, around or near anything to do with the game. But tonight he looks slightly furtive as he approaches the front desk. "Hurry up Gordie, hurry up Gordie," chides his wife Colleen. Howe stops for a minute and casts his eye around, as if expecting someone unpleasant to accost him. Two players in the bar off the lobby trot over to say hello. For a minute all is well. Howe shakes himself like a large puppy and grins at them. "Gee, I'm kinda tired, I just played three games this weekend." The players laugh and make rude remarks about grandfathers and trusses.

Sixty-seven retired players eventually converge on the Ramada Inn. Most were active in the '50s, '60s and '70s, but one of them, former Canadien Glen Harmon, dates back to 1942. The only hint of their purpose is the brief notation on the hotel event board: "NHL Alumni/ Trafalgar Room."

Aside from the miasma of tension hovering in the air, another incongruent note in this gathering is the presence of twenty-six wives and girlfriends. Hockey wives are the most invisible of people: the TV cameras rarely pick them out at games, their names almost never appear in the newspapers, and few show up at old-timers' games or get-togethers after their husbands retire.

But tonight is different. Several of the wives have been instrumental in organizing this meeting, and many have insisted that their reluctant husbands attend. They look businesslike, serious and determined. "The women are much tougher and meaner than we are," observes one of the players. "I'm glad they're here."

Even more jarring, especially to those who know him well, is the presence of former Leafs player Carl Brewer. Bald and still powerful-looking, though slightly portly, he moves among the clusters of players outside the meeting room like a practised host, shaking hands and greeting newcomers. It quickly becomes apparent that this is his show and, for the moment at least, he is the leader.

Brewer's idiosyncratic ways have frequently brought him into the limelight, but he's never sought to be the focal point of any cause. One of the very few genuine free spirits in a sport that ruthlessly culls them, Brewer has often been out of step with his peers. At a 1989 old-timers' dinner in Toronto, he arrived late, long after the several hundred other retired players had quaffed a few pints each. The large hall swam in grey, black and navy blue. Discreet ties cinched every neck. Brewer, head shaven, strode in encased in a pair of jeans so tight ex-Maple Leaf Bob Goldham mused admiringly, "If I tried to get into those pants I'd be singing soprano after one step." Clad in a green sweater (no shirt, no tie), Brewer refused a seat and, while everyone else hunkered down over slabs of roast beef, he leaned against the bar by himself, like a curious bystander.

Hidden behind Brewer's enigmatic façade is a deep "don't tread on me" streak. He guards his telephone number with the fanatical secrecy that a Swiss bank does the identity of its clients. He appears to make a good living, though no one has the faintest idea what he does. Most of all, he doesn't like people poking their noses into his business. "Nobody knows what I'm doing or thinking, and that's just the way I like it," he emphasizes. Yet it's Carl Brewer's initiative, and $25,000 of his and long-time companion Susan Foster's money, that is leading these players into action.

As the players and women slowly file into the room and find chairs, Brewer fidgets near the podium. He starts slightly, as if suddenly realizing everyone is waiting for him to begin. He walks forward and smiles, looking for a moment like a well-fed cherub in his wildly multi-coloured sweater.

Overlooking a sea of broken noses and dental plates, Brewer barks a nervous cough. "It's amazing that we have some of the greatest hockey players ever in this room," he says haltingly. A respectful, self-congratulatory silence is broken when Eddie Shack lumbers to his feet, turns to the crowd and takes a deep bow. The players erupt in wild, tension-releasing laughter. Brewer gestures to the walking proboscis. "I really consider tonight a success when I see Shackie here in a suit when he could be out selling Christmas trees."

Brewer knows better than anyone that this isn't a night for laughs. This is a night for confronting the enemy—the National Hockey League, NHL President John Ziegler, the National Hockey League Players' Association (the NHLPA, their own quasi-union led by Alan Eagleson) and, most especially, themselves.

Hockey players' timidity, indecision and lack of solidarity over many decades has cost them more than $100 million in lost pension benefits, salaries, medical benefits, endorsements and missed business opportunities. Their inaction has had a lot to do with their reluctance to harm the game they love. It is an attitude the owners understand implicitly and have capitalized on again and again.

No sport has controlled its athletes as effortlessly and totally as hockey. Though fabulously profitable over the long term, the NHL has always been able to convince the players—in good times or bad—that the clubs couldn't afford the salaries, benefits and working conditions they demanded, and that if they persisted, the players would kill the sport.

But those days are over. Ninety-three men and women have travelled here, some from as far away as Florida and California, because they are convinced that they've been had by the NHL. This common feeling unites them, but, even so, there is an undercurrent of suspicion. Those present feel betrayed by the NHL, the Players' Association and even their already existing alumni association, set up in the early 1980s to look after the rights and concerns of retired players. They aren't quite sure who to trust.

Several players speculate openly about spies from the League and the NHLPA. "It could be anybody. Maybe Al [Eagleson] sent Bobby," laughs one, jabbing his finger at Bobby Orr, sitting quietly in the very back row. It's an absurd suggestion, since Orr and Eagleson parted bitterly in 1980. Still, all are convinced that at least one player here will report back to Alan Eagleson, and that Alan Eagleson will report to John Ziegler.

Right on cue, a young man rushes in just before the meeting with an armload of papers and thrusts it at Eddie Shack. Shack leaps comically to one side: "Hey, hey, I don't want that! It looks important. Give it to that guy." The young man wheels around and thrusts his bundle at Edmonton lawyer and player agent Rich Winter. Winter takes the material, glances at it quickly and smiles sardonically. Dated that day, it is addressed to "All Retired

Players of the NHL" and signed R. Alan Eagleson, executive director of the NHLPA.

One of the players wanders over, glances at the signature, repeats it aloud and states, "I sure hope he comes tonight, because if he does, we're going to beat the living shit out of him!" A murmur of agreement flutters through the crowd.

This meeting, the hundreds of hours that he's spent on the phone and the thousands of dollars spent on lawyers, represents a personal exorcism for Carl Brewer. It was Brewer who brought Alan Eagleson to national attention way back in 1965, when he shocked the hockey world by abruptly quitting the Toronto Maple Leafs. The team, having won three Stanley Cups in a row, was at its peak, and Brewer, twenty-six, in his prime as a player.

Brewer promptly enrolled at the University of Toronto and, with the help of his lawyer and close friend Alan Eagleson, successfully waged a battle to regain his amateur status in order to play for Father David Bauer's Canadian national hockey team. For Eagleson the fracas greatly increased his profile in the hockey world and set him on the path to the formation of the NHLPA, the basis for his wealth and power.

Carl Brewer has come to see Eagleson's presence in hockey as something less than beneficial. In the car on the way to the Ramada Inn, Susan Foster asked pointedly, "Did you ever expect that this man you brought into hockey would become this monster creation?"

At the core of the players' anger is the NHL pension plan. Since it was introduced by Clarence Campbell in 1947, the players have believed that whatever improvements in salaries, working conditions and benefits they forfeited would be offset by their pension—touted first by Campbell, then Eagleson, and then Ziegler as the best in professional sport.

For more than thirty years, many players—including Gordie Howe and Bobby Hull—have hesitantly asked questions about their wretched pensions. The response retired goalie Glenn Hall got from the Pension Society in 1988 began "Dear Contributor #413" and answered not a single one of his questions.

Many of the players at the Ramada tonight were around in 1957 when Ted Lindsay of Detroit and Doug Harvey of Montreal formed the first, ill-fated players' association. The NHL owners, led by Toronto's Conn Smythe, ruthlessly smashed the association, ruining many careers and embittering many players. The main purpose for that association was to find out how their pension plan operated and how the funds were invested. Thirty-four years later, the same questions remain unanswered.

Red Kelly and Gordie Howe had a lot to do with the 1957 failure. Under tremendous pressure from Red Wings general manager Jack Adams and owner Bruce Norris, they dealt the players' association its death-blow by leading the Detroit team in withdrawing from it.

Kelly—former member of Parliament, Hall of Fame member and eight-time All-Star player—is an honourable man, and what he did was for the best of reasons. Although most players, in their hearts know that not one of them would have responded differently, some still blame him for what happened in 1957.

Gordie Howe holds a special place in hockey. There's no one in the room who doesn't smile when he is around. Yet Howe is answerable to these players for more than the events of 1957. Gordie Howe's contract negotiations were probably the simplest in the history of sport. (His salary was so low it served as a cap on other players' contracts for nearly two decades.)

Each year during training camp, the Red Wings' GM, Jack Adams, would offer Howe a completed contract, with only the salary left blank: "Just fill in what you're worth, Gord." Every year, regardless of his growing list of records and awards, Howe dutifully added a mere $1,000 annual raise. Adams, never deigning to look at the contract, would utter some variation of "You're a good fella, Gord," clap him on the back and, if he were in a particularly expansive mood, take him out to lunch. Adams always warned Howe to keep his salary secret. "It would make the other players jealous," he said, with a conspiratorial wink.

For his part, Gordie Howe trusted Adams and owner Bruce Norris to look after him. "I'd always had an agreement with the Red Wings that, because I was one of the best players in the game, I'd always be the highest paid player of the team—in fact, the highest in the league."

A lesser man than Howe would have been jolted in 1966 when Bobby Orr, a raw rookie, signed with the Bruins for a widely publicized $25,000 annual salary and $25,000 bonus. After nineteen years in the game, Howe had only worked himself up to $27,500, including bonuses. Bruce Norris, who had taken over the signing ritual from Jack Adams, soothed Howe by telling him that the press reports were vastly exaggerated. Even so, he jumped Howe's salary by $10,000.

When Bob Baun was traded to Detroit in 1968, one of the first things he did was set Howe straight. "You've held us back for ten years and perhaps longer," he told a surprised Howe. "Some of the older fellows would probably say you'd held the league back twenty-five years. You set the standard and we all have to live by it and it's from you not negotiating properly. If that's what you think you're worth, then you put a very low price on your ability."

Nonplussed, Howe asked how much Baun thought he was making. When Baun guessed within $500 of his $45,000 salary, Howe was dumbfounded. And when Baun revealed his own $67,000 annual contract, the great number 9 simply gaped in amazement.

Pointing a finger like a bulging bratwurst at the legend before him, Baun asked, "Mr. Norris just gives you a signed contract and tells you to fill in the figures, is that right?"

"Yes," agreed Howe.

"Well, Gord, you're luckier than the rest of us. If you thought more of yourself, you'd get what you're worth. Why don't you try, this year, filling in $150,000 and see what he does?" challenged Baun.

That year, an angry Howe negotiated his 1969 contract with Bruce Norris over the phone. He had considered demanding $150,000, but at the last minute backed off and asked for $100,000, still expecting the sky to fall. Norris, annoyed at being pushed into a corner by his formerly docile star, agreed, but added snidely, "I hope that makes Colleen happy."*

What neither player knew was that Baun's old defense partner, Carl Brewer, had just signed with Detroit for $126,000. Nor did they know that the club had netted $1 million annually on hockey operations since 1946, plus another $1 million running the rink, making it one of the most lucrative sport franchises of the time.

The NHL has never understood the value of looking after its greatest assets, the players, both past and present. It has always had difficulty comprehending the tangible and intangible benefits that accrue when athletes are content, and it has consistently failed to realize how much retired players can do for the game.

Gordie Howe, the most shabbily treated superstar in sport, is the most obvious example. Good-hearted to the core, Howe willingly takes on many small promotions and goodwill appearances at fundraising events that lesser players would sneer at. Through his unaffected greetings and conversation, he has cheered more little boys' hearts—in large and small bodies—than any other player. The NHL often refers to Howe as hockey's ambassador. In truth it treats him little better than a water boy.

In 1987, for instance, Howe was invited by the League to attend Rendez-Vous '87, a two-game showcase series between Soviet and NHL stars held in Quebec City. In return for numerous scheduled appearances and autograph sessions, all to promote the NHL, the League offered to pay Howe expenses plus $100. He and Colleen attended the events and carried out their obligations, but whatever enjoyment they might have felt soured when they learned that arch-rival Maurice Richard was being paid several thousand dollars to attend, and that non-hockey

---

* Colleen Howe is a favourite target of criticism in hockey. She asks questions loudly, demands answers incessantly and runs the Howe hockey enterprises with a firm hand. But in those days, she knew little more about the underside of the game than Howe. Still, Norris assumed it was she who had put Howe up to demanding more money.

celebrities Gary Carter, Wilt Chamberlain, Nancy Greene-Raine and Pele were each paid $5,000 to put in brief appearances.

After twenty-six years in the NHL, the ambassador of hockey receives a pension of less than $13,000 annually. In comparison, a low-level officer in the Canadian military who started at the same time and had the same years of service would be drawing nearly $27,000. For a basketball player, it would be between $30,000 and $35,000, and a baseball player would draw over $42,000.

Another irony of this night, and a mark of the division in the player ranks, is the absence of Bob Baun. The All-Star Toronto defenseman stood up to management in a thousand small ways during his career and again in retirement. Like Brewer, Baun was a close friend of Alan Eagleson's and was instrumental in setting up the NHLPA. But Baun no longer sees Eagleson as the players' saviour.

Baun was one of the first players to become convinced that the munificence of the NHL pension plan was a lie, and one of the first to try to do something about it. In the early '80s, Baun, as determined and immovable off the ice as he was on, spent over $100,000 of his own money to form an NHL alumni association. He wanted to discover why, after sixteen years and 964 games, his pension amounted to only $7,622 a year. "It's a scandal, a criminal scandal," Toronto actuary Lorraine Mahoney told him. Years later, having fought obfuscation, misdirection and stonewalling, he reluctantly gave up.

"I wanted to see whether those boys are putting their money where their mouths are," Baun said of his absence. "They wouldn't spend a nickel to see the Pope go down Yonge Street on a white horse. They wouldn't stick together when I started this alumni association. I was looking for support from within ourselves. We had some of the best pension people advising us, but the players said, 'What's in it for Baun?'"

Since Alan Eagleson became head of the NHLPA in 1967, virtually all of the significant advances he has negotiated for players have been tied to the pension plan.

The players' associations in football, basketball and baseball have all won major concessions or improvements in the areas of free agency, television revenue, grievance procedures or profit-sharing. In hockey, the NHLPA has willingly shelved these crucial issues or traded them away for pension plan gains.

The pension plan came under indirect attack again in 1989 when a group of players, led by hockey agents Rich Winter and Ron Salcer and former head of the NFL players' association Ed Garvey, tried to unseat Alan Eagleson as head of the NHLPA. It wasn't until Mark Zigler, a lawyer and pension expert hired by Carl Brewer, began to turn the doubts and questions about the pension into hard numbers that the players realized how small were the gains and how large the losses.

Zigler dug deeply into the reluctantly proffered pension plan documents and, in September 1990, produced a shocking, five-page preliminary report containing more specific information about the pension plan than the players had been able to glean in thirty-five years. He discovered two major problems.

A surplus of $25 million was sitting in the fund.* Though it had been created by interest earned on the retired players' contributions, only a small percentage had been earmarked to improve those players' benefits.

The plan's members, the players, had never known about the surplus—and for good reason, as it turns out. NHL Pension Society documents and collective-bargaining agreements from 1967 to 1983 clearly state that surplus funds can be allocated *only* to benefit the plan's members. But the owners have used over $13 million to reduce their own required contributions to the plan be-

---

* A surplus is defined as money that is not needed to service the plan's current or future commitments. Actuaries tend to be conservative when estimating what pension funds will earn over a given number of years. In the case of the NHL, the pension's earning estimates were extremely low, around 4 or 5 percent, while the money was actually earning twice that or more. Actuaries normally reevaluate their figures tri-annually to bring them in line with current earnings. But, according to the NHL Pension Plan Society, actuaries have *never* done a formal reevaluation of the plan's investments.

tween 1980 and 1989—in pension circles, this is quaintly called a "contribution holiday."

Only $4.6 million of the $25 million was used to increase the pensions of retired players.* Coincidentally, that increase occurred right around the time that Bob Baun was investigating the fund.

The second problem was more complex. It appeared that money that should have gone into the fund from profits on international hockey might never have made it there.

International hockey has long been trumpeted as the great "cash cow" of the sport, pouring millions into the pension plan. A decade after the seminal 1972 Russia/Canada Series, more than a few players were wondering just whose cash cow it was. "There are some things that have bothered me about that series," its hero, Phil Esposito, remarked in 1982. "I've always wondered where all the money it made went, and I never really have found out."

Eagleson retorted that nearly $4 million went from the NHLPA's international hockey account into the pension plan between 1972 and 1982. But, spread over the '72 Series, the '76 and '80 Canada Cups, the '79 Challenge Cup and two Soviet tours in North America, it seems a small amount from six supposedly lucrative events.

Even so, Mark Zigler couldn't find that money. "The current collective agreement indicates that the Association is obligated to contribute one-fourth of the contributions to the Pension Plan from the proceeds from international hockey," he wrote. "However, the records of the Pension Plan filed with the Pension Commission of Ontario and the financial statements of the Fund do not indicate *any kind of contribution* ever made by the Players' Association to the Pension Fund or the Pension Society. To date there is no explanation for this in any of the documents."†

---

* In Brewer's case, his pension, after 12 years and 604 NHL games, increased from $6,237.48 to $7,781.88 annually.

† Later financial information indicated that the NHLPA provided approximately $2.1 million for the pension plan and $2.5 million for an employee benefit plan.

Because only contributions from players and owners are permitted, according to the NHL Pension Society, the Players' Association presumably paid the money over to the NHL, or the twenty-one member clubs, which then deposited it in the pension plan. But the Pension Society has been strangely reluctant to identify where the various deposits have come from, so it is virtually impossible to verify the NHLPA's claim.

Perhaps the biggest bombshell was inadvertently dropped by secretary-treasurer of the NHL Pension Society, Ken Sawyer himself, in a letter to Mark Zigler. "All-Star game proceeds are not contributed to the Pension Society. Rather, such proceeds are used to pay a portion of pension administration costs incurred by the plan sponsors [the twenty-one NHL clubs]." In many ways, that was the nastiest blow of all to the retired players. The annual All-Star game had been a tradition since then, and though the players were never paid for their appearances, they believed that a substantial portion of the proceeds from each game had been going into their pension plan since 1947.

When Zigler precisely and clinically outlines his findings to the assembled men and women at the Ramada Inn, anger, disbelief, shock and indignation rise from the group like a mushroom cloud. "After all those years . . ." the normally composed and cheerful Andra Kelly mutters, shaking her head.

Bobby Hull is more blunt. "Eagleson," he growls, holding one thumb aloft. "The NHL," he adds, gesturing at his rear end before bending over and ramming his thumb, with a loud grunt, toward his buttocks.

After three hours of presentations, comments and discussions, no doubt remains that the players have to do something. The only question is what. Their first and best attack lies in a lawsuit to claim the surplus funds. The second might be legal action to demand a complete accounting of the international hockey money that supposedly flowed through the NHLPA and into the pension fund.

Even Frank Mahovlich, among the most cautious of

those present, nods in agreement to cries of "Let's do it!"
and "Let's get on with it!" But the players have a problem—money. Such action could take years and cost thousands of dollars. "Let's not spin our wheels," urge Hull
and Howe with one voice. "We have to know what to
say and how to say it and get this thing going." Bobby
Orr, silent and watchful in his seat at the back of the
room, nods vigorously.

Several players suggest boycotting the Heroes of
Hockey old-timers' game, scheduled for January 18, 1991,
the day before the regular All-Star game in Chicago. The
stadium is already sold out and the NHL has signed a
$2.5-million deal with Coca-Cola for sponsorship.

As the plan takes shape, and it slowly dawns on the
players that they are on the brink of dramatic, irrevocable
action, the atmosphere in the room changes. Uncertainty
stiffens many faces, even though only six present have
been invited to play in Chicago. A murmuring undertone
becomes apparent, foot shuffling increases, and the players don't seem quite as comfortable in their chairs.

The players are feeling tremors of the fear that has
been with them throughout their careers. They are afraid
of looking greedy; they fear Alan Eagleson's renowned
vengeance; they fear the wrath of the League; and they
fear looking bad in front of the fans. Most of all, however, they are afraid of losing a piece of themselves. Carl
Brewer addresses this directly: "No matter what, they
can't take the game away from us." Everyone nods, but
many don't believe. "It's tough for them," sympathizes
Norma Shack. "For a lot of them this [the All-Star game] is
their big outing of the year."

The players come by their fear honestly. From the moment they begin their ascent up the ladder to a berth on
an NHL team, they know one thing for certain. They
know it from personal observation, they know it from
legend, and they know it as a kind of osmosis. The NHL
ruthlessly excises malcontents.

Three earlier rebellions led up to the 1957 Lindsay
and Harvey uprising. In 1910, the National Hockey
Association, precursor to the NHL, crushed a proposed

union headed by Art Ross, a fiery, pigheaded rabble-rouser who thought nothing about initiating a fight *before* a game, just to warm up. The league imposed a salary ceiling of $5,000 a season for each team's entire payroll, and vowed to cut any player who didn't agree to the terms.

That made Ross look very bad, since his own salary accounted for more than half of his club's allowable total.

When the governors thoughtfully told the press how much Ross was being paid, the vehement public reaction against him and the other "greedy" players prompted him to write a plaintive letter to the Montreal *Herald*: "While playing hockey the players run the risk, of injury and probably loss of time which is almost bound to affect advancement in business," Ross wrote. "All these things have to be taken into consideration when assessing the value of a professional hockey player. Hockey isn't a gentle pastime. If it were, people wouldn't pay to see it and there wouldn't be any need for salary limits, because there would be no paid players. All the players want is a fair deal." Ross was castigated by the media and public, and the union idea quietly died.

The next insurrection came when the Hamilton Tigers threatened to strike just before the 1925 NHL playoffs. The players had signed contracts for a twenty-four-game season and the League unilaterally increased the schedule to thirty. The players wanted an extra $200 for the six additional games. Utterly refusing to negotiate, league president Frank Calder suspended the entire team for the remainder of the season and the playoffs, even though it held first place. Just in case they didn't get the point, Calder levied a $200 fine on each player for good measure.

In 1946, a group of players began meeting to organize a League-wide pension plan. Newly hired NHL president Clarence Campbell checked this little rebellion in 1947 by taking over the pension plan. In case this group of players didn't get the message, he informed them that "union" members would not be eligible for benefits.

Many of the players at the Ramada Inn remember the

retribution levied after the Lindsay and Harvey uprising in 1957. Their memory of the owners' retaliation has added one more level to the culture of fear in hockey. Fear exists from the day a young player enters the League—fear of injury, fear of embarrassment, fear of being traded, fear of demotion, fear of retirement, fear of punishment, fear of defeat in a fight and fear of the NHL bosses.

Active players tightly compartmentalize their fear, barely acknowledging its existence. They know if it creeps into their consciousness, they're through. When they retire, the fear doesn't entirely go away. Instead, it metamorphoses into a sensory recollection, like the tingling anticipation of impact before a hit. But one fear remains vivid and real—the fear of harming the game.

David Forbes understands this fear. A Los Angeles investment advisor who played six seasons with Boston and Washington, he worried privately before the meeting about how many retired players would support a frontal attack on the NHL. "There are 900 guys out there, and half of them still have their jerseys pinned up over the fireplace," he mused.

As the players refine their All-Star game strategy, the unanimity of moments ago begins to fray slightly. Several suggest, as an alternative, writing a nice letter to John Ziegler, expressing their concerns. Frank Mahovlich brings up the fans. "Yes," chimes in his wife Marie. "If we just don't show up, what happens to them? It isn't going to look very good."

And so it goes, back and forth, finally coming to rest with Bobby Hull. Most of the Chicago fans have bought All-Star game tickets to see the Golden Jet play once again in the stadium he left in 1972 when he joined the World Hockey Association. In their minds, without Hull there really would be no game.

"The Blackhawks! Pah!" Hull spits out. The players' resolve hardens once more.

Eventually, the players decide to demand that a portion of the gate be paid directly to them or they will boycott the game. A group volunteers to direct a fund raising campaign and investigate launching a lawsuit to claim the surplus pension funds.

At midnight, Andy Bathgate, Bobby Orr, Dennis Owchar, Carl Brewer, Allan Stanley, Gordie Howe, David Forbes, Bruce Hood, René Robert, Bobby Hull, Keith McCreary, Ron Wicks, John Miszuk and Fred Stanfield volunteer to form an organizing committee. They congregate around the table to plan their short-term strategy and are joined by Garvey, Winter, Zigler and Alan Dick, Brewer's young lawyer.

Brewer stands to one side as they talk, looking mildly amazed that what he started has gained momentum and a life of its own. The committee shoos everyone else out of the room so they can vote on an approach to take with the All-Star game.

As it nears one o'clock, the ad hoc group prepares to vote on demanding that $50,000 be paid to them from the Heroes of Hockey All-Star game. The room is stifling and the water jugs ran dry hours ago. When the committee began deliberating, Gordie Howe slipped away like a whisper to yarn in the corridor. Colleen pokes her head out the door. "Gordie! Gordie! Get in here, they're voting! The least you can do is come in and vote!" Sheepish, Howe hustles in to cast his yes vote.

The meeting adjourns at 1:30 A.M. The small clutch of remaining players heads for the bar. One asks Orr if he is staying at the hotel. "Are you kidding?" Orr responds. "Stay here?" He waves goodbye and stands fidgeting by the doors, until a cab arrives to take him to tonier accommodations in downtown Toronto. A few players laugh contentedly. Orr always liked the good things in life, and he hated just hanging out. It is comforting to know that some things haven't changed.

In the bar, the lawyers and players sit staring at one another, bemused that something is happening, and wondering how far it will go and how many will join. As they talk, Rich Winter looks through the name-and-address forms every attendee filled out. Suddenly he guffaws, "Look at this, will you look at this!" He waves a sheet of paper.

On it is written the name Shayne Kukulowicz, the son of one of Alan Eagleson's best friends, Aggie Kukulowicz. "Not too subtle," says Alan Dick, with a smirk. Everyone has a moment of satisfaction. They have ruffled Eagleson's feathers enough to prompt him to send a spy—albeit one not well-schooled in the art of subterfuge.

Alan Eagleson's memo to the retired players stated that "the financial statements of the NHLPA have been available for more than twenty years," so David Forbes dropped by the association offices three days later to have a look at them.

The youthful-looking Forbes—lean, wiry and quick-minded—is not encumbered by any rosy vision of the good old days. He is also free of any illusions about Alan Eagleson and the Players' Association. In 1978, while playing with Boston, Forbes was charged with assault after a bench-clearing brawl. When he appealed to the NHLPA for help, Eagleson told him it was not an issue that concerned the association.

This day he got a different reaction. "Dave! Forbsie!" ejaculated Eagleson, bounding out of his office. "Hey, what's this going on with you contacting Ian McDonald [president of Hockey Canada] and running around telling this guy and that guy I won't give you this or that. Every time you've asked me for anything I've always gotten right back to you. When I heard your name attached to Salcer and Winter I was really disappointed, and now that you're involved with them you're turning into a jerk!"

Forbes calmly explained he had come for the information and answers he had a right to as a former player and member of the NHLPA. Eagleson calmed down briefly, but when Forbes mentioned the pension surplus he reddened with anger. "I understand Mark Zigler was saying at your meeting the other night that this surplus belongs to the players. Well it doesn't. It's the owners'. I've retained counsel to look into this and they have assured me that this money is the owners'. However, if someone wants to file a lawsuit maybe they could get it."

"Would you be willing to do that on behalf of the players?" Forbes queried. "No," Eagleson said quickly.

From this conversation, Dave Forbes concluded that Alan Eagleson was unaware that 1967 Pension Society documents clearly state the surplus belongs to the players. "This in itself I found surprising," Forbes later wrote to Brewer. "I mean here I was informing the executive director of the NHLPA about language in the document itself that said surpluses were the players' and he didn't even so much as say, 'Could you get me a copy of that document? I'd like to look into it.' He couldn't care less."

Forbes then ventured into the muddy waters of international hockey. The players' share of revenue has always been expressed as a percentage of net proceeds, and Forbes, as an investment advisor, knew that "net can be just about whatever you want it to be." He asked to look at Hockey Canada's financial statements. "It's none of your business," Eagleson stated, claiming that he was involved in international hockey not as the players' representative but as a board member of Hockey Canada. As such, Forbes had no right to the financial details.

"Alan," Forbes said, "that's really interesting. You were there representing Hockey Canada. Did anyone know you were there and *not* representing the players?" Eagleson simply stared. "I mean, Alan, who was there representing the players if you were there on behalf of Hockey Canada?" Eagleson's stare grew colder.

As Forbes walked out, the question "Who was representing the players?" repeated itself endlessly in his mind.

Before Christmas, the retired players wrote to John Ziegler requesting that $50,000 of the $2.5-million sponsorship deal with Coca-Cola for the old-timers' game be turned over to them. Ziegler told them it wasn't possible adding that his busy schedule would not allow him to meet with them.

On the eve of the All-Star game in Chicago, the retired players had a cause, a plan of action and a growing number of supporters. Money was starting to flow in to relieve Brewer's financial burden, and a few key insiders in the NHL told them confidentially that the League was "very, very worried." What they didn't have was a pledge of support, or even sympathy, from current players.

One of the more pervasive beliefs in professional hockey is that former players are revered. Every rookie has a hero, and every long-standing record that's broken prompts some utterance of respect for the men "who made hockey what it is today." Many insist that hockey is different from other sports in remembering its heritage. But, like so much else to do with the game, it's just a myth.

On January 18, 1991, eleven tense former players, including Brewer, Howe, Hull, Forbes and Ted Lindsay, milled around outside a meeting room in the Chicago Hilton. Inside were the NHLPA executive and player reps. All around the league, whispers had been circulating that Brewer and Co. were out to dismantle the pension plan and strip away the active players' benefits. The veterans were anxious to explain their intentions, provide information to the current players and ask for their support in working toward better pensions for everyone.

Just as the meeting got underway, the veterans tried to enter the room. An uncharacteristically flustered Bob Goodenow, former agent and now NHLPA assistant executive director, waved them out—"Get out of here! You don't belong in here!"—and hustled them back into the corridor. Goodenow returned to the room and the players voted 18 to 16 against allowing their retired brethren in to make a presentation. Goodenow did not explain why, with representatives from only 21 teams, 34 votes were cast and allowed to stand.

Later, a calmer Goodenow promised to meet with the retired players in June. But the damage was done. The current players had pushed aside the very men they held up as icons and heroes. The message was drummed home even more brutally a few weeks later when the Boston Bruins practically ran David Forbes out of the dressing room when he tried to explain his concerns about the pension surplus and the disbursal of international hockey money.

The Heroes of Hockey boycott fizzled. Everyone invited played, except for an obdurante Howe. A slightly sheepish Bobby Hull suited up and played a single shift to the adoring roar of a capacity crowd. "I did it for the fans. The Blackhawk fans are the greatest," he said later, carefully emphasizing *fans* and avoiding any mention of the Blackhawk management or the NHL itself. The retired players failed to get either a penny of the $50,000 they requested or an audience with John Ziegler.

On the surface, it appeared to be just one more rout in a long series of one-sided confrontations between the NHL and its players. But there was a difference this time. Howe's act of defiance seemed to have finally woken up Wayne Gretzky, who has idolized him since boyhood. Gretzky is probably the only man with sufficient stature to influence both the League and the players on behalf of the veterans. "Gordie Howe has told me we all have one thing in common, and that is we will all be retired," Gretzky told a reporter at the All-Star game. "We are going to get it done. Nothing will be swept under the table. It is going to be taken care of."

Gretzky has been well aware of pension issues and the failings of the NHLPA since 1985, yet he's chosen to avoid the controversy. Gretzky's image may be untarnished for the fans and corporations, but a lot of players won't forget his reluctance to get involved when he could have made a difference singlehandedly.

The most recent example came during the 1989 attempt to depose Alan Eagleson as head of the NHLPA. At the showdown in Florida, the players voted on whether to retain him or not. Gretzky, though a member of the NHLPA executive, cited previous engagements and did not attend, instead communicating his vote by phone. Many of the players felt that instead of taking a stand he rode the fence. Regardless of how he voted, they feel that Gretzky should have been more vocal. "He sure ducked that one," a player noted sadly at the time.

Though Brewer's group did not win any quick or easy victories, the retired players convinced the NHL they weren't going away. Typically, the NHL has either crushed organized rebellion or stalled so long that the ringleaders retired or grew discouraged and gave up. When it became clear that there were enough powerful former players behind the pension cause to give it momentum and strength, the League did a startling about-face. Using an intermediary, the NHL made a secret and easily deniable verbal settlement offer of $12.5 million.

The League's sudden and unexpected peace offering backfired. It stiffened the retired players' resolve and started them wondering just how much money was really at stake. The NHL's willingness to settle so quickly, without any real negotiation and before a lawsuit had even been launched, made Brewer's group suspect that $25 million might just be the tip of the iceberg.

What the NHL did not understand was that the retired players were not simply after money: they wanted reform. "No matter who we have gone to for information about our pension plan we have come away with little of substance," David Forbes wrote to John Ziegler. "We've contacted Ken Sawyer at the NHLPS over many years and have come away empty. His view appears to be that the NHL pension plan is his, not ours. For example, after hearing the annual administrative charges to the pension plan were $415,993 in 1987 or 1988, I thought it would be good to call the NHLPS to verify this. I asked Ken if this figure was accurate and, if so, what activities would possibly generate such large fees. He had no real response. . . . I asked if he would provide me financial statements for these plan years and he said he would not. . . . If this is some game we are playing, please, at least tell us what the rules are."

John Ziegler, accustomed to dealing with the docile NHLPA, was not happy. In his tart response to Forbes he wrote, "You have joined your colleague Mr. Brewer in publishing inaccuracies and misstatements, including some which you know are inaccurate. . . . Regrettably, you and your colleagues have chosen the road of threats and attempted boycotts first, rather than that of discussion. Since litigation has been threatened, any further communication will have to come from League counsel."

The high, wide stone wall built by the NHL with assistance from the Pension Society and the NHLPA was, though a substantial obstacle, not the largest one. As it had been at the Ramada Inn in December, the divisions among retired players was their greatest impediment. Not only did they face the opposition of their own Players' Association, but also the differing philosophy of the 700-member National Hockey Alumni Association and its president, Larry Regan.

According to Regan, he has been working on the pension issue since mid-1989, but he has shrouded his efforts with war-like secrecy, refusing to say whether he had been directly negotiating with the NHL, and even refusing to explain what information his research had uncovered. He would only reveal that he was waiting for Ontario premier Bob Rae to come up with a general statement about pension surpluses. "It's a very dicey thing, this pension business, it's a slow process, and I'm not about to say anything to anyone that will jeopardize it." Regan's approach must have pleased the Pension Society, which has always viewed information as a privilege, not a right.

Though Regan purported to be deeply concerned about the players' welfare, he called the investigation into international hockey money—an issue with far larger financial ramifications than just the pension surplus—a "witch hunt."

In the background, hundreds of former players wondered which side, if any, to join. Glenn Hall was pessimistic about the outcome and supported a cautious approach: "Hell, we've been patient for 40 years already. The NHL is probably waiting for us to die anyway." He suspects the players behind Carl Brewer have "an axe to grind" against Alan Eagleson and may be as interested in skewering him as getting increased pension benefits.

Other retired players, not yet committed or actively working against Brewer's group, are convinced the presence of Rich Winter and former NFL players' association head Ed Garvey is hurting their cause. "A pair of fucking hotheads," a former Montreal Canadiens forward pronounced. Others side with Eagleson, who has successfully inculcated the idea that Winter, as an agent, is simply out to get more hockey clients.

Carl Brewer has heard that statement so many times over the past year that he merely shakes his head wearily. He agrees that Winter has the reputation of being a loose cannon and an impetuous irritant. Then he pauses and delivers his next words carefully and softly. "They have no idea how hard and unselfishly he has worked for us. Whatever he gets out of this, if anything, will never compensate for what he has done."

The divisions and uncertainty among the retired players, even those initially supportive of action, have made it difficult for Brewer's group to raise money. A fundraising dinner scheduled for March 27, 1991, and featuring four retired stars was cancelled after two players, including former stalwart Gordie Howe, said they would not attend. Though they were among the first to ante up cash for the cause, the Howes ran hot and cold. One minute they were wholly committed, the next seemingly disgruntled. "They want eighteen things done at once and they want them all done now," moans one of the insiders.

Others were carefully putting a little cushioning distance between themselves and the organizing committee. "I have an association with Hartford so I had to pull back a little bit," Bobby Orr explains quietly. But most of the players were in the twilight zone of fear and indifference.

Norma Shack tries hard not to get aggravated by all the wafflers and cowards. "I've heard so many of them say, 'I hope you get us some more money, but I don't want my name associated with it.'" Then she sighs. "But I guess we have to expect it, hockey has always been that way."

"When it came time to stand up the players just didn't," agrees Bobby Orr resignedly. "Why do you think we're in trouble today? Nobody paid any attention including Bobby Orr. We didn't pay any attention. It was *our* pension and it was *our* association."

But the core group of retired players and women—

Brewer, Susan Foster, Eddie and Norma Shack and
Bobby Hull—pressed on. At the end of April 1991, they
filed suit in the Ontario Court of Justice to recover the
pension surplus. "In round figures, we're talking $40 mil-
lion," Carl Brewer told reporters. "But the actual amount
has to be determined by actuaries. With interest that $40
million could become $60 million or even $100 million."*

The chief irony in the efforts of Brewer, Howe, Hull,
and the rest lies not in what they are doing, but in who
they are. For the most part, they are players who entered
the NHL in an era considered to be hockey's greatest.
The game was run by a handful of men, just enough to
fit around a poker table. These hockey bosses controlled
the destiny of every player on the continent, from the
moment he was out of short pants until the day he died.
It was an age of a purer, more glorious sport, unsullied
by big business and unspoiled by greedy young men encased in plexiglass armour.

At least, that is what most people think.

The concerns of these retired players have welled up
out of a system made possible by a single man, Jim
Norris, a Chicago grain baron. While Norris was responsible for keeping the game alive during the bleak '30s, the
system he set in place, and which was perpetuated by
his sons, sowed the seeds for the confrontation more
than half a century later.

---

* The seven former players filing the suit were Carl Brewer, Andy Bathgate, Bobby
Hull, Allan Stanley, Eddie Shack, Leo Reise and Gordie Howe.

Chapter 2

One Man Rule

Ironically, the man who controlled hockey utterly for decades and set the National Hockey League on its modern course is barely remembered. James E. Norris is afforded little better than footnote status in the NHL's official Hockey Hall of Fame history. His two sons, James Dougan and Bruce, and even his junior partner, Arthur Wirtz, are routinely credited with his accomplishments.

The control Jim Norris exercised over the National Hockey League is unequalled in the history of professional sports. No doubt, the NHL would have continued in some form without him, but three of its teams—the Chicago Blackhawks, Detroit Red Wings and New York Rangers—owe their existence to Norris. And the Boston Bruins, which he didn't own, likely would have folded in the '30s had it not been for the quiet loan Norris gave owner Charles Adams.

A fierce vitality radiated from Jim Norris. Even when he was an old man, few doubted he could square off with anyone if the mood took him. He came by this side of his character honestly, for the Norrises were a clan of hard men. Jim Norris's great-grandfather, also James, was one of the horde of relentless Scots who settled Upper and Lower Canada in the 1830s.*

The family was a Victorian success story, rising in three generations from farming to owning a huge fleet of ships on the Great Lakes, flour mills, roller mills and tracts of land in the Western U.S. By 1898, when Jim's father moved his business south of the border to Chicago, Norris Grain Inc. was one of the largest combined shipping and grain companies on the continent. When his father retired just after the turn of the century thirty-one-year-old James E., usually called "Jim" or "Big Jim," made his first bold decision. In 1909, he took Norris Grain into "the Pit," the cutthroat world of grain trading in the Chicago Board of Trade building. Until then, the company had simply bought and sold grain at par from other brokers; now Norris could indulge in the risky but extremely profitable game of short-selling and trading in futures and options.

At that time, the midwest exchange was notorious worldwide for its orgies of speculation, ruination and fabulous gains. Though the Board of Trade regularly instituted stringent rules, the blatant fraud, thievery and corruption that plagued the exchange before the turn of the century still proliferated.

At six feet, two inches tall, and ranging anywhere from 250 to 300 pounds, Norris thrived in the frenetic Pit. He loved the danger and excitement, and he never backed away from a promising gamble. Conflict exhilarated him. "He loved to argue, he loved to be cross," recalls his daughter Marguerite fondly. Even into his sixties, Norris could still physically dominate the floor. Though he swelled from big to massive in later years, the physique that made him the Chicago Athletic Club squash-racquets champion in middle age served him well during the exhausting hours of shouting, haggling, shoving and intimidating.

---

* Jim Norris's great-grandfather once injured his leg in a logging accident and amputated it himself.

After the Pit closed, Norris often stopped by one of his favourite haunts, the Chicago Boxing Club, set up in the basement of the Board of Trade. There he'd relax, pummel a few bags, slap a few backs, lay down a few bets and generally revel in the sweaty atmosphere.

The Norris companies had always been cash-rich. Though he would have scoffed at the term, Jim believed in horizontal integration—if you owned a shipping firm, you purchased your own goods to ensure that you had a cargo, and so on. Using Norris Grain's ready cash, Jim quietly began buying grain elevators, building up an enormous storage capacity. If he went long on grain futures and the price dropped, he simply stored the grain in his own elevators until the mistake went away. During a time of oversupply, he bought cheaply and held the grain back to force prices up. In essence, he couldn't lose.

Norris hedged his bets further by purchasing large numbers of rail bonds, railways being the best and most inexpensive way to transport grain. The bonds peaked in 1912, and when a recession hit in 1913, many of America's railroads were stuck paying high interest rates on too many bonds. One after another they slid into receivership and bankruptcy, at which point Norris tore up his bonds in exchange for taking over the mortgages that most railroads of the day carried. In this way, he became one of the largest shareholders in the Chicago, Rock Island and Pacific Railroad. He also held a large stake in J.J. Hill's Great Northern Railroad, and many of his grain elevators were strung across its transcontinental route.

Aside from skill and daring, Big Jim had more than his share of plain luck. In 1917 his elevators were brimming with corn, already sold to Germany. When the United States entered World War I on April 6, 1917, all contracts with the enemy were immediately cancelled. It would have meant ruin for most, but because Norris owned the elevators, he was able to wait a few months. Soon the war sent prices skyrocketing, and he sold domestically earning massive profits. Sometimes Norris's luck, or feel for the market, seemed supernatural. He bought a seat on the New York Stock Exchange in January 1929 for $575,000, a record price. In July he sold the seat for $718,000, just before the market crashed.

Norris strode through life with a bull-like arrogance, but his demeanour masked considerable subtlety. When no one was looking, he could slide off with the hush of a snake, negotiate some quiet but monumental deal and reappear in another place entirely, with neither his name nor his fingerprints visible anywhere on the transaction. When Norris wanted something, he had the money and power to kick down the front door to get it. More often than not, however, he'd tiptoe in the back way, snatch it up and be away before anyone realized it was gone.

Though a Chicago celebrity by 1920, and well known in business circles, Norris liked to keep his business to himself. Only the most general outlines of his affairs ever made it into the papers, and he was rarely quoted.

Many of North America's great fortunes were made during the Depression. Norris was rich when it struck and richer when it finished. Throughout the spring and summer of 1929, he ruthlessly sold grain futures short, buying them back for pennies on the dollar when the market crashed to fulfill his short position. By 1935, such tactics had turned Norris Grain into one of the biggest cash grain dealers in the U.S.

Norris worked the bankruptcy courts with the skill of a card-shark hustling an easy mark. In the summer of 1935, the powerful Rosenbaum Grain Corp., with assets of $2 million, succumbed to years of losses and declared insolvency. Norris moved in first with a bid to take over for the corporation, and others, like the giant Cargill Inc. of Minneapolis, soon followed. Rosenbaum tried to fend them off with loans to shore up is crumbling empire, but the Cook County court awarded Norris control. After swallowing Rosenbaum, Norris became the largest cash grain buyer in the world.

Norris bought heavily all through the '30s: thousands of acres of ranch land in Indiana, Florida, Montana; entire forests in New York; the Upper Lakes and St. Lawrence Transportation Co. Ltd.; and any wheat-storage facility

that became available. The family referred to his purchase of vast tracts of land in North and South Dakota as
"the time we bought the Dakotas." Whatever Norris acquired fit into the same pattern. He picked up brokerage
firms for his trading, elevators to store the grain, and
Great Lakes freighters and shares in railroads for shipping it. He bought cattle to eat the grain in bad markets
and land for his growing herds. His Norris Cattle Co.
owned three of the largest ranches in North America. By
the time the Depression was over, Norris ranked among
the richest men in the country, with a net worth of more
than a quarter of a billion dollars.

Sport was Norris's main interest outside of business.
He played a ferocious game of squash and had been a
capable hockey player in his Montreal days. He and his
young son Jimmy regularly attended boxing matches,
football games, baseball games, horse races and tennis
matches. Together they watched an undersized Jack
Dempsey beat Jess Willard in Toledo. They saw the last
game that Notre Dame's George Gipp played, and they
sat a few rows up from the field to watch the Black Sox
throw the 1919 World Series. Like many rich men of the
time, Norris dabbled in boxing and horse racing, but it
wasn't until the mid 1920s that he came to see sport as a
serious investment.

Ironically, a vicious feud with Major Frederick
McLaughlin, the wealthy son of a coffee merchant and a
prominent Chicago citizen, spurred Norris's hockey interest. No one knows the origins of the animosity, but
Norris family members knew it as a fact of life from their
earliest recollections. In newspaper reports, the feud is
written up as a playful affair. In truth, the two men were
out to get each other. Reedy, prune-faced, erect and mili-
tarily brisk, McLaughlin looked as if he had been born
with pursed lips. He considered Norris—big, sloppy and
boisterous, with a voice like a load of gravel being
dumped—to be rude and common.

In 1926, encouraged by Tex Rickard, the colourful hustler, fight promoter, impresario extraordinaire and head
of Madison Square Garden, McLaughlin spearheaded a

group of one hundred prominent locals who raised $120,000 to buy an NHL franchise for Chicago. Pointedly, McLaughlin did not invite Norris to participate. With $150,000 in seed money, the syndicate bought player contracts, mostly from the recently collapsed Western Hockey League.

The National Hockey League, originally an all-Canadian league, had existed since 1917, when it had been formed to force the collapse of the National Hockey Association. The motivating force behind the new league was not a vision for the future but a desperate desire to get rid of the argumentative owner of the Toronto Arenas, Eddie Livingstone. The other team owners were all fractious freebooters, but Livingstone, who'd rather have cut out his tongue than agree with his fellow governors, drove them all to distraction. "Don't get us wrong, Elmer," Sam Lichtenhein of the Montreal Wanderers told sportswriter Elmer Ferguson when the NHL was formed. "We didn't throw Livingstone out; he's still got his franchise in the old National Hockey Association. He has his team, and we wish him well. The only problem is he's playing in a one-team league."*

The number of NHL franchises increased steadily to reach a high of ten in 1928, including five American teams: Chicago, Detroit, Boston and two New York franchises—the Americans and the Rangers. The League, though relatively profitable throughout the '20s, wasn't the only show in town. There was competition from two other leagues—the Pacific Coast Hockey League and the Western Canadian Hockey League—players bargained freely with all three for the best salaries and working conditions. By 1926, however, only the NHL, headquartered in Montreal, was left.

In the spring of 1928, eighteen months after the Blackhawks began playing, Norris applied to the NHL for a second Chicago franchise. He had reached a tentative

---

* Only three franchises were granted—the Ottawa Senators, the Toronto Arenas and the Montreal Canadiens. Toronto was given a franchise on the condition that Livingstone not run it.

agreement to buy the financially ailing Ottawa Senators for $250,000 and move them to Chicago. Major McLaughlin, furious that the Senators had made such a deal without letting him know, quickly vetoed Norris's application. Foolishly, he also taunted his rival publicly, saying that Norris couldn't "put another team in Chicago unless I give my permission, and besides he can't get another team together."

Norris grinned wolfishly and snorted, "Watch me!"

Six weeks later, Norris formed the Chicago Shamrocks, a semi-pro team in the American Hockey Association, referred to as an outlaw league by the NHL. Norris also injected several hundred thousand dollars into the AHA to ensure its stability.

McLaughlin discovered, to his dismay, that Norris had secretly purchased playing dates in the Chicago Coliseum, where the Blackhawks were also playing. But the Major had the satisfaction of knowing his team would soon move into the new $6.8-million Chicago Stadium at the beginning of 1929, and leave the Shamrocks behind. Norris, however, had other plans.

In October, the backers of the new stadium told the League that the venture was nearly bankrupt and the building would not be completed in time. McLaughlin was forced to play for several months in Fort Erie and Windsor because his lease in the Coliseum had expired. The Major didn't realize that Norris was using his influence and money to tilt the playing field.

Behind the scenes, Norris had pressured the Coliseum management to deny the Blackhawks new playing dates. He was also busy making his voice count at the new stadium as well. NHL president Frank Calder and the city of Chicago were frantically searching for a white knight to shore up the stadium's finances until completion. They referred to the man they found only as a wealthy Canadian who came up with a $600,000 immediate bailout and promised to underwrite a percentage of the operating costs. He was, or course, none other than Jim Norris.

The bailout made Norris the primary creditor and gave him tremendous leverage, guaranteeing that his Shamrocks would have priority over the Blackhawks in the grand 16,000-seat facility, the largest in the world. The stadium was finished in February 1929, and McLaughlin, who had managed to renew his Coliseum lease, fumed as his team played in the rickety old building while his rivals revelled in luxury.

The Blackhawks were finally admitted to the new facility before the end of the 1929 season, but on several nights the Shamrocks outdrew them. Norris goosed McLaughlin at every opportunity and in 1932 had the gall to issue a challenge for the Stanley Cup.*

At first, Norris was just having a good time aggravating McLaughlin, but he quickly came to understand something that many modern hockey owners have tumbled to only recently. While hockey teams can be immensely lucrative if run well, the key to real riches is owning the rink itself. In 1927, for instance, Madison Square Garden netted an astronomical $1 million, even though Tex Rickard probably sliced off half again as much through his various scams, which included privately scalping large numbers of his own tickets.†

When Tex Rickard unexpectedly died in 1929, Norris, through nominees, purchased a major piece of Madison Square Garden. At the same time, he carefully monitored the fortunes of Detroit's troubled Olympia Stadium and the city's equally troubled NHL hockey team, the Falcons. The Olympia, built in 1928 for $2.25 million, lost money in four of its first five years. When it declared bankruptcy

---

* The Stanley Cup was originally a challenge cup, and the rules of competing for it were governed by a group of trustees who were independent from the NHL board of governors. The last Team to challenge for the Cup had been the Victoria Cougars in 1926. The Cup's trustees agreed to Norris's challenge in 1932, but the NHL refused to let a League team compete. The matter was postponed for a year, during which time the AHA conveniently folded.

† Rickard's most famous scam was selling 15,000 high-priced "ring-side" seats, that stretched thirty rows back, to the 1921 Carpentier/Dempsey fight.

in 1932, Norris picked up both the stadium and the team for $100,000—in his words, "loose change."

As soon as he bought the Falcons, later renamed the Red Wings, Norris put the Chicago Shamrocks up for sale. There were no takers and both the team and the league folded. The loss of revenue, not incidentally, put added pressure on the troubled Chicago Stadium, which Norris intended to buy when the time was right.

Almost immediately, the sporting press began making unflattering comparisons between McLaughlin and Norris. One writer took issue with the army discipline the major forced on his players. "He seldom speaks to his players and insists that they address their manager as Mister." Norris, on the other hand, was a "democratic" owner who "goes into the dressing room to carry his praise direct to the players, and calls them all by their first names."

McLaughlin discarded coaches like used Kleenex, twelve of them in the team's first ten years. Players would show up for practice and ask their mates, "So, who's coaching us today?" Norris, in contrast, stuck with Jack Adams in Detroit through good times and bad, and was never stingy with the team. In 1933, when the Red Wings beat the Rangers for the first time in seventy-eight games, a joyous Norris paid out fifty-dollar bonuses to each of the players. He once even dispensed a fifty-dollar bonus when Detroit lost. Winning *or* losing, bonuses were an unheard-of extravagance among hockey owners of the time.

Having Norris as a rival owner was bad enough, but the poor Major was appalled when his nemesis swooped in and bought complete control of the Chicago Stadium. Dubbed "the white elephant of West Madison Street," it had, despite Norris's 1929 bailout, been steadily going broke. The situation worsened when the Shamrocks folded. On January 20, 1933, Norris applied to Cook County Federal Court for ownership, offering $250,000 cash and promising to invest a further $250,000 to $300,000 into the venture—a pittance compared to the stadium's cost.* McLaughlin was so upset at having Norris as his new landlord that he promptly resigned as an NHL governor.

As with his grain business, Norris tailored his entertainment empire so that he couldn't lose. He purchased or financed a dizzying array of events, including circuses, ice acts and musical revues, to fill up his arenas. He took over Sonja Henie's Hollywood Ice Revue and, in partnership with Hopalong Cassidy, bought the Cole Bros. Circus, then the second-largest in the world. Norris also had a stake in Ringling Bros. and sponsored a string of vaudeville troops. For added insurance, he bought into many of the major booking agencies, which handled everything from boxing to bicycle acts.

By the time Norris officially took control of the Chicago Stadium in February 1935, he had committed bookings for 250 days including 21 days of his own circuses, 14 days of bicycle races, 6 wrestling matches, and 24 hockey games. He persuaded the city newspapers to sponsor another 14 days of events, and in 1935 staged an unprecedented 20 boxing cards in Chicago. In contrast, the building had been booked for a bare 65 days the previous year. By the mid '30s, America was hailing Norris as the "virtual Dictator of U.S. Indoor Events," with an entertainment empire covering Chicago, Detroit, New York and St. Louis.

Norris habitually cloaked his ownership behind nominees and front men. This was particularly so in the entertainment business, where his front man was Arthur Wirtz, a Chicago real estate entrepreneur who had made a small (compared to Norris) fortune during Prohibition. Wirtz ran Norris's entertainment interests, often taking a minority position in many of the companies Norris bought, formed or underwrote, including a 30 percent share of the Chicago Stadium. By 1936, he and Norris owned or

---

* This would be the first of a long series of NHL suits heard in Cook County court in Chicago. The NHL in coming years would show an affinity for filing there. According to famed Chicago columnist Mike Royko, Cook County was, for many years, the most corrupt court system in the United States.

managed nearly a hundred buildings in Chicago, many of which they had "rescued" from receivership.

The skating shows gave Wirtz a very high profile, and Hollywood columnists regularly commented on the lavish production numbers. The costumes and sets for the Ice Revue alone cost half a million dollars each season. By the time Sonja Henie became a headliner, Wirtz had assumed full credit for the idea and the development of Norris's entertainment empire. Norris didn't mind this, but his wife did. "Mother used to get cross," recalls their daughter, Marguerite. "We would go to see the Hollywood Ice Revue at the Chicago Stadium and on the marquee would be 'Arthur Wirtz Presents.' Well, you would never know that Father and Jimmy had anything to do with it."

Norris and Wirtz rarely gave interviews and were almost never directly quoted, but the press liked the bluff "robber baron" Canadian and disliked his dry, acid partner. While Norris was often described as bailing out a failing company, the papers managed to imply that Wirtz, in identical circumstances, was a parasite feeding off the misfortune of others.

A major component of Norris's plan to fill his arenas was the expansion of his considerable presence in boxing. Boxing historians have forgotten—or ceded to Jimmy Norris—his father's position in the sport. Though Norris was involved in the boxing as early as 1919, no one knows how many fighters, managers and promoters he owned. In 1935 he demonstrated his power by unilaterally moving the centre of boxing from New York to Chicago, where he hired matchmakers Nate Lewis and Jim Mullen to arrange fights. Between November 1934 and March 1935, the pair organized four championship fights in Chicago and one in Detroit.

One of the rare times Norris's name surfaced publicly in connection with boxing was in 1936 when he stepped in to save the Max Schmeling–Jimmy Braddock fight. The match had foundered over the bitter personal animosity between the two fighters' promoters, the powerful Mike Jacobs of the Twentieth Century Sporting Club and

Jimmy Johnston. Norris controlled Johnston, but when he saw the prospect of a juicy gate start to disappear he collected Scott Griffiths, another Madison Square Garden shareholder, and paid a call on a surprised Jacobs. "You own Schmeling. We own Braddock," Norris stated bluntly, "Your word is good. So is ours. Forget the petty personalities and we'll go fifty-fifty on everything, and we'll both make money."

Meanwhile, back in Chicago, with Norris firmly in control of the Stadium, McLaughlin's status plummeted from major tenant to bit-player. The Blackhawks' rent increased by 50 percent at the peak of the Depression, and the team could no longer book preferred dates or times. The players often arrived at the rink for practices to find the dressing room full of bicycling and boxing equipment, or debris from one of the travelling shows. Other times they discovered that attendants had neglected to clean circus refuse off the ice.

To the Major, these tribulations were nothing compared to the indignities of the actual games. The Red Wings quickly became competitive with the Blackhawks, and the Norris clan were always loudly present in the section next to McLaughlin's raucously cheering for Detroit.

Big Jim adored hockey games as much as he loved the vicious battles on the floor of the Chicago Grain Exchange. On the day of a contest he would happily poke his large, fleshly face into anything that looked interesting. Anyone sitting near Norris could be assured of an off-ice spectacle.

He enthroned himself right at rinkside, not as today's owners do in the plush surroundings of enclosed suites high up above the ice. More than one companion had to duck quickly to avoid his waving fists. Those nearby would often leave the Stadium with their ears ringing, not from the crowd but from Norris's bellows at the referee and opposing players.

During a December 1939 game between Chicago and Toronto, Norris took exception to referee Bill Stewart and heckled call after call. "You're a disgrace!" shouted

Norris. Stewart ground his teeth and said nothing. Then Norris taunted "Homer!"—an insult meaning that the official favours the home team. Stewart whipped over to Norris's rinkside box. "You should be ashamed of yourself for such conduct by a League governor." Norris waded in. "I'm going to turn you in for your terrible work tonight," he bellowed, inches from Stewart's nose. "I'm going to have you fired!" "Do as you please," returned the referee, "but you can't referee games from a box while I'm on the ice." Little fanfare accompanied Stewart's removal from League officiating shortly after the incident.

Hockey mythology has it that Norris bought into hockey out of his "unquenchable love for the game," but the simple fact is, though hockey was his favourite game, he viewed the sport as an investment, first, last and always. He enjoyed football, and his own son Jimmy played it avidly, but, at the time, no one made money in it. Baseball looked promising. At least twice he came close to buying major league teams—the Chicago Cubs in 1920, before they were bought by the Wrigley family, and the Brooklyn Dodgers in 1934. He backed away because baseball prohibited ownership of more than one club. The NHL also expressly forbade multiple ownership, but the League allowed a corporation rather than an individual to be named as owner. Conveniently, the rules didn't require the disclosure of who was behind those company names.

When Norris became an NHL governor in 1934, he found the meetings disorganized and discordant: a bunch of "nasty little boys at each other's throats," he once said. He felt the other eight governors were constantly feuding over minor things that had little to do with running a hockey league, or making money.* Leo Dandurand of the Canadiens argued with Boston's Charles Adams, Art Ross, the Bruins' GM who became a governor in 1937, fought furiously with Conn Smythe of Toronto, and McLaughlin

---

* The NHL Board of governors consisted of a representative from each club, usually an owner but sometimes the general manager.

bickered with everyone.

During these years, the feud between Smythe and Ross, who didn't speak to each other for twelve years, even at governors' meetings, reached epic proportions. At one point, Ross hired two longshoremen to rough up Smythe at a game. On another occasion, Smythe took out a large ad in a Boston paper mocking Ross. "If you're tired of what you've been looking at, come out tonight and see a decent team, the Toronto Maple Leafs play hockey," it stated.

The *coup de grâce* came at a game in the Boston Garden. Smythe, ostensibly as a peace offering, had King Clancy skate across the ice in front of the crowd and present a bunch of roses to Art Ross, who had just recovered from a painful hemorrhoid operation. "Insert these up your you know where," read the attached card, written in Latin. Ross, who couldn't read Latin, nodded his thanks to Smythe and grandly passed the bouquet over to the matron of a powerful Boston family, who, unfortunately, could.

The other NHL owners naturally gravitated to Jim Norris, who reeked of power and authority. With Norris as a governor, NHL meetings magically became less fractious and more concerned with the League's overall financial health. But not everyone approved of Norris's ascension to the NHL leadership. Constantine Falkland Cary (Conn) Smythe felt that the mantle of leadership was rightfully his and didn't like it one bit.

Smythe had become accustomed to the status of sage and hockey demigod in Toronto, but Norris viewed him as small-time and mean-spirited, and treated him with disdain. He had no patience with Smythe's inclination to fight bitterly for pennies when there were dollars to be made. Smythe became increasingly irritated by the other owners' deference, especially when he noticed that General John Reed Kilpatrick, governor for the New York Rangers, suddenly began voting in lock-step with Norris. He didn't discover the reason why until a 1936 newspaper article revealed that Norris was a "heavy" shareholder in Madison Square Garden.

Even more aggravatingly, Charles Adams, the irascible and normally independent Boston owner, quickly fell into Norris's camp. Smythe probably never knew that Norris had underwritten a series of mortgages that Adams couldn't pay in the early years of the Depression. When Norris quietly bought Chicago after McLaughlin died in 1944, his control of the NHL, now stable at six teams, was complete. He owned three of the teams and a fourth was beholden to him.

Jim Norris never really cared about the Rangers or Blackhawks beyond the number of dates they represented in the buildings he owned and the votes they represented on the board of governors. He devoted none of the time or money to them that he lavished on the Red Wings, and neither club developed a farm system, which Norris encouraged Adams to create in Detroit.*

Norris allowed both clubs to languish under ineffectual management. Kilpatrick in New York, and his son Jimmy in Chicago. In eighteen years of the much-maligned Major McLaughlin's ownership, the Blackhawks won the Stanley Cup twice and only missed the playoffs six times. In twelve of the first fourteen years of Norris's ownership, the Blackhawks didn't make the playoffs at all, and in the other two years the team didn't make it past the first playoff round.

Though Smythe, Leo Dandurand, Fred McLaughlin and Charles Adams all squabbled with NHL president Frank Calder, who they believed didn't know his place as an employee of the governors, Norris carefully supported him. When Calder died suddenly in 1943, Big Jim immediately suggested installing Calder's longtime friend Mervyn (Red) Dutton as interim president.

Dutton, former governor for the Brooklyn Americans, a team that had folded in 1942, never felt comfortable as president. He didn't like answering to so many masters,

---

* The Montreal Canadiens were the first NHL club to develop a sophisticated network of sponsored clubs, both amateur and semi-professional. Detroit and Toronto followed. In these pre-draft years, a farm system was the best way to develop players, protect them from being signed by other teams and, most importantly, limit their ability to market their services independently.

especially fractious ones like Smythe and Art Ross. Twice he offered to resign, and once he begged to be allowed to. Each time the governors persuaded him to stay a few more months until the designated successor, Clarence Campbell, returned from Europe. A Rhodes scholar, lawyer and former NHL referee, Campbell had spent most of 1945 and '46 in Europe as one of the Allies' prosecutors during the war crimes trials. When he returned, the League offered him the presidency for a handsome $15,000 annually. Campbell accepted and vowed to make hockey his life's work.

Stately and dignified, Campbell personified integrity, wisdom and leadership, an image that has survived to this day. But as far as hockey was concerned, Campbell functioned as a servant; the only independent judgment he exercised concerned the fit of his collar and the length of the leash. "Operating on his own," Conn Smythe later observed, "Campbell sometimes made mistakes, but he was the perfect second-in-command." A friend of Smythe's son Stafford once complained about a disciplinary decision Campbell had made, and asked, "Why the hell don't you get another guy to run the League?" Stafford replied, "Where would we find another Rhodes scholar, graduate lawyer, decorated war hero, and former prosecutor at the Nuremberg trials, *who will do what he's told?*"

Though far from an inspiring speaker, Campbell's crisp delivery, his command of reams of unrelated statistics, his legalistic jargon and circumlocution never failed to cow both sportwriters and players. He had a slow way of smiling and a knack of cocking his head slightly and looking hard at people, as if weighing their merits.

Campbell looked the part of president and acted it. He dressed with such impeccable taste that the uniformed could be forgiven, when seeing him together with the NHL governors, for thinking he was the boss and the owners his minions. The only time Campbell's classy demeanour slipped was when he absentmindedly stuck his hankie in his sleeve and left it flapping around on his arm.

Though a proud man, Campbell had no illusions about his position. He carefully described himself as the manager or the executive officer who didn't formulate policy but carried out the wishes of the owners. Most writers of the time considered Campbell's disavowals an example of his admirable humility rather than simple statements of fact.

One publication, *Sports Illustrated*, had a more sceptical view of the situation. "National Hockey League chief executives are chosen for their meekness in the face of authority," observed one writer. "Clarence S. Campbell, president of the league since 1946, is a former referee who learned early in his career that if he wanted to get ahead in hockey he should never sass a magnate back. The Board of Governors, made up of a representative of each club, runs the league, usually according to the plans and specifications of the Norris interests; and Mr. Campbell, who besides being league president is also the secretary-treasurer, has to do little except look respectful and nod his head in the right direction at the proper time."

Campbell buffered the owners from each other and, more important, from the public. He successfully presented the image of a cohesive, unified League with the incorruptible Nuremberg prosecutor at its head. But from the owners' point of view, his most critical job was to keep the players in line. Campbell enforced the rules, dispensed justice with an immaculate *savoir faire* and shaped his own image as the players' protector, their last resort in any negotiation or grievance with their teams or the League.

The NHL rules established the president as final arbitrator—a provision intact to this day—and Campbell made it seem that he would stand up and fight for the rights of players. If the players were grateful, they never showed it by approaching him. In his later years, Campbell could not recall a single instance of any player coming to him for help or arbitration in a dispute.

Jim Norris's steadfast support of Clarence Campbell, coupled with his leadership, gave the NHL stability.

Unfortunately, he was unable to exercise the same guidance with his son Jimmy. Hoping to find a place for Jimmy in his vast empire, Norris Sr. gave him innumerable odd jobs with the Red Wings and the minor-league Detroit Olympians. But in the '30s, Jimmy was best known for pitching pennies with the teams, playing challengers to a standstill in poker and laying players' bets at the racetrack. He would invariably greet the players with a big, warm smile and "Where's the action?"

According to sportswriters who followed the teams, Jimmy's principal job as a vice-president of the Red Wings "was to call his father long-distance the moment a game was over and give him a blow-by-blow description." Still, Jimmy's hockey reputation has come to overshadow his father's. Many accounts credit the growth of the Norris hockey empire to Jimmy rather than his father. Hockey histories have him partnering his father, or even leading him into the purchase of arenas.

Born in 1906, James Dougan Norris was deeply attached to his father. Their affinity was made all the stronger by the death of Jimmy's mother in 1910. Until Norris remarried in 1919, the two were inseparable, playing vigorous and often viciously competitive games of squash, softball and tennis. When Jimmy wasn't in school—and he boasted of spending more time skipping classes than attending them—his father often took him along on business.

Jimmy enjoyed watching his father in the Pit or listening in on the hockey business, but he adored it when they dropped into the gym in the old Chicago Board of Trade building to watch the boxers spar. Big Jim was treated like a celebrity and one of the boys at the same time. Grizzled, bent old trainers slapped him on the back and joked with him, and young boxers raised their gloves in salute when he walked in.

The boxers interested Jimmy, but the grifters, touts and pimps that surrounded boxing like flies in a stable mesmerized him. In his early teenage years he spent as much time as possible hanging around with them. Initially, Norris wasn't too alarmed by his son's obvious infatuation with lowlifes. During Prohibition years, no one who did a sizeable business in Chicago and New York could avoid coming into contact with gangsters.

The mob moved into sports like horse racing and boxing as offshoots of their gambling and numbers rackets. Norris knew more than his share of underworld denizens, but he also knew how to keep them at a distance, and how to use them to his advantage. Jimmy never learned those lessons, and early on his companions were bookies, con artists and hit men.

Jim was nearly fourteen when his father married Marguerite Loris, a graceful and elegant woman who had had a brief career as a Broadway "gypsy."* Young Jim and his stepmother, only thirteen years his senior, disliked each other on sight. The second Mrs. Norris didn't appreciate the companions Jimmy brought home, nor, in later years, did she approve of the girls he liked, with their hard eyes, extravagant clothes and racy language.

The second Mrs. Norris was not cut from the same rough cloth as her new family, but she had her own sense of humour. "She gave him [Jimmy] suitcases I guess every Christmas," chuckles her daughter Marguerite. "He certainly didn't quite get the message."

By the time he was sixteen, Jimmy, already well over six-feet tall with the physique and strong features of a man and an outgoing personality, had easy access to the speakeasies and gambling joints in Chicago. He always had a big roll of money and gladly flashed it around to smooth his way. Gambling played an integral part in his life from the moment he learned the game of pitch-penny; a poorer man would have been called an addict.

Jimmy wasn't content just to place his bets, he wanted to be part of "the action." In the '30s, Norris Sr. purchased a magnificent Fontainebleau-like estate in the exclusive Chicago suburb of Forest Lawn, but for a while

---

* "Gypsies" in the Edwardian years were not strippers but prancers and posers. They would strut silkily around the stage in large, fantastic hats, strike attitudes then slide off into the wings.

he hung on to his city apartment as well. One day, Mrs. Norris went into Chicago to retrieve some belongings and returned to complain to her husband, "Well, Jimmy is still in the apartment, and I can't understand what all those phones are doing in the nursery!" Her daughter laughs. "Well, he had a bookie joint is what he had. She couldn't understand the phones!"

In later years, Jimmy would be portrayed, or excused, as a "dupe" of gangsters, but they were his closest friends and business associates from an early age. Sports people well remember "a tall, slender, bespectacled man with the mien of a minister and the voice of a confessor" who accompanied Jimmy everywhere, opened doors for him, booked rooms and made sure they were well stocked with drink and the kind of female companionship he preferred.

This austere figure, who lurked in the corridors at NHL board of governors' meetings, was Sammy "Golfbag" Hunt, a vicious hit man in the Al Capone era. Hunt acquired his nickname by carrying his machine-gun in a golfbag. Before each execution, he reportedly hollered "Fore!" Hunt met Norris at the race-track. The twenty-four-year-old had just been relieved at gunpoint of $1,100 he'd been flashing around a little too ostentatiously. The gunmen were only too glad to return the money when Hunt politely asked for it.

Jimmy Norris's other close friend from organized crime was Frankie Carbo. No one knows when they met, but it's clear their relationship dated back to Jimmy's friendship with Hunt. While Hunt became Norris's underling, Carbo was a peer who partied with Norris and made mutual investments. Jimmy once named one of his favourite horses Mr. Gray, Frankie Carbo's mob nickname.

Carbo, a member of the infamous Murder Inc., was a gunman even more notorious than Hunt. His first recorded kill was in 1924 at the age of twenty. In 1939, Carbo and Bugsy Siegel terminated Harry "Big Greenie" Greenberg, a small-time enforcer who had been threatening to turn state's evidence. Carbo later gunned down

Siegel for Meyer Lansky in one of the biggest gangland assassinations of all time.

The track was Jimmy's earliest and most enduring passion. At nineteen he secretly invested in a horse-racing stable with two of his cronies. Later it was reported, though not proven, that Eddie Coco, another well-known gangster, was one of the partners. The mob was partial to horse racing too. The Chicago family controlled Continental Press Service, a racing wire on which the nation's bookies depended. Using Continental as leverage, the mob took over numerous bookmaking firms, like the once-legitimate S & G Syndicate in Miami. Using front men, organized crime bought into many of the major race-tracks in the United States. Eventually, they came to control trainers, stables, jockeys, bookies and the tracks themselves.

Though Jimmy and his father remained close until the day the older man died, tension developed between them. Big Jim was accustomed to dominating people, but Jimmy, being a Norris, wasn't about to be dominated.

Jimmy was constantly reminded that he was a rich and powerful man's son. Articles about his father frequently tacked on mention of "his personable giant of a son, who goes for horseracing." The giant in question, while his father was alive, was usually referred to in the diminutive: "Young Jim," "Little Jim," "Jim Jr." and most often "Jimmy." There was never any hint that Jimmy did anything independent or useful.

Norris decided that Jimmy should be educated at the prestigious Colgate University. Some weeks after the start of the first semester, he phoned his son and said he wanted to meet his teachers. Jimmy stalled and stalled until his aggravated father exploded at him. They finally agreed to meet at the train station near the university. They walked around campus, had lunch and saw the sights—but no teachers.

Finally, an exasperated Norris demanded, "Well, let's go and see these teachers of yours!" As it turned out, Jimmy hadn't even registered at the university and had never even visited it previously. Hoping to fool his father, he'd travelled up to Colgate that day on the same train.*

Jimmy floated in and out of the Norris empire throughout the late '30s, often appearing on the society pages looking dashing and carefree in his straw boater at Hawthorne and Washington Park race-tracks. Norris Sr. tried to interest Jimmy in cattle, but his son preferred horses. Big Jim made him a vice-president of Norris Grain, but Jimmy rarely showed up at the office. He offered him positions with the Detroit and Chicago hockey teams, but Jimmy found baseball more appealing.

When the Yankees came up for auction in 1945, Jimmy decided to bid for the team, but Norris, who intended to turn the Blackhawks over to his son, pronounced, "You can have a hockey team or a baseball team but you can't have both, and this is your father talking. So what's it to be, the Blackhawks or the Yankees?" Jimmy chose the Blackhawks, not because of the sport itself, but because of the stadium, which was to become a cornerstone of his boxing empire.

Throughout the '40s, Jim Norris, plagued by a deteriorating heart condition, organized his affairs so his family wouldn't be at each other's throats over control of his estate. He also knew he had to settle an inheritance on Jimmy and move him as far out of the picture as possible, for the sake of his wife and three other children, Eleanor, Marguerite and Bruce.

In 1946 he turned over control of the Chicago Blackhawks to his eldest son. Though Jimmy professed to love the game, he left Bill Tobin in place as governor for the team and spent little time on Blackhawks business.† The next year, Norris signed over his controlling interest in the Rock Island Railroad to Jimmy. The following year, he purchased a seat on the New York Stock Exchange and a brokerage firm, transferring the seat to

---

* Though Jimmy never did register at Colgate, he didn't trouble to correct articles that described him as a graduate of the university.

† Norris Sr. was still the majority shareholder, but he backed away from decisions about the team, leaving that up to Jimmy and the other major shareholder, Arthur Wirtz. After he died, his shares were split equally among the rest of the family.

Jimmy for the token sum of one dollar.

From 1946 to 1948, Norris turned over virtually all of Jimmy's inheritance to him. Other little bits and pieces included his 40 percent interest in Madison Square Garden, arenas in Indianapolis, Omaha and St. Louis, a 25 percent share in Detroit's Olympia Stadium and the Red Wings, three thoroughbred farms in Florida and Kentucky and several hundred thousand acres of real estate in North and South Dakota, St. Louis, Chicago, New York, Florida and Kentucky.

Now a rich and independent man, Jimmy could afford to pour money into the ever-failing Blackhawks. However, it wasn't hockey that received his attention, but boxing. Together with his father's old partner, Arthur Wirtz, Norris bought pieces of several heavyweights, none of whom distinguished themselves.

The old man had mixed emotions about Jimmy's relationship with Wirtz. "Mr. Norris pretty quickly realized that Wirtz had the head for business that his son Jim lacked," a Chicago businessman who knew the Norrises and Wirtz explained to the *Wall Street Journal.* "The old man saw he needed someone to keep the young man from spending every cent he had. After a while, Jim rarely made a move without clearing it with Arthur."

Jimmy was attracted to Wirtz, but not for his business sense. It was his involvement in show business and liquor distribution, that dovetailed with the worlds of boxing and horse racing that excited the young man.

Jimmy's closeness to, and dependence on Wirtz piqued his father, who occasionally lashed out if Jimmy came to visit and spent more time on the phone to Wirtz than he did talking to Norris. "How much is that call?" the old man would snap. "Why do you have to phone him all the time? You just left him!"

Everywhere Jimmy went, his father had been before him. Norris Sr. had lost interest in boxing after the Depression, and by the mid-'40s the sport had fallen into a shambles. Joe Louis could no longer pack the arenas, and the public, disgusted by revelations about the sport's seamy underside in the hands of the mob, stayed away from boxing in droves. Jimmy's big opportunity came when the mob moved in to shut down the Twentieth Century Sporting Club, which had been the major force in boxing since the early '20s.

In 1946, Twentieth Century had hired Teddy Brenner as assistant matchmaker. Shortly afterward, a group of fight managers set up the Boxing Managers' Guild and demanded a much larger cut of the money the Gillette Company paid to sponsor the Cavalcade of Sports TV broadcasts every Friday night. "Each time I made a match, the Guild got wind of it and before long I would get word that this or that fighter had hurt his head or his back in training and could not keep his date in the Garden," Brenner recalled in his autobiography. "You'd have to be stupid not to know that there was something wrong, and what everybody knew was that Frankie Carbo was operating on the side of the Guild. Soon as he heard that I signed a fighter, he got word to the fighter's manager that it would be unwise, if not unsafe, to cooperate with the Garden." Twentieth Century suddenly could not deliver fighters to honour its contract with Gillette, and by early 1948 the club faced ruin.

On March 1, 1949, Jimmy Norris, Arthur Wirtz and Joe Louis formed the International Boxing Club (IBC), headquartered on the second floor of Madison Square Garden, absorbing Twentieth Century at the same time. Interestingly, Frankie Carbo and the Boxing Managers' Guild had no problem with this arrangement. Within a year, IBC had branches in Chicago, Missouri and Michigan, and within two years the authorities were moving in to investigate.

Not only did the IBC own and manage almost every important American boxer by 1951, but it owned the agencies that promoted them, the agencies that put together the rights and television packages and, of course, all the key arenas. The few fighters who weren't connected directly or indirectly to IBC were coincidentally owned by Jimmy's old pals. Blinky Palermo and Carbo had lightweight champion Ike Williams, Eddie Coco ran Rocky Graziano and Carbo controlled Jake LaMotta.

Two years after IBC was established, publications across North American crowned Jimmy as the "Mr. Big" of boxing. *Life* magazine accorded him "more control over boxing than any man since the Marquess of Queensberry laid down the rules 84 years ago. . . . There has not been a big bout in the U.S. in two years, including the last Robinson-Turpin fight, which drew 61,370 people, that Jim Norris has not run."

By 1954, Norris had been accused of fight-fixing once, consorting with known criminals twice and operating a monopoly three times.* His response to these charges must have had Frankie Carbo, his frequent dinner companion, choking with laughter. "It's rather like the diplomatic service," Norris blandly described his work in IBC, "this bringing managers together for matches. And like the diplomatic service it's subject to investigations."

Many chaffed at IBC's monopoly, but not even the powerful seemed able to do anything about it. Six of the fifteen Madison Square Garden board members, including Bernard Gimbel of department store fame and Walter Chrysler, resigned in 1954, protesting that they were "captives" of Norris. Jimmy accepted their resignations, then installed himself as president and General Reed Kilpatrick, longtime family friend and Garden employee, as chairman.

Curiously, while the Chicago Blackhawks' fortunes dropped from dim to dismal in the early '50s, IBC and Norris's horse-racing interests threw off money like a Catherine wheel shoots sparks. IBC ran the Gillette Friday Night Fights on CBS and had a second match televised weekly by NBC.

Jimmy grossed $10 million annually from these two contracts. That amount didn't include the under-the-table cuts IBC took from boxers whose rights he owned and whose careers his agencies managed, both in flagrant contravention of boxing regulations stipulating that no

---

* Only one charge, an anti-trust suit, was ever laid against Norris during this time, and a federal judge threw the whole thing out of court forty minutes after proceedings began in February 1954.

promoter could own a boxer. Then there were the gate percentages taken by his arenas and by IBC as promoter.

On top of it all was the gambling action, the bribes and the fight-fixing run by his friends Carbo, Coco et al., which probably doubled Norris's boxing take.

Still, throughout this period, Jimmy often repeated a favourite line: "I'd rather win a Stanley Cup than a world heavyweight championship or the Kentucky Derby."

Chapter 3

The "Good Old Days"

Six teams comprised the NHL after 1942, but only three counted: the cool and methodical Toronto Maple Leafs, the searingly brilliant Montreal Canadiens and the multi-dimensional Detroit Red Wings. All were hugely successful financially, and in any given year any one could have won the Stanley Cup. Between 1942 and 1957, the three teams won the Cup five times each.

The rest—the New York Rangers, Chicago Blackhawks and Boston Bruins—existed only to round out the schedule and provide the odd bit of drama. During the same fifteen years, these three teams got to the Stanley Cup finals just six times. The most successful, Boston, made it four times, and the Blackhawks and the Rangers only once each.*

As far as Norris Sr. was concerned, if his teams didn't actually lose money, he was content to let them stumble along as glorified player warehouses. "[Detroit] was definitely the team he was most interested in," his daughter

---

* Over the entire period of the six-team League (1942 to 1967) Montreal, Detroit or Toronto failed to win the Stanley Cup only once, in 1961, when Chicago captured it.

Marguerite confirms. "The others were just an investment. He just didn't really care."

Norris did care deeply about the Red Wings. He saved them from bankruptcy and pumped hundreds of thousands into the club, content in the knowledge that his ownership of the team had given his foe, Major McLaughlin, a decade-long case of heartburn.

Jack Adams, the most colourful and powerful general manager in the League, ran the team for Norris. Fawned over by the media, feared by his players and deified by the public, Adams sculpted a legend for himself as "Jolly Jack" the trade master—the hockey genius with the heart of gold.

Adams began his professional career in Calumet, Michigan as a fiesty, scrappy hockey player. There was nothing elegant about the way he played, but the Toronto Arenas added him to their roster for the first NHL season of 1917-1918. In those days, teams kept a bucket of icy water on the bench. When a player was cut, he skated to the bench and had his wound sponged off. Games were rated by how red the water in the bucket became. Adams's rubbery face took a terrific beating during his eight pro seasons, but he gave as good as he got, leading the League in penalties in one season and ending up near the top in most others.

In 1927, while playing for the Ottawa Senators, Adams heard that the fledgling and already foundering Detroit franchise desperately needed a new coach and general manager. In 1926, the team had played just across the border in Windsor, Ontario, waiting for Detroit's 14,000-seat Olympia Stadium to be completed. That season the Cougars lost $83,000, and a depressed Charlie Hughes, president of the club, confided to NHL president Frank Calder that the team might soon go under. During the playoffs in Boston, Jack Adams boldly approached Calder and asked to be considered for the Detroit job. Calder hesitated, but thought a scrapper like Adams just might pull the ailing team together, so he sent him along to Hughes.

Stuck with a nearly bankrupt club of ageing and

marginal players, Adams's first five seasons were dismal. Everyone perked up when the team posted a handsome profit of $175,000 after a year in the new Stadium, but from then on the losses mounted year by year. The club paid the players sporadically, and several times Adams dug into his own pocket to meet the payroll.

The players were so pathetically equipped that they often had to borrow opponents' sticks. Even worse, the fans were so objectionable that the Cougars prayed for small turnouts and looked forward to road trips. At home, spectators crossed the river from Windsor to watch with bloodthirsty pleasure as the Canadian teams beat up on the Cougars. On the rare occasions Detroit did win, the crowds booed and hissed.

By 1932 the Detroit team, now called the Falcons, was in such desperate shape that the NHL governors discussed transferring players from other teams to prop them up. Then along came Big Jim Norris. Fortunately for Adams, Norris saw his potential and renewed his contract for a year, but placed him "on probation."*

It was hardly a vote of confidence, but Norris gave Adams something far more valuable—$100,000 to spend on players. It was a staggering sum at a time when the entire team's payroll was capped at $62,500, and no single player could be paid more than $7,000. Out of that $100,000 was born Jack Adams's reputation as a hockey genius.

Norris and Adams appeared to have little in common. Adams looked like a walking coronary case history. Standing only five feet, seven inches tall, he eventually pillowed out into 225 very soft pounds, a considerable portion of it squeezed into three huge neck jowls. Norris's tall, hulking presence looked firm in comparison and dwarfed the squat, rotund profile of his employee.

Adams's public jolliness thinly overlaid an inner core of darkness. When angered, he reacted violently. Temper tantrums—punctuated by objects sailing through the

---

* The probation term with the Norris family stretched to thirty-one years. Big Jim never once offered a contract, nor did Adams ever ask for one.

air—became legendary in his office. After an Adams "fit," as one of his secretaries called them, his office looked as if a lawnmower had roared up and down its walls.

Norris, worldly and subtle, took a longer view. His gruff heartiness hid a cold, controlling and unsentimental underside. When crossed, he used his vast, interlocking businesses to slowly squeeze opponents to death. Then, at the critical moment, he'd "rescue" his victims at fire sale prices.

In their twenty years of association, Norris acted as a balance to Adams. He often cautioned against precipitous action, and he helped Adams control the seething cauldron of bitterness that turned many of his business decisions into personal ones. Each day after the Chicago grain market closed, Adams conferred with Norris, and he phoned him, without fail, after each game. Every summer they spent as much as a month together in Florida, often talking hockey until well into the night.

Norris made many suggestions about team management, especially in the early years. He added a business dimension to the management of the team and stadium that was then unknown in professional sport. (The Red Wings, for example, were one of the first teams in the '30s to travel by air, which thoroughly terrified a number of players.) But when it came to the game itself, Norris deferred to Adams and allowed his inventiveness full rein. Adams developed or promoted a number of revolutionary techniques, including resurfacing the ice between periods, televising home games and the rule allowing a penalized player to leave the penalty box once a goal is scored.

Adams always had an eye out for anything to give his team an edge. During a particularly hot playoff series in Detroit, he produced oxygen for the players. In the middle of another muggy series he decided his team would perform better if they freshened up between periods. Instead of the normal fifteen minutes of relaxation, the players were appalled when their rest period was taken up by a complete change of clothes, right down to underwear and socks. Some of them barely made it back to the bench in time for the next period.

The contrast between Norris and Adams extended to their treatment of players. Norris preferred the carrot, his employee the stick. Adams responded to his team's failure to make the playoffs in the 1937-38 season by doing away with "contracts of guaranteed figures." Instead, players were signed to "figureless or small-figure contracts." Added remuneration would be in the form of bonuses, at Adams's discretion.

Singled out by the new "bonus system" were injured players such as Mud Bruneteau, whose performance that season had been hampered by a badly broken arm. This was the same Mud who, just two seasons before, had scored the winning goal against the Montreal Maroons in the ninth period, after a record 116 minutes and 30 seconds of play.

Jack Adams based his management strategy on dependence: he liked a healthy dose of it in his players and was a master at instilling it. He used example and anticipation to weaken autonomy and create fear. Coaches in all sports have always benched players for performing badly, having a poor attitude or breaking team rules, but Adams was unpredictable. Players never knew what infraction would earn them time on the bench or for how long. That way he kept them offbalance and created a domino effect of anxiety within the team.

If harangues or benching didn't work, a quick trip to the minor leagues provided an effective shot of adrenaline. Demotion was a lot cheaper than having a player loaf around Detroit. The salaries of those sent down automatically dropped to half, or even a third of the major-league figure.*

Adams sent players to the minors for the most arbitrary and quixotic reasons, and he kept his charges, particu-

---

* A trip to the minors put a terrific strain on marriages, as the club provided neither moving allowance for families nor any compensation for broken leases. It is the nature of athletes to be optimistic, so many ended up maintaining two households, confident they'd be brought back into the franchise's bosom once Adams realized his error

larly the fringe players, in a permanent state of agitation
by carrying around a sheaf of one-way train tickets in his
front pocket. There was a corps on the team who called
themselves "the suitcase brigade." These unfortunates
weren't necessarily the dregs of the League, but they
clashed regularly with Adams, which was worse. "I'm on
the suitcase express," members of this unhappy lot
would observe. More than one was sent down for nothing more than missing a pass at a key moment.
Distractions as well as infractions fell into Adams's large
catch-all category called "disciplinary reasons." Seeing the
wrong woman, or worse, seeing her too often, came under this broad umbrella.

Little of Jack Adams's true nature has ever surfaced,
largely because he courted and seduced sportswriters so
skilfully. Cold beer awaited underpaid and travel-weary
reporters on the train after every game, and they could
always count on Adams for a free dinner on the road.
They could also rely on him to say nothing when they
submitted expense invoices to their papers for those
same meals. After every playoff game, Adams hosted a
large troup of writers and stood them a fine meal with
plenty of beer and whisky at the best restaurant in town.

Even more important, from a reporter's perspective,
Jack Adams always provided a good quote—the lifeblood
for writers facing a daily deadline. "Jack Adams was, in
the parlance of the sports world, a great guy," wrote one
of the grateful scribes after his retirement. "To a young
reporter, he was the perfect hockey foil. He would talk to
you and tell you things about hockey that provided you
with enough material to write endlessly about the game.
He was never too busy to sit down and have a cup of
coffee with you, or to talk about 'my kids' as he always
referred to his Red Wings."

Adams, like many hockey people, privately loathed
most sportswriters but thought of his generosity as
throwing a little bread upon the water. In return, writers
overlooked questionable trades and the periodic appearance of the dark side of his personality. They nicknamed
him "Jolly Jack" and "Genial Jawn" and described him as

an "overweight cherub," a "jolly fellow" or a kind and "genial guy." They felt honoured to be the conduits for Adams's criticism of individual players. Comments attributed to "sources close to the Wings" invariably came from Adams himself.

Adams's arch-enemy, Conn Smythe, refused to mollycoddle reporters. When he wanted them, he summoned them. At press conferences he restricted questions and would only discuss "the facts," the facts being whatever he wanted to talk about. For interviews, he often demanded that questions be submitted in advance, whereupon he'd rewrite the questions and return them to the reporters.*

Smythe took advantage of the fact that "sportswriters were very low paid and always had their hands out." He boasted that he could get "any story I wanted in the paper for $50 or less," but he resented having to pay to ensure "honest" reporting.

When reporters erred, in Smythe's view, he retaliated by making them pay for their game tickets and withdrawing all Leafs advertising from their paper. During one conflict with the Toronto *Star*, *Star* owner Joe Atkinson approached Smythe to end the stand-off, asking him how much hockey writers might expect in cash handouts from him. "I mean," Atkinson quickly added, "you're not giving our men money, but if you did what would you expect the figure to be?" Smythe told him $20,000. Atkinson promised to pay his writers more, for "honest" writing, if Smythe agreed to spend $20,000 on advertising annually. "That deal lasted maybe twenty years," Smythe observed.

The genesis of the Adams-Smythe feud dated back to 1934, when the two men shared a Pullman on the trip to New York. "I thought there was no nicer guy to travel with!" Smythe later wrote in his autobiography. "He seemed content to take second place all the time to me,

---

* When Gordon Sinclair wrote sports for the Toronto *Star* in the '30s, he had the audacity to call the Maple Leafs "yellow" after a game in which the team had been thoroughly trounced. Smythe publicly offered to fight Sinclair and, when the reporter demurred, barred him from the Leafs' dressing-room.

which was nice; nobody else trying to hog the limelight."

As Smythe talked expansively about race horses and world affairs, Adams gently probed him about his hockey prospects for the coming year. Smythe admitted he had been watching an awkward young lacrosse player named Bucko McDonald who could barely skate but handled the ball with rare finesse and displayed marvellous defensive anticipation.

On his return to Toronto, Smythe wired NHL headquarters to "list" McDonald, which meant no other team could claim him. A return wire informed him that Jack Adams had just listed McDonald a few minutes earlier. Smythe simmered over the next five years as the ungainly but talented athlete helped the Red Wings to two Stanley Cup victories.

Adams habitually referred to Smythe as "the little shit" when talking privately to reporters. For his part, Smythe deeply resented the fact that Adams, a mere hired hand, had an entrée to the inner circles of power through Jim Norris, while he, an NHL governor and owner, had less real power and influence.

The enmity between Adams and Smythe infected their teams. By the late '40s, the competition between the Maple Leafs and the Red Wings had grown so vicious that sportswriters devoted as much space to gleeful speculations about potential bloodletting as to the games themselves. "Detroit and Toronto are clashing again tomorrow night," drooled one writer in 1947, "and lots of blood is sure to flow."

Though the balance of power shifted back and forth between the three dominant clubs, the years between 1948 and 1957 belonged to the Red Wings. Anchored by Gordie Howe, Sid Abel, Ted Lindsay, Red Kelly and Alex Delvecchio, the team made Jack Adams one of the most successful coaches and general managers in hockey history.

Gordie Howe, talented, tough and dextrously mean, remains the team's greatest star, and the one Red Wing fans remember best. But Howe never possessed that indefinable quality which transcends merely great play. Ted Lindsay, a pit-bull of a player described by *Look* magazine as "a blood-red flash of cold fury," was the club's fulcrum.

Lindsay, aged nineteen, turned pro in 1944 amid widespread predictions that he would be "carried out on a board." That belief had as much to do with his personality as it did with his five-foot, nine-inch frame and 160 pounds. Even in the rawness of youth, Lindsay was a walking, talking smirk. He never knew his place and he never, ever gave his elders or betters their due.

Adams cruelly initiated Lindsay by assigning him to check the legendary Maurice "Rocket" Richard, then entering his prime. Richard played and looked like a demon, with deeply set coal-black eyes that burned a path from goal crease to goal crease. Unforgiving of insults and injury, the Rocket was quick to retaliate with the kind of finality that sent so many players hobbling from the game. Even teammates gave him wide berth.

But Richard found his match in Lindsay. For all his manic play, the Rocket had a streak of caution. He was calculating about his scuffles and cared more than a little about the state of his own hide. Lindsay wasn't burdened by any such considerations. During that first game, he imprudently drove the much larger Rocket to distraction, pestering him with nudges, thumbs to the eye and chops to the legs. Richard finally tired of the rookie's insolence and squared off to rid himself of the disrespectful gnat. To everyone's surprise, Lindsay fought the Rocket to a bloody standstill, establishing a lifelong enmity. Today, Richard, given to bitter, brooding moments, won't even utter Lindsay's name, much less talk about him.

Weasel-fast, Lindsay wasn't a great fighter, but one of unrelenting ferocity. Hockey fights, then and now, are often relatively tame, even stately affairs—an unsteady waltz, a stream of obscenities, a spray of spittle and an offbalance, off-speed punch or two. But when Lindsay was in the fray, more telling blows landed, more blood flowed and someone *always* got hurt, including fans when he ploughed into the stands to silence hecklers.

Those few who emerged victorious over Lindsay were invariably in far worse shape than if they'd *lost* a fight with someone else. Early in his career, he used his knees and elbows so viciously on opponents that the League created "Rule 51 (Elbowing and Kneeing)," informally known as the Lindsay rule.

Sportswriters doted on "Terrible Ted." "Hockey's most spectacular bloodlettings in recent years usually have involved Lindsay," crowed *Look* magazine's Tim Cohane in 1952. Calling him "a picture of unmitigated villainy," Cohane enthusiastically described his favourite slaughter, a January 25, 1951 epic starring Lindsay and Bill Ezinicki, the Boston Bruins' tough guy. The two men usually vied with each other for the most penalties every year. Even a slightly cross-eyed look was enough to spark a brawl.

On this night, after a series of preliminary scuffles, elbows and retaliatory shoves, Ezinicki pool-cued his stick into Lindsay's left eye. In return, Lindsay axed Ezinicki "eyebrow to hairline." With the gentle stuff out of the way, they went at it with their fists. Lindsay was leading on points by the time the officials separated them.

Ezinicki slipped away from the scrum and circled wide around Lindsay, whose back was turned. Lindsay saw him coming but feigned unawareness. At the perfect instant, he wheeled and landed a right that felled Ezinicki to the ice head first. "Lindsay leaped on him like a jaguar," Cohane exalted, "and was pummelling him before he realized Ezinicki was unconscious from his fall. Then Ted got up and skated off the bloody ice to the screams of the hockey heathen."

Clarence Campbell's public outrage over the incident—or, more accurately, over the widespread coverage of it—echoed throughout the six NHL cities. The public believed that if a man with the credentials of Campbell got upset, then, by God, there was something to get upset about. The NHL president handed each player a much-heralded three-game suspension without pay and a $300 fine—the stiffest bit of disciplining in eighteen years. But after Adams finished lobbying Campbell, the penalty was quietly reduced to $100, which Adams paid for Lindsay.

The real truth behind the president's anger lay in his intense dislike of Ted Lindsay. Lindsay represented everything Campbell abhorred in a hockey player: cockiness, irreverence and disrespect. Worst of all, Lindsay could not be controlled by money, threats or example.

Conn Smythe loathed Lindsay even more than Campbell did. His animosity began when Adams swiped Lindsay, who was playing as a junior for St. Michael's College School in Toronto, out from under the Maple Leafs' nose. The rancour soon became personal. Smythe's famous motto was "If you can't beat 'em outside in the alley, you can't beat 'em inside on the ice" and he prided himself on dressing the toughest sons of bitches who had ever tied on skates. He took it personally when one of his strong men came out the worst in a fight. Ted Lindsay could beat his big boys in the alley, on the ice or in the stands and still walk away. What's more, Lindsay flaunted his victories. After a scuffle with one of the Maple Leafs, he'd stand grinning and pointing up at the stands where Smythe sat.

Lindsay had a large measure of talent leavening his aggression. He quickly became the best left-winger in the NHL. He scored seventeen goals over forty-five games in his first season. In comparison, Gordie Howe scored only seven goals in fifty-eight games during his 1947-48 rookie season. Howe wouldn't surpass Lindsay's first-year goal totals until his fourth year.

The Red Wings were a unit that stuck together on and off the ice. In many ways, the club resembled the Edmonton Oilers of the Gretzky years. As rookies, most of the players lived at Minnie (Ma) Shaw's boarding house, less than three blocks from the Olympia Stadium, built on land owned by Shaw's father.

Shaw specialized in rookies and unmarried players. In all, she played surrogate mother to more than 175 Red Wings between 1938 and 1959. A strict disciplinarian, she reported regularly to Adams on the players' deportment, but she also knew how to have fun. "She wasn't just a landlady," Marty Pavelich recalled on her death. "She was one of us. If we went out for a beer after a game she went with us. We never left her alone. And she had just as much fun as any of us."

The Russian coach Anatoli Tarasov has often maintained that Bob Gainey embodied the perfect player. In truth, that accolade belongs to Gordie Howe. There was no aspect of the game that Howe didn't master. At six-foot one and 205 pounds, he was one of the two or three biggest players of his day, a faster than average skater with an excellent wrist shot made all the more dangerous because he was ambidextrous. His backhand was as hard and accurate as the average player's forehand.

Moreover, Howe's passes were executed with a rare anticipation or foreview of the game, one of the characteristics that makes Wayne Gretzky the dominant player of his day. Some players can hit and fight, while others can whirl, dodge and feint. Howe could do it all and score, too. Just as important to Adams, few players were tougher and none more cleverly dirty. At a recent old-timers' dinner, a small argument broke out concerning the number of jaws Howe broke over the years with his elbows; the most often quoted figure was five.

Adding a sheen to the Howe perfection, from Jack Adams's point of view, was the star's childlike subservience. Adams loved to tell the story of how he'd picked Howe out of a crowd of young players and then nearly lost him.

He said to me one day, 'Mr. Adams, I'd like one of those windbreakers the Red Wings wear.' I said, 'Okay son. I'll get you one.' Then it promptly slipped my mind.

Next fall at training camp I decided I wanted him to turn pro and I offered him a contract. He looked at it but didn't sign it. So I asked him what was wrong, wasn't it enough money? He just looked at me and said 'I'm not sure I want to sign with your organization, Mr. Adams. You don't keep your word.'

Naturally, I was flabbergasted, and I asked him what he meant. 'Well' he said, 'you promised me a windbreaker and you never gave it to me.' You can imagine how quickly I got that windbreaker. But that's how close I came to losing him.

That one act of defiance was to last Howe for twenty years.

One of Adams's skills as a manager lay in his ability to use his team against itself, and each player against himself. His favourite monologue revolved around the self-sacrificing athlete who did his all for the team with no consideration of money. Through the years, he invariably held up Gordie Howe to the other players as the shining example of team spirit, loyalty and, most important, lack of greed.

It is a measure of how genuine was Howe's humility, off-ice geniality and love of hockey that he isn't the most hated man of his era.

During the 1961 training camp, apparently feeling that Howe was getting a bit uppity, Adams observed casually to a Detroit writer, "When I signed Gordie Howe the other day, I asked him if he'd thought he had a good year—of course, 36 goals, that's a great year for some people! But I asked if he's had what he could call a good year for Gordie Howe. He's an honest big guy. 'No,' he said. 'Too many dry periods.'"

As a result of Adams's finesse, Howe happily remained the most underpaid player in the history of pro sport. Colleen Howe wasn't nearly so impressed with the humility of the League's seven-time MVP. "We had four children to support! We had to scrimp. I made our clothes. I cut the kids' hair. We used skate exchanges. It was strictly no-frills. I couldn't even afford to make long distance calls to Gordie when he was on the road."

Though the '50s unfolded in idyllic fashion for Jack Adams and the Red Wings, the ground was shifting imperceptibly under the fat man's feet. When Big Jim Norris died in December 1952, shortly after taking his regular phone call from Jack Adams, the vital glue that bound his family and his business empire began to dissolve.

Jimmy already had his $45-million inheritance, and Norris had organized his affairs so that when he died his estate, for tax purposes, was valued at less than $5 million. Before his death, he had shuffled off nearly $200 million into a complex trust that kept the bulk of his fortune out of the hands of the U.S. Internal Revenue Service. The trust was to be managed by the other family members, Mrs. Marguerite Norris and her three children, Eleanor, Bruce and Marguerite, who had equal shares and an equal vote.

The only NHL team Jimmy controlled outright was the Rangers, through his majority block of Madison Square Garden shares. Though he didn't own controlling interest in the Blackhawks, Jimmy had been in charge since the mid-'40s.

Though neither Jimmy nor Bruce had shown any particular interest in hockey, both wanted the Red Wings. Bruce liked the games, the parties and the back-slapping maleness, but he had no inclination to learn the business side of pro hockey, or the business side of anything, for that matter.

The question of who would run the Norris hockey empire, especially the Red Wings, was complicated by a little gambit Conn Smythe had played when he realized that Jim Norris was dying. Smythe had always believed the leadership of the NHL was rightfully his, and so he set out to loosen the Norris family's grip on the NHL and, most importantly, to neutralize Jimmy Norris. He wasn't afraid of any other member of the Norris clan, but he knew that if Jimmy took over ownership of the three teams from his father, he and partner Arthur Wirtz would run the NHL like a fiefdom.

On February 21, 1951, Smythe astounded the other NHL owners by talking publicly about League business and casting aspersions on the Chicago Blackhawks. "I do not know who owns the club," he told the *Globe and Mail*, "and I am beginning to think that the lethargic manner in which things are being run in Chicago is part of a plan. Looks as though someone is waiting to step in and buy the club at a bargain." Two days after the editorial appeared, Clarence Campbell responded to Smythe with dignified outrage. "The reference to the ownership of the Chicago Club and its management clearly implies that they are suspect of dishonourable conduct."

Unfazed, Smythe pressed harder to flush out the Chicago ownership, which was masked by an anonymous corporation represented by NHL governor Bill Tobin. "I have several times asked you who are the owners of the Club and you have answered that you are unable to tell me who they are," he wrote to Campbell. "Surely our constitution is very clear regarding the registration of ownership, change of ownership and how it must be arranged. The Maple Leaf Gardens are very anxious to have this matter cleared up."

It was all shadow-dancing, of course. Smythe well knew that the Norris family had owned Chicago since 1944 and that Jimmy Norris had run the team since 1946, though his father still held the majority of shares. Jimmy Norris even attended board meetings, and Bruce Norris was vice-president of the club. This multiple ownership was against League rules, but the governors accepted the convenient fiction that Bill Tobin was the owner.*

Smythe's action threatened to force the League, through court if necessary, to adhere to its by-laws on multiple ownership once Jim Norris died. At the March 14, 1951, owners' meeting in New York, Smythe brought up the Chicago ownership issue so vigorously that the other owners voted to censure him for failing to act "in the best interests of the NHL" after he left the meetings early to attend to other business.†

---

* Although Jim Norris never broadcast the fact, his purchase of the team from Fred McLaughlin's son *had* been reported in 1944. And, when he turned over the management of the stadium and the club to Jimmy in 1946 that too had been made public. Interestingly, though Jimmy's partner, Arthur Wirtz's name is occasionally associated with the club in the late '40s, Jimmy's never is. Jimmy was also on the Blackhawks board of directors as was Wirtz. Though William Tobin had been president and governor of the club since 1944 there is no evidence that he owned more than a token number of shares.

† According to Smythe, the censuring was "expunged" from the record shortly after it was voted on.

An infuriated Smythe continued pushing Campbell to "make a proper investigation at Chicago." Attempting to muzzle Smythe, Campbell produced a report from Tobin on April 27. In Smythe's absence, the governors decided that Campbell should give a verbal summary about who owned Chicago, but only to those owners who made the request. No information was to be put in writing and, curiously, none of the governors asked for it.

Smythe was far from satisfied. The Chicago ownership still hadn't been *publicly* unmasked, and Smythe had expected Campbell to fall in line behind him much more easily. He instructed Maple Leaf Gardens lawyer Ian S. Johnston to contact Campbell, suggesting that legal action would follow if Smythe didn't get what he was looking for. Then, on August 2, 1951, he wrote a short and very threatening letter to the NHL president. "Up to the present it has been the policy of the writer to support the President of the League on any position he has taken. I wish to advise you that in future the policy will be for the writer to vote for what he thinks will be in the best interests of the League." To punctuate his threat, Smythe pointedly included a year-by-year summary of Campbell's salary and expenses since 1946.

Campbell responded with puzzlement: "I do not know what prompted your letter at this time, but if it has any sinister implications so far as I am concerned I appreciate the warning."

Campbell might have been puzzled, but Jimmy Norris got the message. With his immense boxing interests at stake, he couldn't afford a potentially embarrassing public showdown with Smythe, nor could he afford to lose control of the various NHL arenas that were vital to the IBC. He signalled his submission with a single, unheralded September 1952 announcement in which he stated that he and Bruce Norris, together with Arthur Wirtz, had bought out seven unnamed Blackhawks shareholders.*

---

* There probably actually were seven shareholders, but six of them were Norris family members who owned virtually all the shares. The other one was Wirtz. In essence, the three men bought themselves out.

With the Norris ownership of the Blackhawks forced into the open, Jimmy couldn't immediately increase his part-interest in the Detroit team when his father died in 1952. The obvious face-saving solution was to have Bruce become the figurehead president of the Red Wings. Unfortunately, Bruce was already a declared shareholder and also vice-president of the Blackhawks.

Jimmy had two choices. He could persuade Bruce to publicly "sell" his interest in Chicago, resign as vice-president and then take over in Detroit. Or he could support an interim Red Wings head while he waited for a better time to squash Smythe and take over. Selling his Chicago interest was not an alternative, as the city was a critical boxing centre and key to his International Boxing Club activities. On the surface, Bruce was the best alternative, but Jimmy found his dissolute twenty-nine-year-old brother unreliable and increasingly difficult to control.

Jimmy chose to support his twenty-four-year-old half-sister Marguerite. Ten days after Norris Sr. died, she took over as president of the Red Wings. The papers spent more time on how the first female owner in professional hockey would rearrange the office furniture than on how she intended to run the team. "The handsome young Amazon is so perfect for her spectacular role," gushed a women's page writer. "Wow—what a gold mine of pictures and stories can be foreseen in her good looking 5-foot-11 person and pleasantly cocky personality!"

Few took Marguerite's position seriously, and most treated her as a temporary phenomenon. "When I kept calling her 'honey' and 'dearie' my wife asked if that was a dignified way to address our new president," chortled Adams at Marguerite's first introduction to the media. "I said, 'How can I be dignified with a youngster I trotted on my knee when she was five years old?'"

Marguerite had other ideas. She made no secret of her inexperience in hockey, but she had her father's canny deal-making instincts, bolstered by her own headstrong intelligence. And she had travelled extensively with her father, which gave her a clear idea of how the Norris empire worked and how hockey fit into it. Marguerite also inherited her father's dislike of pomp and pretence. Once, when asked in a telephone interview about the colour of her hair, she replied bluntly, "I'm a dishwater blond."

As a result of the confidence and closeness between Norris and his daughter, Marguerite had turned out far more like her father than either he or his wife had wanted. "I was supposed to be a debutante and marry a Vanderbilt boy," she says, wrinkling her expressive eyebrows at the absurdity. By the late '40s Marguerite had had enough of all the "society things" her mother tried to thrust upon her and had left the family home in Lake Forest for a job in New York with Dunn and Bradstreet.

With a powerful mixture of determination, business acumen and common sense, Marguerite would no doubt have kept the Norris empire together had she been born a man. As president of the club she proved extremely adept; the players and other team officials remember her with tremendous respect. The Red Wings finished first in each of the three seasons she ran the team, and won the Stanley Cup twice. Marguerite controlled the team utterly, moving to Detroit and vetting every decision made by Jack Adams and Lincoln Cavalieri, who ran the arena.

Things were vastly different at the League level. When Norris died, Conn Smythe began exerting his new power. He tried to humiliate Marguerite by refusing to let her sit as governor, quoting a non-existent NHL by-law forbidding women from holding that position. Marguerite deftly turned it around by appointing Smythe's rival Jack Adams in her place, and communicated her votes with hand signals.

As the months went by and Marguerite showed no sign of stepping down, Smythe, irritated by the Red Wings' continued dominance over his Maple Leafs, stepped up his campaign. He made snide comments about the management of the Detroit club, the cleanliness of the players' uniforms and the condition of the Olympia Stadium.

"Your ladies' rooms are a disaster!" he accused Marguerite on one occasion. "Why do you go in them? What are you doing in my ladies' rooms?" Marguerite shot back. Smythe's bathroom badgering continued until she casually mentioned to a Toronto hockey writer that Mr. Smythe had an unusual interest in women's washrooms. That was the last she heard on that subject.

Marguerite kept close tabs on Jack Adams. She wasn't enamoured with her general manager's personality or overwhelmed by his reputation as a hockey genius. "Rotten, just really evil," is her capsule description. She knew, from years of watching and listening to her father, how much guidance Adams needed.

Right after taking over in Detroit, Marguerite decided to replace Jack Adams, now nearly sixty, with Tommy Ivan. She knew Ivan, who had been the Red Wings' coach since 1947, was looking to advance himself.

"I cannot fire Jack," she told Ivan confidentially. "We have to talk him into retiring." "When?" Ivan pressed recognizing that Jack Adams would never leave the Red Wings voluntarily. "I have to think of myself," he said apologetically, reminding her he had just married. "Jimmy [Norris] can hire me."

Marguerite smiled thinly. "I know, that's why I'm talking to you now." In 1956, Ivan became coach of the Blackhawks, "stolen" by Jimmy.

In the two years it took to sort out the vast legal complications surrounding Big Jim's will, a number of odd events occurred indicating serious rifts in the Norris clan. Today, Marguerite contends that her relations with her half-brother, whom she respected, admired and looked up to, were amicable. But Jimmy's actions and words don't bear out her view of things. Shortly after he hired away Tommy Ivan, the Chicago papers quoted Jimmy as saying he intended to "go all out to buy Gordie Howe, Ted Lindsay and Red Kelly."

"I didn't know Jim was 'sniffing the stuff' these days— at that rate they might as well buy the whole club and close up Olympia," Jack Adams commented peevishly.

If Jimmy had any hopes of one day taking over the Red Wings, he soon abandoned them. In order to do so he needed the support of his step-mother who had an equal vote in the trust, and he knew he'd never get it. In the spring of 1953, Jimmy bought out his family's interest in the Blackhawks and Chicago Stadium in return for selling his interest in the Red Wings and the Olympia. It seemed a happy arrangement, but comments from Jimmy had a bitter edge. "I was forced to divorce myself entirely from the Red Wings," he complained, "a team I had helped my dad build up to its present status as a champion hockey squad for five years in a row."

Jimmy also shot a barb at the rest of the family, claiming that he had to take sole control of the Blackhawks to prevent the team from folding: "Someone had to come up with the $210,000 in 1953 to keep the club alive." He insinuated that he couldn't count on Bruce or Marguerite to help stave off disaster, though both, through the trust, had owned shares in the team and the Stadium. No one thought to ask why, if the Blackhawks were in such desperate shape, he hadn't put in some money years before. A cash injection of that size wouldn't have caused a ripple in either his personal or IBC fortunes.

A week later, Jimmy delivered another kick when he told the Chicago *Sun-Times* that he wouldn't be surprised if the executors of his father's estate sold both the Red Wings and the Olympia. "It is not necessarily a family decision, since I would be in a position to take it over completely myself, if I wished," Marguerite responded tartly.

Then in 1954, Jimmy withdrew IBC from Detroit and staged no more fights in the Olympia. Since Detroit had proved an excellent boxing venue, the vengeful move cost him hundreds of thousands while knocking a considerable amount off the Olympia's gross revenue.

In 1955, Bruce suddenly announced his intention to run the Red Wings. Marguerite had been quite happy as president of the franchise and the last thing she wanted was to hand everything over to Bruce. She had little faith in his judgment and none in his management ability. "He always felt that if he met somebody and chatted with him—whether it was in a bar or a boardroom—he could tell by talking to them whether they were good guys or bad guys. Whether they were smart or not smart, sincere or not sincere. He thought he had this intuition. Well, he wound up with the worst collection of these sycophants you can imagine. Real ne'er-do-wells. The joy boys we called them."

Knowing her mother would side with Bruce, Marguerite had no choice but to hand over the presidency to him. She became executive vice-president and continued to play an active role with the team for a few years, though tension mounted and disagreements escalated between them.

Jack Adams got a stay of execution, but something fundamental had changed. Even though she detested him, Marguerite had been partly successful in controlling his darker impulses. Bruce, on the other hand, neither understood nor was capable of handling Adams. The fine line between motivating and bullying his players started to blur, and trades, ostensibly made to improve the team, were increasingly used to punish players. After Jim Norris died in 1952, the master trader made many questionable deals, but the Red Wings were so strong that the impact wasn't seen for years to come.

Nowhere was the change in Jack Adams more apparent than in his dealings with Ted Lindsay. Adams had never really liked Lindsay, but had suppressed his feelings because Lindsay was far too valuable to get rid of. "He was like a father to me," Lindsay recalls. "I could walk in in the morning and I could kick him right in the butt and he'd put his arms round me and kiss me."

Every year Lindsay played so relentlessly that he simply wore down at season's end, just when Adams needed him most. His weight would drop to 150 pounds, and the back pains he held at bay in the fall would grip him fiercely by mid-winter. In the early years, Adams compensated by resting his prize winger from time to time, even sending Lindsay to Florida in 1951 for an unprecedented holiday halfway through the season.

The bloom went off the romance early in 1952 when rumours surfaced in the press that Lindsay had lost some of his infamous fire and that his temper had mellowed. Though his statistics were as good as they had ever been, reporters, primed by Adams, began writing about

Lindsay's supposed "subpar" performance. When asked privately about the problem, Adams didn't attribute it to anything so innocuous as a beaten and battered body. He blamed sex—and too much of it at that.

The topic preoccupied the Red Wings' brains trust in those days. Many players drank themselves into a stupor with impunity after games, but if they violated the sex taboos they were in deep trouble. At the time, everyone, from armchair athletes to physicians, was convinced that athletes lost their "legs" or endurance if they engaged in sexual intercourse before competition.

When the Detroit management huddled to discuss a poorly performing player, the conversation invariably turned to the player's sexual proclivities. "If they thought one guy was screwing around with his wife too much they'd call him in," chuckles Lincoln Cavalieri, then manager of the Olympia. The scouts, Ma Shaw and even other players would be consulted and then someone, usually a trainer with a veneer of medical knowledge, would be delegated to approach the player, his wife or both to discuss their "problem."

Management didn't have much to worry about because on top of everything else, hockey players were and are sexually the most conservative athletes—at least according to the professionals. At the 1989 NHL draft, in Minneapolis, four hookers who specialized in servicing athletes celebrated the addition of a new sports team to their market. "It's so terrific now," enthused Sherry of Baltimore. "With four teams there's no dry period."

The hookers all agreed that hockey players are the least egotistical and demanding of their clients. They also approved of their lack of ornaments. "Ya know how it is with the other guys," ruminated Lindy. "They've got to have ten gold chains around their necks and they're always hitting you in the face with the goddamn things. Hockey players now, they're real nice and basic; two balls, one handle and one chain."

As for their performance ranking, "Hockey players do pump pretty good," observed Lindy. "Yeah!" chimed in Sherry, "but that's about it, pump, pump, pump. S'okay

by me though boring can be beautiful in this business."
All retailers agreed that hockey players were a little short
on imagination. "I don't think most of those hockey studs
would know what to do with snatch if you hung it off
the end of their noses," assessed Molly, a diminutive,
busty redhead.

The three women weren't maligning hockey players
who, after all, tipped better than their football colleagues.
"Those boys from Saskatchewan and Quebec, they give
real nice presents," says Sherry. "One of them gave Molly
a pink rabbit's foot. He told her he'd always played with
it stuffed in his jock." Molly wrinkled her nose, "Yeah,
still smells like it too."

"We *never* call these boys Johns," notes Sherry primly.
"We see what we do as part of their education (some of
them are *so* young) or part of their physiotherapy."

But Jack Adams saw no place for sex in *his* hockey
players' lives. A firm proponent of the sexual-intercourse-
damages-legs school of thought, he objected vehemently
to players getting married during the season. Nuptials
should be reserved for the day after the playoffs, giving
players four clear months to get sex out of their systems
before training camp.*

Glen Skov, traded to Chicago in a 1955 airlift of eight
players to the Blackhawks and Bruins, thinks his marriage in 1954 had something to do with Adams getting rid
of him. "Marriage was really taboo with Jack. If the team
lost a game he'd come into the locker room after and
point to all the married guys: 'You lot are spending too
much time pushing grocery carts and baby carriages and
it's ruining your game.'"†

Adams, thinking that Lindsay's ferocity had slipped be-

---

* Adams was far from alone in his obsession. Conn Smythe kept Bill Ezinicki down
on the farm in Pittsburgh for years, even when it was clear he could help the
Leafs, because he'd had the temerity to get married during the season.

† Hockey wives occupied an uncomfortable status with Jack Adams, who claimed
he could only remain impartial to them if he didn't know their names. If he happened upon a group of them in a hotel corridor he would turn to his own wife and
ask, "Which ones are those?" eliciting an affectionate "Why you big clown" as she
proceeded to brief him. However, during the playoffs, if a wife visited a cloistered

cause he was spending too much time with his fiancée, sent a trainer to sort him out. (It had apparently slipped the general manager's mind that Lindsay was playing with a separated shoulder that Adams had kept quiet, "so that the other teams don't take advantage of you.") Lindsay responded so truculently that Adams felt compelled to summon him for some personal instruction. The relationship between the two men became even more icy after Lindsay told Adams to "fuck off" and stormed out.

"I think he's so much in love, he may be softening up," Adams told reporters in saccharine tones.

Lindsay's independence rankled Adams, but his influence on the other players, and most particularly his closeness to the "big fella," Gordie Howe, was what threatened Adams the most. Howe and Lindsay roomed together at home and on the road, and at the start of the 1949-50 season, they agreed to pool their winnings from the NHL scoring leadership and share them equally, no matter who won. This infuriated Adams, though he carefully said nothing to Howe at the time.

When Lindsay brought his parents to Detroit from Kirkland Lake, Ontario, he bought them a house, and he and Howe moved in too. After Lindsay got married in April 1952, most assumed his relationship with Howe would change. "Gordie's awfully nice, next to Ted," joked Pat Lindsay on her wedding day. "I suppose he'll suggest he move in with us. Maybe he'll just show up at meal-time every day." She never dreamt how prophetic her words would be. Howe did move in with them just a few days after their return from a five-week Florida honeymoon, and he stayed until the end of the 1952-53

Detroit player in his hotel room, Adams had an uncanny knack of knowing who the offending woman was, how long she had stayed and whether any clothing had been removed.

When the team was on the road, Adams instructed the hotel switchboard not to accept any calls from players' wives under any circumstances. "The wives were just nobodies in the grand scheme," recalled Colleen Howe in *After the Applause*. "I remember once when I wanted to reach Gordie during the playoffs, I had to explain to the general manager what I wanted. *Just to talk to my husband.* As far as they were concerned, my only purpose in life was to make sure that Gordie was well fed, well rested, and well taken care of."

season, when he married Colleen.

Lindsay then committed another sin, as serious as enjoying too much sex. He and teammate Marty Pavelich
began their own plastics business and, if that wasn't bad
enough, they included Howe in the operation. Early in
the 1955 season, articles quoting the usual unnamed
sources charged that Lindsay and Howe had grown "too
wealthy to maintain zest for Stanley Cup playoffs."

Colleen Howe and Pat Lindsay were more angry than
their husbands. One evening, without telling Howe and
Lindsay, they turned up at a game in borrowed mink
stoles. "If we are that wealthy, we should look the part,"
they explained to reporters.

Checkmate to the wives, thought the writers, who
didn't count on Jack Adams's retaliatory zeal. Adams
phoned the paper's editor, called in a few favours and
got big dollar signs overlaid on the photo, with the wives
standing up to their knees in a superimposed flood of
paper money.

Lindsay's influence on the younger Red Wings also
bothered Adams. A fond myth circulates in hockey lore
about veteran players taking rookies under their wings,
nurturing them, seasoning them and helping them along
the way. In fact, a Darwinian struggle for position exists
on every team. Who's going to help a rookie who might
well take your job? "None of the older players would
ever tell you anything," Toronto defenseman Bob Baun
recalls of his first few years in the NHL. "They wouldn't
disclose anything that they said in negotiation, talk contracts or give you advice."

Lindsay was different. He talked to the younger players, bought them beer and dinner, interceded to prevent
the worst of the hazing by teammates, and generally tried
to make them feel at home. Before long, he exerted
tremendous, though informal, influence on the team, and
could often be heard contradicting Adams during tête-à-
têtes on the bench. Instead of trying to co-opt that influence for the benefit of the team, Adams sought to destroy
it. He warned rookies like goalie Glenn Hall against talking with Lindsay when they signed their contracts.

Adams made a mistake when he tried to dominate Hall. The rookie's big, cosy, rubber-faced demeanour masked a quiet and steely individuality. The puck terrified Hall—he regularly spent the last few minutes before a game with his head in the toilet—but he couldn't be intimidated or manipulated by mere mortals. Though his words flowed jerkily and he gave every impression of a not-too-bright, raw-boned farm boy, Hall's mind was very much his own. "I wasn't prepared to say, 'Yes, you are right, Mr. Adams, the great and glorious Adams.' I didn't say that. But that got you into trouble, everybody knew that."

Adams frequently called in his charges to discuss a particular play or point out a bad habit. Hall ignored every summons. Even when Adams spoke directly to him, Hall passed on his answers through the coach. Adams blamed this kind of impertinence directly on Ted Lindsay.

Lindsay, for his part, didn't make much of an effort to avoid trouble. Insolent, quick-witted and insightful, he became one of the most sought-after interviews around the League. In 1955 he breached one of hockey's inviolable codes by publicly criticizing the trade of Glen Skov to Chicago.

Just before the season opened in 1956, Adams threw down the gauntlet and humiliated Lindsay. Citing a previously unknown but "longstanding policy" of rotating the captaincy, Adams summarily announced that Lindsay's four-year tenure had ended. "Shifting the responsibility to another will help ease the tension on Ted and will help us develop leadership for the future," he explained. Lindsay only discovered the move when he read the papers the following morning.

From that moment on it was war. Neither spoke directly to the other, except during their increasingly combative contract discussions.

Chapter 4

Lindsay's Dream

From 1952 onward, Ted Lindsay's relationship with Jack Adams steadily deteriorated. At the same time, he was expanding his horizons and learning more and more about the world outside hockey. Running the business with Howe and Pavelich had taught him about bookkeeping and the costs of employing staff. He'd also begun to realize that his hockey salary wasn't as high as it seemed. He saw that while he was playing hockey, his contemporaries were building their futures. In the '50s, changing careers was difficult for any man in his late twenties or early thirties. When they retired, hockey players invariably spent years earning far less than their peers.

The Standard Player's Contract, a repressive masterpiece, made it almost impossible for players to capitalize, either directly or indirectly, on their hockey careers. Though players were paid only for the six-month hockey season, the contract dictated their lives for the entire year. Moreover, the contract expressly forbade earning money during the off-season from "football, baseball, softball, hockey, lacrosse, boxing, wrestling, or other athletic sport without the written consent of the club." In many cases, athletic ability was the only marketable skill players had. Even when a player worked up the nerve to ask his general manager, consent was rarely given.

On the other hand, the contract committed players to take part "in any and all promotional activities of the Club and the League" without pay. For example, in 1957 Maple Leaf Gardens received $9,300 from the St. Lawrence Starch Company and the Parkhurst Bubble Gum Company for use of the players' pictures. The players got nothing. Should an entrepreneurial player get any ideas about picking up a little change in the same manner, however, the contract prohibited him from making public appearances, having his picture taken, writing articles or sponsoring products "without the written consent of the Club." Again, such consent was rarely granted.

The draconian nature of the contract, coupled with the fact that few players had anything more than a high school education, meant that most were limited to off-season jobs as golf caddies, door-to-door salesmen, parking lot attendants and carnival barkers. One of the more fortunate was Toronto's Jimmy Thomson, who worked in and eventually took over his father-in-law's home heating oil business. The rare few, like Ted Lindsay, started their own enterprises, despite management opposition. During that era, when the season was shorter, players could have improved themselves with correspondence courses or summer school, but even that caused friction with their clubs.

In return for virtual servitude, the NHL provided precious little. The League's average 1957 salary of $8,000 seemed munificent compared to the $4,800 earned by sportswriters and the $5,500 paid to the average teacher. But out of their salaries, the players had to pay expenses most employees didn't. Many had to support two residences, especially if they had families or were traded in the middle of the season. If they wanted their wives to attend training camp, they paid the fare plus accommodation, and after training camp they paid their own way back home. As well, $900 came off the top annually for their pension, and many carried additional insurance to cover a career-ending injury. By the time all the little bits and pieces were taken away, their real gross salaries dropped by about 25 percent.

The hockey clubs did pay reasonable hospital costs, providing the hospital and the doctor were selected by the club, but their contractual obligation ended "at a period not more than eight weeks after the injury." Compensation also stopped if the injury stretched into the off-season, even if it prevented a player from earning further income. As a result, severely injured players, or those unlucky enough to get hurt at the end of the year, had to rely on the largesse of their general managers and owners. There were no guarantees that such charity would be offered, particularly to players who weren't on good terms with management.

Hockey teams perpetuated their image as a "family" that "looked after" their players, but the facts suggest this was the exception rather than the rule. According to Conn Smythe's records, three of his players, injured during the season, missed all or part of their off-season employment in 1956. Tod Sloan dislocated his shoulder in the playoffs and missed six weeks of his summer job, as did Hughie Bolton. Tim Horton broke his leg and couldn't work at all. None of them received *any* compensation.

Players were under tremendous pressure to play while hurt. No one has expressed hockey's attitude to injuries better than Punch Imlach. "If he can fuckin' walk, he can fuckin' play," he told the Leafs medical staff. "But I don't want you sendin' him back to me unless he can fuckin' walk."

Players who refused to play because of injuries were contractually guilty of withholding services. They could be benched, sent to the minors or "terminated," effective as soon as the notice was "delivered" or on the date it was "mailed," regardless of whether he received it or not.

The contract did provide an appeal procedure, with the League president Clarence Campbell to preside as arbitrator.

To compound the problem, most players had no idea

what their legal or contractual rights were, in large part because they weren't allowed to have a copy of their contract. With permission from their general manager they could look at it, but simply requesting the opportunity branded them as troublemakers. Several players recall examining their contracts with the club's secretary hovering nearby to ensure they didn't take notes.

In the end, any nagging concerns players had about their salaries and working conditions were offset by the knowledge that they would retire with an NHL pension, touted by the League as the best in professional sports. But Ted Lindsay was starting to change his mind about even that. In 1955, he and Canadiens defenseman Doug Harvey were appointed to the five-member National Hockey League Pension Society board; player representation was a requirement of the Society's by-laws.

Campbell, chairman of the board, personally administered the plan through ManuLife in Montreal. He was supported by two owners' representatives, General John Reed Kilpatrick, the Norris family's hired gun who had been running the New York Rangers since 1936, and Ian S. Johnston, a lawyer and secretary of Maple Leaf Gardens. The three men provided an admirable buffer between the owners and the players.

At first, both Lindsay and Harvey felt honoured by their selection, but pleasure quickly turned to frustration. Questions about owner contributions, pension size, All-Star game deposits and plan expenses and investments were never answered directly. Instead they were referred to the governors, then promptly forgotten. Pressing Campbell, the awe-inspiring war-crimes prosecutor, for answers was an intimidating task. "Campbell was a very, very powerful man with the players. He was a man of stature, and he wasn't going to give anything to anybody he didn't feel like giving," emphasizes Leo Reise, a self-assured war veteran and chartered accountant who succeeded Lindsay on the Society board. "There weren't many people who were going to stand up to Campbell and say 'Look, you lied,' or 'You pulled a boner' because a guy has to play hockey."

Campbell's droning legalese and obfuscation left the most intelligent and motivated players feeling insignificant and confused. "He used to come and visit us once a year," recalls Lindsay. "When he was through speaking for two hours, everybody would say, 'What did he say?'"

After a year on the Pension Society board, Lindsay, now a businessman, asked more pertinent and pointed questions about the plan. When he couldn't get direct answers, he requested that an outside expert be hired to examine its investments and yields. Voting on such issues invariably went three to two against the players. Interestingly, NHL records show all votes as unanimous.

The NHL players' pension plan dates back to 1946, when C. Jean Casper, a Detroit insurance agent and avid hockey fan, suggested the idea to a few players. Until then, he and other local independent agents had restricted themselves to selling injury insurance to the Red Wings. Dubbed the "per stitch" policy, one of the provisions awarded players compensation based on the number of stitches required to repair their injuries. Consequently, visible damage was always preferred to hidden problems like twisted knees and wrenched backs. Players occasionally asked doctors to add a few extra stitches to close a cut.

Casper gathered together a group of players to form an association to administer the proposed pension. They talked about asking the NHL owners to contribute some of their profits to the fund. There was nothing secret about their intentions. When a group of Red Wings asked his advice, Jack Adams quietly sent Casper $2,500 start-up money.

But Conn Smythe, who understood money and power rather better than Adams, did not intend to let the players have any control over anything—particularly money. He lobbied the other owners to convince them that something had to be done to stop their efforts. Clarence Campbell had been hired a few months earlier, and the owners gave him his first big job—head off the players. In late 1947, Campbell announced that the League intended to form its own plan, giving Casper no choice but to hand over the funds he had collected.*

Between 1948 and 1957, all NHL players paid $900 annually into the plan. It was a huge bite considering that the average NHL salary was less than $5,000, and some players were paid as little as $3,500. The owners' contribution of $600 per player didn't come out of profits. Instead, the League took two-thirds of the gate receipts from the All-Star game and added in the proceeds from a new twenty-five-cent surcharge on playoff tickets.

The players weren't paid for the All-Star game, so, in essence, the owners donated the players' own wages to fund their pension plan. As a result, in some years there was little if any real owner contribution. In 1956, for example, the League turned over $28,261 from the All-Star game and a further $32,000 from the surcharge. In contrast, the players contributed nearly $130,000. Since the players were never allowed to look at the Pension Society's books, they had no idea about the real state of their pension. Nor did they know that by February 1957 the plan, after fulfilling all current commitments, had a huge surplus of $1,527,708,† a surplus that the owners would soon begin quietly distributing to themselves.

Harvey and Lindsay developed a grudging respect for each other. Harvey admired Lindsay's refusal to be intimidated by Campbell's sharp sarcasm. In turn, Lindsay enjoyed Harvey's laconic manner, which masked a penetrating mind. One day, after a particularly aggravating Society meeting, they commiserated over beers. Their conversation turned to money, and, after considerable fencing, they breached the NHL's biggest taboo—akin to fondling each other in public—salary disclosure. (Billy Harris and Bob Pulford of the Toronto Maple Leafs, for instance, were close friends and roomed together on the road for seven years. Pulford was best man at Harris's

---

* It appears that Campbell vaguely promised Casper a role in managing the plan, at least the assets pertaining to the American teams' players. But Campbell turned the whole thing over to ManuLife in Montreal and shut Casper out.

† Current commitments refer to benefits paid to players and costs associated with administering the plan.

wedding and Harris was an usher at Pulford's. They talked at length about every conceivable topic but never once asked each other how much they made.)

Lindsay and Harvey spent hours calculating attendance figures, estimating profits and comparing them with the players' share. Before parting, they concluded that the much professed "fragility" of professional hockey was nothing more than a big lie, and that they were being cheated out of a fair return.

One of the NHL's most unwavering contentions is that hockey teams make very little money, even in good years, and that "excessive" player demands will bring about the collapse of weaker clubs. In bad times, such demands could threaten the very existence of the entire League. The teams trot out this argument whenever individuals or groups of players make any kind of demand. And it works astonishingly well; so well that the League's fragility was, and is, an accepted fact among players, sportswriters and fans. But it is nothing more than a ruse.

During the 1950s, every club made money. And even the Chicago operation was profitable because Jimmy Norris owned the stadium and many of the events booked into it. "The arena and the team always made at least a million bucks each [annually]," emphasizes Lincoln Cavalieri, former vice-president in charge of operations for the Detroit Olympia Stadium. "If you don't make money in an arena, you don't know how to operate an arena."

"We were absolutely coining it," Marguerite Norris recalls happily.

The Toronto Maple Leafs likewise were a private mint for Conn Smythe, who after Norris's death became the League's most powerful owner. By gambling on horse races, hockey games and other sports, Smythe had parleyed his $10,000 severance cheque from his very brief stint as coach of the New York Rangers into $40,000. He and several partners then purchased the franchise and the players in 1927 for $160,000.

In 1931, Smythe performed a neat trick, worthy of the penny stock market. The company formed to build

Maple Leaf Gardens was trading on the Toronto Stock Exchange, with Smythe as one of the founding shareholders. He and his partners vended in, or traded, their ownership of the $100,000 hockey franchise for controlling interest in the $2-million Maple Leaf Gardens.*

Smythe often talked about the hardships of building the arena during the height of the Depression. In fact, Maple Leaf Gardens Limited, incorporated on February 24, 1931, turned a $40,535 profit, thanks to advance ticket sales, even before construction was finished. And it profited handsomely every single year thereafter, netting $3,418,467 between 1932 and 1957. Moreover, in those years the Gardens paid dividends of $2,577,906, at least half of which went to Smythe and his partners. By 1957, the Gardens was debt-free and had been for years. That year's operation netted $214,586, down from the previous year's $289,786 but still a respectable amount.

Smythe played a subtle game for years. At first glance his management of the arena doesn't make sense. It was sparsely rented in the early '50s, with only the occasional non-hockey booking. And even though the games were sold out long before the season began, he resisted all efforts to have the Gardens expanded beyond its 12,737-seat capacity. Smythe's behaviour was always attributed to his being a hockey purist, but in truth, keeping the Gardens underdeveloped and under-utilized deflated the share price and allowed him to slowly pick up undervalued stock at a bargain.

The Maple Leaf Gardens books were poked, prodded and curried masterfully to show no hint of either the hockey team's or the arena's real profitability. In 1957, for instance, after paying $176,000 in dividends, the Gardens carried an impressive earned surplus of $1.2 million, but the real figure was far higher. Part of the surplus was held in marketable securities—Massey-

---

* Smythe and his partners were guaranteed a 7 percent return on the 10,500 preferred shares they got in the trade. They also received 23,100 common shares, which meant they could still participate in any profits the team made. Smythe also personally bought 3,880 shares of common stock.

Ferguson, Noranda and International Nickel—which were carried on the books at their original purchase price of $254,800, instead of their real market value of $473,000.

Also that year he listed both the hockey franchise and player contracts as being worth $100,001—a figure that hadn't changed since 1931. The players alone were insured for $400,000. Smythe also inflated his expenses, charging $396,788 for players' salaries, travelling expenses, promotion and training. As the actual total of players' salaries was $164,535.28, including bonuses, and the actual travelling expenses no more than $60,000, Smythe was unloading an impressive $172,252.72 in other expenses on the Leafs.

The most misleading figure on Smythe's books is the value of the Maple Leaf Gardens site, almost an entire city block in downtown Toronto. The company paid $350,000 for it in 1931, and Smythe, in the prospectus, said it was then undervalued by $150,000. He listed all the property the company owned at $467,138, and that figure included four parcels of land entirely separate from the Gardens and purchased between 1954 and 1957 for a total cost of $247,500. In 1957 those parcels alone were worth nearly $400,000 and the Gardens site about $5 million.

Smythe wasn't the only owner to hide profits and undervalue assets. The New York Rangers' earnings were shunted through a labyrinth of Norris companies and Madison Square Garden subsidiaries. Though MSG admitted to profits of half a million dollars in 1955, the real total was far higher, because a portion of it was siphoned off in extraordinarily high dividends paid to Jimmy Norris, Arthur Wirtz and the other shareholders in 1954, 1955 and 1956.*

Owning an arena, in addition to being immensely profitable in its own right, provides many opportunities to make the resident hockey team appear to lose money. The simplest method is to have the arena charge the club

---

* The Rangers contributed heavily to those profits as revealed in anti-trust actions against Jimmy Norris in 1957 and 1958.

exorbitant rent for the facilities. Another equally effective technique is for ancillary revenues from beer sales, souvenirs and other concessions to end up in the arena's books, or in a separate branch of the parent corporation. Suddenly, the team that sells out every game chronically loses money or breaks even at best.

Jiggery-pokery with attendance figures has long been a staple of arena management. Under-reporting totals is an easy way of reducing revenue, something several franchises indulged in during the '50s and '60s. In an annual report, the NHL listed the Rangers' 1954-55 attendance figures as 235,000. The real total was 313,026—a difference in gate revenue of as much as $500,000.

Another technique, beautiful in its simplicity, is to have more actual capacity than the arena is rated for. If it seats 14,500 but is only listed as having 14,000, then the price of 20,000 seats over a forty-game schedule never enters the books. At $5 a seat, this is a net profit of $100,000 annually, not including playoffs. Even better, revenue from seats that don't exist isn't taxed.

Jimmy Norris, with his underworld connections, was an experienced skimmer. When his International Boxing Club set up the Sugar Ray Robinson–Randy Turpin fight in 1951, Norris surreptitiously installed an extra four rows in the ringside sections, numbering them 1a, 2a, 3a and so on. Someone must have squealed because the normally toothless New York State Athletic Commission found out and fined him a token $5,000. It amounted to a slap on the wrist because IBC grossed over $1 million for the event, not including the $200,000 under-the-table cash Norris netted from the ringside-seat scam.

A major reason for the NHL's historical profitability is its dominance over the players. From 1955 to 1965, one of the most profitable periods in the League's history, the players' percentage share of revenue actually declined.

Lindsay and Harvey didn't know any of this, but still they seriously doubted that the franchises were as unprofitable as the League maintained. Their revelations and speculations probably would have remained just so much talk except for a chance meeting between Lindsay and Bob Feller during the summer of 1956. Feller, star pitcher for the Cleveland Indians and founding president of the baseball players' association, told Lindsay about the ground-breaking contract that New York lawyers Norman J. Lewis and Milton Mound had just negotiated on the players' behalf. Fascinated, Lindsay flew to New York at his own expense to meet Mound and Lewis.

Believing themselves inured to the peculiarities and meanness of baseball's eccentric owners, Mound and Lewis were thunderstruck when Lindsay revealed hockey's "normal practices." "Plain and simple indentured servitude," was Lewis's assessment. "Conditions were far worse than any other sport."

Lewis baldly stated that television, still in its infancy, would be the major vehicle of change in professional sport, and he explained to Lindsay how he and Mound had negotiated an unprecedented deal to turn over 60 percent of $9.75 million in World Series broadcast revenues to the baseball pension fund. Lindsay shook his head in wonderment and said it couldn't apply to hockey because the owners didn't make any money from television. Lewis wheeled around and snapped, "How the hell do you know?" Lindsay shrugged feebly. "The owners told us."

In fact, hockey was on the verge of a television breakthrough. CBS had televised a ten-game series during the 1955-56 season, paying each of the four American teams a total of $100,000 for the privilege. The players received nothing. The initial popularity of the games amazed television executives. "Even businessmen's clubs in Florida set earlier luncheon dates so they could watch the hockey show," Pete Molnar of CBS marvelled. "We got one call from a girl in Cincinnati who wanted to start a women's hockey league. We referred her to NHL president Clarence Campbell who told her hockey was too rough for gals."

Newspapers across the state of Florida scrambled to dig up snowbirds from the north like Bullet Joe Simpson, one of the original players for the New York Americans, and ran interviews explaining the exciting "new" game.

One Miami paper ran a cartoon of a scantily clad tourist sitting under a palm tree, mint julep in hand, ogling a game of hockey on TV. In New Orleans, sportswriter Tom Fox enthused, "Boy! When they gang up on the poor goalie and everybody's pushing that little puck at the wire cage, your pulse just has to pick up the beat." Midway through the '56-'57 season, CBS announced its intention to broadcast twenty-one games the following year, paying the League $210,000.

In Canada, the pot was much richer. The Maple Leafs and the Canadiens each received $331,000 for television and radio rights in the 1956-57 season, information they did not intend to share with the other clubs. Weston Adams, who inherited the Bruins from his father, Charles, and New York's General Kilpatrick regularly suggested all teams pool their television revenues, but Smythe regretfully explained that he couldn't get his sponsors to agree.

The players had no idea how much money Montreal and Toronto were making from television, but Norman Lewis suspected it was substantial, certainly enough to fund higher wages and a better pension. Excitable, vociferous and passionate, Lewis hammered away at the inequities the players suffered. His aggressiveness frankly scared Lindsay, who had only wanted some questions answered. Lewis promised to "snowplow" their cause right up to the U.S. Supreme Court if necessary.

More than once, Lewis uttered the dreaded word, *union.*

Compared to today's multimillionaires, pro athletes of the '50s were charmingly, if naively, devoted to their sports and to their heroic image as professional athletes. At all costs, they wanted to avoid being seen as grasping trade unionists. The neophyte basketball and football associations promoted themselves more as fraternal clubs than labour groups. "If we begin operating as a union," explained National League player Bob Friend, "we immediately will begin antagonizing the owners. . . . It would tend to destroy the image of the baseball star for the youngsters because of the haggling between the players and the owners."

Lindsay didn't want to start a union, nor did he want to create any more trouble than he already had, but he felt something had to be done. "The reason we were doing it was not to be upstarts or to be controversial or be detrimental to hockey," Lindsay recalled more than thirty years later. "We were doing it because there was a need for it—not for the guys who were forming it—but for the average hockey player—the fringe hockey player."

Twice more, Lindsay flew to New York at his own expense. He was relieved when the quiet, fatherly but shrewd-eyed Mound took over the hockey cause from Lewis. Mound was no less aghast at life in the NHL than his partner. "Outrageously corrupt, outrageously wrong—far worse than baseball," he exclaims, still indignant more than thirty years later. "Hockey was so medieval—as if it were a dynasty. When you are born, you are already indentured to the lord and master. Hockey children belonged to the lord and master and he could tell them what they had to and what they shouldn't do. The fellow who was the president of the team was God to them."

Lindsay explained that the players wouldn't be able to pay them much, but Mound and Lewis, who ran a well-heeled Manhattan law practice, loved a good, righteous fight. Mound laid out the steps necessary to set up an association and prodded Lindsay to draw up a list of potential representatives on each team.

During the pre-game skate at the Montreal All-Star game in October 1956, Lindsay made his move, gingerly approaching Doug Harvey. Harkening back to their earlier conversation and describing his talks with the lawyers, Lindsay proposed that they form a players' association. To his relief, Harvey was enthusiastic. After the game they casually drew Bill Gadsby of New York, Gus Mortson of Chicago, Fernie Flaman of Boston and Leafs captain Jimmy Thomson to one side and arranged a meeting.

The idea of these men talking together, let alone conspiring, was nothing short of a miracle. "Fraternization," as the League by-laws called it, with members of other teams was strictly forbidden. Coaches treated any hint of it with the same derision and censorship that a boot camp staff sergeant would direct at a male army recruit who showed up wearing pantyhose. Professionally, and often personally, players loathed each other. Sometimes management even publicly put prices on opposing players' heads.*

The hostility between teams was so great that when they travelled on the same train they were separated by a dining car and scheduled to eat at different times. Occasionally, the cars couldn't be organized this way and the players had to pass each other to get to their meals. Usually they accomplished this in frosty silence with a minimum of eye-contact.

A walking, sneering affront, Lindsay always made eye-contact in the trains, and he never shuffled past but strutted like a cock among a pen of brood hens. The atmosphere was always ominous, and on several occasions he came close to blows with Montreal or Toronto players. "Ted always seemed to be seething," recalls sportswriter Jim Eathorne. "Every time he walked through the dining car, you felt something was going to happen."

No one would ever have dreamt that Ted Lindsay would lead a players' organization. He'd fought every one of the players he called together to meet after the 1956 All-Star game. He'd had particularly bloody bouts with Thomson and Flaman, and, just a few days previously, had beaten a Boston player so badly he'd ended up in the hospital.

But the players put aside their animosities and plotted long into the night. The next morning they returned to their clubs, pledged to take action. Under intense secrecy they began soliciting support among their teammates and collecting $100 annual dues. They were careful not to talk in earshot of the trainers, many of whom they be-

---

* Canadiens coach Toe Blake once put a price on the head of Boston defenseman Ted Green. Though chastised for it by Clarence Campbell, the threat heated up team feuds and was viewed as an acceptable weapon of war and an excellent attendance enhancer.

lieved to be management informants. Within four months they had signed up every player but one, Ted Kennedy of the Toronto Maple Leafs, and the association treasury totalled $12,000.

Outwardly the League went on as always. Battles were fought, trades made, careers broken and stars born. But the pressure of the players' terrible secret grew as each day passed. Remarkably, not a single man leaked information to the owners or the press.

On February 11, 1957, after a Montreal–New York game, the conspirators assembled in New York to meet Mound and to put the finishing touches on their plans. At a press conference on February 12, Lindsay announced the formation of the National Hockey League Players' Association. He presented himself as president, with Doug Harvey as first vice-president, Fern Flaman and Gus Mortson the second and third vice-presidents, Jim Thomson as the secretary and Bill Gadsby as the treasurer.

The players' association announcement was so uncontentious it could have been Lord Baden-Powell outlining the formation of the Boy Scouts. "The association will be news to the NHL owners, I believe, but we get along fine with them. We are very happy, but we want to make the league so popular that youngsters in both Canada and the United States will want to grow up and play professional hockey."

When one sportswriter referred to the fledgling group as a union, the collective intake of breath sounded like a snake's hiss. "We're not a UNION!" six voices shouted almost in unison. "We're not out to make trouble."

The six men boarded their respective trains that evening, stomachs churning over a sickening mixture of elation combined with the corrosive fear that is bred into hockey players. They'd signed up every player in the League but one. It was the most support ever given to a professional sport association, before or since. And they had neither said nor done anything even slightly offensive. Still, they felt like plantation workers who had sassed their masters.

The League reacted with astonishment. "I'm completely surprised. I honestly don't see where players have a grievance," confessed Lynn Patrick, general manager of the Boston Bruins. Conn Smythe, contacted at the Breakers Hotel in West Palm Beach, said curtly, "The players on the [association] executive have done a lot for hockey, and hockey has done a lot for them. It's been an even deal up to date." Jack Adams snapped, "I don't know what they need a lawyer for!"

The day after the announcement, an eerie tension crackled in the six NHL arenas. There was no sign of "Jolly Jack" in Detroit as Adams rampaged around the dressing room, every centimetre of the considerable expanse of his face beet red. His breathing came in staccato gasps as he confronted *his* boys. After a harsh tirade on the subject of loyalty and ingratitude, he stalked from one half-clad player to another.

"Are you for this? Are you for this?" he shouted, stabbing his finger at one after the other. The rookies and fringe players blushed, fidgeted or looked away. Badger as he might, Adams couldn't get a yes or no out of any of them. "Well, see, he doesn't want it!" Adams crowed over each bowed head before moving on.

When he came to Gordie Howe, Adams put his hand on the player's shoulder and said, with a quivering voice, "I know you're not for this Gord, big fella, I don't even have to ask." Howe's eyes stayed rivetted on his skates and not a sound escaped his lips.

Standing before Marty Pavelich, Lindsay's close friend, Adams stared for a long moment, looked around the room and then pointed. "Time will take care of him." Then he moved to Lindsay and stood for a longer moment as a rictus sneer folded his face. "Time will take care of him." Lindsay alone met Adam's stare.

Adams then summoned every Detroit writer of consequence to his office for a private conversation. Bill Brennan, a distinguished hockey writer for the Detroit *News*, remembers his meeting with a clarity that defies the years. Cheerful and relaxed at first, Adams's calm quickly degenerated into a bitter denunciation of Lindsay:

"a bad apple," "a cancer" and "the ruination of the team." Brennan nodded sympathetically, but said nothing.

Abruptly, the tirade stopped and Adams tiptoed furtively over to shut his office door, then returned to rifle through a file on his desk. "Look what this bastard is making," he snarled, flipping him a contract with Lindsay's name and $25,000 written prominently on it, "and he's still bitching!"

Brennan couldn't help but compare this munificent figure with his own $6,800 annual stipend. "I lost a lot of sympathy for Lindsay that day," he admits. Brennan has never doubted the authenticity of the contract Adams showed him, but when pressed admits the irregular nature of the event. "It was the only time a GM ever showed me a salary." Lindsay actually made $12,000 that year.

The Detroit papers, which had initially treated the formation of the players' association as a straight news story, suddenly began larding their accounts with tidbits about Lindsay's "lavish" $40,000 home in an "exclusive" subdivision and his "rich" but unspecified salary.

When Lindsay remained unbowed, Adams stepped up the attack by giving reporter and close friend John Walter unsolicited and "hitherto unrevealed salary figures" for quotation and attribution. "Lindsay has averaged $14,500 a season (or $188,550 for his 13-year career) all the years he's been with the Wings. He's built up other businesses, founded on his hockey earnings and reputation."

Not content with leaking false salary figures to the press, Adams listed his "untouchables," players too valuable to trade. He pointedly excluded Lindsay, who had just finished the best season of his career, indeed the best season of any left winger in the history of hockey with thirty goals, fifty-five assists and eighty-five points.

Things were no better for Jimmy Thomson. Upon returning to Toronto, he found a telegram ordering him to appear in Smythe's office the next morning at 9:30. When he arrived, he found Smythe sitting waiting for him, rigid as a corpse. Thomson steeled himself for a tongue-lashing, but Smythe simply stared in frigid silence.

Finally the harangue began. "Traitor," Smythe spat out early on; "quisling" and "communist" he added later. He ranted on about gratitude or lack of it and the family nature of the Leafs. "We all look after each other," he said sanctimoniously. On top of the treachery, disloyalty and insurrection, it was the intrusion of "New York lawyers" and "Jews" that infuriated him. "Of course that boiled Smythe," laughs Thomson. "Jewish lawyers telling him what to do. He was just a little bit prejudiced." It quickly dawned on Thomson that Smythe was castigating him not so much for participating in the association as for failing to inform on the others.

Smythe, a self-made millionaire, had scrabbled all his life, challenging anyone who got in his way. "The truth is, I never shared things well with anybody, all my life," he admitted in his 1981 autobiography. "I would give something freely, didn't mind giving it, but nobody was going to take it away from me, or just move in and use it."

When crossed, Smythe, the "utterly charming man, funny, expansive, warm and outgoing," became snake-mean, with ball-bearing eyes and condor lips. On such occasions he turned his formidable organizing skills against his opponents and, more often than not, went for the kill.

For a relentlessly practical man, Smythe had a romantically ideal portrait of the perfect hockey player, and King Clancy embodied it. He had "guts" and could score, but it was Clancy's disregard for money that Smythe most treasured. In 1930 he purchased Clancy from Ottawa for the equivalent of $50,000, an unheard-of sum at the time. "What do you want to be paid?" Smythe asked. "Anything you say," Clancy shrugged obligingly. "Anything you say!" Smythe later wrote. "I never had any trouble with Clancy about money in my life. He was the most *amateur* athlete I ever had. Just loved to play."

Smythe did his best to keep his hockey players amateur. In 1931 he wrote to potential Maple Leaf Gardens shareholders: "We cannot tell you the actual value of the Toronto players. We consider them pals rather than business associates and do not care to place a price on their hockey ability." By 1957, Smythe's "pals" were the lowest-paid team in hockey, and had been for years.

In 1956, Smythe had slowly begun to turn over control of the team and Maple Leaf Gardens to his youngest son, Stafford. But Smythe, not trusting him to fight Lindsay's players' association, brusquely shouldered him aside.

Immediately after his confrontation with Thomson, Smythe unleashed Ian S. Johnston, the Maple Leaf Gardens' lawyer and the man he most trusted to handle dirty work. His instructions were to find a way to beat the association no matter what the cost. Johnston's first job was to recruit an informant on the team to tell them what was being planned. Using a combination of bribery and blandishment, he recruited one of the club's most trustworthy players and used his information in compiling a dossier on every player, rating them for loyalty.

Smythe, with Johnston's information in hand, summoned each player to his office for interrogation, and berated them for their lack of loyalty and gratitude. For emphasis, he read aloud a meticulously prepared list, citing precisely what the Maple Leafs had done for that player. Frank Mahovlich slouched into Smythe's office to hear a detailed report of every penny the club had spent on his behalf.

In the four other NHL cities, the reaction was similar, if somewhat more civilized. In Montreal, an ageing Senator Donat Raymond had just sold the Canadiens and Canadian Arena Company to his friend Senator Hartland de M. Molson. The Molsons had long experience with unions and knew that even the strongest did little damage to a monopoly. Hartland Molson, who saw no real harm in allowing the players to organize, was the only owner to express any support or understanding.

But Frank Selke, the Canadiens' operating manager, was cast from the same mould as his former employer, Smythe. Initially apoplectic about the association, he soon calmed down and decided, as Montreal has always done, that winning was the primary issue. Let the other teams do the heavy punching, he reasoned, and Montreal would reap the benefits without harming the team or spending any money. Selke knew he could take his revenge when it suited him.

The association also infuriated Boston owner Weston Adams, but he had no close friendship with any of the other owners, so his attack was limited to veiled threats in the paper: "They'll be sorry if they continue this line."

The response from Chicago and New York was blunted by the quicksand that trapped Jimmy Norris. Mired in lawsuits and facing racketeering accusations concerning his International Boxing Club, Norris viewed the new association as just one more aggravation, and a minor one at that.

On the surface, the NHL projected a business-as-usual placidity, but a few days after the association's New York press conference, Clarence Campbell threatened a group of players, saying that the owners could and would "terminate" the pension contract if they stepped out of line.

Campbell understood the players better than anyone. His prescription for defeating their attempt at organization was simple: frighten them, starve them and then ignore them. After that, the association would fall apart on its own. "As I told you before, Jack, the really important thing is to win the ultimate battle," Campbell later wrote to Jack Adams, explaining his philosophy. "And that will be won when the players have found that they have been taken in by Lewis & Mound and the only way to do that is to make it cost them some money."

Conn Smythe, on the other hand, favoured a scorched-earth policy. He was obsessed with crushing the association, *immediately*. His harassment of Thomson didn't end with a lecture. The Leafs' captain suddenly found himself sitting out games, playing with strange defence partners and practising with the rookies. Smythe further humiliated Thomson by ordering Hap Day to leave him home for the team's last road trip. At the end of the season he put Thomson on waivers. Suspiciously, there were no takers.

Smythe had always viewed Day as "soft" on the players but ignored it because he got results; between 1940 and 1950, with Day as coach, the Leafs won five Stanley Cups. But Day might as well have organized his own execution when he privately told Smythe that he didn't believe that the players' association should be exterminated like an infestation.

The 1956-57 season was one of the Leafs' worst in years. At a March press conference, Smythe grandly took "complete responsibility" for the "year of failure," but then proceeded to blame Thomson and, by implication, his old friend and partner Hap Day for everything. "I find it very difficult to feel that there is time during a hockey season for the Captain of my club to go around and influence young players to join an association, which has, as far as I can find out, no specific plans or ideas of how to benefit hockey. I also feel that anything spawned in secrecy as this Association was, certainly has to have some sort of odour to it."

At the press conference, Smythe talked about Day as if he weren't there.* "Whoever signs my men next year, will have to know whether they are going to understand that they have to give 100 percent hockey loyalty to the Maple Leaf association and also that they know that they are going to play; when, how and where, our organization tells them."

Day, who had been Smythe's "whoever" for years, was dismayed at the clear message being given to the assembled reporters. His dismay turned to anger when Smythe, showing his own brand of "100 percent hockey loyalty," repeatedly refused to endorse Day as general manager or Howie Meeker as coach, claiming he had to consult his "very active Board of Directors" before deciding on the futures of the two men.

"My legs have just been cut out from under me," Day said afterward. A proud man, he told reporters that he

---

* Many claim that Day, who owned 16 percent of Smythe's gravel business, had more to do with the success of the hockey and gravel enterprises than Smythe himself. For decades, Day arrived at the gravel pit at 5 am to dispatch trucks. After a full day's work there he went to the Gardens and stayed until lock-up. When Smythe went to war, he left Day with all the coaching duties as well as responsibility for the gravel business.

would be "unavailable" to the Leafs in any capacity in the future. It is a fixture of hockey mythology that Smythe regretted what he did to his friend Day, but if so, there's no hint of it in his autobiography or in his private papers: "As far as I was concerned, nothing changed between me and Hap. I counted him as the best friend I had." Day went on to be a successful businessman and largely ignored Smythe for the rest of his life.

Smythe temporarily elevated Howie Meeker to general manager for the 1957-58 season, but fired him a few months later in favour of Billy Reay, "a true soldier of the old school." Reay promptly demonstrated the right attitude by mocking the association. "I think they should be tickled to death to play in this league. Most of them don't even know why they need an Association. Ask them what their beefs are and they don't know."

Publicly, the League treated the players' association as if it didn't exist. It refused to negotiate, answer phone calls or respond to letters. Early in April, Milton Mound politely wrote to Smythe asking for clarification of comments he'd made in the Maple Leaf Gardens annual report and at a recent press conference concerning Thomson and the players' association. Smythe answered sarcastically, "Any resemblance between the reports you have heard and the truth is only coincidental. However, don't let that stop you."

On June 14, 1957, the NHL agreed to a secret meeting with Mound in Montreal. The League sent lawyer John Chisholm with simple instructions: "Let Mound talk and say nothing." Mound had prepared twelve legal-size pages of specific demands, ranging from compensation for injuries and reimbursement for travelling expenses when traded during the season to the reinstatement of Jimmy Thomson. Two weeks before the meeting, he sent an abbreviated version to the League. "Rank impertinence," sputtered Ian Johnston when he read the section requesting Thomson's reinstatement.

Smythe was outraged to learn that the players wanted to take control of the pension and have the All-Star game broadcast revenues going directly into the pension fund.

From there, he knew it was a very small step to demanding a share of regular-season television money. He could barely contain himself when he discovered that the players had already written to CBC and CBS "to call to your attention that despite the players' financial interest in the proceeds of such broadcasts, to date you have failed to obtain their consent to such broadcasts."

At that point, Smythe convinced the NHL to go on war footing. Lindsay, Harvey and the rest of the player reps were privately told that they would "rot in hell" before they got what they wanted. The governors agreed to levy a special fund—5 percent of net gate receipts—to combat the players. Publicly, the NHL explained that the fund would be used to bolster the weak Chicago club.

The governors also agreed that something had to be done about Lindsay. Jack Adams was more than happy to take care of that problem. On July 24, 1957, he shocked the hockey world by trading Ted Lindsay and "the young pest" Glenn Hall to the Chicago Blackhawks. He described his action as part of a "youth movement." Normally, a player trade is a time for unctuous platitudes, but Adams turned the knife, claiming that Lindsay had "outlived his usefulness" and was "over the hill." But the fans weren't fooled; if Lindsay was losing it, they saw no indication. At the age of thirty-three, he was as fit and belligerent as ever and had finished the best scoring season of his career. Both he and Glenn Hall had just been named to the first All-Star team, the eighth time for Lindsay.

Infuriated fans overloaded the Detroit Olympia switchboard with a deluge of angry phone calls. Red Wings staff kept as low a profile as possible, and for several weeks, if anyone asked their place of employment, they made something up. The newspaper switchboards were also jammed, and so many protest letters arrived that the Detroit *News* had to pull staff from other departments to help out the mailroom.

Marguerite Norris, still the Red Wings' executive vice-president, read about the trade while in New York on business. Livid, she grabbed the phone and dialled her brother, Bruce. "You can't do that!" she exclaimed. "Well, I've done it," he replied unperturbed. "You just can't do that!" she repeated louder. "Do you want to have a fight about it in the papers?" he challenged. Marguerite paused for a moment, then offered a limp "No" before dropping the phone into its cradle.

Today, Marguerite acknowledges that she might have won had she accepted Bruce's challenge. But the prospect of dragging the Norris name into the papers for a family feud appalled her, especially considering the highly public problems her half-brother Jimmy was having with the International Boxing Club. Furthermore, her mother who had always disapproved of Marguerite's independent spirit would have sided with Bruce. A public war might have destroyed the already fragile relationship between mother and daughter.

After the phone call, she realized her career with the Red Wings had ended. "I quit," she says, her voice still charged with emotion after nearly thirty-five years. "I just walked."* It was a sad end to a promising career. Neither of her brothers even remotely approached her hockey success, but the NHL treats her as if she never existed. She isn't in the NHL Hall of Fame, despite many dubious and far less successful entries, nor is she mentioned in the official NHL history.

Naturally, Ted Lindsay did the unexpected, calling his own press conference to denounce the trade, something no player had ever done. "I wanted to close my hockey career in Detroit," he stated, "but derogatory remarks about myself and my family showed me that the personal resentment on the part of the Detroit general manager would make it impossible for me to continue playing in Detroit."

The writers, desperate for a happy ending, frantically tried to coax "a word of praise for the dean of hockey managers" from Lindsay, but he wouldn't bend.

---

* Though Marguerite had no further involvement with the team or the Olympia, she was listed as executive vice-president until 1973.

Throughout the interview he refused to mention Jack Adams by name, much less praise him.

Reports of the trade were curiously muted, covering only the facts and offering little comment on the implications of the deal. Even details of Lindsay's press conference were buried at the bottom of a story headlined by Jack Adams's rebuttal: "There is no place in sport for a disloyal or selfish athlete. And it would appear from Lindsay's statements, which are vindicative and untrue, that he is apparently putting self above hockey."

Not satisfied with trading Lindsay, Adams banished Marty Pavelich, Lindsay's close friend and business partner, to the minors as another part of his so-called "youth movement." Pavelich, though quietly supportive, hadn't been particularly active in the association, and demoting him offered a terrifying object lesson to the other players. Interestingly, the previous year's Red Wings media guide, zealously vetted by Adams and written just before the fateful union announcement, described Pavelich as an "untradeable." With Lindsay in Chicago, Pavelich had to run their business by himself, impossible from a minor-league outpost. Rather than knuckle under, he quit hockey.

Smythe wasted no time in getting rid of Thomson. "I didn't want anyone telling us what we had to do," he wrote in his memoirs. "I traded Thomson to Chicago, bang."

In Montreal, Frank Selke considered trading Doug Harvey. "Mr. Selke phoned Jack Adams," recalls Jimmy Skinner, then coach of Detroit and present for the call. "They were going to make a trade; Doug Harvey to Detroit. Selke finally phoned Jack back and said, 'Jack, you have more guts than I have. I can't trade Harvey.'"

Guts, of course, had nothing to do with it. Selke hated the idea of a players' association just as much as Adams or Smythe, but no one could replace Harvey as the firing-pin of the Canadiens' offense and power play, and Selke would not deliberately weaken his team for any reason. Besides, with Smythe and Adams decimating their squads, Montreal, still intact, would be even stronger in comparison.

Selke seemed to know, to the second, when a player's value was used up. Twice a year he gave the team's owners his brutal assessment of each player's weak points, character flaws and trade value. Three years later, in 1960, when he was convinced that Harvey was in fact "over the hill" and the club would not get a good "return on our investment salarywise," Selke lost no time dispatching him to New York.* Until the day he died, Harvey believed that Selke traded him as punishment for his activities in '57, but waited until he got every last bit of performance out of him before casting him off. Harvey took particular pleasure in the fact that his career lasted another seven seasons.

In September 1957, the NHL owners shuffled the deck some more, creating an unprecedented 32 percent change-over in team rosters through trades and the promotion of rookies. One or two rookies making a team in those days was cause for comment. Never before had so many newcomers been added or veterans moved.

In Toronto, before players signed their 1957-58 contracts, Smythe summoned them one by one to his office. Once again he reviewed at length their debt to the team before digressing to the general themes of disloyalty, communists, Jews and New York lawyers. Each player was asked to sign a "loyalty pledge" promising unequivocal allegiance to the Maple Leafs. Only then were they given their contracts to sign.

Throughout this period, Ian Johnston was in almost daily contact with his Maple Leafs spy, a man only identified in his reports to Smythe as the "pipeline" or "our informant." The pipeline provided richly intimate detail about the inner manoeuvring of the players' association, and occasionally dropped in a divisive tidbit or

---

* In the same memo Selke described Jacques Plante as "almost a mental case in his exalted ego and we must give serious thought to a replacement as he is not very amenable to discipline." Another star's "I.Q. is so low that we must not let ourselves count too highly on him." Bernie Geoffrion "can't even check his suitcase." Dickie Moore was a "disappointing worker at training camp and as you know I had quite a session with him at contract-signing time."

two at Johnston's behest. The pipeline's information allowed the owners to put tremendous pressure on specific players who were wavering, and to isolate and discredit the players who weren't.

The association should have been stopped dead in its tracks, but the players demonstrated a backbone the owners didn't believe they had. Lindsay remained outspoken, even after being traded to Chicago, and those who replaced the traded players didn't buckle under. In Toronto, no one Leaf was willing to be the player rep and suffer Thomson's fate, so three were chosen: Tod Sloan, Dick Duff and Sid Smith.

Despite the appearance of strength, Lindsay and Mound felt that time was running out. Detroit in particular seemed to be wavering now that Lindsay, Hall, Pavelich and several other association supporters were gone. Late in the summer of '57, both Lindsay and Doug Harvey sent personal appeals to Clarence Campbell, pleading with him to use "your good offices" to schedule a meeting between the association and the League.

Campbell didn't trouble to answer. Instead, he called a press conference on September 12, 1957, to announce that the League had, just a few days earlier, adopted a reform program. "It may come as a surprise that these provisions for NHL players should be placed in the contract at this time," Campbell said blandly, "but in point of fact this has been the invariable practice in the NHL during its past twenty years of operation." None of the so-called reforms were ever introduced.

Throughout their dispute with the owners, the players were painfully conscious of "the good of the sport and the benefit of all concerned," as Lindsay put it in a letter to Clarence Campbell. They never once publicly criticized the NHL. The owners, however, weren't concerned with such niceties. Smythe kept the kettle boiling when he summoned three newspaper editors, read them a prepared statement, allowed them each to ask a single question and then sent them on their way. After casting numerous aspersions on Ted Lindsay's character and ethics, he "revealed" that the players' association was "a smoke screen to enable a small group to get control of the NHL Pension Fund, which now amounts to about $1,750,000—and this group might be more interested in its own welfare than that of the players."

The players' association retaliated by filing suit in New York and Toronto, accusing the NHL of failing to bargain in good faith. After waiting three weeks for the League to respond to the action, the players unsheathed their most powerful weapon, an anti-trust suit.* The suit charged that, since 1926, the owners had "monopolized and obtained complete domination and control and dictatorship" of hockey.

Nothing could—or can—send a jolt of fear through the belly of pro sport like the word "anti-trust." By 1958, every major professional sport except basketball had been faced directly or indirectly with a suit, and all had been filed within the previous five years.

"I cannot believe that players on our team, players I associate with or have associated with would be a party to any such thing," sputtered Smythe, in his best "after all we've done for you" tone. "Some of these accusations don't make sense. No player has to sign a contract unless he considers it satisfactory. And there's even the possibility that the players themselves might be in breach of contract in this instance. My personal opinion is that if this thing degenerates into a legal hassle between the NHL and lawyers in New York it could mean the end of hockey."

The owners might have been shocked, but not enough to abandon their deadening strategy of stonewalling the association. Hoping to goad the League into responding to them, Mound applied to each NHL city for certification of the association as the players' legal bargaining unit. The Ontario approval hearing was scheduled for November 18.

On Monday, November 4, Clarence Campbell, Conn

---

* Named, in addition to a plethora of holding companies, in the American federal court action (under the Sherman and Clayton Antitrust Acts) were the National Hockey League, Walter Brown (Boston), James D. Norris (Chicago), Bruce Norris (Detroit), Frank J. Selke (Montreal), Reed Kilpatrick (New York), Conn Smythe (Toronto) and Clarence Campbell.

Smythe, Stafford Smythe and Maple Leaf Gardens' solicitor Ian Johnston materialized unexpectedly in the Leafs' dressing room, just before practice. The dumbfounded players, all in various stages of undress, gaped as the powerful quartet entered.

A locker room plays an integral role in shaping a team's character. Every day, a hundred small power struggles are enacted in the course of dressing and undressing. Even more than the ice itself, the locker room is a touchstone for players. While in it, they occupy that middle ground between the game and real life. In it they are vulnerable, as naked men are. In it they are in transition between athlete and man, enforcer and nice guy, superstar and shy recluse. But above all, in the locker room, the players are vulnerable. No one felt that fact more than those seventeen men in skates, tape, jockstraps and padding when the four immaculately clad hockey bosses pushed open the door.

Conn Smythe, leading off the proceedings, harshly demanded to know if the players really wanted to be led by "outsiders from New York" who were trying to "wreck hockey" and put them all out of jobs. He worked himself into a fever with his short, explosive narrative. At the culmination of his talk, he was so agitated he grabbed a chair and heaved it toward the ceiling, where it broke through the plaster and stuck fast. Throughout the meeting, the chair hung dangling over the players' heads like the sword of Damocles.

In stentorian tones, Johnston read an eight-page statement, heavily larded with legalese "proving" that the players were throwing away their right to bargain individually. Again and again he drove home the point that their "union" would result in a single salary for them all. Woven throughout Johnston's statement was the implication that the players' actions were criminal.

A frosty silence fell when Johnston turned the last page. The players shot awkward glances at each other, wondering whether to speak up or keep quiet. A few brave ones admitted to confusion about the purpose of the anti-trust suit and certification application.

Stafford Smythe barked a nasty laugh and attacked Lindsay and Harvey. "Those guys are in it for themselves," he sneered. "They don't give a crap about you."

Clarence Campbell, looking like a seer, stood tall and erect and trotted out his favourite saws about "the fragility of hockey" and how the players were endangering "the finest pension plan in sport."

After the two-hour presentation, Conn Smythe called for an immediate vote, urging the players to withdraw from the "union." To his astonishment, they voted ten to seven to wait until they could talk to their lawyers before making the decision. Smythe's chiselled jaw rose, his mouth flattened into an ominous line and his eyes veiled over with an opaque darkness.

The next day, the players, Milton Mound, Ian Johnston and a group of lawyers met in secrecy at Maple Leaf Gardens. Two of the Leafs had personal lawyers, and George Armstrong was so nervous he had two. Reporters were banned, not only from the meeting but from the building itself. For three hours, both sides hammered away at the issues, with Mound patiently correcting management's charges.

When it ended, the players voted unanimously to "certify that we the undersigned members of the Toronto Maple Leafs hockey team are all presently members in good standing of the National Hockey League Players Association and request you [the Ontario Labour Relations Board] to certify the association as our representative for collective bargaining and the regulation of relations between us and our employers."*

It was a stunning victory for the association, made all the sweeter when Johnston agreed to support an independent investigation of the Pension Society's finances. It should have been the decisive battle. Mound and the executive felt that it would be just a matter of time before

---

* The players present were: Tod Sloan, Dick Duff, Barry Cullen, Ron Stewart, Al MacNeil, Jim Morrison, Sid Smith, Frank Mahovlich, Marc Reaume, George Armstrong, Brian Cullen, Rudy Migay, Peter Conacher, Bob Baun, Billy Harris, Ed Chadwick, Bob Pulford and Tim Horton.

the other teams fell into place.

But they didn't count on Jack Adams.

Three days after the Toronto players had defied management, a vicious Detroit newspaper article, datelined New York, revealed the Red Wings players' "real" attitude to Lindsay's trade. The writer was Lewis Walter, a close friend of Jack Adams. He quoted an unnamed "former Red Wings star" who told Adams, "I see you finally made the move, Boss. But I'm afraid you may be a year late. I think he has already spoiled some of the other players." The *coup de grâce* came from another unnamed "long-time player," who reportedly said in the dressing room, "I'll bet there isn't a man in this room who isn't glad Lindsay's gone, even if we finish last."

The day the story appeared, the Red Wings arrived for practice to find copies of the paper, conveniently folded to the Lindsay article, tucked into their lockers. No sooner had they digested the article than "Jolly Jack" appeared with owner Bruce Norris in tow. Under his arm, Norris carried a stack of heavy ledger books.

Fat lidded eyes brimming with tears, Adams launched into a soliloquy about the value of loyalty, starting off with loyalty to the family, traversing through loyalty to God and religion and finishing off with the rightness and justness of loyalty to the team, management and owner.

"Yes! Loyalty to this good man standing over here with the broken heart," he sobbed, pointing to the thirty-three-year-old Norris standing awkwardly to one side. Though hung-over, as he often was, the six-foot five, 225-pound Norris, dressed in a three-piece, navy-blue suit, still cut an imposing figure.

Adams frequently found occasion to refer to the "recently departed" Ted Lindsay as "a cancer" who had repeatedly shown particular "disloyalty" in spite of the incredible generosity of Adams and "this good man over here."

If the players weren't sold by Adams's performance, Bruce Norris put the capper on it. Face set in an uncharacteristically funereal expression, he spoke glumly. "Boys, we don't take any money out of this hockey club.

It's a hobby for us. We put it right back into the hockey club. And anyone who doesn't believe me can look at these books."

To punctuate his comments, Norris slammed the heavy ledger books down on the floor. The challenge went unanswered. There was no way a bunch of athletes clad in their underwear were going to call him a liar by taking a look at the books, even if they could understand them.

Still moist-eyed after his impassioned oration, Adams pulled himself together for a few last words. "Boys, I know you'll do the right thing." With that, he and Norris abruptly left the room. By this time quite a number of the players—who had been squirming in their seats—were teary-eyed as well. "From then on we never had any trouble," recalls coach Jimmy Skinner. "The players were so ashamed. They'd been led astray."

On November 13, 1957, the Detroit Red Wings, led by Red Kelly, Gordie Howe and Marcel Pronovost, withdrew from the players' association. The stated reason, given by Kelly, was that the anti-trust suit had been filed without their consent. But in truth, Adams had succeeded in making Ted Lindsay the issue. He convinced the players that Lindsay had betrayed them and was battling the owners for his own ends. Adams and Norris, who attended the press conference, could barely contain their glee.

The association reeled. Running out of money and scenting the rank breath of defeat, the stalwarts desperately sought a compromise, offering to withdraw the unfair labour practices suit if the League would meet with them. Clarence Campbell and the owners, sensing complete capitulation, didn't give an inch, sticking to their condition that no meeting would be held if the players' lawyer was present, and adding a new one, that the players drop all legal action before they met.

At the same time, management stepped up the tremendous pressure on the players' association executive, attempting to separate them from Mound and Lindsay, who by now were the only ones resisting the owners. At the beginning of January 1958, the owners' strategy was clearly working. Doug Harvey and Bert Olmstead were meeting secretly with Clarence Campbell in Montreal, making calls to the other executive members from his office and trying to find ways to force Lindsay and Mound into giving up what was now their only weapon, the lawsuits.

By mid-month, only Lindsay and Mound had any fight left in them. A face-saving compromise had been worked out that called for each side to telegraph the Ontario Labour Relations Board, asking that the certification decision be delayed until after the owners and players had met. The owners knew that the minute they sat down with the lawyerless players it would be all over.

Lindsay stubbornly refused to send the capitulating telegram. "I understand that [Jimmy] Norris will speak to Lindsay and try to straighten him out," Johnston reported happily to Smythe. "In my opinion this is all working in our favour, even though Lindsay refuses to send the telegram. The Montreal players are getting fed up with Mound and so is [Tod] Sloan. I think that if Sloan gives up on Mound then Armstrong can take our players away from him."

Norris's conversation with Lindsay was short and sweet. He told him that, though he wasn't particularly against the players' association, he didn't want any more aggravation. He was "up to his ass in alligators" with lawsuits, rackateering investigations and now the players' association. And he was so upset about it all he had a rash all over his body. If the whole business wasn't settled, and soon, he intended to close down the Blackhawks team. "I'm losing money anyway, so I don't give a fuck."

Finally beaten, Lindsay sent the telegram. The owners then invited the association executive to a conference in Florida on February 4.

The players got almost nothing. In exchange for a few trifles—a $7,000 minimum salary, a marginally increased playoff pool, moving expenses for a traded player and a meaningless affirmation of the right of the player to be the sole judge of his fitness after an injury*—they agreed to drop all pending litigation and their attempts to have a legally recognized players' association.

The much-trumpeted concessions included an increase in the clubs' contribution to the pension plan. The players didn't know it, but the total cost of the settlement was less than the owners were spending on lawyers to fight the association. No change in the arbitration or conciliation procedure was agreed to, leaving Campbell firmly in place as the final voice in any dispute, on or off the ice.

Though they had made little progress, the players professed delight. "We'll have two or three meetings a year with the owners," Bill Gadsby explained triumphantly. "The important thing is that we have the right to ask for a meeting anytime we want. That way, if anything is really wrong, we can talk it over right away. Right now we are closer to the owners than we've been since I've been in the league and we've got things we've never had before. Maybe this all should have been done five to eight years ago but wasn't. Now we've started."

Even Lindsay claimed not to notice that the players had been castrated. "In fairness to our owners, we want to say that at the meetings in Palm Beach, they did not ask or suggest that we drop the association," he said gratefully.

Gadsby made light of the players' failure to make any significant inroads into sharing television revenue. "They told us they weren't making any money on TV. They said if they started to make anything they would tell us. We had to take their word for it. These things will come in time."

Thus, on February 5, 1958, a week short of a year after it was formed, the National Hockey League Players' Association died. Essentially, everything important was left up to the goodwill of the owners. The player-owner meetings did happen, but the players had no power. No questions about the pension fund were ever answered.

The annual "Clarence Campbell Dog and Pony Pension Show" continued as before, and somehow, the owners

---

* Though players could now decide whether they were fit or not, nothing could stop clubs from exercising the clause in the contract allowing them to terminate players who refused to perform required services for the team.

forgot to let the players know when "they started to make anything" from television.

Chapter 5

The Lost Years

The final years of the six-team League are among the most cherished by hockey fans. When hockey followers get together, their conversation inevitably turns to the glories of that era, often portrayed in sharp contrast to the present state of the game. Die-hard fans wax eloquent about the tremendous battles fought among the original six teams. They extol the high quality of the play and the simplicity of hockey unsullied by the current complications of agents, corporations, rival leagues, international players, endorsements and expansion. And they recall their certainty that the game they loved so much would never change, that it was frozen in time.

The autumn years of the six-team league were a marvellous time to be a hockey fan, but beneath the surface, those were dark days for the game itself. The NHL's victory over the players' association in 1958 proved a Pyrrhic one. The real cost, to both the League and the players, was tens of millions of dollars in lost opportunities, lost salaries, lost revenues and diminished pensions. After the death of the players' association, professional hockey drifted into a greedy, grasping era of cynicism that eventually brought the NHL to the brink of disaster.

The financial troubles of the '70s can all be traced back to the events of 1957 and '58.

Though the pretence that the owners acted "for the good of the game" had been brilliantly propagated by Clarence Campbell for decades, hockey's true nature began to emerge in the 1960s. Virtually all major decisions in that decade were made either to put money into the owners' pockets or to keep it out of someone else's. From the thievery of Harold Ballard and Stafford Smythe to the opportunism of expansion, the dying years of the six-team League were, in reality, a sorry mess.

A fortress-like mentality pervaded the NHL. Amid the winds of change coursing through professional sports, hockey alone stood firm and unbending. In the '50s, hockey had been more profitable than football, basketball or baseball. The Montreal and Toronto arenas had been sold out since the end of World War II. Even in Boston, where, by 1966-67, the lacklustre Bruins had been out of the playoffs for eight straight years, the team outdrew the perennial National Basketball Association champions, the Boston Celtics.

In New York, sportswriters marvelled as fans regularly trooped into Madison Square Garden to watch the wretched Rangers, who had finished out of the playoffs eighteen of the past twenty-four years and hadn't won the Stanley Cup since 1940. "It must be obvious by now to anyone interested in the game that New York just plain doesn't *want* to have a good hockey team," moaned writer William Leggett. "The Ranger management, an amorphous group of capitalists who own the Knicks basketball team and Madison Square Garden as well, does not waste much time on hockey fans."

Yet the fans came in droves. In 1964-65, the Garden sold out nine times and had near sell-outs on eight other nights, even though ticket prices had gone up 30 percent in the previous two years and the price of programs had doubled in one year. Then, in the middle of one March 1965 game against the Blackhawks, the frustrated fans threw hundreds of orange, green and red balls onto the ice in the middle of the action. It was "like a man who has finally cracked up and sits thrumming his fingers over wet lips," wrote an anguished Leggett.

Even so, they still came to the games.

As the '60s progressed, every aspect of the game—from status and popularity to player benefits and working conditions—slid further and further behind other sports. Though one of the first pro sports to be televised regularly, and one of the most popular, hockey lost its CBS network contract in 1959. Instead of trying to persuade Jimmy Norris, with his connections and savvy, to lead a concerted effort to regain the coverage, the NHL governors voted to dissolve their broadcast committee completely in 1960. More than thirty years later, hockey is still striving desperately to regain this lost momentum. Hockey's U.S. network revenues, once on even terms with those of other sports, were dwarfed by the 1990s. Hockey signed a $51 million three-year deal, which expired in 1991, from SportsChannel America. In comparison, the NFL in 1990 received a $3 billion four year contract from CBS to broadcast Sunday games, and gets another $900 million from ABC for Monday night games and the 1992 Superbowl. The NBA broadcast revenues are $1 billion and major league baseball revenues have reached $1.6 billion.

In the '60s, the NHL's Canadian owners had television money, and lots of it, but they were determined not to share it with the U.S. teams. After 1960, the Maple Leafs and Canadiens boasted nearly $1 million each in annual broadcast revenue. Boston, one of the two strongest hockey cities in the U.S., could pull in only $187,000 from television in 1962. Every time Bruins owner Weston Adams tried to bring up the subject of revenue sharing, he was quickly torpedoed by Stafford Smythe. "Weston has been at me again on his favourite subject," Stafford noted in a report to his father, then staying at the Breakers Hotel in Palm Beach, Florida. "You'd think he would get tired of beating that poor old nag to death. He won't find much good cheer from me about it but I am getting tired of his bleating."*

The American owners wanted television revenue, but they could never get their minds around a strategy that would win over the networks. Other professional sports bent themselves into pretzels to accommodate television, readily changing the days and times of games, scheduling breaks to fit commercials and even tailoring the rules to make the sports more appealing to viewers. Baseball experimented with different-coloured stitching on the ball. Football leap-frogged all over the week to find the time slot that most appealed to viewers, and the American Football League tried a variety of ball colours to make it easier to follow the game. Several basketball franchises happily ripped out or rearranged seats to accommodate the cameras, but hockey's Bruins flatly refused when a local television station asked to have five seats removed to provide a better camera angle. The NHL considered such suggestions to be meddling.

In 1963, the NHL was still without a U.S. network contract. That year, CBS proposed a "Hockey Game of the Week" to run on Saturday afternoon during the football season, then on Sunday afternoon after football ended. The network reasoned that such timing would build a viewing pattern for hockey, with fans already hooked on watching football in the same Sunday time slot. And it would allow CBS to promote hockey during the football broadcasts. The NHL rejected the idea outright, claiming that it would cause too many schedule and travel problems.

Even after expansion in 1967, the NHL did little to persuade the franchises to cater to television. When the Canadian Sports Network (CSN)† broadcast games out of American cities, its producers were forced to use inex-

---

* There's something terribly pathetic about Stafford Smythe's letters to his father. They always had the tone of a report. He occasionally signed them "Your son," as if Conn might forget who he was. He also addressed his father as Major, Sir or even Mr. Smythe, less frequently Dad.

† "Hockey Night in Canada" was originally produced by MacLaren Advertising, first under the name Videotape Productions and later as Canadian Sports Network.

perienced local technicians. By offering a fifty-dollar bribe, the CSN crew could usually persuade the cameramen to spend the evening in the bar. But it didn't always work. Before a playoff game in St. Louis, CSN president Ted Hough and a producer went up to have a few words with the cameraman in the balcony. "Well, we discovered he had never seen a hockey game in his life," laughs Hough. "He was a Cuban refugee wearing this baseball cap all askew and chewing a great big fat cigar." When offered the fifty dollars, the man told Hough to "fuck off." CSN had to eliminate coverage from that camera for the entire game.

After years of exerting tremendous pressure, in 1962 the American owners persuaded the Canadian clubs to pool all broadcast revenue and divide it six ways. But, because there was no auditing procedure, the teams all suspected each other of grossly underestimating their revenues. Conn Smythe made a deal to pay Jimmy Norris a percentage of his revenues if Norris supported Smythe's underestimation of his broadcast money. "Toronto and Chicago were playing games," confirms Hough, who was nominated to talk to Norris about structuring a more equitable deal.

On a Sunday, late in November 1963, Hough arrived at the elegant old brownstone on Lakeshore Boulevard in Chicago where Norris had an apartment. "I knocked on the door," recalls Hough, still amused at his apprehension. "A little peephole opened. I was ushered in by a chap that I recognized as being his chauffeur, having driven him to and from hockey games on occasion. A great big strapping black man with a bulge under his arm." Hough spent the next several hours watching the television coverage of John F. Kennedy's lying in state, trying to find an opening to broach the delicate topic. In the end he left, unable to summon the nerve to raise the issue.

But the NHL's major problems with television had nothing to do with time slots, the colour or size of the projectile, or camera angles. The NHL owners remained adamantly opposed to allowing players to become celebrities and rise above their teams, as was happening in other sports. They kept their players' salaries low, discouraged self-promotion, forbade players from taking part in beer advertising and quibbled about paying them for having their pictures on bubble-gum cards. When Conn Smythe finally agreed to pay $100 each to the Maple Leafs players for their participation in his lucrative card deals, he insisted that it be paid in quarterly instalments. He personally double-checked each $25 payment, prepared by his general manager, lest a player get something he didn't deserve.

Football's "Broadway Joe" Namath was the perfect example of the star-system's effectiveness. He signed with the New York Jets for a record-breaking $400,000 in 1965. The huge contract, coupled with Namath's telegenic face, provocative personality and racy lifestyle, made him a television celebrity overnight. The New York Jets aggressively used Namath's popularity to promote the team, boost ticket sales and increase the TV audience, not only for the Jets but for the entire league. Namath's signing, together with skilful marketing on the part of the team and the league, ensured the survival of the American Football League until it merged with the NFL.

The impetus to develop aggressive marketing and licensing plans in other professional sports grew directly out of the increasingly powerful voice of the players. Their demand for more money, visibility and power was part of the star-system that network television capitalized on in the early '60s and turned into a multi-billion-dollar bonanza over the next thirty years.

For the most part, hockey players still believed that the owners were wise guardians of the game. They naively thought that the new Owner/Player Council would be the instrument of change. The first Council meeting was held at the Queen Elizabeth Hotel in Montreal in June 1958. It was a congenial gathering, with each player representative sitting snugly between his owner or general manager and at least one team lawyer.

By the October meeting, also held in Montreal, the

owners felt comfortable enough to leave their legal guns behind. "A very amicable discussion took place in which the decisions taken on several matters at the previous meetings were reviewed but no changes were made," read the minutes, which sound more like garden club deliberations than labour-management negotiations. "It was agreed that in the absence of some 'emergency' there would be no occasion for holding any further meeting during the current playing season."

The tone was thus set for the future. Ensuing owner-player meetings were one-hour gatherings slotted into the NHL board of governors' meetings, between various committee reports. The annual dinner or golf game were invariably on the agenda, but little was discussed and even less accomplished. Every now and then, some brave soul would bring up a slightly more contentious point, such as pension benefits or travel money. Without exception, such items were "taken under advisement" or "referred to the governors." No one asked why this was necessary since the governors themselves were sitting in the room.

At the October 1963 meeting held in Toronto, the players politely asked if they could have a copy of the NHL by-laws, the secret text governing every facet of League operation and player conduct. Clarence Campbell told them "that the President of the League and their own General Managers would be happy to make the by-laws available for reading in their office."

Between 1958 and 1965, the players, wanting to be nearer their families over the holidays, put the Christmas playing schedule on the agenda six times; six times they were fobbed off. First they requested that each team play the geographically closest club—New York and Boston, Toronto and Montreal, Detroit and Chicago. Then they asked that each team play at home on Christmas every second year. At each meeting their proposals were put forward for further discussion, but each year, when the subject was raised anew, it was treated as if it had never been discussed before.

In 1965, the players asked the clubs to set up a

committee, comprised of team people and outsiders, to advise them about the "going rates" for endorsements. Once again, they were told to consult their general managers.

Of all the problems undermining the NHL, by far the most insidious was the lack of leadership. A leader with vision could have yanked hockey out of the '50s and into the modern era, but none emerged. As a result, the owners bickered and squabbled among themselves, jealously guarding their profits and blind to the future.

Conn Smythe was the League's strongman from 1952 to 1961, but he was a reactionary, determined to maintain the status quo. His view of hockey was frozen in the pristine days of the '30s and early '40s, when "men were men" and gladly played for next to nothing. Had Clarence Campbell been a different person, he might have been able to unite owners and guide them toward badly needed change.

Since 1946 he had represented a cohesive ownership to the public. For decades, the owners had quarrelled among themselves but presented a seamless front to outsiders. In the '60s, however, the NHL's façade began to crack.

The new pack of owners in the '60s apparently didn't understand the value of a good front man, or the importance of maintaining his dignity. Increasingly, Harold Ballard, Stafford Smythe and even Bruce Norris made public statements commenting on League business without warning Campbell in advance. As a result, the president, who abhorred surprises, was continually embarrassed by reporters' unexpected questions. Though formidable once his arguments were lined up, Campbell didn't think well on his feet, and his trademark lawyerly precision rapidly gave way to cranky responses and sarcasm.

Even in Montreal, the NHL headquarters, Campbell found himself stumbling over obstacles thoughtlessly strewn in his path. On one occasion he steadfastly maintained to a reporter that expansion would create impossible scheduling problems. But just across town, Frank

Selke, managing director of the Canadiens, was happily advocating expansion to a *Gazette* reporter, even outlining the easy mechanics of an interlocking schedule between eastern teams and a sister western conference. When Campbell saw the story the next morning, he fired off a series of letters to the governors begging them, in a dignified way, to muzzle their managers.

Just as embarrassing to Campbell was Canadiens owner Senator Hartland Molson's highly public campaign to cut down on hockey violence. After complaining internally about stick fouls, fighting and poor refereeing, Molson stunned the League in 1963 by going public with a letter outlining his criticisms. He correctly predicted that escalating hockey violence would eliminate the smaller, more skilled athlete in favour of the larger, tougher player. He urged fellow NHL owners to "either start playing the game according to the rules or rewrite the rules to fit the game."

Molson listed twenty rules that he felt were flagrantly violated in every NHL game. "My fellow owners probably think I'm a panty-waist," he observed. "But I still believe that hockey is a rough game when played strictly by the rules: it could not be otherwise. But in the absence of strict observance of the rules I cannot see any argument against criticism of unnecessary roughness."*

Panty-waist was the insult of choice in hockey circles that year. Clarence Campbell made a veiled jab at Molson's charges during a Vancouver radio interview, calling the game "almost panty-waist" compared to the rough, tough stuff of days gone by. When a brave *Globe*

---

* The heretical words of Senator Molson sparked a frenzied and sympathetic response from hockey fans across North America. Though convinced of the rightness of his crusade, he began to have private regrets about the tempest he had stirred up when letters flooded his desk daily.

One man from Willowdale, Ontario, wrote not only to support Molson's comments but to offer a unique, though bizarre-looking solution to officiating problems. He included an elaborate sketch detailing a bubble, containing the referee, which could travel on tracks above the ice. The referee would sit on a swing attached to a swivel for a bird's eye view of the activities below. An added bonus, concluded the writer, would be to restore the referee's dignity, which "suffers much [lost] prestige when he is forced to cling to the glass at the side of the rink, when someone bashes into the boards beside him."

and Mail reporter asked Leafs coach Punch Imlach if the game was too violent, the snort of derision echoed all the way through the Gardens. "That's the way hockey should be played. Some guys may like the panty-waist stuff but I don't and I don't think the fans do."

But Imlach, like most of the men running the game, was wrong. The fist-first hockey that reached a bloody crescendo in the mid-'70s with Philadelphia's "Broad Street Bullies" and their trademark bench-clearing brawls had already begun to disgust and turn away fans.

An opportunity to improve and update the game lay naked and inviting, but the League turned its back. Instead of reviewing its rules and penalties, the NHL hired Fred Corcoran, a New York public relations man, to polish its image. Clarence Campbell explained that Corcoran's job would be to woo TV executives and major advertisers. "Our goal is a national television contract," he said. He was irked when Corcoran, interviewed for the same article, said his job had nothing to do with TV and everything to do with putting a prettier face on hockey. "Hockey has been looked on in some quarters as a sport with brawn, no brains and brawls, this is the type of thing we are trying to correct."

Jimmy Norris could have led the NHL. When he did turn his attention to hockey, after being forced out of boxing, the Blackhawks became a winning team, finally capturing the Stanley Cup in 1961, something they hadn't done since 1938. But by then, the charismatic, bushy-eye-browed boxing king was a spent force and only six years from death. He had been under anti-trust investigation since 1952 but had managed to put off hearings and a trial with dozens of legal stratagems. On March 8, 1957, he and Arthur Wirtz were found guilty of operating a boxing monopoly and conspiring to restrict trade.

Judge Sylvester Ryan ordered Norris and Wirtz to sell their 39 percent share of Madison Square Garden stock and ruled that IBC be dissolved. Ryan restricted the two men to promoting only two championship fights a year for five years. Though he allowed Norris to continue operating in Chicago, he insisted that independent promoters be allowed to stage fights in the stadium. "I intend to stay in boxing," a grim-faced Norris said after the verdict.

Shortly after Ryan's decision, Norris suffered a heart attack, his second. Throughout the next season he appeared regularly in the Blackhawks dressing room, but the life seemed to have fled his once handsome and convivial face.

Norris and Wirtz sold their Madison Square Garden shares to the Graham-Paige Corporation for $4 million in 1959. Most assumed that was the end of the Norris name in boxing. But Jimmy couldn't let go. He tied to revive his empire with a new venture, National Boxing Enterprises (NBE) Inc. Norris, and partner Wirtz, even captured a contract with ABC to televise Wednesday night fights. But they were kicking a lifeless corpse. More investigation haunted Norris as Senator Estes Kefauver launched a far-reaching probe into boxing's association with the underworld.

Testifying before the Senate subcommittee, Norris admitted to having given Frankie Carbo's wife a $45,000 job as a "goodwill representative." Norris claimed he only did it to ensure the co-operation of Carbo, who owned a great many fighters and managers. Norris also told the subcommittee that he'd offered J. Edgar Hoover a $100,000 job to get rid of the hoodlums in boxing. ABC, embarrassed by the controversy, abruptly cancelled his TV contract, forcing NBE to fold.

"I'm sorry I ever got into boxing," Norris lashed out bitterly. "I tried my best to bring good boxing to the public of America. My enemies—as vague as they were—beat me down."

Slightly more than a year before his death in February 1966, Norris talked to Red Smith of the New York *Herald Tribune*. "I like boxing, that's why I was in it. But what I got was abuse for myself and humiliation for my family. They bracketed me with hoodlums," he complained. "That was the main rap on you," Smith commiserated. "You were always the rich kid fascinated by hoods." Norris grimaced. "Fascinated? I inherited them, I didn't bring them into boxing." Smith gently reminded him,

"Some of us thought at the time that the one man who could freeze the hoods out was Jim Norris."

There is no evidence that Jimmy Norris made the slightest effort to clean up boxing. He was willingly involved in bribery, fight-fixing, racketeering and numerous other illegal activities. "There was a great charm about the swashbuckling Norris, and this new cringing fellow, whining in the corner that 'I'm sorry I ever got into it,' turns this particular stomach a little," commented prominent sportswriter Doc Greene of Jimmy Norris's attempts to revise history.

Arthur Wirtz, who bought out Norris's hockey interests, had no interest in being the sport's leader. The Blackhawks rarely saw Wirtz. Each year when the team picture was taken he'd arrive at the last instant, step into a space left for him and vanish when the shot was over. Once, when the players had had a particularly long wait, the door at the end of the rink clanged open and his car drove out into the ice. The instant his photograph was taken, Wirtz got into his car and was driven away.

Bruce, Jimmy's half-brother, only thirty-one when he took control of the Red Wings from his sister in 1955, badly wanted to be the NHL's strongman, but he had neither the aptitude nor the strength of character for it. The truculent boy who chafed beneath the firm hand of his father grew into an equally truculent man with no idea of how to make his own mark. Bruce's thin veneer of bonhomie disintegrated quickly when he was crossed, and he had no patience for sitting down and thinking a problem through.

Norris Grain, now headed by Bruce, continued to be immensely profitable in the '60s. He had enough money and power to buy virtually anything he wanted, and at the top of the list was a Stanley Cup team. But the damage he and Jack Adams had inflicted on the Red Wings in order to crush the players' association would never be repaired.

Jack Adams revered James Norris Sr., but he had little use for his oversized second son. Bruce Norris vacillated between an impetuous generosity that drew many friends and a boorish, bullheaded demeanour that few dared criticize. He loved women (he married four), fast cars (he had at least a dozen recorded accidents) and parties. Norris also loved to drink and had difficulty knowing when to stop. And he was a mean drunk. Adams liked rowdy social gatherings too, but he didn't drink or smoke and abhorred Norris's drunkenness. Adams habitually left parties after Norris had two drinks, and instructed all other Red Wings personnel to do the same.

Adams listened, with heavy tolerance, to Bruce Norris's suggestions about running the team and then promptly forgot about them. Norris, accustomed to the kind of deference only a multimillionaire can inspire, became increasingly irritated by Adams. Three decades of service aside, treating the owner as a quasi-employee is something you can only pull off as long as the team is winning, and the Red Wings stopped winning shortly after Ted Lindsay was traded.

One day in 1961, Norris hailed Adams, who waddled into his office as "jolly as the dickens," recalls Jimmy Skinner, at that point the Red Wings chief scout. Five minutes later, "Jolly Jack" stormed out again, slammed the door, stormed into his own office and slammed that door, too. For once, only silence emanated from Adams's office.

After the briefest of intervals, Norris stuck his head out, glanced around at the shocked staff, cheerily announced that "Mr. Adams is going to retire" and then retreated. In his office, a suddenly very old Jack Adams, with tears streaming down his face, slumped like a slowly deflating balloon until Jimmy Skinner came and led him off.

By elevating Sid Abel from coach to general manager, Norris freely insinuated himself into the club's affairs. He called two and three times a day to give Abel suggestions and get reports. He had a phone hooked up between his private box in the south-west corner of Olympia Stadium and the bench, so he could dictate line changes and strategies to the coach.

Bruce Norris wanted the players to like him, respect him and view him more as a friend than a boss. He appeared in the dressing room at home games, and afterwards, win or lose, he'd often hand out expensive cigars while he joked with the team. Several times he took the players to Homosassa Springs, an unprofitable Florida resort he'd purchased in 1963. Once, he paid for wives and children to come along too, as well as the water boys, trainers and the entire Red Wings management.

He even lent the players money. "He was the easiest touch I have ever seen," recalls longtime friend and employee Lincoln Cavalieri. "Anybody that wanted to say, 'Bruce, I need $100 or $2,000,' or whatever, they'd get it." One of the Red Wings' defensemen, originally from Montreal, had been deported after the war for desertion. A compulsive gambler, he spent everything on the horses. Several times a year he'd call Norris and ask for help. Bruce always sent him something, and even set up a pension for him. There were many such stories: players who couldn't get jobs, players who drank too much and players who had been unlucky in business all found a sympathetic ear and an open wallet when they turned to Norris.

The problem in Bruce's ownership of the Red Wings was that he never could decide whether the team was a hobby or a business. Sometimes he'd tinker with it like a toy; other times he'd throw himself into it as if it were the only thing that counted. And worst of all, Bruce would never admit to what he didn't know, confusing good intentions with sound action.

The Red Wings didn't go sour immediately after Adams left. Indeed, the vestiges of the great team of the '50s took the club to the Stanley Cup final three times in the four ensuing years. But, lacking the critical element that propels a good team into greatness, they lost all three.

At the end of the 1964 season, Detroit played against an old-timers' team in the Olympia. The old-timers, supplemented by Gordie Howe, almost beat the NHL club. What caught Sid Abel's eye was forty-one-year-old Ted Lindsay, who was by far the best player on the ice.

Desperate to win back the Stanley Cup, Abel asked Lindsay to return. Lindsay didn't need hockey, thanks to his successful plastics business. Though his wife Patricia and his business partner, Marty Pavelich were adamantly against it, and Abel offered him a paltry $12,000 a year, barely half of what he'd been getting four years earlier in Chicago, Lindsay jumped at the chance to play again. He gave no thought to the punishment his 165-pound body would take in a sport where the players were getting bigger every year. He won't admit it today, but the only reason he returned was to prove once and for all what a mistake Jack Adams had made.

More than 15,000 people, the largest crowd in the Red Wings' history, jammed the Olympia and howled their approval when Ted Lindsay skated onto the ice. The howl shook the building when Tim Horton, Toronto's heavily muscled, two-hundred-pound defenseman, welcomed him back with a thundering hit. Lindsay picked himself up, skated toward Horton and decked him with a roundhouse elbow to the cranium that had Horton seeing double till he staggered out of a bar later that night. Referee Vern Buffey promptly sent Lindsay to the penalty box and added a ten-minute misconduct for the stream of invective Lindsay sprayed over him.

Not everybody cheered Lindsay's return. "It's a black day for hockey," screeched the normally composed and self-contained Clarence Campbell at Sid Abel during an altercation outside the Red Wings' dressing room.

After each game, Lindsay dragged himself into the whirlpool bath and stayed for hours, even conducting interviews there. He was so stiff and sore that he could only get out of bed in the morning by rolling onto the floor. Before practices and games, he arrived early to be doused in liniment and cocooned with electric heating-pads to loosen up enough to get into his uniform and skates.

In a typical week, Lindsay worked Wednesday morning in his office, flew to New York in the afternoon and returned to Detroit late the same evening after the game. Thursday and Friday, while the other players relaxed, he worked at his office. He'd fly to Montreal Saturday morning for a game and then travel with the team to Boston for a Sunday evening game. He returned on the midnight flight and made it to his desk at nine o'clock Monday morning.

It was one of the great comebacks of all time. Lindsay played with gusto, scoring critical goals and sparking the Red Wings into a semblance of their old precision and fire. "The little SOB beat us," commented the Boston Bruins' Tom Johnston after Lindsay had inspired Detroit to victory by roughing up the much larger Gary Dornhoefer. But the Red Wings talent had deteriorated too much for the spark to last. Lindsay retired for good at the end of the 1964-65 season when Detroit narrowly missed the finals. The following year, the Red Wings lost in the finals and, in the ensuing sixteen years under Bruce Norris, only made the playoffs twice.

An increasing air of desperation permeated the Red Wings as Norris resurrected every old star who could still walk and talk as coach or manager; the club ran through seven coaches in the next ten years. The Detroit executive turned into a giant snake pit, with the occupants frenziedly biting each other and occasionally themselves in their exuberance to draw blood. For years, a joke circulated around the Olympia that the last person in the sauna with Bruce really called the shots. That joke lasted until the appearance of John Ziegler, a slender, young Detroit lawyer whose firm represented the Red Wings on various matters. Ziegler—a mean partier himself—one-upped all the "joy boys," as Marguerite called Bruce's entourage, and bought a condo next door to Norris in North Miami, Florida.

It was a clever move, and the first step in driving the unknown thirty-year-old Ziegler into the League presidency. By 1966 he was a powerful force in the team's affairs and had been appointed to the board of directors of the Red Wings and of Detroit's two farm clubs. That year he also became the alternative NHL governor for the Red Wings and governor for the Virginia Red Wings, the club's American Hockey League franchise.

As the years went by, the most persuasive voice whispering in Norris's ear was increasingly John Ziegler's. The Red Wings were an excellent training ground for him.

Ziegler proved to be an extremely adept lawyer, particularly skilled at negotiations and drawing together diverse interests in smoky backrooms.* He was, for example, instrumental in negotiating the lease to the city-owned Joe Louis Arena, where the Red Wings played after moving out of the outdated Olympia in the '60s. The agreement was considered a masterpiece of one-sided deal-making.

The Red Wings were already losing money in the mid-'60s, but that didn't stop Bruce from promoting the European Ice Hockey League. Aided by John Ziegler and New York lawyer Joe Besch, Norris outlined a plan that would put pro teams in up to eight European countries, each paying $500,000 for the privilege. Norris announced his intention to buy Wembley Stadium in London, England, and, when that fell through, proposed building a $15-million arena in London, despite the fact that hockey had a minuscule following in Britain. A crowd of five thousand for any game was considered an excellent gate.

Norris poured hundreds of thousands into the venture and, in 1973, put together a British team called the London Lions, installing them in Wembley. His grand scheme fizzled in 1974, though the Lions proudly posted a winning record in their one and only season.

When his father died in 1952, Bruce Norris stepped into a ready-made empire worth close to $200 million, and he spent the next twenty-five years eroding it.† Merely managing his father's vast empire didn't satisfy him. He began to buy an odd assortment of businesses and prospects, using the family trust to finance them.

"Bruce was such a jerk," sighs his sister, who watched

---

* As adept as he was at backroom dealing, he was a little short on hockey knowledge. As an economy measure, Ziegler, over the vociferous objections of the scouting staff, decided that the western scouts didn't need to travel to the east and vice versa. As a result, there was no basis for comparison between players in the west and players in the east. The system was soon changed, but the damage was done. The Detroit scouts claim that this was the reason the team had dismal drafts for several years afterward.

† Though he owned only his inherited share of the estate, he managed it all, through the trust his father had set up.

her own fortune evaporate with her brother's. "Bless his heart, he was sincere but it was just one bad call after another. It was always going to be great the next time."

Bruce's biggest problem was cash. He could never get enough. He borrowed heavily against the trust and sold whatever assets he dared. His holdings were so massive that no one paid any attention when he sold the cornerstone of the family fortune in 1961. In a multi-million-dollar transaction, he turned over the family's grain elevators to John J. Daniels and used the money to finance his purchase of fifteen insurance companies.

Marguerite took a dim view of his legerdemain. "I was getting more and more stormy about the situation. I said to Mother, 'I think you have to do something. Tell our little darling we are not too thrilled with these manoeuvres.'"

"There is nothing we can do," her mother replied.

"Yes, we can," Marguerite shot back. "You are supposed to have the swing vote." She wasn't prepared for her mother's answer.

"Well, I don't any more. I signed it all over to him."

Under Bruce's control, the essence of the Norris empire steadily slipped away as he jettisoned assets like ballast from a sinking ship. In the mid-'70s he decided to get out of insurance and financial enterprises and go back to his father's original interests, grain and food production. He sold his flagship company, Norin Corp., to Canadian Pacific Enterprises in 1977. Ian Sinclair, who negotiated that purchase for CPE, recalls feeling very sorry for Norris, whose long-time alcoholism showed in his vein-shot face, reddened eyes and the grey pallor beneath his tan.

Eventually the Red Wings went as well. Rumours had regularly surfaced since 1962, that Norris intended to sell the team, but he consistently denied them and reaffirmed his love for and dedication to the game. In 1979 he privately put a $20-million price tag on the team. Two years later, he dropped the price to $13 million. Finally, in 1982, after several years of $3- to $4-million losses Norris sold out to Mike Ilitch, owner of the Little Caesars pizza chain, for $8 million.

Norris loyalists, notably John Ziegler, stoutly defend Bruce's business and hockey acumen. The facts, however, suggest otherwise. There is no way of knowing how much money Bruce Norris went through, but there is little hint of the once-great wealth in the Norris family today. Lincoln Cavalieri estimates that Norris lost about $150 million on his various enterprises over a twenty-five-year period.

On January 1, 1986, the sixty-one-year-old Bruce Norris died of liver failure in a Stony Brook, New York, hospital. "He just couldn't get it right," says Marguerite Norris today, a little sad, a little bemused and a little angry.

The disintegration of the Red Wings in Bruce Norris's hands wasn't the only, or even the most obvious, example of the NHL riding hard toward self-destruction. The dismal descent of the Toronto Maple Leafs into a laughing-stock was a consequence of the arrogance of first Conn Smythe, later his son Stafford and then Harold Ballard. The easy profitability of the Leafs fuelled Stafford and Ballard as they milked the team of money and good times while completely ignoring the overall good of the game.

Stafford and Ballard were as vehemently opposed to expansion as Conn Smythe had been. Bill Jennings, governor for the New York Rangers, spent many fruitless hours trying to convince both men that the NHL should add at least two new teams to thwart the creation of a rival league, protect themselves from anti-trust action and lure network television. At least seven times between 1962 and 1964, Jennings tried to persuade the other governors to put expansion on the agenda at annual and semi-annual owners' meetings.

"Great idea," responded Smythe. "You figure out a way to put the franchise fee in my pocket and I'll go along. But a bunch of guys in San Francisco who have never seen hockey aren't getting any of my players." His partner, Harold Ballard, was more succinct: "Fuck 'em!"

Though Ballard's name became synonymous with hockey in Canada, his interest in the game was largely financial. He once confided to Jim Kearney, then lead sportswriter for the Vancouver *Province*, "If I could get dog racing licensed in Ontario I'd have the Leafs out of Maple Leaf Gardens just like that!"

The cynicism infecting the League during the '60s is perfectly illustrated by Stafford Smythe's sudden development of interest in helping Vancouver acquire an NHL franchise, eighteen months after spurning the idea. Edward deJong, a real estate developer, approached Smythe claiming that he had Vancouver's city council "in my pocket" and could deliver to Smythe, virtually free, a prime building site for a new arena.*

Expansion wasn't a new idea to the NHL, but the last serious brush with it dated back to 1952, when the League had toyed with the possibility of granting a franchise to Jim Hendy, owner of the highly successful Cleveland Barons of the American Hockey League.

Hendy and Cleveland lusted after a franchise and were prepared to grovel in whatever direction the NHL desired. One of the League governors suggested that a farm system was essential to a successful NHL club. Hendy diligently set about building one that compared favourably with those of the League's two second-rung teams, Boston and New York. When another governor intimated that Cleveland's arena looked a little shabby, Hendy spent thousands giving it a complete overhaul. Then the League demanded that Hendy raise $425,000 in cash—separate from a $50,000 franchise fee—to prove he had operating capital.

The League governors nodded beatifically at every mention of Cleveland's bid, even giving tentative approval pending formalities. This show of encouragement was so convincing that a Cleveland newspaper writer devoted a column to the premature announcement that a

---

* In return for a guaranteed $150,000 finder's fee, deJong promised to convince the council to turn over $2-million worth of choice downtown Vancouver real estate to Smythe as the site of a $8-million, 20,000-seat arena. Vancouver eventually turned down the proposition, mainly because of opposition to giving a carpetbagger a hand-out of downtown land.

franchise had been granted. But, behind the scenes, the governors were only feigning interest to avoid charges of monopolistic practices. They hoped that Hendy would just give up and go away.

Finally, the NHL ended their fan dance, rejecting Cleveland's application with the specious reasoning that a small percentage of the $425,000 Hendy raised was in guaranteed advances from local TV and radio revenue, rather than cash. Behind closed doors, Jimmy Norris queered the deal by claiming that "gambling money" was behind the Cleveland bid—a laughable assertion considering his own mob connections and the fact that he and Conn Smythe regularly laid bets together on hockey games and horse racing.

Throughout the early '60s, Campbell tirelessly asserted the NHL's opposition to expansion. "Right now we're a pretty successful operation. When you come right down to it, nobody can match it. We'd only be buying a headache and what for?" he repeated endlessly.

Campbell further hardened the League's stance in 1964 when he announced that the board of governors had no committee studying expansion—hadn't had one since he'd become president in 1946—and what's more, the topic most definitely was not on the agenda for the June 8 owners' meeting. "Increasing the league doesn't increase your revenue 5 cents per club," he told the press. "You'd simply have more hockey, and all diluted. If you expanded by only two clubs, each NHL team would have to provide six players. You just tell me what the result would be if you took six players off any team in the NHL. Any team! And what the hell do you think it's gonna do to the spectacle? . . . It has to dilute it. These six players at the bottom echelon couldn't sell tickets, they couldn't sell a show, you couldn't put them on the ice by themselves. They are the fillers."

According to Campbell, the addition of even two new teams would create insurmountable scheduling problems. In a monumental display of illogic, he maintained that arrangements routine in other sports would somehow ruin hockey. "You can't schedule Montreal or Toronto at home on Saturday and then on the Coast on Sunday Who the hell would run the risk? You could get snowed in. . . . And in order to go to the Coast, Toronto would have to give up three or four of its Canadian television dates, and *that's revenue.*"

The NHL's longstanding intransigence about expansion made the sudden about-face on March 12, 1965, all the more amazing. On that day, Clarence Campbell emerged from the governors' meeting in Montreal to announce that the NHL intended to expand, not by one or two teams, but by an entire six-team division. What's more, the insoluble problems of finding players and scheduling games had magically disappeared.

The normally excruciatingly precise president floundered in imprecision, answering the most innocuous questions with unusual prefaces like "I presume" and "I suppose." So hurried was the decision that the NHL hadn't even discussed the most basic of details. "No definite time limit has been set for the expansion program but it would be highly unlikely it could be implemented by next season," Campbell stated.

There was only one thing the NHL was clear on. "The teams that come up with the best offers are going to be the teams that will be taken into the new division."

The NHL was galvanized into action only when the U.S. television networks told the governors point-blank that the League would never get the coverage they wanted without more American teams, particularly on the west coast. The NHL owners had noticed that television contracts were starting to bring in serious money for other sports. ABC had recently paid $12.35 million for the rights to broadcast a Saturday afternoon major-league baseball game of the week. CBS paid the fourteen-team National Football League $28 million for the television rights to the 1964 and 1965 seasons. But most concerning to the NHL was NBC's contract for $35 million, over five years, to the eight-team American Football league, the NFL's upstart rivals.

Immediately before the surprise expansion announcement, Bruce Norris had organized a top-secret governors' meeting with several network officials. The executives politely watched a hockey highlights tape and just as politely told the hockey men to call them after the NHL expanded. The governors were further dismayed when one executive offhandedly mentioned that he had been talking to the minor Western Hockey League, and that the WHL had as much chance of getting a national contract as the NHL did.

The NHL had long been operating on the comforting assumption that no rival league could get a national contract because it would be offering an inferior product. The case of the American Football League demonstrated the opposite. Though that league was clearly inferior to the existing National Football League, the teams were competitive with each other, and the high-scoring, exciting games appealed to fans. Most important, the AFL officials were willing to go to considerable lengths to accommodate television. Their attitude paid off with the $35-million national contract.

The Western Hockey League had been actively seeking promotion into a separate division within the NHL since 1960. Five of the six teams in the league—Portland, Seattle, San Francisco, Los Angeles and Vancouver—played at near-capacity and had been steadily building toward a big-league organization with stronger financial backing.* Most minor-league teams relied on players lent to them by NHL clubs, but Portland owned sixteen of their eighteen players outright, and all other cities, except Vancouver, owned at least half of theirs. That made the WHL far more independent than the NHL would have liked.

In 1964, the Western Hockey League owners, tired of the NHL's expansion stonewalling, began making plans to move to major-league status on their own and started courting cities like Quebec, St. Louis, Pittsburgh, Buffalo and Baltimore to join them.

Clarence Campbell dismissed their efforts. "They'd

---

* The sixth team, the Victoria Cougars, was owned by the Toronto Maple Leafs.

have to do it with the okay of the National Hockey League. Otherwise they'd be competing for players and I don't think they could do that dollarwise. And I don't think they have the earning power at the moment to warrant the expense of junior clubs either." But the WHL teams had no intention of saddling themselves with expensive farm clubs. As the World Hockey Association did years later, the teams would simply poach players from the NHL's farm system and junior clubs, leaving the League to bear the cost of developing talent.

The Western Hockey League owners obliquely threatened an anti-trust suit if the NHL tried to block them. "I haven't met with any NHL people lately, but there are other ways of presenting our case forcefully," warned James Piggott, owner of the WHL Los Angeles franchise. "And we do want in. And I can tell you it's not very far off, either."

Faced with the rapid emergence of a rival league, possibly anchored by a network television contract, the NHL moved with extraordinary speed. Once the decision to add teams was made, the League galloped ahead, producing a thrown-together game plan that included a $2-million franchise fee for each new team. To their surprise, no one balked at it. Campbell announced that a new division would play in the 1967-68 season. Los Angeles and St. Louis were named as the first two acceptable cities, though several governors admitted they had not yet examined any of the twelve bids received. St. Louis hadn't even applied.

Initially, the NHL owners fell all over themselves promising that the new teams would get a good start. "We don't want any set-ups coming into our buildings," emphasized Stafford Smythe. "Keen competition is necessary for success in sport. We can assure such competition by making good players available to the new clubs." He was later more specific. "We might protect say five players and then allow the new division to draft." Jimmy Norris did him one better by offering to let the new clubs have a shot at all his players except for the "top three or four."

Campbell cautioned, "The formula has not been established for drafting these players. Naturally, the players will be of NHL calibre. The teams realize this is essential. It would be a built-in formula for failure if the players were not competitive." But it was clear that he was far from comfortable with the idea. When asked if any franchises would be awarded when the 1966 governors' meetings were finished, Campbell snapped, "I'm not a policy-maker. I don't have a dollar invested in the NHL, except my life. It's not inconceivable that some will be awarded, but it's not for me to say how many if any."

Normally, Campbell faced the press with a prepared statement, but this time he spoke off the cuff, telling writers that "expansion would dilute the product for a generation." Angry owners, led by Stafford Smythe, burned up the telephone lines from the six League cities to Montreal. They told Campbell to say something, anything, to change the tenor of his unfortunate remark. A few days later Campbell explained, in classic bafflegab, that he meant a generation to be just five years, the time reasonably expected for the new franchises to get on their feet.

Three months after the March 1965 expansion announcement, the League had twelve applications in hand, each accompanied by a $10,000 deposit. There was still no plan for stocking the teams or scheduling the season and playoffs—all critical factors to the eventual financial well-being of the League.

Once a group of prospective new owners was hooked, all the generous talk of protecting only the top three or four players disappeared. "The governors feel each of the present clubs could give six players—a pool of thirty-six bona fide big-leaguers," stated Campbell, carefully neglecting to mention what rung the players would come from. He did offer buyers some inducement, saying that once each of the new teams had their six "bona fides" the NHL would "then build the new clubs up through preferential draft treatment."

As the months passed, statements about the player pool became less and less specific. In January 1966, when the governors began considering what were by then fifteen franchise applications, the players weren't mentioned at all.

It's clear from the minutes of their own meetings that the NHL owners could barely contain their excitement at the glitz and apparent wealth of some of the people associated with the applications. Press accounts focused on bids from cities like San Francisco, backed by Bing Crosby and the giant Shasta (soft drink) Corporation. A Los Angeles bid came from TV producer Tony Owen, husband of actress Donna Reed. Though the backers of a Philadelphia bid owned neither a rink nor a site for one, the League entertained the application because one of the group was Jack Kelly, former Olympic oarsman, son of a financier and brother of Princess Grace of Monaco.

Conspicuously absent from the list of prospective owners were people with any previous hockey experience at any level. A few claimed to have seen a hockey game, though none seemed quite sure when. The list of applicants—with its plethora of brothers and sisters and friends and cousins of someone who was or had once been famous—more closely resembled the come-on of a penny-stock prospectus than a list of professional sport expansion prospects.

On February 9, 1966, only eleven months after the decision to expand, the NHL granted six franchises: Los Angeles, San Francisco, Minneapolis–St. Paul, Philadelphia, Pittsburgh and St. Louis. The owners explained that the decision to ignore rock-solid applications from Baltimore, Buffalo and Vancouver in favour of St. Louis, which still hadn't even applied, was made to make the new division "geographically viable."

No explanation was given of how a franchise without owners would add viability to the League, geographic or otherwise.

Supportive sportswriters valiantly tried to defend the choice of St. Louis, suggesting that there was some unseen, superior wisdom at work, and that it was "*unlikely* the franchise was awarded blindly." In fact, that was precisely what happened. Reporters, casting their nets far and wide, could come up with only the vaguest hint that anyone at all was the slightest bit interested in owning a franchise in St. Louis. The best they could dredge up were rumours of rumours that a sixteen-man syndicate, headed by baseball legend Stan Musial and his restaurant partner Biggie Garganani, would materialize soon. Biggie and Stan the Man were never heard from.

The real reason that St. Louis was given a franchise had little to do with "geographical viabilities" and everything to do with money. As it happened, Jimmy Norris and his partner Arthur Wirtz owned the decrepit St. Louis Arena and wanted $4 million for it. A franchise for that city was their price for supporting expansion. Norris was characteristically blunt about his intentions. "St. Louis is an attractive NHL area but somebody has to come up with a franchise bid. I don't want to rent the rink to whoever wants in the NHL. I want to sell it."

As for the failure to grant Vancouver a franchise, Clarence Campbell was a lot more specific. "[It] was not a good situation out there," he explained. "There was no real head to the Vancouver organization. The operation was, financially, controlled by a group of five percenters. How was the league to deal with a group of that size and variety of ideas?" No one asked Campbell what special arrangements were being made to "deal with" the twenty-one different investors in the Pittsburgh franchise. Heading that group were Art Rooney, owner of the NFL Pittsburgh Steelers, and Jack MacGregor, a state senator, both of whom owned less than 5 percent.

Aside from payment schedules, the actual plans for expansion were still nebulous, though it was made clear that play would begin in the fall of 1967 and the draft would be held in June. With the next instalment of "good faith" money due in April, the governors were once again talking expansively of allowing the original six to protect only five skaters and a goaltender.

Perhaps the NHL owners originally did care about the competitiveness of the new franchises, but any charitable impulses they might have had evaporated when faced with applicants so desperate for hockey franchises that they'd take whatever they could get.

If the original owners had really been serious about fairness, they never would have put a general manager, much less the likes of the Canadiens' Sam Pollock, in charge of drawing up the provisions for drafting players. As a group, general managers had no phoney ideals about competitiveness. After all, *they* didn't get a penny of the $12 million in expansion money, and, unlike the wealthy owners, their welfare and the welfare of their families depended directly on the success of their teams, not on the parity of the League.

Sid Abel, Detroit's general manager, summed up the prevailing attitude. "The new teams will be weaker and they ought to be," he emphasized. "Why should the Red Wings spend millions to build up a franchise and then let these new guys move in on the same level?" Pollock dismissed the whole exercise as a "forced sale rather than an expansion draft," stating that "property rights of the six present owners" had to be protected, and scoffing at the very idea that the established teams would each protect only five or six players.

"We have our own interests and fans to consider," he snorted. "What is desirable, for the first few years, is that the new teams have an equality among themselves. Why should we give up a good kid to a new team when we haven't had a chance to look at him in the NHL ourselves?"

Putting Sam Pollock in charge of the draft was akin to loosing a weasel in a henhouse. The plan he developed was so patently unfair and one-sided that the appalled owners sent it back for revision. Even Stafford Smythe, hardly a philanthropist, gagged at Pollock's proposal to protect fourteen players per team. "What we really need are rules to protect us from our own selfishness. I want the new teams to be competitive because they've got to be an attraction when they play in our buildings."

Even so, the final plan was so prejudiced in favour of the old NHL teams that it guaranteed five of the six new clubs decades of ineptitude and financial difficulty.

Chapter 6

The Young Lions

The Toronto Maple Leafs, a once-in-a-generation team, rose from the ashes of Conn Smythe's 1957 anti-union pogrom and flourished in the easy profitability of the pre-expansion '60s. The Maple Leafs of that era included veterans like Andy Bathgate, Red Kelly, George Armstrong, Johnny Bower and Allan Stanley, but at the heart of that great team was a group of unusual youngsters—Dick Duff, Bob Nevin, Bob Pulford, Billy Harris, Bob Baun, Frank Mahovlich and Carl Brewer. They entered the League within eighteen months of each other, and many had played together as juniors with the Toronto Marlboros.* As it had been with the Red Wings, was with the Canadiens and came to be with the Islanders and Oilers, these players became the nucleus of a dynasty.

Frank Mahovlich was the only one who ranked as a superstar, but the rest fused into a rare critical mass that elevated them far beyond their individual capabilities.

---

* They were the last important group of Toronto players to sign with the Leafs. The 1967 NHL entry draft which largely did away with territorial protections eventually ensured that each franchise would get its players from all over the continent.

They were eccentrics, iconoclasts, individualists and men of above-average intelligence. They worked together, played together and powered the Leafs to four Stanley Cups in six years.

The Maple Leafs reigned in an era of calm for the NHL. So it is all the more surprising that this team was the catalyst of the turmoil and dissent that gave rise in 1967 to the second National Hockey League Players' Association.

The Young Lions were moulded in the anti-union fire of Conn Smythe, Stafford Smythe and Leafs coach Billy Reay, but they were tempered on the Imlach anvil. George (Punch) Imlach, a short, explosive and profane cockatoo of a man, won Conn Smythe's confidence immediately. Hired late in the summer of 1958 as assistant manager until he "proved himself," Imlach quickly demonstrated his mettle by relieving Billy Reay of his coaching duties at the first opportunity and taking over the job himself. It was just the kind of Darwinian competition Smythe admired.

"I sat up in my private box halfway up the stands, which the sportswriters called Berchtesgaden, and for the first time in my life a strange thing was happening," Smythe revealed in his autobiography. "I was there, always, with a handy messenger; Clancy or Tommy, Stafford's son, or somebody. I would see a line that wasn't working, a player below par, all the things I'd been seeing for years and telling coaches about—except that with Imlach, before I could get the message down to him, he would have done exactly what I wanted him to do. He was the best coach I ever saw. It was as if he were a mind reader."

Imlach the coach made Smythe very happy. Imlach the general manager made him ecstatic.* Even after the minimum-wage agreements won by the players' association in 1958, Imlach managed to decrease substantially the team's already paltry payroll, paying 25 percent of the

---

* Smythe wrote in his autobiography that Imlach was the best coach and the worst GM he had ever seen. Unfortunately, like many autobiographies, that book is full of revisionist history. Smythe was initially delighted with Imlach's iron fist.

players less than the League's $7,000 minimum. Relations between Imlach and the players were always tempestuous. At any one time, Imlach's stable admired, loathed, revered, respected or resented him—often all at once.

Billy Harris is convinced that Imlach "turned back the clock of hockey twenty years" with his tartar personality, his unbending philosophies and his inability to understand anything except in relation to the game. Imlach became a rallying point for his players; they were united as much in spite of him as because of him. Without him, the Maple Leafs might have remained just another talented group of hockey players. Without their hatred of Imlach to focus on, the Young Lions might never have had the backbone to lay the groundwork for the second NHL Players' Association.

Members of the Young Lions came and went, but the central figures—Billy Harris, Carl Brewer, Bob Baun and Bob Pulford—were there during what Harris calls "the glory years." Skinny and lanky, with a clean, boy-next-door look, Billy Harris is one of the most distinguished men ever to have played hockey. He went on to touch every level of the sport, as broadcaster, writer, coach and manager.

Harris had a fine NHL career, but Imlach always believed he underachieved. According to Imlach, Harris "thought too much," meaning he couldn't be easily bought or coerced—a cardinal sin for a hockey player. Even as a teenager, Harris was a problem to the hockey establishment. When asked by Leafs scout Bob Davidson to sign the standard C-form,* Harris cheekily replied that he would, if the team threw in four tickets to a Nat King Cole concert in addition to the usual $100 signing fee.

Only nineteen when he joined the Leafs, Harris rapidly developed into a clever, play-making centre. He had an

---

* The C-form was a simple document that bound a player to a specific team when he turned professional. No other team could then approach that player, and he could not sign with another club unless traded. Some boys signed the C-form as early as age fifteen. Though almost certainly legally unenforceable, the C-form was never challenged.

incisive and analytical mind that he exercised happily with teammate Bob (Pully) Pulford. The two roomed together on the road and spent hours dissecting the most minute details of every game.

Harris and Imlach co-existed peacefully until contract time. Hap Day had signed Harris in 1955 for a respectable $8,000. It seemed a large amount to the young man, made all the more attractive because it was a one-way contract, quite rare in those days for a rookie.* Still, Harris had the nerve to ask for a $500 bonus if he scored fifteen goals. "Look, Billy," Day told him, "this is the NHL. We are the best hockey league in the world. We don't talk hundreds, we talk thousands. I'll give you $1,000 if you score fifteen goals."

During the Imlach regime, the thousands quickly reverted to hundreds, and Harris found himself arguing futilely over $250. Though his play steadily improved during his first three professional seasons, Harris was able to lever only marginal salary increases out of Imlach. By the 1960-61 season, the only players getting less than Harris's $9,000 were the rookies. That fall, he went to training camp confident that his twenty-two-goal, thirty-assist year and his strong performance in the Stanley Cup playoffs would earn him a big jump in pay.

The players were summoned, one by one, into Imlach's room at training camp headquarters in Peterborough's Empress Hotel. Without wasting time on the preliminaries, Harris boldly asked for a $5,000 raise. Imlach gaped, as if Harris had become unglued. Then he laughed and began to curse him up, down and sideways. Though shaken, Harris stuck to his position. The next morning a mortified Harris read in the papers that "one of the young Leaf players had the audacity to ask for a $5,000 raise."

Of the many fears that are a permanent fixture in a hockey player's life, being publicly branded as greedy and ungrateful ranks high on the list. Afraid of what

---

* In a one-way contract, if a player is sent down to the minors the team must maintain his NHL wage.

might appear in the papers if he delayed any longer, and worried that the other players would discover the identity of the "young Leaf," Harris hurriedly settled for the $2,500 Imlach had offered.*

Though Imlach considered him "difficult," at least with Harris he knew he was dealing with a rational being. Defenseman Carl Brewer, in Imlach's view, was completely irrational. A genuine free spirit in a sport that relentlessly squashes them, the enigmatic and eccentric Brewer baffled and infuriated Imlach, who confessed he never knew what Brewer was thinking.

Most people who are afraid of flying would avoid airplanes. Brewer hated leaving the ground, so he took flying lessons. Most hockey players are thrilled if a general manager singles them out for congratulations after a game. Brewer was just as likely to shrug it off.

After a game in which Toronto squeaked past Detroit, Imlach, in a rare moment, unbent enough to shake Brewer's hand in the dressing room and congratulate him on the "best" game he'd ever played. Brewer looked up casually and took the offered hand as if Imlach were a small boy begging for an autograph. "Well, I don't know that it was the best game," he said with an insouciant smile.

"What the hell! Of course it was, whaddya mean?" sputtered Imlach, who had expected the requisite gratitude and forelock-tugging.

"Every game's the same to me," Brewer responded heretically. Bristling and red-faced, Imlach stalked out.

Though often a mass of nerves before games, once on the ice Brewer played with such coolness that observers wondered if it was the same man. He also played with a flash of humour. During one penalty-laden game in Detroit, Warren Godfrey lost his helmet during the play.

---

* Harris still feels he was very well paid in those days. His first contract netted him $20,000: $7,000 for the first year, $8,000 for the second and a $5,000 signing bonus. In comparison, his high school principal was making less than $5,000 at the time. But Harris, like most players of the day, never considered the intangible factors: the risk of injury, the relatively short career and the difficulty of finding well-paying work after hockey.

Brewer cruised by, flipped it into the stands with a flourish and positively preened as the Red Wings fans hooted their disapproval.

Though Brewer could rough it up, he was a poor fighter and relied more on finesse. "In the space of two seconds," marvelled writer Scott Young, "he would unlace the other player's skates, break two buttons on his braces, start his sweater unravelling in three places, saw his stick in half, and grab the man by the elbow."

To management, Brewer was the personification of cheek. To the players, he presented an inexplicable façade that simultaneously attracted and repelled. Brewer carried with him the taint of scandal, of going too far, of insufficient reverence for the game, and for the owners. He was the first player to use a lawyer in negotiating his contract and the first to investigate setting himself up as a corporation.

Brewer came to the Leafs in 1957 at the age of nineteen, and though Imlach always appreciated his speed and defensive finesse, he quickly came to resent him as a troublemaker and a rebel—too irritating to keep and far too good to trade. Stuck with a conundrum, Imlach resorted to belittling Brewer, portraying him as a delicate creature, "an emotional high strung kind of guy." But Imlach never saw anything beyond the game itself, and Brewer saw too much. In 1965, after a between-periods argument with Imlach, Brewer abruptly quit the team and quit hockey. Imlach's response was curiously muted when he discussed the event in later years. He had been angry at the time, but his dominant feeling later was bafflement. As an explanation, he hinted that Brewer had a nervous breakdown; it never occurred to him that Brewer had simply had enough of Punch Imlach.

Standing foursquare at the rock-hard centre of the Young Lions was Brewer's defense partner, Robert "The Boomer" Baun. As with the rest of that group, Baun didn't quite fit the typical mould. At a time when a hockey player's preferred drinks were rye whisky and beer and his favourite meal meat and potatoes, Baun became a Cordon Bleu chef, even travelling to Paris in the off-season to learn the intricacies of the art. He built up a huge wine cellar, and every bottle had a cork. In the summer, while other players switched pads and skates for polyester and golf clubs or just hung out at the bar, Baun took General Motors management courses and enrolled in the Wharton School of Business. Imlach sneered at Baun's off-ice interests, calling them "perverted" examples of a "deviated personality."

For all his eccentricities, Baun epitomized one of hockey's most dearly beloved images—the relentless bruiser on the ice who is just the nicest boy in civvies, unfailingly self-effacing and a little bit shy.* Built like a tree stump, he was the archetypal NHL warrior and one of the game's great bodycheckers. Timing a collision between two fast moving bodies on skates is a matter of considerable skill. Like all the best checkers, Baun got within striking range of his target with skill and instinct. But once there, his hits were more the application of a blunt instrument than technical expertise. At the moment of impact, his victim sounded, and looked, like a bagpipe abruptly deflated. Telecasters loved Baun's checks, replaying them again and again—often in slow motion—accompanying the action with orgasmic squeaks and grunts.

Baun mastered the art of "getting a piece" of the other guy. Unfortunately, every piece he took cost him a chunk of his own hide. In an occupation that treats debilitating injuries as normal wear-and-tear, Baun's inventory is singular. A partial list includes numerous broken toes from blocking slapshots (he is credited with having coerced manufacturers into adding a metal plate in the toe of the

---

* The media endlessly promulgate this image. In the 1987-88 playoffs, for example, Marty McSorley, then playing for the Oilers, nearly gelded Mike Bullard of the Flames, who was harmlessly skating toward the bench far from the action. A scythe-like stick to the groin dented Bullard's cup. After a few ritual "tut-tuts," the commentators inundated viewers with tales demonstrating "what a really nice, quiet, respectful young man" McSorley was. They trotted out tales of his farm days and examples of his kindness to his mother, young children and strays.

McSorley, explaining his action, quickly fell back on an NHL classic, the "temporary amnesia defence"—a never-fail explanation for an other wise inexplicable atrocity.

skate), torn ligaments in both knees, two broken fingers and a thumb, a broken leg, a broken cheekbone, a gruesome near decapitation and, of course, the requisite flattened nose and missing teeth.*

Part of the patented NHL tough-guy mystique is a quick return to action after injury. No one came back sooner than Baun. But he admits it had more to do with fear than valour. "Before expansion [1967] there were always far more players than there were jobs," he points out. "If I didn't come back, some guy took your place and you'd wind up in the minors. I remember once that Moose Vasko of Chicago hit Larry Hillman on our club. Larry went from us to the Rochester farm [team] and he didn't get back for five years."

Baun's most famous moment came on a steamy April evening in 1964 at the Detroit Olympia during the Stanley Cup playoffs. With the Red Wings leading three games to two and the score tied at three, Baun took a heavy wrist shot from Gordie Howe directly on his ankle. By the time he reached the dressing room, the ankle had swollen into a thick cuff of flesh. The team doctor cut away some padding, shot him up with novocaine and watched grimly as Baun gingerly headed back to the bench with a few minutes remaining in the period.

With the game in overtime, Imlach sent in Baun. He took a pass and drilled the puck at Terry Sawchuk. Deflected off Bill Gadsby, the puck slid past the surprised goalie and ensured a seventh game, which the Maple Leafs won. Only after that game did Baun have his fractured ankle x-rayed and treated.

Imlach gushed about Baun's heroics, promising he would place him forever on his very short list of "untouchables." Imlach's "forever" proved to be a bare three years. In 1967, when he left Baun unprotected in the draft, a reporter reminded Imlach of his pledge. "Well, shit!" he exploded. "I woulda played with ten broken

---

* When he retired, Baun decided to get himself fixed up. He checked himself into hospital and ordered the works—except for his nose which he had grown fond of.

bones. What the fuck's the big deal?"

Baun recoils infinitesimally each time the broken ankle incident is mentioned. He loathes the insinuation that his entire career, and character, can be summed up in one neat anecdote. Privately, he judges people—writers especially—on whether they bring it up or not.

What sets Bob Baun apart is a deeply imbued sense of his own self-worth, which he attributes to a loving, comfortable, middle-class upbringing in Toronto. "My dad was fairly successful, we had a nice home and everything else," he says. "So when I turned pro I expected the same thing. I couldn't believe how these teams treated their players." At fourteen, when most NHL hopefuls could think of only two things—hockey and their young male urges—Baun started his own construction business and maintenance company. "Mr. Smythe always said I was the only junior player who drove a Cadillac," laughs Baun. "But I saw very quickly that I didn't want to live like the rest of the guys."*

In 1956, to stir up excitement over the signing of highly touted junior Frank Mahovlich and thumb his nose at Jack Adams, who had lost Mahovlich to Toronto, Conn Smythe leaked Mahovlich's two-year $20,000 salary to the press. It was a highly unusual event, as secrecy about salaries was one of management's most powerful and effective weapons. When he read the details, Baun was determined to get more than the League's minimum wage, then $6,000. He made a deal to negotiate in tandem with his friend, Al MacNeil. "I would prepare my presentation based on what Hap Day had said to Al MacNeil. Then after I came out we'd go off and have a chat. . . . We ended up with around $16,000 for the two years with a $4,000 signing bonus, so we were pretty pleased." Years later, Baun told him that story to Day who retorted, "I

---

* Baun's drive hasn't made him the most successful ex-hockey player. He's gone through several businesses and a painful bankruptcy. "Bob's good at making money," observes a former teammate. "But he's even better at spending it. He's too quick to take off his shirt, lend it to you, then forget to ask for it back." Today he owns two Tim Horton franchises in the Toronto area.

thought you little buggers were up to something!"

In those days, contracts were decreed, not negotiated. Often no discussion at all took place: the general manager made an offer, the player nodded acquiescence and the paper was produced for signing. Contracts usually had a duration of only one year and were invariably negotiated during training camp when a player was most vulnerable to pressure. Baun's salary, like that of the other Young Lions, crept up infinitesimally in his first years with the Leafs. By 1961, he realized that he was only going to get ahead by bargaining, and bargaining meant preparation. He put together cards containing details of his performance, stressing the high points, ignoring the low ones. He winnowed out information about other players' salaries, made estimates, comparisons and generally behaved rather unlike a hockey player. As a result, though not among the League's most talented players, Baun was one of the most highly paid in his final years.

Baun became known among his teammates as the man to talk to before sitting down with the general manager. By the 1966-67 season, the practice had become institutionalized. At training camp, the rookies, after receiving their contract offers, would line up outside Baun's room for his advice. That year, Punch Imlach happened along and saw a group of players milling around in the hall. "What the fuck are you assholes doing?" he snarled. "Oh, we're just waiting to talk to Mr. Baun about our contracts," they chorused.

Imlach's jaw flapped like a castanet, his face convulsed and his lips pulled up in a sneer, bringing his nose, like a dagger, toward his chin. "You fucking little ungrateful pricks," he shrieked. "You get your fucking asses out of here and back to our fucking rooms before I fucking well lose my fucking temper and really do something you fuckers will regret." The players dispersed.

"Punch called me in and threatened to send me to the minors right then," recalls Baun. "So from that point on we never got on very well." Imlach's idea of holding a grudge was to use Baun erratically that year and hardly at all during the 1967 Stanley Cup, though the previous season had been Baun's best ever. Baun protested by refusing to take part in the Leafs' '67 Stanley Cup festivities.

The fourth Young Lion, Bob Pulford, was also the quietest. Although many hockey players were talented, all-round athletes, few had time to devote themselves to another sport, let alone star in it. Pulford was an exception. Even playing in his spare time, he became a superb lacrosse player.

Hap Day signed the highly touted young centre in 1956. Big, mobile and sly, Pulford excelled defensively *and* offensively, and he had the enviable knack of putting the puck in at critical moments. Nearly every season during his career with the Leafs he made or came close to the twenty-goal mark, considered excellent for the time. Even during his periodic spats with Pulford, Imlach conceded that he was the team's most valuable player next to Frank Mahovlich. Still, Pulford rarely garnered the headlines and was often described as the player no one ever really noticed.

Like Harris, Brewer and Baun, Pulford saw life beyond hockey. Though Imlach loathed the very idea of higher education, Pulford, stiffened by his father's unbending "no school, no hockey" attitude, enrolled in McMaster University and, after years of part-time and summer school study, completed a bachelor's degree in 1963. "Mr. Smythe always told me you couldn't have two bosses. But I liked going to school, it was a break from hockey," Pulford recalls. "With Punch it was just another thing to argue about."

The Leafs often made the slow-talking, good-natured Pulford the butt of their jokes, and they particularly enjoyed poking fun at his excessive thrift. "He was always the last one out with his wallet and the first one to count his change," smiles Billy Harris. Today, those who know him agree that Pulford appreciates a nickel more than most people do a twenty-dollar bill.

Other players moved in and out of the Young Lions, notably Dick Duff, Bob Nevin and Frank Mahovlich, who was as big a cipher to the players then as he is now. "To tell you the truth," admits one member of the group, "we didn't know whose side he was on then and we still don't know." When Imlach wanted the team to do something, he always enlisted Mahovlich first and exhorted the other players to follow. When the players wanted to do something that Imlach might oppose, they also enlisted Mahovlich first.

The final member of the Young Lions was not a player at all but a lawyer by the name of Alan Eagleson. His association with the Maple Leafs gave him a foothold in hockey which, in turn, became the basis of an empire.

Eagleson had been tagging along with hockey players ever since his teenage friendship with fellow lacrosse player Bob Pulford. The parsimonious Pulford was perfectly teamed with Eagleson, who could always get a discount on anything, had a solution for every problem and could find a way out of every scrape.

On the surface, Eagleson appeared unimpressive, except for his hyperkinetic verbal skills and his ability to talk in entire paragraphs consisting almost entirely of expletives. But by the time the Maple Leafs won their first of three consecutive Stanley Cups in 1962, he had become a dominant fixture in their high-spirited little clique.

Born in St. Catharines, Ontario, in April 1933, Eagleson was the only boy among three sisters, Margaret, Frances and Carol. His parents had immigrated from Northern Ireland in 1929, settling first in St. Catharines, then Port Dalhousie, Guelph and finally, in 1943, New Toronto, a bustling, working-class suburb with, as Eagleson has described it, "small houses and big mortgages."

Like most young boys, Eagleson had a different career idea virtually every day. "When I grow up I'm going to be a minister," he once announced to his mother after a church outing. "Only I won't make sermons, I'll just take the collection and leave." "The Eagle," as he called himself, later declared that he intended to become a professional boxer. His mother scoffed at the idea, pointing out that he looked more like a sparrow, and a scrawny one at that, than a bird of prey. "He was just like a little bird, with legs like toothpicks," she said of her undersized son.

The career that eventually held enduring attraction for Eagleson was the law. "Lawyers around New Toronto lived in nicer houses than we did, so they were making money. That was an attraction," he revealed in a 1981 interview. One of the Eagleson family's favourite childhood stories revolves around the mock-trials he conducted, complete with paper-cut-out attorneys and witnesses. He cast himself permanently in the role of judge, and it was always a hanging judge who presided.

He created an elaborate penal system with clerks, opposing lawyers, a jury, reporters and the accused all posturing and capering on a variety of structures created out of discarded wooden crates, cigar boxes and hat boxes. The jury was sequestered in the hat box and the guilty were banished to a dung-encrusted old birdcage in the basement. One of the most interesting aspects of Eagleson's criminal justice system was the fact that the accused were invariably individuals who had crossed him in everyday life.

In those days, a lot of people crossed Alan Eagleson, and a lot of retribution had to be handed out. He regularly returned home from school in tears after being tormented by neighbourhood bullies. Bony, short and already possessing his trademark wicked, wise-cracking tongue, Eagleson was the perfect target. Ironically, considering his future profession, athletes picked on him most, questioning his masculinity and entertaining each other in the locker room by throwing Eagleson, his clothes or both into the showers.

Eagleson solved most problems with native wit and what he remembers as a well-developed running ability, but occasionally, when there was no risk of retaliation, he let his native aggression flare. In a high school basketball game, an opponent persisted in tripping him. "Don't try that again," Eagleson warned. "What are you going to do about it?" sneered the other boy. "You'll see." The next time Eagleson got the ball he charged down the court and went in for a lay-up. At the last moment, he turned and drove the ball into the boy's face. "He never bothered me again," he states flatly.

School was easy for Eagleson, a fact he didn't trouble to hide. He raced through to grade five at the age of eight, skipping two years along the way and catching up to his older sister, Margaret. Eagleson flaunted his speed with schoolwork, which didn't endear him to his classmates. "If the rest of his class took thirty minutes to do an assignment, it only took Alan five," recalls Marguerite Weir, his high school teacher. "Then he would clown. He would even stand on his desk . . . he had to get attention some way and he certainly couldn't get it on the football field or with girls . . . he simply couldn't compete."

Only fourteen years old in grade eleven, Eagleson weighed less than eighty pounds. "There's no question that I overreacted to my deficiency in size," he once admitted candidly. "I always talked louder and tried harder." He also compensated by throwing himself into out-of-school activities, desperately striving to become popular, an attention-getter, a leader.

Eagleson became known as the fast-talking, fast-moving Duddy Kravitz of his neighbourhood—the kid who always had a deal cooking. He took to the role of middleman as if it had been genetically imprinted on his character. When the bus picked the children up for their swim lessons at Humberside Collegiate pool, Eagleson collected the ten-cent fares each week. If someone forgot their money or spent it, he grandly smoothed it over with the driver. He never lost track of the debits and credits and never let anyone's tab run up. "He was a regular little monopolizer," his mother told his biographer. "If a kid showed up without his money a second time, Alan took it upon himself not to let him get on the bus."

Just before he entered university, Eagleson finally got what he most wanted: he grew nine inches and gained fifty-five muscular pounds. "When I got to U of T it was an absolute picnic!" he exults. "Suddenly I was the same size as everybody else! And got into more fights and trouble than the next ten students."

Overnight, Alan Eagleson became the aggressor, getting into fights at swimming pools, locker rooms, during intramural games and just walking down the street. Sometimes there was provocation, sometimes not. Robert Mackay, then a lecturer at the U of T law school, often gave Eagleson a lift to classes. One day, on the way into Toronto, another car whizzed past them. A short while later they caught up to the car at a stoplight and Eagleson yelled, "Just a minute!" He jumped out and pounded on the adjacent car's window. When the occupant foolishly opened the window, Eagleson pummelled him, ran back to the car and exhorted Mackay to get going. "Boy did I ever go!"

On another occasion, a driver made the serious mistake of cutting Eagleson off. At the first stop, Eagleson leapt out of the car, leaving the startled Mackay behind, dragged the offender clear out of his car window and pummelled him into a bloody mess. Then he calmly walked back to the car and drove away.

During an intramural basketball game, one of the law school players, Lionel Schipper, had his badly injured knee heavily wrapped in tape. Eagleson, a reserve player, watched from the bench. When an opposition guard deliberately fouled Schipper—a pal of Eagleson's—with a blow to his knee, Eagleson sprang to his feet, marched over to the scorer's table and declared himself a substitute. Before anyone realized what was happening, Eagleson walked up to the offending player and flattened him. Then he returned to the bench and sat down.

Even Eagleson's most protective friends agree that he's never heard of the Marquis of Queensberry, but they rationalize his aggressiveness as a strength—something to be admired and envied—rather than a character flaw. "Al told me that he worked on the premise that if you hit them with everything you had with the first blow they really questioned coming back at you," explains former law partner Bob Watson, in the manner of a grandfather relating tales about a favoured but naughty grandson.

But the same friends admit that being with Eagleson could be a nerve-wracking and dangerous experience.

They never knew when he would explode, and the prospect of a brawl was never far from their minds. One day, Eagleson and a group of lacrosse players arrived at Toronto's Hart House for a practice. A basketball team had the floor and showed no sign of relinquishing it. Eagleson loudly demanded that the "faggot" basketball players get out of the gym. One of them innocently inquired, "Where's your permit?" Eagleson strode over and, lightning-fast, landed a roundhouse right to the young man's head. "There's my permit," he replied, stepping over the fallen body on the way into the gym.

Eagleson's unpredictable fisticuffs gained him notoriety, but it was his capers, his tricks and his ever more sophisticated wheeling and dealing that earned him a large group of friends and admirers. He cultivated a host of useful contacts, such as an usher at varsity and Argonaut football games. At the beginning of the game, the usher would throw his armband, which gained him free admission into the park, over the fence. On the outside, Eagleson would round up a promising clientele and collect a fee for the use of the band. After each use, the armband would be tossed back for the next in line. "That was part of being Al," laughs Bob Watson, "and the fun of being with him. . . . We had wonderful times. Al was proof to me that if you have the nerve to pull things off, there is not very much that you can't pull off."

If Eagleson had a connection or even just a name, he used it. When he went to Exhibition Stadium he rarely paid to get in or park. He'd simply tell the guard that the president of the CNE gave him permission to enter and park. He said it with such authority the guard never doubted his word.

Few would dare to use a sister's wedding presents for a prank. The day Eagleson's sister got married, the gifts were laid out on display, as was the custom. Eagleson gathered up the presents, unwrapped them and took them out to a nearby field where a fair had erected its tents. He and a friend set up a booth with the presents tantalizingly arranged. But they had also bought a supply of cheap novelties, and those were the only things their eager customers won. At the end of the day they pocketed their earnings, rewrapped the presents and carefully put them all back.

Then as now, Eagleson repels at least as many people as he attracts, but the ones he attracts become addicts. Eagleson did everything in extremes. He talked louder and swore louder and more frequently than anyone his friends had ever met—or, for that matter, ever would meet. Those who knew him talk of those days as if they were touched by a god, far from a perfect god, but a god nonetheless. For many, their association with Alan Eagleson, however brief and distant, was a highlight in their lives.

After graduating with a B.A. in 1954, Eagleson stayed at the University of Toronto to study law. It was a magical time to be a U of T law student. In 1949, Bora Laskin, later Chief Justice of Canada, and Caesar Wright, an unparalleled legal scholar, abandoned the hallowed, tradition-bound Osgoode Hall to set up a maverick school on the U of T campus. Wright feuded for many years with Osgoode and the Law Society, which required his students to attend Osgoode for a year after graduation before being admitted to the bar. The students, and many faculty members, revelled in the image of themselves as outlaws. "We felt our little school was fighting the great big bad Law Society," says Lionel Schipper, "trying to get them to move into the twentieth century in terms of legal education." When Eagleson was admitted, the eighty-odd students had enough esprit de corps to challenge a dozen law schools.

Eagleson thrived on conflicts with clearly delineated sides—us versus them. Where they didn't exist he created them, and where they did exist, as in sport, he raised the stakes. Half of the eighty law students were fervent athletes, and the renegade little faculty's tremendous spirit ensured a law team for every event, competition or league. Some, like Eagleson, spent far more time competing than studying. Though he played for intramural teams, not the varsity squads, he developed a reputation as an athletic superstar that persists to this day.

Eagleson brought his fierce determination and lack of respect for the niceties of fair play to the athletic field. "It didn't matter how big they were, how many there were, he was fearless," recalls Lionel Schipper, still in awe more than thirty years later. "That's the way he is. He is bright and if he was on your side he was fun, he would protect you. If you were on the other side, I suspect you didn't like him at all."

Lacrosse became Eagleson's game. Never the most skilful player on the team, he was often the most valuable. Lacrosse is a sport that rewards quickness and ferocity. In hockey, cross-checking with the stick is penalized—or supposed to be at any rate. In lacrosse it is an integral part of the game. Bodychecking, the bread-and-butter of hockey, is rare in lacrosse, where most of the work—scoring, hitting and checking—is done with the stick.

When Eagleson's friends reminisce about university days, they invariably end up talking about a single game, an intramural lacrosse playoff that epitomizes everything they adore about the man. The injury-riddled law team had no offense left except Eagleson, and the opponents keyed on him, working him over systematically. His friends recall Eagleson's valour, the goals he scored against all odds and every elbow, knee and stick that landed on his steadily weakening body. At one point, Eagleson's father, a small man, rushed out to tackle the referee before being restrained by several law students.

At the end of the game the law team had lost by one goal, and a battered, barely conscious Eagleson had to be carried to the dressing room and laid down on the training table, where he lay quietly gasping and moaning. His pals gathered round to commiserate and pay homage in hushed tones, until one of the opposing players turned up to taunt Eagleson. The law students waved him away in disgust. The prostrate Eagleson offered no response at first, and then a barely audible "Go fuck yourself."

The other player foolishly leaned a little closer to hear. "Poor old Eagleson, who was slumped over with no energy, leapt off the bench, grabbed the guy and started to throttle him and kept smashing him against the locker," says Schipper. "That was Eagleson."

As it became clear to Eagleson that beating up future pharmacists and divinity graduates during lacrosse games wasn't the route to fame and fortune, he increasingly gravitated to management. In the relatively closed fraternity of '50s varsity sport, the only way to land cosy positions like team manager was by knowing the right people. So Eagleson cultivated John McManus, the varsity basketball coach. He ran errands, picked up sandwiches and even cleaned the coach's furnace, gratis.

Eagleson's approach wasn't subtle, and McManus well knew that the twenty-six days the team spent in Florida every year attracted Eagleson far more than any desire to be helpful. Still, something about the all-too-obvious young man intrigued him and he gave him the job. "He was a belligerent little rooster, but he knew how to handle a dollar. When he went into a hotel everything was taken care of right away—the rooms, meals, everything."

In Florida, the team stayed near the beach, which was usually filled with party-minded students. Eagleson would patrol the area and tell likely prospects that the team was hosting a party that night. He collected a dollar from each. Out of the forty or fifty dollars he would buy ten dollars' worth of soft drinks and potato chips and then pocket the rest.

When asked if the players liked Eagleson, McManus pauses, groping carefully for the correct words. "He was respected," he finally concedes, "held in awe."

Eagleson was every bit as partisan a manager as he was a player. During a close game against Queen's University, the trombonist in the pep band continually spoiled the Toronto players' foul shots with perfectly timed blasts. "Are they allowed to do that?" Eagleson asked McManus. "Nope," McManus replied, "I'll go over and speak to the referee." The appeal failed, and the next time a Toronto player stepped up to the foul line the trombone again sounded. "*I'll* go and have a word with him now," Eagleson said. He walked over and without a word knocked the musician into the next section.

After Eagleson was called to the bar in 1959, he

stepped into a partnership at the firm he articled with, a rare feat then as now. Then, in 1960, he and Bob Watson joined the young firm of Blaney, Pasternak, Luck and Smela and opened a branch office in a little corner of north Etobicoke called Thistletown. Surrounded by a handful of houses and a police station, Eagleson and Watson weren't exactly inundated with work.

The partners in the firm managed to pay themselves $75 a week, but most of them lived as if it were far more. "Oddly enough," muses Watson, "Al and I were the conservative partners. Absolutely. Al was very cautious with his money because he didn't come by it very easily. But we always expanded when we couldn't afford it. We were all driving vehicles we probably couldn't afford. The whole history of our firm was we always went ahead by getting ourselves into jackpots that we had to live up to."

Though he did legal work for Bob Pulford and Billy Harris in the early '60s, the Maple Leafs of that time can't recall how Eagleson became such a permanent part of their circle. What they do remember is that once he attached himself he was as immovable as a tick. "He was very, very dominant," recalls Harris. "Socially—there could be six or seven conversations going on and his would be the loudest."

Eagleson was always ready and willing to run out and get beer, organize a party, provide free legal advice or help the players move. He seemed to know how to fix things, how to get them new cars at a good rate, presents for their girlfriends at a discount and custom clothes at off-the-rack prices.

In some respects, hockey players haven't changed at all in twenty-five years. Then, as now, high on their wish list on turning pro was a fancy car. Fancy cars meant lots of speeding tickets, and Eagleson proved adept at removing that little aggravation. "In those days, with the brush-cuts, we all looked the same," chuckles Bob Baun. Eagleson would walk into court with one of the Leafs and the policeman would point, "There he is. Yes that's Bobby Pulford." Then Eagleson would introduce Baun, and that was the end of the ticket.

Getting clients was critical for the fledgling law firm, and no one excelled at that more than Eagleson. Already a master at constructing a network of people who owed him favours, he proved equally adept at bringing people together for mutual gain. In 1959 he cemented his relationship with the Young Lions by forming the Blue and White Investment Group, which included Billy Harris, Bob Baun, Bob Pulford, Carl Brewer, Bob Watson, Herb Pasternak, George Graham of Ostranders Jewellers and Hern Kerney of Hern Pontiac. The businessmen were thrilled to be rubbing shoulders with hockey players and the players got good deals on cars and jewellery for their wives and girlfriends. When Eagleson was elected to the Ontario Provincial Parliament in 1963, the circle around the players widened to include politicians too.

Eagleson, in turn, got tremendous mileage out of his connections with the players in hockey-addicted Toronto. "People like to be around hockey players. People like to be around people who act for hockey players. Especially in Toronto. It's a unique city," points out Watson. "You go into any other city—like New York—and it wouldn't mean anything, but in Toronto, we could have a party or a 'do' for our clients—we could call on eight or ten players—that's something."

On average, hockey players are the most conservative of professional athletes. The Maple Leafs of the '60s were a give-no-quarter team, but, like most hockey players, they left their aggression behind when they took off their skates. Eagleson's lack of inhibitions enthralled the Maple Leafs.

Though no one has ever known Eagleson to lift a hand against—much less strike—a hockey player, it remained open season on everyone else. When pressed, Eagleson's friends admit his incendiary out-bursts often embarrassed or discomfited them, but they reasoned away the incidents because he appeared to be fighting for someone else's greater good. One night in Maple Leaf Gardens, a group of Pulford's friends came to watch him play. A raucous fan booed and hissed when Pulford came on the ice. After the fan and Eagleson exchanged a few blue words, Eagleson turned to one of the group, said "Here, hold my glasses," then turned and leapt at the fan's throat.

The most interesting insight into Eagleson's time as an honorary Maple Leaf comes from the recollections of the players. Most have come to the conclusion, and are surprised at themselves for it, that Eagleson never really liked them. "Eagleson has always looked down on hockey players," maintains Harris. "I think underneath he thought we were all a bunch of dummies." Even Eagleson's law partner, Bob Watson—still an Eagleson loyalist—recalls how malicious he could be with the players, using ridicule, thinly veiled as humour, to dominate them. "Al would be relentless if he ever got the players in a situation where he was having fun with them," he says. "Then he would just never stop."

By the mid-'60s, the Young Lions had coalesced into a strong core of veteran players. Thanks mainly to Imlach's bullying, they had developed a view of the game different from that of the generation before. They weren't quite as grateful for the opportunity to play as their predecessors had been. Many afternoons, a group of them would congregate in the office of Jim Blaney, Baun's lawyer. Other times they'd meet at their favourite hangout, George's Spaghetti House, on the corner of Sherbourne and Dundas. Inevitably the conversation would turn to hockey, then to Punch, then to the owners and eventually to the inequities in the game.

Favourite stories would circulate, like Eddie Shack's early experience with the Rangers. After several terrible games, coach Phil Watson came into the dressing room and told the players to speak their minds. He assured the team that nothing they said would be held against them. But player after player said not a word. Then came Eddie Shack. "Are you sure nothing will be held against me?" he asked. "Yeah, sure, sure. That's what I said." Shack smiled, "Well Phil, everything you've ever told me has gone in one ear and out the other." Watson exploded

and stormed out. Next day Shack got word he was to report to Springfield.

Players who crossed a coach or general manager had a
net worth of zero because they were completely at the
mercy of the team that owned them. Mike Walton, a
small but incredibly deft player, was one of those.
Named rookie of the year in two different minor leagues,
he looked like a certainty to join the Maple Leafs. But
Walton was as combative off the ice as he was on, and
he argued about everything, especially his contract.
During a Central Hockey League game, Harold Ballard
and Stafford Smythe came down to watch. "Walton will
never be a Maple Leaf the way he's playing," Smythe told
the coach, who promptly told Walton.

The mini-volcano inside Walton exploded. Going out
for the third period, he spotted Ballard and Smythe. "The
guys had to hold me because they thought I was going
to punch the shit out of them. I just screamed and yelled
at them out on the ice." Smythe retaliated by keeping the
volatile youngster on the protected list so he couldn't
play for any other team, but told Imlach to leave him in
the minors. Had it not been for a scoring slump the Leafs
hit early in the 1966-67 season, Walton might have spent
the rest of his career riding the buses in the minors.*

The Young Lions had all suffered or witnessed such incidents and realized that their working conditions were
arbitrary and, what's more, there was no vehicle for
change. Though they were all relatively new to the
League in 1957, they had seen what happened when
players tried to improve their lot. Unaware of it at the
time, they had been sensitized and, to a degree, politicized by the fate of men like Lindsay, Thomson and
Harvey.

Increasingly, the players' talk centred around money.
The young men who had been delighted with $8,000 in
1960 began to think their pay cheques in 1965 didn't

---

* Walton did do something that helped improve his career outlook. He married
Stafford Smythe's niece.

represent a fair share of the League's tremendous profitability. After one grumbling conversation, Eagleson approached Clarence Campbell with a plan for saving the players' tax. The NHL president listened with interest and promised to take the idea to the League. "My relations with Mr. Campbell were very cordial," said Eagleson after meeting with the president. After Eagleson left, Campbell cordially filed his proposals in the wastebasket.

By the 1964-65 season, Eagleson and his partners were advising at least half of the Maple Leafs players on their contracts and doing other routine legal work for them. It has often been written that the turning point in Eagleson's career came when he negotiated Bobby Orr's NHL contract in 1966. But the foundation for his hegemony over hockey was laid a couple of years earlier, when that core group of Leafs stuck with him, despite management's growing opposition to the relationship.

It was actually Carl Brewer who first brought Eagleson's name into prominence in hockey circles in 1964 when he asked Eagleson to help him negotiate his contract. During training camp in Peterborough, Brewer mentioned the new arrangement to Imlach.

"Can he fucking play hockey?" Imlach demanded.

"He's a lawyer, not a hockey player," Brewer answered with exaggerated patience.

"If he can goddam well play hockey, I might talk to him. But I'm not going to waste my time on some son of a bitch who can't fucking play hockey."

"But Punch, he's my lawyer. Don't you understand? He's not another hockey player. He's my lawyer."

"That doesn't matter shit to me! I'm not gonna talk with the son of a bitch if he can't play hockey! And that's that!"

Imlach flatly refused to negotiate through Eagleson and Brewer ended up signing for $9,500. In 1965, unable to budge Imlach and growing sick of his oppressive tactics, Brewer did the unthinkable—he quit in the middle of the season and enrolled at the University of Toronto. A year later, Brewer enlisted Eagleson again, this time to battle both the Maple Leafs and the League, in order to play for the legendary Father Bauer, coach of the national amateur team.

"I was very religious at the time," Brewer says, as if observing the actions of someone else from a great distance. Eagleson got credit publicly for Brewer's eventual success, but the two-year fight to regain his amateur status would never have been won without Brewer's incredible persistence.

Despite Eagleson's inability to negotiate contracts with management, more and more players, primarily Maple Leafs, asked him to do their legal work. By 1966, nearly half his clients came from hockey. But Eagleson might have remained simply a lawyer with a lot of NHL clients had it not been for a series of events that altered the course of the game.

The first was expansion which created the climate for change. The next three were directly tied to Eagleson: the signing of Bobby Orr by the Boston Bruins, the formation of a new players' association and the squashing of the Captain Queeg-like Eddie Shore, then owner of a professional minor-league team, the Springfield Indians.

Stories about Eagleson's feats during this period have grown to proportions rivaling those of Paul Bunyan, who created the Grand Canyon just by dragging his pick on the ground. "Any one of those moves, people would have predicted was impossible," Eagleson later said.

Representing Bobby Orr certainly gave Eagleson visibility and laid the basis for his considerable wealth. The formation of the Players' Association undoubtedly gave him tremendous power and leverage. But it was the much-heralded defeat of Eddie Shore that demonstrated to hockey players that it was possible to beat the owners, and that Alan Eagleson was the man to do it.

Until the Shore–Eagleson confrontation in 1966, the players had never won anything of consequence during the NHL's forty-nine-year history.

Chapter 7

Slaying the Dragon

A throwback's throwback, Eddie Shore makes Ted Lindsay look like a pussycat and Philadelphia's "Broad Street Bullies" look like so many ballerinas. Billed as "the Babe Ruth of Hockey," Shore filled rinks during the Depression when professional hockey was desperately struggling to survive. When he charged down the ice in the Boston Garden, the fans rose screaming for a goal. In the NHL's other nine rinks they screamed for his blood.

Many name Howie Morenz as the greatest star during this period. No doubt the Montreal forward had more all-round talent, but no player before or since has had the same combination of skill and personality as Eddie Shore. "It's nice to know that Edward is still bad," wrote John Lardner in 1939, at the end of Shore's career. "For twenty years, man and boy, this evil fellow has been punching people, hitting them over the head with his stick, chewing their ears, butting, gouging, shoving, and generally bedeviling his fellow men and always for handsome fees. No one has ever made malevolence pay better money. . . . Mr. Shore has lowered the late Cesare Borgia's record for all-round evil-doing and developed the role of Villain to such an extent that professional wrestlers gnash their teeth with envy."

Tex Rickard, who ran Madison Square Garden, promoted games against Shore's Bruins by hiring a fleet of ambulances to race through New York's "theatre row" en route to the Garden with sirens blaring and lights flashing. Drawn by this graphic promise of bloodletting, the crowds deserted the shows and headed for MSG. Once Rickard advertised a Bruins–Rangers game by overlaying Shore's face on a "Wanted Dead or Alive" poster.

An excellent skater with a wicked wrist shot, Shore was a rushing defenseman in an era when the breed was virtually unknown. His bodychecking was devastating, and often he blocked as many shots on the net as the goalie did. Playing fifty to fifty-five minutes of every game, he fascinated and terrorized the NHL for thirteen and a half seasons, scoring 105 goals and setting up 179 others, the latter figure all the more impressive as only one assist was awarded per goal. Shore won the Hart Trophy as the League's most valuable player four times, in 1933, '35, '36 and '38—the most for any defenseman. Additionally, he made the NHL's All-Star team eight of the nine times he was eligible.

Shore was born in Fort Qu'Appelle, Saskatchewan, in 1902. His father, Thomas John Shore, ran a prosperous, thirty-five-section farm with 400 head of horses, 600 head of cattle and an annual wheat yield of 100,000 bushels. Shore usually attributed his fight-to-the-death toughness to bronco-busting as a ten-year old, but in later years he obliquely hinted at ferocious beatings by his father.

Nothing about Eddie Shore was typical. Like most prairie boys he skated shortly after he walked, but unlike most he showed no particular interest in hockey. His older brother Aubrey adored the game and played for the Manitoba Agricultural College in Winnipeg. During an argument with Eddie, who also attended the school, Aubrey taunted, "You could never be a hockey player, let alone one as good as me!" "Hah!" shot back Eddie. "Anybody can be a stupid hockey player!"

Every evening and every weekend after that, Shore laced up his skates, took a stick and puck and systematically made himself into a hockey player. Even when the temperature dropped to minus-thirty degrees and the wind cleaved off the prairies, a solitary figure would drive up and down the ice far into the night.

Shore made the college team for the last three games of that season, but the next year he was forced to leave school when his father went bankrupt. He went to Melville and played for the amateur Melville Millionaires during the 1923-24 season, supporting himself with odd jobs. His skating was still rudimentary, so he concentrated on the physical side of the game. In the championship playoff against the Winnipeg Monarchs, the coach told Shore not to retaliate, no matter what the provocation, because the team couldn't afford to take any penalties. During the game, Shore was knocked cold three times, suffered a broken jaw and nose and lost six teeth. Even so, he played fifty of the sixty minutes. His team won, but after the game Shore vowed that he would thereafter be his own hockey boss.

In 1924, he signed on with the Regina Capitals of the Western Canada League and the next year moved to Edmonton in the Western Hockey League. His skating had improved dramatically by then, enabling him to place fourteenth in league scoring with twelve goals in only twenty-nine games. When the WHL folded at the end of the season, Art Ross, the Boston Bruins' general manager, purchased Shore's contract.

In the fall of 1926, the twenty-four-year-old Shore attended Boston's training camp. Also debuting was Billy Couture, a ten-year Montreal veteran known as "one of the roughest defensemen in hockey." Coutu, as his teammates called him, sought to establish himself with his new team by intimidating Shore.

The rock-hard 190-pounder hit the 160-pound Shore on the first play of the first scrimmage, and at every conceivable opportunity thereafter. Shore, being Shore, retaliated using knees, elbows and the butt of his stick. By the fourth practice, the bodychecks were little more than mutual muggings. Late in that session, Coutu picked up the puck and started an end-to-end rush heading directly towards Shore, the waiting defenseman. Halfway down the ice, the puck slipped off Coutu's stick but he continued on, picking up speed.

Some primordial instinct caused everyone in the arena to stop and watch.

An elementary principle of physics dictates that, all other things being equal, a larger, heavier object, travelling at speed—Coutu—will overpower a smaller object—Shore. But Shore had his own physics. An instant before impact, he crouched low, coiled and launched himself head-first in a football-style tackle at Coutu's upper body. The impact lifted Coutu six inches off the ice. He landed, unconscious, like a bag of cement. Shore then skated over to an admiring Art Ross and suggested in his gravelly voice that it would be best if he had someone scrape the "garbage" off the ice.

Shore stayed for the rest of the practice, but he wasn't completely unscathed. The shearing motion of the hit had almost completely ripped off his ear. The club doctor told him they had to amputate, but Shore had his own medicine. For the rest of the day, hand clasping his ear to his head, he trudged from door to door until he found a physician who would do what he was told.

"What kind of anaesthetic do you want—gas or local?" the doctor asked.

"First I want a mirror," Shore replied.

"Now what?" the doctor asked again.

"Just start sewing," growled Shore. White with pain, he watched until the doctor finished. "That last stitch is wrong, take it out. You left a little pucker there."

"You're a surgeon? You know more than I do?"

"Yes I know more than you do. Take it out." The aggravated doctor took it out and did it over.

Forty years later, his ear smooth and uncauliflowered, Shore was asked about Coutu. "I'm sorry to say, he wasn't so good after that."

Shore pushed everything further than anyone else— that was his edge. "A fanatic, almost psychopathic urge to excel," one writer observed. Shore's eerily inhuman lack of concern for personal safety freed him from the normal, healthy fear that restrained others. As a result, he could execute plays no one else even envisioned.

When speed, skill and daring weren't enough, the grim reaper took over. His admirers used to say you could put "Old Blood and Guts" down *sometimes* but you could *never* keep him down. "My memories of Shore come through a haze of red," marvelled Jimmy Powers, a New York columnist. "He bled almost every night. His blood dripped on the ice of Chicago, Montreal, Boston, and countless other rinks." Shore's bloody inventory included 978 stitches, rounded out by a fractured back, a fractured hip, a collarbone broken at least twelve times, a nose broken fourteen times and five broken jaws. The only teeth he had left were far—very far—back in his head.

Hockey's enforcers tend to be on the large side with big, obvious muscles. Tall, lean and whipcord tight, Shore didn't look dangerous or even particularly strong. He never started the season weighing more than 170 pounds and usually ended it at barely 160. The only giveaway were his large hands and Popeye-like forearms. Shore's muscles were wrapped tightly around his body like armour.

Rushing down the ice, his deep-set eyes black and glowering, Shore resembled an advancing death's head. His manner was equally immovable. Soft-spoken, he chose his words carefully and precisely before dropping them at the feet of listeners like chiselled hunks of granite.

The Shore saga is punctuated by bloody incident after bloody incident but inevitably comes back to December 12, 1933, when the Maple Leafs played the Bruins in Boston Garden. The teams had been feuding for several years, thanks to the long-standing enmity between Conn Smythe and Art Ross. The game started off as a brawl and escalated. Halfway through the second period, Toronto's Red Horner blind-sided Shore, who hauled himself up and immediately sought vengeance. The first moving object he found was Irvine (Ace) Bailey. "Bailey went down hard," an eyewitness observed. "His head struck the ice with a loud, dull, sickening thud. You could hear it up in the peanut gallery. You could feel it in the pit of your stomach. You knew the man stretched out on the ice, his limbs quivering convulsively, was really hurt."

For ten minutes, the team doctors desperately tried to revive Bailey. Finally, with some bare signs of consciousness returning, they carted him away. Shore received no penalty and returned to his position when play resumed. As the referee dropped the puck, Red Horner skated over to Shore and levied his own penalty with a right to the head. The butt of the stick protruding through Horner's glove tore a seven-stitch cut on the side of Shore's face.

Shore claimed that he hadn't even seen Bailey, and that in any event he had been dazed and couldn't remember exactly what had happened. It was the first recorded use of the "temporary amnesia defense" that has become the time-honoured NHL explanation for any particularly gruesome bloodletting. The NHL characteristically circles the wagons in such instances, uttering some variation of "It was an accident / It's part of the game / The aggressor feels as bad as the victim." In Shore's case, even Bailey, who recovered, completely absolved him. "That's the style of hockey Shore plays. I was just unlucky enough to be on the receiving end," he said, as if he had been a stray piece of raw meat careless enough to get in the same cage with a carnivore.

Art Ross relentlessly capitalized on the box office potential of Shore's villainy. "He never missed an opportunity to further the legend of Shore," observed one sportswriter. "Shore the Hockey Hoodlum, Shore the Tough Guy. Any newspaperman interviewing Ross could be certain of going away with his notebook filled with anecdotes of Shore's lust for combat and thirst for the blood of his opponents."

Ross even baited the other teams with Shore. Once Ross kept his star in the locker room until both teams were on the ice. A spotlight then hit the players' entrance as a brass band struck up "Hail To The Chief." After a suspense-building pause, Shore appeared, clad in a richly colourful matador's cape. Behind him stood a fully liver-ied manservant, who gently eased the cape off his shoulders.

The stunt drove the crowd and Shore's opponents into a frenzy. Ross kept using it until the New York Americans one-upped him. After the Shore theatrics, several of the Americans slipped away and returned carrying a large roll of carpeting which they laid portentously on centre ice and unrolled with a flourish to reveal "Rabbit" McVeigh, a tiny forward with an oversized set of ears. McVeigh, rose clamped between his teeth, pirouetted daintily all over the ice, curtsying and blowing kisses to the cheering crowd and snarling Bruins.

Shore never complained that Ross's tactics made him a target. The other players called him "the butcher" and viewed any atrocity committed against him as simple justice. Managers offered bounties for his head. One year the Americans' players even formed a lucrative pool on who would "get" Shore—it went uncollected. When he walked down the gangway after the games, Shore was sometimes so coated with spittle and beer that thrown popcorn adhered to him in clumps. Fans from opposing teams often tarried into the wee hours hoping to waylay him.

Through it all, Shore strode with the sombre dignity of a Caesar among the hordes.

But what did gall Shore was the owners' unwillingness to share the profits they made out of his hide. Every year, Ross attempted to freeze or even reduce Shore's salary. Shore invariably held out for more and, just as invariably, League president Frank Calder, at Ross's urging, suspended him. When training camp finished, Ross would give in, and Shore would receive precisely what he had demanded in the first place.*

Shore knew his value to the team and the League down to the last cut and bruise he suffered. In 1934, de-

---

* This tactic had a particular upside for Shore, as he loathed training camp. Unlike most of his contemporaries, he kept himself in superb condition and he didn't want to chance injury during training camp when the players weren't paid.

spite an excellent 1933 season, Art Ross tried to cut Shore's salary by $3,000. On November 3, Shore abruptly left training camp and returned to his farm in Daugh, Alberta. Frank Calder promptly suspended him "indefinitely." Every day, the Boston papers printed stories featuring Shore and his buddies going hunting, or Shore and his family enjoying life on the farm.

"You see, here is the way I have things doped out," Shore told an Edmonton *Journal* reporter, pausing while he butchered a three-hundred-pound Poland China pig. "Boston has used only three defensemen each year. The other NHL clubs have always had at least four. The reason, of course, they do not need more than three men is myself. I say this modestly enough. Anybody can look over my record. I am a 60 minute man and with the exception of penalties received I am on the ice continuously. Therefore I feel this way about things. If Boston is going to get twice as much work out of me as they do out of the other men on the team why should I not cut in on a portion of the extra salary that ordinarily they would have to pay."

While Shore was holding out, he practised in the evening with the Edmonton Eskimos, a minor professional club. The team drew standing-room-only crowds during practices while Shore was around. It occurred to him that if he owned the team, he would make far more money than he did playing for the Bruins. He began secretly negotiating to buy the Eskimos, and though the deal fell through, the idea was firmly lodged in his mind.

Art Ross made light of Shore's holdout, claiming it would have a negligible effect on the team. His resolve lasted until the Bruins' first game—a 6 to 1 thrashing by the Toronto Maple Leafs on November 8. The next morning, Ross wired a contract offer to Shore, meeting all his demands. A few minutes after Shore accepted, Frank Calder lifted his indefinite suspension. That year Shore earned $13,000, though the NHL's official salary cap was $7,000. In his best year, 1936, Shore made $17,500, including secret bonuses. In contrast, the largest contract

Howie Morenz ever signed was for $6,000.*

After 1933, Shore made repeated attempts to buy an NHL team. Notoriously parsimonious, he had been squirrelling away his money for years. In 1936 he made an offer for the New York Americans. He also came within a whisker of buying the Boston Bruins for $300,000. He had an option from owner Charles F. Adams, calling for $150,000 down and the remaining $150,000 to be spread over a number of years. But when Adams changed his mind and demanded the additional $150,000 be paid after only one year, Shore couldn't complete the deal. For the rest of his life, Shore felt that the deal had been torpedoed by Art Ross and the other NHL owners.

After 1936, firmly convinced that the NHL owners weren't going to let him have a team, Shore turned his eye to the minor leagues. In 1939, at the age of thirty-seven, he quietly bought the Springfield Indians of the International–American Hockey League for $42,000, paying $16,000 cash and signing a $26,000 note.

When the NHL governors found out, they were angry, mainly because Jack Adams wanted Springfield as a Detroit farm club. They were aghast when Shore announced that he intended to manage, coach *and* play for Springfield while continuing to play for Boston. "Where do the Bruins come in?" Ross plaintively asked the Boston media. The NHL quickly cobbled together a by-law prohibiting a player from competing in two different leagues.

Shore responded by packing his bags and moving to Springfield. The beginning of the 1939-40 season came and went with no Shore. Ross, whose Bruins were off to a good start, thought he could starve Shore out, but just to make sure, he prodded Frank Calder to force the International League to suspend him as well. Shore was caught on the horns of a nasty dilemma. By not playing for Boston he forfeited his $17,500 salary, and if he

---

* It was reported numerous times in the '30s that other teams had offered Ross $100,000 for Shore. It is interesting to note that Conn Smythe evaluated Gordie Howe's worth at $100,000 more than two decades later.

couldn't play for Springfield, he estimated that his gate would decline by $25,000 annually. Even so, he preferred to see his franchise die and his hockey career end on this dismal note than knuckle under to Art Ross.

As it always does in hockey, money had the final word. Fed up with the stalemate, Charles Adams told Ross that his stand was akin to burning money and instructed him to bring Shore back. Adding urgency to the situation was the fact that the Bruins were starting to lose and the fans were getting restive. "Shore has a heavy investment in the Springfield club and we want to give him a hand," Ross said, piously explaining his abrupt about-face.

Knowing he'd be lucky to get a season out of Shore, Ross called Red Dutton, general manager of the New York Americans. On January 25, 1940, the Bruins traded Shore to New York for $5,000 and Eddie Wiseman, an exciting, high-scoring forward.*

On March 8, 1940, Shore played against the Bruins for the first time. He was thirty-eight years old and playing his fifth game in six days. Still, Shore was the best man on the ice, playing for thirty-five of the sixty minutes, including fourteen of the last twenty. "He shone more brightly than any of the Bruins' luminaries—Clapper, Schmidt or Brimsek," raved one reporter.

In a typical week that season, Shore played for Springfield on Saturday night and for New York on Sunday night. On Tuesday he played in Springfield, on Wednesday there was a road game in Philadelphia and on Thursday he returned for a game in New York. During one period he played eight games in eight nights. Despite the burden, Shore starred for the Americans, driving them into the playoffs against all expectations, although the team folded two years later. The following season, to Dutton's vast annoyance, Shore retired from the NHL, though he played in Springfield for three

* The cash amount would have been larger but Shore would only commit to play the remainder of the season, and only on the condition that he could play for both the Americans and the Indians.

more years.

Eddie Shore spent the next twenty-six years as the owner, coach, trainer, team doctor and sometime seer of the Springfield Indians. His legend as an owner has grown to such dimensions that it has completely overshadowed his hockey career. The players on his teams came to be every bit as afraid of him as any opponent ever was.

Being sent to the minors—never a happy event—took on an entirely new meaning thanks to Eddie Shore. Some players insisted on a "no trade or demotion to Springfield" clause in their contracts. In 1963, Brian Smith found himself traded to Shore. Rather than report, he decamped to Innsbruck, Austria, and played there until Shore found out and had him suspended from international play. In the end, Smith dutifully reported to Springfield.

Even players on other teams weren't safe from Shore. One day he had his charges duck-walking on the ice to improve flexibility and build up their groin muscles. Jimmy Bartlett, with a visiting team, sat up in the stands catcalling and guffawing throughout the entire practice. Within a week, Shore had traded for Bartlett.

During his first years as an owner, Shore was desperately short of cash because he didn't sell his farm until 1942. As a result, his reputation for miserliness became legendary. He parked cars before the games, then rushed in at the last minute, dressed, played virtually every minute of every game and returned to the parking lot afterwards to direct traffic, often still wearing his uniform.

He cut costs beyond the bone by having his spare or out-of-favour players—called "Black Aces"—sell programs, paint seats, make and bag popcorn, clean the ice after games, park cars, man the concession and even cut inner tubes into substitutes for bandages.* When one of

---

* Shore always carried twenty-four or twenty-five players, even though he could only play eighteen, because he liked the pressure it put on the regulars to perform. He also seemed to have a large number of players either hurt or in disfavour at any one time.

his players suffered a broken arm, Shore had him paint-
ing lines on the ice with the other one. Ralph Tattion, a
player then under League suspension, spent his penalty
time walking all day long up and down in front of the
arena clad in a giant sandwich board reading "HOCKEY
TONIGHT."

When the Ice Capades came to town, Shore personally
operated the spotlight and, on several occasions, had the
players blow up balloons for the grand finale.

Shore eased up marginally as the hockey team became
profitable—he stopped using inner tubes as bandages—
but he still never let a penny slide past him unnoticed.
For years he bulk-ordered the cheap, heavy and durable
Wally sticks universally loathed by the players. Each one
had a short, seven-inch, perfectly flat blade making most
shots on the net and many passes about as easy as shooting with a two-by-four. Some players bought their own
sticks while others traded with sympathizers from other
teams. Once, Gerry Foley slipped out on the ice and
gathered up all the opposing players' sticks while they
were involved in a brawl.

Though Shore's economy measures included leaving
the lights off during the visiting teams' practice time,* he
always overheated the rink during games. He sold
peanuts and popcorn cheap but made a large profit on
the resulting beer and soft drink sales. To further pump
up concession profits, intermissions in Springfield routinely went five or ten minutes overtime. Third periods in
Shore's rink seemed to stretch forever, particularly if the
home team was behind.

Referees dreaded Springfield games. If Shore didn't
like a call, he'd get on the public-address system and denounce the referee and his family antecedents, not to

---

* Visiting teams hated playing in Springfield as much as the Springfield players did.
On sunny days, Shore refused to turn on the interior lights for their practices.
Since the only light came from strip-like windows near the ceiling, they muddled
around in an errie twilight. One visiting player had the temerity to complain and
Shore dismissed him with "Light? You don't need light to see the puck. You
should be able to feel the puck. I'm doing you a favour, I'm helping you concen-
trate."

mention the play in question. More than once, Shore locked a referee in his dressing room between periods or after a game.

Shore's cheapness extended into the executive suite. In 1949, he fired two public relations directors in a row because they refused to clean the ice after games. He solved the problem permanently by hiring his nephew Jack Butterfield. Butterfield, just out of the RCAF and grateful to have a job, willingly sold popcorn, swept the stands and washed the jockstraps, as well as issuing press releases. He still marvels at his uncle's parsimony forty years later. He once mailed some papers on a Friday and met Shore on the road the next day. "Did you mail those papers?" Shore asked. "Yes," replied Butterfield. "How did you send them?" "By airmail." Shore reared back disapprovingly. "Don't you know that was Friday? It would have gotten there just as cheap by regular mail."

That night Butterfield met Shore and a group of newspapermen for dinner, and Shore picked up the huge tab. "I don't understand you," an exasperated Butterfield said. "You just finished eating my ass off because I spent three cents to send a letter airmail and you went out and spent $200 for some goddamn meal and you're giving me hell!" Shore calmly returned, "Young fella, when you learn to look after the pennies, the dollars will take care of themselves."

Shore's frugality paid off in spades. Springfield had been losing heavily when he took over, but by 1947 he was netting $100,000 annually from the Indians alone. He also built a mini-empire by purchasing all or part of an American Hockey League team in New Haven, a United States Hockey League team in Fort Worth and an Oakland, California team in the Western Hockey League. Shore also owned a sizable piece of the Ice Capades. That year, the Boston *Record* hailed Shore as "the richest man to come out of modern hockey."

Survival as a minor-league owner wasn't easy. At any one time, at least half of Shore's team were reclamation projects: players with drinking problems, development problems, lack-of-talent problems and discipline problems. Some years he'd have a working arrangement with an NHL team whereby they'd provide him with a number of their young players. Other years Shore owned all the players. If one of his own reclamation projects worked out, he'd sell the player to an NHL team for a tidy profit.

Shore had a long series of coaches, but they were coaches in name only. Shore ran everything. Planted in the stands, clad in his overcoat, he surveyed the play looking like the grim reaper of old. If something struck him the wrong way, he'd blow his whistle and summon the players over, even if the coach was right in the middle of a drill.

The players were so well conditioned that they stopped in their tracks when they heard Shore's whistle. "I swear he used to blow it about every fifteen seconds," laughs Glen Sonmor, recalling his first practice as a Springfield coach. "He came out on the ice. I'm not trying to exaggerate. He had one guy showing where to put his foot down and he was saying, 'You're putting your foot down an eighth of an inch too far forward.' He spent all this time talking and everyone else is standing there and I don't know what to do and then pretty soon the kids start getting restless and they're slamming pucks against the boards.

"I said to one of the players who'd been there a while, 'Geez, maybe we should get the guys to stop that, the old man will really flip his lid,' and he said, 'No don't worry Glen, once he starts one of those explanations, he's in his own world. He can't hear anything.'"

Shore called practices without bothering to inform his coach, and during games the coach was little more than a marionette; Shore sent his own instructions via a runner. The more malleable the coach, the longer his tenure.

At once brilliant and malevolent, Shore was a rare student of the game. Many of his most bizarre seeming theories are now common practice. He believed, for example, in "visualizing." His goalies spent hours stopping imaginary pucks, shot from all angles and at all speeds. Today it is a common technique advocated by sports psychologists for every sport from basketball to archery.

Shore also favoured dancing as a training device for professional athletes decades before it came into vogue. The players didn't mind the dancing as much as *where* he had them do it. During training camp in Hamilton, Ontario, guests of the Royal Connaught Hotel were startled to find players tap-dancing in the lobby wearing only their pyjamas.

But as revolutionary as Shore's ideas were in theory, they often reeked of sadism in practice. He insisted that his forwards skate up and down their wings like ducks in a shooting gallery. When Otto Schmidt, a young winger, strayed too often from his appointed lane, Shore built an elaborate canvas harness, fastened it to Schmidt and then attached it to the arena's rafters. During scrimmage, if Schmidt wandered even a millimetre, Shore yanked him up off the ice and swung him back to his proper spot.

Though Shore himself skated upright with extraordinary, long strides, he insisted his players adopt a semi-squat and place their feet exactly eleven inches apart. "Like a boy scout on hike, who has to move his bowels. Bend your knees and squat," he drilled into them.

If a player skated with his legs a fraction too far apart or too close together, Shore took a piece of rope and hobbled him like a horse. Often players had their arms strapped behind their backs to improve arm position and their gloves taped to the sticks to ensure proper hand placement. Particularly slow pupils practised for weeks trussed like Christmas turkeys. "If you fell down, it was an adventure getting back up," recalls Brian Smith, who played for Shore during the 1964-65 season.

Goaltenders suffered particularly from Shore's Rube Goldberg contrivances. Twenty years before it became NHL gospel, Shore demanded that his goalies stand up as much as possible to stop shots. If verbal instruction failed, he tied them to the net. When one goalie still couldn't get the hang of it, Shore tied a rope around his neck and fastened it to the crossbar. "Now fall down!" he dared.

Shore also believed goalies should plant themselves well out in front of the net to cut down the shooter's angle. "He made us design an iron brace that would fit on the net in a semicircle so they couldn't back into the net," chuckles Butterfield.

Players who couldn't or wouldn't obey Shore's dictates became Black Aces who sat on the bench and endured extra practice time, made all the more onerous because their fewer numbers allowed more of Shore's undivided attention. A Black Ace could only return to the squad if a regular was injured or had disgraced himself worse than the Black Ace.

Ken Schinkel, temporarily a Black Ace, once thought he had an opportunity to get a little of his own back at the "old man." While preparing for an ice show, Shore balanced on a special wheeled ladder to install lights high in the rafters. It was a tricky process as Shore steadied himself with one arm hooked over a rafter. Schinkel, in charge of moving the ladder along as needed, eased it completely away, leaving Shore hanging in a particularly awkward spot.

Shore, then sixty, serenely pulled himself hand-over-hand, seventy feet above the ice, until he'd installed all the lights in his pockets. Only then did he glance down at Schinkel. "Mister Schinkel," he rasped, "Please return the platform to its rightful place." Finally aware that he was dealing with an altogether different order of being, Schinkel meekly pushed the ladder back.

The Springfield players feared Eddie Shore the medical man above all else. Crediting his skill to castrations and other operations he performed on cattle in his youth, Shore believed his potions and manipulations cured everything from stretchmarks to prolonged scoring slumps. Shore was, of course, his own best testimonial, claiming to have cured himself of bowel cancer with a starvation diet in 1940.*

The players were particularly terrified of Shore's so-called "Martel Treatment," a vile-smelling concoction prescribed when lesser methods proved ineffective. Shore diagnosed a lethargic Kenny Schinkel as having yellow fever and dosed him with the miracle cure. Schinkel cautiously drank only half of it and claims to have lost twelve pounds overnight. "I could have shit through the eye of a needle," he says, still wincing. The next day Schinkel, wan, weak and still ailing, dragged himself out to practice, lest Shore provide another dose.

Far worse than the Martel Treatment were Shore's back massages, an excruciatingly painful technique that defenseman Bob McCord, among others, says nearly ended his career. In the peculiar gallows humour of hockey, players considered it a particularly fine joke to sic Shore on each other.

"Gee Barclay, is that right—*is your back really bothering you?*" Brian Kilrea said loudly to his teammate just as Shore walked into the dressing room. Despite Barclay Plager's near-hysterical protests, Shore insisted "GET ON THE TABLE MR. PLAGER!"

The players executed an orderly retreat to a nearby bar and were downing a few when a teammate hurried in. "Did you hear what happened to Barclay? They put him in an ambulance and took him to the hospital. His back was so bad he couldn't straighten up. You better look out, Brian. The last thing we heard while they were putting him into the ambulance was Barclay screaming, 'I'm going to kill Kilrea.'"

No one could ever predict Shore. In 1958 the Indians had a particularly bad road trip, losing their last two games to Providence. When the long bus ride home ended at 2:00 AM, Shore announced a 9:00 AM practice. After an easy warm-up, the tired players were dismissed.

---

* When goalie Don "Nipper" O'Hearn told Shore that his wife had just given birth to twin girls he didn't get congratulations but a classic lecture. "If you'd come to me you'd have had boys," Shore told him matter-of-factly. "I'd have shown you how to screw by the moon." Shore also told O'Hearn's wife to rub cocoa butter on her abdomen to avoid stretchmarks, and after five children she had none.

Returning to the dressing room, they were astonished to find the training table laden with beer, whisky and other drinks. "I've been driving you too hard," Shore told them, "let's relax." Later in the afternoon he took the players and their wives to dinner at the best local restaurant.

When the team hit a slump, or Shore's tactics pushed them to the breaking point, the players would discover a hand-lettered sign taped to the locker room door: "RE-PORT BACK TO THE DRESSING ROOM AT THE THREE O'CLOCK WITH YOUR DRINKING CLOTHES ON." Shore would sit in the corner sipping brandy from a shot-glass. It didn't take long before the players were drunk. "As these guys progressively got a little more stiff, he allowed them—just this one day—to tell him off in spades," recalls Glen Sonmor. "They would go and say, 'You bald headed old son-of-a-bitch, you've ruined my career.'" Far into the night, the players heaped vile epithet upon vile epithet, competing with each other for the worst slur. Through it all Shore sat benignly, a half-smile on his face.

Like many of his generation, Shore believed that the old devil sex was often the culprit when a player or a team fell into an extended losing-streak. After one such period, he invited the players' wives to meet him at the rink. Expecting one of Shore's periodic surprise parties, they all arrived in their best clothes. Instead of a party, they were ushered into the locker room, which was festooned with stale jock-straps and ripe underwear and redolent of the searing combination of sweat, liniment, blood and the ghosts of thousands of stale farts.

When all the women were assembled, Shore walked in and launched into a lengthy and pointed harangue. "The club is not doing too well and there's a very good reason for this state of affairs. *You ladies are giving your husbands too much sex!*"

When he had finished his lecture, Shore wheeled around and fastened his eyes on Audrey Smith, the wife of Floyd Smith, then mired in a particularly deep slump. "To prove my point," he announced, "I'm going to ask Floyd Smith, who is newly-married, to send his wife home." Shore then turned on his heel and left the room.

"It wouldn't be so bad if it were true," the humiliated young woman later confided to Don Cherry's wife Rose, "but it's not. I wish it was."

For all Shore's assaults on his players' dignity, there were unexpected displays of sensitivity. He reinforced his object lessons with fines, the standard being $100. But at the end of every season, he usually returned all the money while swearing the surprised recipient to secrecy. And it wasn't uncommon for Shore to give players a bonus, simply because he felt like it. "When I left Springfield for the New York Rangers [in 1959]," recalls Schinkel, "I went into his office to say goodbye and he gave me a $700 bonus—serious money in those days." Most of Shore's charges believed he hadn't a compassionate cell in his body, but when one of his players' children was severely injured in a car accident, Shore quietly paid the nine-month hospital bill.

When goalie Don Simmons fell into a protracted slump, Shore summoned him to the office. Fearing a lecture or the administration of a purgative, Simmons tarried until Shore was forced to come looking for him. Instead of a dressing-down, Shore sent him home to help his mother and "take your mind off hockey."

Shore jealously guarded the legend of Eddie Shore the ogre. Once, Jack Butterfield suggested telling the media about some of his good deeds. "You will like hell!" snarled Shore. Butterfield never dared raise the matter again.

Shore might have ruined Floyd Smith's sex life, but he also turned him, along with a legion of others, into a hockey player. "Studying with Shore is like getting your doctorate in hockey science," extolled Kent Douglas. "He taught me things about the game that nobody else ever mentioned."

Even Brian Kilrea, who spent nine long years with Shore, came to see the light. "As a teacher, he was the best hockey man ever. He put me in the NHL. I was a late developer. Shore gave me a chance to play and worked with me each day. Nobody else would have bothered." Shore's team was also very successful. The

Indians won an unprecedented three championships in a row, from 1959 to 1962. Also, at least two dozen of his former players have become professional coaches, scouts or managers, unmatched in NHL history.

But as the '60s progressed, the uneasy balance between Shore's eccentricity and genius began to shift. His health deteriorated: he had his fourth heart attack and his hearing started to go. Conflicts with his players rapidly escalated and his punishments became harsher. Gone were the blowout parties that had so effectively eased the tensions in earlier years.

One night, during the 1964-65 season, Brian Smith was woken up from a deep sleep by a phone call. "Mister Smith, come down to the rink and see me immediately." Thinking he had been traded, a delighted Smith jumped into his car and drove to the old brick arena, which squatted in inky blackness, not a light visible anywhere. Smith groped through the rink and down pitch-black corridors until he noticed a wedge of light under the dressing room door.

"When I opened the door, it was like something out of a horror movie. There was Eddie Shore, Mr. Hockey as he was known in Massachusetts, looking more like Mr. Clean. His sleeves were rolled up to his elbows, revealing those massive forearms, his tie loosened, the bald head wet with sweat, and a wild look in his eye."

Seeing Smith, Shore bellowed, "Mister Smith. Why, Why, Why? . . . would you tape your stick from the heel to the toe instead of the toe to the heel?" Smith stood there speechless until Shore fired the stick into a pile at the other end of the room. "Look at this one," screamed Shore. "Not enough tape! And this one! And this one!" until the pile had grown large.

"Here," Shore growled. "Take a roll of tape and let's go!" "The two of us retaped every hockey stick in that room with Shore yelling and screaming the whole time. To this day, I still tape my stick from the toe to the heel."

Over the years, many drunken lynch mobs had formed in the middle of the night only to dissolve the next morning in the face of the cold reality of Eddie Shore. But during the 1966 training camp, long-simmering pressures reached their bursting point.

Emboldened by the promise of new opportunities brought by the announcement of NHL expansion the previous year, three of the Indians' defensemen—Bill White, Dale Rolfe and Dave Amadio—refused to play until they got pay raises. To their surprise, Shore agreed, but a few weeks before Christmas, he suspended all three men for "indifferent play." The suspension had no effect on the team standings since they had a seven-day lay-off, but it did put a dent in the three players' pay cheques—an amount, coincidentally, exactly equal to their raises.

The next morning, the team gathered and deputized two reluctant players Gerry Foley and Brian Kilrea to approach the dragon. They gingerly knocked on Shore's door. Kilrea spoke first: "The players have asked us to represent them . . ."

Before he could finish, Shore spat out, "You represent fuck-all." He ordered Kilrea out of the building and sent Foley to tell the players to mind their own business, while they still had one.

The team, now worked up to a fever-pitch of indignation, rebelled and walked out. That was Monday. By Wednesday, the strike was big news, but the players' bravado was shrivelling fast. Shore, who refused to talk to them, had quickly assembled an entire replacement team by calling in favours from other minor-league owners. The players were also told that Shore intended to sue them for breach of contract.

Uncertain and nervous, the Indians gathered to discuss their next move. "What about that guy, that guy who signed Orr and did the Brewer thing?" Bill White suggested in desperation. "Eagleson, that's his name. Why don't we contact him?"

Once again Kilrea was deputized. "I hear you guys are having a little fun down there," said Alan Eagleson when Kilrea called. "Can you help us?" asked Kilrea. "What the fuck! Sure, I'll help. I'll be on the next plane." Eagleson and two of his law partners—Ray Smela and Bob

Watson—immediately flew to Springfield, where they found a very agitated group of men.

The players were quite clear in their demands. They wanted to play with modern, well-fitting equipment ("Some of the stuff still had Shore's name on it from his playing days," snorts one former player) and they wanted the right to consult a doctor or go to the hospital if *they* felt they were injured, rather than be forced to accept Shore's tender ministrations.

Eagleson had them swear out affidavits as evidence of Shore's mistreatment. The exercise turned into an emotional outpouring of grievances much like a group-therapy session. Donny Johns described how he had once cut his knee badly. After surgery the doctors told him he needed four days in the hospital plus several weeks to recuperate before skating again. Immediately after the operation Shore informed him, "Get out of the hospital and get back here now or you're off the team." Kilrea revealed that after he'd broken several ribs Shore had refused to let him get an x-ray. On another occasion he had a double fracture of his jaw. The day he was released from hospital, Shore insisted he attend practice and put his equipment on over his plaster head cast.

Goaltender Jacques Caron, who once had a fistfight with Shore when he was refused a trip home to visit his sick wife, testified, "When I first arrived in Springfield I took a size 13 skate. This was interfering with my leg exercises and tap-dancing according to Mr. Shore because they were too large. I was given a pair of skates size 11, and thus lost all my toenails when stopping a shot with my skates."

Only after four years, when Caron could barely walk, did Shore finally relent and allow him to wear a size 11 1/2.

The stories went on and on, each more grotesque than the last. "When you hear one Shore story you smile as people seem to have been doing for years," Eagleson later told sportswriter Trent Frayne. "When you hear ten you might grin weakly. When you hear a hundred—and there were a hundred—you want to throw up. If the players were dogs, you'd pick up the phone and call the humane society."

Oddly, Eagleson's partners, whose razor-sharp memories can dredge up minute details of many other Eagleson escapades of this period, are remarkably hazy about his critical confrontation with Shore. About all Bob Watson remembers was that he was there. "I'm sure we weren't there too long," he says. "Al may have stayed and I may have gone back. I just don't recall."

Ray Smela will only talk about the incident through another lawyer, and his memory is also cloudy. "We met with all the players in our hotel suite," he told Eagleson's biographer in 1981. "They weren't on strike yet but were pretty heated up and talking nothing but strike, strike, strike. Strike was an unthinkable action at that time. They were still part of the old farm system and even the players didn't want to strike, but they were unhappy with the manner in which they were being treated."*

The partners are vague about the details because there were few to remember. They did indeed meet with the players, but there is no evidence that Eagleson ever met, or even talked to, Eddie Shore. "Eddie never met with Eagleson, he never talked to him," Jack Butterfield states unequivocally. "I talked to Eagleson and then I talked to Shore."

Butterfield was in a quandary. Not only was he manager of Springfield, but that year he had reluctantly agreed to become acting president of the AHL until the league found a replacement for the outgoing president.† "That's when I first started taking tranquillizers," he says, not entirely in jest. "I never knew what the hell they were till then."

As a first step to settling the crisis, Butterfield went to the players and talked tough. "You guys are in violation of your contract and I've got the league constitution here

---

* But Gerry Foley and Brian Kilrea insist the players were already on strike. They didn't miss any games because of the seven-day break in the schedule.

† After twenty-five years, Butterfield is still the president.

and I have the authority to expel you. If I expel you you're out for the rest of your lives. So you'd better think about the consequences of your actions." Butterfield didn't expect the players to cave in after a few threats, especially with Eagleson there to bolster them. His intention was to "soften them up" a little, so that they'd be grateful for whatever crumbs he was able to wheedle out of Shore.

Then came the conversation he dreaded most. "Screw'em," Shore roared when Butterfield told him that the team was being torn apart. "I couldn't care less. I don't give a shit. They'll either do it my way or they won't do it." Butterfield pressed on. "I know, Eddie, but I'm going to meet with Eagleson."

"If you do I'll fire you," Shore shot back. Butterfield shook his head sadly. "Okay you gotta fire me. Eddie, I've been very loyal to you but I'm now in another capacity. I'm president of the league and I have to do what I think is best from a league point of view."

"You're going against me," Shore said ominously. "Maybe I am but I'm wearing two hats and I have to put the other hat on," Butterfield explained. Shore wouldn't budge. "Okay, I guess you're right, I understand but I'm not going to give in."

Butterfield had his own agenda. He didn't believe the players would stand firm and he knew that the league would survive whatever was done that day, but he was less certain about his uncle. Shore's doctor, a close family friend, told him privately that the "old man," then sixty-four, was on the verge of another heart attack, and this time it would probably be his last. Butterfield met with Eagleson and told him that the best he could do was *maybe* get Shore to agree to step down.

During the ensuing conversation with his uncle, Butterfield wisely steered clear of Eagleson and the players' demands, stressing instead the state of Shore's health. Woven throughout his argument was the insinuation that if Shore died the players would win by default. To Butterfield's everlasting astonishment, Shore did agree to resign as president of the club.

Once he'd heard the news from Butterfield, Eagleson informed the jubilant Indians that they'd won. The Toronto papers obligingly trumpeted Eagleson's great victory over "Old Blood and Guts" and the story quickly reached legendary status. It was the pivotal event in Alan Eagleson's subsequent career, playing a major role in providing him with the status and credibility to form the National Hockey League Players' Association. "We proved that we could do it in Springfield, that if the guys stuck together success would result," Eagleson said in 1989. "We used that as the test case. If they had broken down that and had we not been able to get Eddie Shore fired, the union would probably not have taken place—the Association wouldn't have come into being."

But just what was really achieved and who was the victor isn't so clear. To a man, the Springfield players feel that a great victory was won and that Eagleson forced Shore into numerous concessions, including new hockey equipment, the right to outside medical consultation and a $10,000 team bonus at the end of the season. Butterfield adamantly denies that any of this was ever discussed. "I talked with Eagleson and the only thing we discussed was Shore stepping back from the team."

Though Bill White, Dale Rolfe and Dave Amadio were reinstated without repercussion, no new hockey equipment was ever purchased, nor was there a new medical regime. Some players remember being paid a bonus, some not. But most remember paying Alan Eagleson roughly $6,000 in total legal fees. Shore did eventually step down as president but provocatively named his twenty-year-old son Ted—who had most recently been running errands and staffing the food concession—as his replacement.

Even with the pleasant, earnest Ted Shore as president, there was little doubt who was running things. Butterfield still got his orders from the "old man," who lurked like a ghostly spectre in the back of the rink watching practice. Sometimes peculiar things happened, and the players knew Shore was behind them. Once they were told to report to the bus for a road trip. They loaded up and then sat for three hours before the bus moved. "That was his way of letting us know he was still the boss," says Kilrea. "He did it just to aggravate us."

On the face of it, the idea that a thirty-three-year-old upstart lawyer could defeat Eddie Shore in just a few days seems ridiculous. Oddly, Eagleson has never shown any of the magnanimity towards Shore one expects from a victor. In fact, he's jumped at any opportunity to discredit him. In 1970, when Shore won the Lester Patrick Award "for outstanding service to hockey in the U.S.A.," Eagleson sneered at the choice. "It's incredible," he told the media at the event. "Shore may have been one of the greatest hockey players, but as a general manager and a manager of men, he wasn't my idea of an award winner."

Whenever Eddie Shore was asked about his most humiliating defeat, he simply flashed a Cheshire cat grin and changed the subject.

Shore smiled because he had already agreed to sell the players in November 1966, before the strike, to Jack Kent Cooke, the owner of the Los Angeles NHL expansion team, for $1 million—a fact unknown even to Jack Butterfield. It was a stupendous sum considering that the NHL expansion franchises, including the players, were selling for $2 million.

In truth, Shore had been in an extremely weak negotiating position from the beginning, and he knew it. All he really had to sell were the players, and if they were on strike or refusing to report, the deal with Cooke would have fallen through. Also weakening Shore's position was the threat that player disruption would bring to the NHL's impending expansion. Part of the NHL's sales pitch to the new entries was the docility of the players. The NHL owners weren't going to let Eddie Shore, or anyone else, get in the way of their expansion pot of gold.

When the sale to Cooke was announced in the summer of 1967, Eagleson took credit for that, too. "I ended up negotiating Shore's retirement," he stated. "Getting Shore and Butterfield out of hockey was the best thing that ever happened to it." But considering the high stakes of the game—Shore's $1 million and the NHL expansion—players had risked their careers for precious little return.

Until he died in 1985 at the age of eighty-three, Eddie Shore remained the toughest guy around. Well into his seventies he'd stand at the door of a bar and physically keep "longhairs" out. In 1974, at the NHL summer meetings, Aut Erickson, a thirty-six-year-old former player, made the serious mistake of slapping the seventy-two-year-old on the back. "Don't ever do that again, mister," Shore threatened.

When Erickson slapped Shore on the back a few minutes later, the seventy-two-year-old wheeled and knocked him ten feet over a nearby table. Onlookers had to pull Shore off the unconscious Erickson. "He was ready to give him the *coup de grâce*," recalls a not entirely disapproving Don Cherry.

In 1975, seventy-three-year-old Shore bought the Springfield Indians back from Jack Kent Cooke without a whisper of protest from Alan Eagleson. He ran the team for the rest of the season. Then, having proved his point, he quietly sold it again that summer.

Chapter 8

The Man Who Would Be King

Of all the people who helped propel Alan Eagleson to his unique position of influence in professional hockey, the most important was unquestionably Bobby Orr. It was Orr's unblinking faith in the man he saw as a "father" or "brother" that sped him on his way to wealth.

Bobby Orr was the most highly sought-after young player to come along in generations. The inept Boston Bruins stumbled upon the twelve-year-old while scouting two fourteen-year-olds who never made it to the NHL. "There were players in the NHL who couldn't feather a pass the way Orr did that night, and Orr was only twelve years old," recalled Lynn Patrick, the Bruins' general manager. "He always caught his teammates in stride and put the puck right on their stick. He was amazing. He could have played for the Bruins that year without embarrassing himself at all."

The Bruins' head scout, Wren Blair, built up a close relationship with the Orr family and fended off the frenzied advances of the other NHL teams until Orr committed himself to Boston for life by signing the League's standard C-form, in 1962. Instead of the usual $100, the Orr family negotiated a $2,800 bonus, including a $900 stucco job on the family home.

The next year, Alan Eagleson gave a speech in McTier, Ontario, a small resort community where ten years before he had worked as a summer recreation counsellor. Eagleson spoke passionately about the evils of the NHL system, and afterwards, Doug Orr, who had met him briefly in the past, asked for advice about his son turning pro. Eagleson agreed to represent Orr. Just before the season started, Orr asked if Eagleson could get him a ten-dollar-a-week raise in living expenses from his junior team, the Oshawa Generals. Eagleson failed.

No one who saw Orr start behind his own net and glide through the entire opposing team to score a picturesque goal will ever forget it. In flight, Orr was as close to a work of art as the rough-hewn game of hockey has ever produced.

Early in 1965, *Maclean's* magazine hailed the junior sensation with a cover story. Later that year, Toronto hopefully offered the Bruins $1.5 million for his professional rights. "We wouldn't trade Bobby Orr for 1.5 million dollars and all the players on the Toronto hockey team," snorted Hap Emms, who had replaced Lynn Patrick as general manager. "Orr will make the Boston franchise a winner and keep it that way for years."

The Bruins had finished last in the NHL for five of the past six seasons. Management placated mutinous fans by holding up Bobby Orr as the team's saviour. But when it came time to sign Orr, Boston saw no reason to treat him differently from any other young player. Late in the summer of 1966, Emms sent a routine 'take it or leave it' offer, by mail. It was a two-year contract for $10,250, including bonuses. Eagleson reacted with righteous outrage, publicly lamenting that football's top rookie, "Broadway Joe" Namath, had signed in 1965 for $400,000 over three years with the New York Jets, and that Cazzie Russell, the first draft choice in the NBA, had signed for $65,000 annually.

When Eagleson then announced that Orr would likely be attending university and playing for the Canadian Olympic team instead of turning pro, the firestorm of protest from fans and the media forced the Bruins into hasty reconsideration. In September, Emms came up with a more appealing figure: a $25,000 signing bonus, $25,000 the first year and $30,000 the second. It was a landmark contract. No rookie had ever received such a generous package, and many predicted dire consequences for the NHL. One writer called it an "obscene precedent."

Until Orr came along, Eagleson had done legal work for hockey players but had had little success in negotiating contracts. Four months after Orr signed, Eagleson boasted to *Hockey News* that his "lucrative" agent business now included nearly fifty NHL players, over a third of the entire League, and 60 percent of the junior Ontario Hockey League players, the major talent pool for the NHL.

Orr's blinding talent, combined with his unrelenting humility—the teenager called virtually everyone, including his fellow teammates, "sir" or "Mister"—defused any resentment towards his salary or his instant superstar status. When Orr gave Johnny Bucyk the "Mister" treatment, the long-time veteran was dumbfounded. "For a moment I thought he was putting me on," Bucyk recalls, "but then I realized he was serious. I told him to forget the Mr. Bucyk stuff. Heck, if what I'd read about him was even halfway right, I knew I'd probably be calling him Mr. Orr before the end of the season."

In his first practice with Boston, Orr undressed All-Star defenseman Ted Green so badly with deeks and feints he could have been naked on the ice. Towards the end of the practice, Green skated menacingly toward Orr. Onlookers anticipated a mauling of the rookie who had made him look so inept. "Kid," Green growled, "I don't know what the fuck they're paying you but it's not enough."

Orr also gracefully endured the initiation rites faced by every rookie, and he didn't flinch when subjected to hockey's classic initiation—the full body shave. Rick Heinz, a rookie with the St. Louis Blues in 1979, describes in horrifying detail his own experience with this brutal bit of fun.

"Six naked hockey players walked up to me disguised with masks on their heads, armed with scissors, shaving cream, razors, tape and other paraphernalia. . . . They picked me up and carried me to the shower room. I was laid down on the damp floor, with my hands tied together over my head taped to a hockey stick and my feet taped to another one. They put a wet towel over my face and I began to hyperventilate.

"After that, they shaved all the hair on my body: chest hair, armpits, legs, head and groin area. In the meantime, they kicked and punched me in the stomach and pretended to urinate on me to get me to struggle, scream in pain and resist their efforts. . . . They covered my head with vaseline and put hot liniment on my testicles, which burned to no end. I wished I could have died . . . I've never felt such pain and humiliation before in my life."*

Orr suffered this indignity with good humour and constant applications of salve to his nether regions. He also bore up well under the relentless locker room banter, which typically centres around genital size or lack thereof, and who was sleeping with who's wife, girlfriend or sister.

From the beginning, Orr was a walking advertisement for Alan Eagleson. He quickly became his best salesman as well, eagerly answering endless questions from teammates and opponents alike. "What's Eagleson like anyway?" "Do you think I should talk to him?" Or, more frequently, "Do you think he would talk to me?" The Orr-Eagleson saga rippled through the League, generating excitement, anticipation and not a little greed. By the hundredth telling, Eagleson's negotiating feats had achieved epic proportions.

Orr frequently brought Eagleson into the locker room and introduced him as though he were a cherished older brother. He willingly ceded credit to Eagleson for virtu-

---

* Interestingly, one of the things that the hugely successful Edmonton Oilers players did was outlaw the practice of hazing, still widespread in the NHL, on their team.

ally everything but his playing skill.

The currency of Bobby Orr turned to pure gold for Eagleson when it became apparent that, unlike so many hot young prospects, he would not only fulfil the wildest predictions of his talent, but exceed them. In his first season, Orr easily won the Calder Trophy for rookie of the year and made the second All-Star team. An ageing Gordie Howe was asked what he thought were Orr's best moves. "Just putting on those fucking skates," he replied with a thin smile.

In only his second year, Orr won the Norris Trophy for most valuable defenseman, and he went on winning that accolade for an unprecedented eight years in a row. He also won the Hart Trophy as the NHL's most valuable player three years straight and became the League's scoring leader twice, in 1970 and 1975—the only defenseman ever to do so.

Orr's magic sparked a renaissance in the historically miserable Bruins team. His talents, combined with those of the recently acquired Phil Esposito, Ken Hodge and Fred Stanfield, vaulted Boston out of the League's basement and to the 1970 Stanley Cup—the club's first in twenty-nine years. The Bruins won it all again in 1972, by which time the Orr legend had eclipsed virtually every hockey great of the past.

In 1971, just five years into his career, *Sports Illustrated* anointed the twenty-four-year-old Sportsman of the year, calling him "the greatest player ever to don skates; not the greatest defenseman, the greatest player at either end of the ice."

Eagleson wielded the acquiescent Orr like a human sword, using his name and image to carve a path to some of the biggest companies in North America— Standard Brands, General Foods, Coca-Cola, General Motors. He lost no time in turning Orr himself into a corporation. On December 22, 1966, he registered Bobby Orr Enterprises Ltd., reportedly owned 85 percent by Orr, 10 percent by Eagleson and 5 percent by Mike Walton, though Walton now confesses he didn't then and doesn't now know if he was actually a shareholder in BOE.

Doug Orr, Bobby's father, was one of the directors.

The investments came thick and fast: real estate; Marty's, a high-end men's retail clothing outlet; the stock market; car washes; an interest in Pony Sporting Goods Ltd. and the Owaissa Lodge in Orillia, Ontario. Known as the Orr-Walton Sports Camp, Eagleson called it "the best pension plan I could have given Orr."

Eagleson's own investments also proliferated. He formed Sports Management Ltd. in 1972, and Marvin Goldblatt, an accountant who did the books for Eagleson's law firm, ran it for him. A large percentage of the players Eagleson negotiated contracts for turned around and gave their cheques to Sports Management, which offered a complete financial management package, from bill paying to wills. The same year Orr became a client, Eagleson set up Nanjill Investments, named for his wife Nancy and daughter Jill. By 1978 its real estate assets were worth about half a million dollars. Another company, Rae-Con Consultants, was owned and run by Eagleson's wife, Nancy. Curiously, it competed directly with Sports Management in offering financial planning to athletes. Goldblatt was both treasurer and an employee of Rae-Con.

One of Eagleson's greatest talents is his ability to form an interdependent web-like network of personal and business interests. The signing of a hockey player produced a ripple effect throughout his various companies. When Eagleson negotiated a player's contract, that client would then go either to Sports Management or Rae-Con for advice and services, paying roughly $100 an hour. If that player was a star, then Eagleson could refer him to Sports Representatives, run by Bob Haggert, former Maple Leafs trainer and a longtime friend of Eaglesons.

Sports Representatives organized corporate endorsement and merchandising packages for athletes. Often players who came to Haggert first would be referred to Eagleson, who, more often than not, would end up negotiating their contracts. Though the Toronto *Star* reported that Eagleson and Haggert had set the company up together in 1976, both men now vehemently deny that Eagleson has ever had any financial interest in it.

Another old friend who became part of Eagleson's business circle was Arthur Harnett, who stage-managed Eagleson's successful bid to become president of the Ontario Progressive Conservative Association in 1969. Eagleson asked Harnett to assist him in organizing the 1972 Russia-Canada Series, and suggested his friend form a company to sell the broadcast advertising rights. It was a tremendously lucrative venture. Harnett's company, Harcom, went on to become the broker for TV rights and board advertising for seven ensuing international events. In 1980, Eagleson became a 50 percent partner with Harnett in selling the advertising rights for Toronto's Exhibition Stadium. Harnett bought him out six years later.

The players gave Eagleson his power base, and his tight corporate and political network helped keep it in place. The NHLPA gave Eagleson unparalleled access to every single professional hockey player. In turn his sports agency and financial management company serviced a large number of NHL players, including a majority of the stars. Endorsement work went to one friend and big-league advertising to another. One of Eagleson's employees admiringly observed, "Al's into hockey right down to its underwear," referring to the fact that many of his clients bought their suits at Marty's, which Eagleson had a share in.

Bobby Orr knew very little and rarely asked questions about what part he played in these various business deals. Though his money was central to many of Eagleson's ventures in the early '70s, Orr didn't even know what stocks he owned. "I obviously have a lot of faith in him," he explained confidently whenever asked about it. Eagleson felt secure enough in that trust to make substantial investments without consulting Orr in advance. In 1971, Bobby Orr Enterprises bought 60 percent of the Canadian closed-circuit TV rights for the Cassius Clay–Joe Frazier fight for $250,000. Though a week passed between the time Eagleson expressed interest to Jack Kent Cooke and the time he closed the deal, he did not tell Orr until the money was already committed.

In those days, Orr was invariably portrayed as a nice, fun-loving, not-too-bright young man who loved to play hockey and had every young man's disregard for retirement planning and financial management. He didn't worry about details because his "brother," Eagleson, assured him he was "fixed for life." No caveats, no qualifications, just "fixed for life."

Eagleson was a drug to Orr, who became increasingly dependent on him as a shield from the pressures of life. During one particularly difficult contract negotiation with Boston, Orr called Eagleson before breakfast every day. In one month alone during that time, Eagleson claimed he spent $3,000 talking to his star client.

No one doubted that Eagleson was Orr's friend, confidant and mentor. But those outside the small inner circle never saw the flip side of their relationship. Beneath the brotherly love rhetoric, Eagleson denigrated and undermined Orr in a thousand small ways. He spoke of him as if he were some inanimate possession, promising to turn him into this or that, get him involved in this or that. Most often, he predicted that he would make Orr a millionaire, first within five years and, when that didn't happen, by the time he was thirty.

Eagleson referred to Orr as "the perfect client" and enjoyed repeating their standing public joke that they split Orr's earnings 90-10, emphasizing the punch line: "Orr lives very well on the 10 percent." Bobby often told the same joke with a self-mocking twist: "Al lets me keep 10 percent."

Recently, Bobby Orr has been criticized for being careless in business, for relying on Eagleson too much and for hiding his head in the sand where his finances were concerned. In truth, it would have been a very unusual young man who could have seized control over his blossoming affairs while associated with a dynamo like Eagleson. It would have been an even more remarkable accomplishment for a young sports superstar, swamped by adulation and envy. For most young hockey players, then and now, the meaning of money starts to blur after the first five zeroes. Add to that the intoxicating burden of being a demigod, and the relevance of investment plans and income tax strategies falls into perspective. In short, Orr's primary concerns were playing hockey and having a good time—the future was left to his "brother."

Eagleson assigned Marvin Goldblatt to look after Orr's financial affairs, virtually a full-time job in itself. There were equipment suppliers, corporate sponsors, politicians, travel agents, coaches, other players, car salesmen, old friends, friends of friends and friends of friends' friends—all of whom wanted a piece of Bobby Orr. "There were all these people approaching trying to put some type of deal together. Somebody had a puck on a ball bearing!" laughs Goldblatt, who sometimes felt like a venture capitalist under siege from a horde of penny-stock promoters.

Insiders called this group the "floaters' ball." "People were all over him," recalls Rick Curran, formerly an Eagleson employee and now a player agent. "It got to a point where Bobby got so inundated with these types of people that he had a very difficult time in dealing with people in general because he never knew where a person was coming from."

The Orr-Walton Sports Camp, Eagleson's first investment for Orr, swarmed with members of the floaters' ball, including a large contingent of Eagleson's friends and family. "Al always had these people hanging around and on the payroll who never seemed to do anything," says Doug Orr, describing the camp. "The kids were mostly from the States and a lot from rich families who dropped them off while they took off for Europe. We had a lot of drinking and stealing and fighting but we couldn't send them back home because their parents weren't there."

Eagleson made his father-in-law head of maintenance and hired Mike Walton's father as "head of clean-up," according to Walton. He also convinced Doug Orr to resign from his work in high-explosives with CIL. "He told me there would be work for me with the camp, and he said he had a trust fund set up for us so if we didn't want to we'd never have to work again," he states earnestly.

Doug Orr's new career never materialized nor did the trust fund. "He pretty nearly ruined my life," the sixty-six-year-old says of Eagleson. "I quit after thirty years and four months on the job, lost my pension and now I'm still working. I'm a liquor salesman!"

Though Mike Walton remembers the camp as "great fun with great instructors," he now concedes that beneath the surface things were different. "There was too much funny stuff going on there." He explodes into anger when the subject of his father's job is raised—"My Dad got fucked!"—but lapses into silence when asked "By whom?" Walton also says bitterly, "Doug Orr never worked there. He *supposedly* had a job there. He was on the payroll."

Orr Enterprises appeared to grow and prosper in those days, but at least one member of the board of directors, Doug Orr, didn't receive reports or financial statements, and at the handful of meetings, he attended all he heard were vague statements from Eagleson of the "things are going great, guys" variety. "He never asked me for any advice," recalls Doug Orr. "Al did everything. I was there just in name only."

Mike Walton, also both a client and a business partner, had little idea how "the accountant stuff" worked and to-day hotly describes the business side of the Orr-Walton Sports Camp as a "complete screw-up."

The fairy tale relationship between Alan Eagleson and Bobby Orr ended in 1980. It wasn't until ten years later that Orr made public his reason for leaving. "Bobby Orr Enterprises was worth the goose (egg)," he stated baldly. But according to his "brother," it was all his own fault. "Bobby Orr should have been a millionaire by 30," Eagleson told the Toronto *Sun* in 1990 ". . . if his cost of living had been reasonable. If he hadn't spent lavishly on everything, he would have been."

But if Orr's spending was out of control, or his future security threatened, there was no hint of it while Orr was still playing. In 1973, for instance, Eagleson said he and Orr—then only twenty-six—were already millionaires. "I suppose either of us could be called millionaires if one of us wanted to turn everything into cash but we're not about to do that," he told Tim Burke of the Montreal *Gazette*. "We're like brothers in our relationship. Money has never been the primary consideration."

As it turned out, there was only one millionaire left standing when the dust settled.

Sorrow and recriminations were far in the future in the late '60s and '70s as Orr opened door after door for Eagleson. Orr was even instrumental in the birth of the National Hockey League Players' Association, or so the story goes. According to all accounts, three Boston Bruins—Orr, Murray Oliver and Eddie Johnston—approached Eagleson in Montreal on December 28, 1966, when the Bruins were slated to play the Canadiens.

"They said, 'Come on up to the room, the guys want to talk to you,'" Eagleson explained recently. "I got up there. The whole team was there. They said, 'Al, it's about time we had a union. We would like you to take a look at getting it going.' This was based on what was happening in Springfield."

In the years to come, Eagleson repeated "The Bruins asked me to start a union" story so often that it has become accepted as fact. "I don't think that's true at all," Orr states emphatically. "The guys in Canada did much more work and were much more involved. I wasn't involved in the players' association. I'd be only eighteen years old at the time. I didn't know anything about any association." Murray Oliver, supposedly one of the NHLPA instigators, agrees that the impetus came from Toronto and doesn't remember any Montreal meeting with Eagleson.

The Bruins, however supportive they may have been, didn't spearhead the drive to create an association. That accomplishment belongs to the Young Lions of Toronto, in particular Baun, Brewer and Pulford, a fact rarely mentioned, then or now. From the early '60s on, they spent hours discussing unions and how to form one with Eagleson and his law partners.

In 1964, the Young Lions talked seriously about starting an association with key players on other teams. By the time Eagleson talked to the Bruins in Montreal, the Maple Leafs were close to action. The biggest name omitted from the accepted version of the Players' Association story is that of the conservative and quietly effective Jim Blaney, one of Eagleson's partners. "If Jim would talk, even a little, the whole story would unravel," says Bob Baun. "He was the silent steering wheel that directed everything."

Throughout early 1967, Eagleson crisscrossed North America talking to players. "I visited every NHL club, every American League Club, every Western League club, which was a pro league then, and a couple of Central League clubs," he said during a 1989 interview. Though the work took Eagleson away from his law practice, his partners supported him fully. They understood the benefits that could accrue to their firm with one of them heading a hockey union. "Jim Blaney and Bob Watson and the boys—and later myself—believed that anything that Alan did that helped Al would help the firm because he was a partner, that some day he would be in a position to be very successful and that would be very helpful to the firm," says Bill McMurtry, a former partner.

Eagleson's young law associates were also, to a man, die-hard hockey fans, and Eagleson's connections put them on a first-name basis with the elite of the sport. It was a heady time. Very quickly, they began rubbing shoulders with their heroes and came to be insiders at key events: the Orr signing, the '72 Russia-Canada Series, the World Championships, the Olympics. They got great deals on international air fares, the best seats at games and preferential hotel rates. They attended important cocktail parties, hobnobbed with politicians and got invitations that never would have come their way without Eagleson. Those perks were worth far more to them than any number of dull but lucrative corporate clients. The partners did not foresee that Eagleson would become hockey's pre-eminent potentate. Just getting close to the sport they loved was reason enough to support the big chunk of time he spent talking up a union in NHL and minor-league cities across North America.

Travelling around under the Players' Association banner was a godsend for Alan Eagleson. It gave him cachet and a legitimate reason to speak to every team in the NHL without anyone accusing him of furthering his player-agency ambitions—that would come later. With few exceptions, players greeted him with open arms. "We all thought, here was a guy who'd find out about pensions and take the heat off the players," recalls Harry Howell, then with the Rangers.

At every stop, Eagleson told the players how badly they were being paid and treated. He promised to protect them from the owners' backlash if they formed an association. "He convinced us all in one meeting," Howell says. "We certainly couldn't have been any worse off." In Chicago, Bobby Hull introduced Eagleson with a ringing endorsement. "This man has done more for the players in the last three months than anyone has done in the last twenty years."* Murray Oliver is still bemused about how little persuading the Bruins needed. "We were just like puppy dogs."

Eagleson sold the players at every conceivable level. Though highly educated, a lawyer and a member of the Ontario provincial parliament, his youth, aggression and ease in the sports world convinced them to accept him. He looked smart and tough and talked smart and tough. In professional sport, profanity is a second language, but for every expletive uttered by the players, Eagleson summoned up ten and spit them out faster and more authoritatively.

In truth, the players didn't need much selling. They eagerly signed a simple form giving Eagleson carte blanche to negotiate on their behalf. Within a few months he had the authorizations of all but a handful of the 120 current players in the NHL. At the same time, Eagleson signed up players in gross lots to be personally represented by his agency.

---

*   Sometimes Hull vehemently denies ever having introduced Eagleson claiming that
    he was suspicious of him from the start. Other times, when reminded of the event,
    his wide and ready smile twists into a grimace: "Some asshole I was, huh?"

Eagleson maintains that he organized the NHLPA and signed up every club under the strictest security. "It was very secret. Nobody knew," he emphasized in 1989. "I just told the players that the element of surprise is everything: 'Don't say anything to anybody.' It's amazing. We had 500 players and it was kept a secret."*

Eagleson does allow that one particularly clever reporter discovered his mission. "The only person who got wind of it was Red Fisher. He always reminds me of it. 'Did you think you could get in and out of Montreal without me finding out?' But he was the only one. I made them [Montreal] the last team."

But the story, worthy of a John le Carré espionage novel, strains credulity. Eagleson was hardly stealthy. On March 5, 1967—a full three months before he "surprised" League owners with a full-blown and fully organized association—he told his great secret to an Associated Press reporter. "Eagleson," the ensuing wire story stated, "is in the forefront of the formation of a players' association."

"The players need an association to get a fair shake from the owners," Eagleson explained. "There's a good chance that it will be a reality next season." AP sent that story to hundreds of affiliated papers in North America, but the League owners and general managers were already aware of events unfolding. "We knew about it almost from the first day," confirms Emile Francis, then general manager of the New York Rangers. "We just decided that its time had come."

Asked why the NHL put up so little resistance to the association, Sam Pollock, then general manager of the Montreal Canadiens, pauses to consider and releases one of his peculiarly feline smiles. "It was all part of doing business." More to the point, the League sensed that Eagleson was a man they could do business with.

Alan Eagleson displayed none of the militancy and uttered none of the union rhetoric so distressingly evident

---

* There were actually only 120 players in the League. Eagleson has cited many different figures over the years for the total number of players signed up. In this case, he may be referring to *verbal* support from the minor leagues.

in basketball and baseball. Clarence Campbell, who had had several dealings with Eagleson, liked what he saw of the neat, well-dressed and respectful young lawyer. Even Conn Smythe, who had so ruthlessly crushed the 1957 players' association, would come to endorse Eagleson. "I don't like unions but I'm glad it's Eagleson at the head of the Players' Association rather than somebody else."

At that time, Smythe's "somebody else" could have been a whole host of rather threatening people. Early in 1966, Jimmy Hoffa and the Teamsters had announced plans to unionize professional sports. The Teamsters were the most powerful union in the world at this point, and Jimmy Hoffa was nothing if not a man who could smell money from a great distance. The Teamsters, and their partners in organized crime, had long been interested in sports and arena management. Unionizing workers had proven to be a lucrative and efficient way of taking over other industries, like garbage collection.

Clarence Campbell dismissed the possibility that the Teamsters could organize the NHL, but behind closed doors the NHL owners were very concerned—and for good reason. In 1967, Bernie Parrish, fed up with the ineffectual National Football League Players' Association, formed the rival American Federation of Professional Athletes and vowed to affiliate with the Teamsters. When Parrish's intentions became public, the NFL owners, who had fiercely resisted any form of collective bargaining, immediately agreed to negotiate with the NFLPA.

Just as worrying to the hockey bosses was an association led by the likes of baseball's formidable Marvin Miller. Miller, hired in 1966, had spent sixteen years with the 1.25-million-member United Steelworkers of America, serving most recently as chief economist and assistant to the president. In comparison, butting heads with Alan Eagleson, a young lawyer with no labour experience, was hardly worth getting excited about.

The first confrontation between the supposedly ultra-secret National Hockey League Players' Association and the owners occurred on June 6, 1967, immediately before the NHL governors' meeting and the historic first expansion draft in Montreal. Six players, twitching with nervous energy and recently acquired bravado, filed into the meeting room to face Bruce Norris of Detroit, David Molson of Montreal, Bill Wirtz of Chicago, Senator Jack MacGregor of Pittsburgh, Walter Busch of Minnesota and Barry Van Gerbig of Oakland.* Also present was Charles Mulcahy, secretary of the NHL's board of governors.

"I have been directed to tell you that we want Alan Eagleson to speak on our behalf," Bob Pulford, NHLPA president, read slowly from a prepared statement. "A players association has been formed and he is our executive director. Talk it over among yourselves. If you agree to meet with Eagleson, fine. If you don't—our meetings this year won't last for five minutes."

The owners flatly refused to talk to the players through Eagleson, and the small group turned around and trooped out of the room. After a bare five minutes, the governors sent out an emissary to ask the players—who had only retreated to the hallway—to return. The subsequent discussion lasted just fifteen minutes and concluded with formal recognition of the NHL Players' Association.

The whole thing had the air of a set piece, staged for the benefit of observers, and perhaps, of the participants as well. Several owners described themselves as being "happy" and "elated" at this sudden turn of events. In a picture taken after the meeting, Bill Wirtz resembled a cat who'd just swallowed a juicy canary. A sanguine Sam Pollock, who carries shrewdness around with him like a set of matched luggage, best captured the mood of the day. "Everything is negotiable," he said.

The players were characteristically respectful. "There was no ultimatum involved," emphasized Norm Ullman, "but there are some things we want negotiated. I can't at this time say what they are."

Despite all the revisionist history about Bobby Orr and

---

* The players were Bob Pulford, Norm Ullman and Bob Nevin from Toronto, Eddie Johnston from Boston, Harry Howell from New York and J.C. Tremblay from Montreal.

the Boston players being the catalysts for the NHLPA, the owners well knew the real strength lay in Toronto. And, though they may have felt comfortable with Alan Eagleson, they had no intention of letting the NHLPA become the least bit effective. With a tidy bit of housekeeping, they stripped Eagleson of his key supporters in Toronto. It was a simple task: all they had to do was give Punch Imlach his head.

Imlach loathed the very idea of an association. He had already served notice of his vehement opposition in the latter half of the 1966-67 season, well before the supposedly secret association had even been announced. "Imlach weeded out problems," observed Brian Conacher, a former player. "He didn't face problems, he just got rid of them."

Imlach took the rookies aside and harangued them about the danger of being led by "a bunch of fucking hotheads." He met with key veterans like George Armstrong, Marcel Pronovost and Johnny Bower, reminding them bluntly that they owned their careers to him. Practices turned into feuds. "Guys like myself, Bobby Pulford and Mike Walton, Jimmy Pappin, Tim Horton—we practised at one end," says Conacher. "Then the guys that were in Punch's camp, all of the older players—the Marcel Pronovosts—practised at the other end. There was nothing in the players' association for them but aggravation." Defenseman Kent Douglas estimates that eight of the Leafs were not only opposed to the formation of an association but actively working to undermine it.

Though the Maple Leafs went on to win the Stanley Cup that season, the rift between "Punch's boys" and "the shit-disturbers" widened. At the expansion draft, Imlach let association stalwarts like Baun and Douglas go while protecting creaky old-timers like Marcel Pronovost and Allan Stanley, who supported him. He did hang on to some of the "shit-disturbers" like Brian Conacher, but got rid of them at the first opportunity.

It was a serious blow to the NHLPA but a crippling one to the Toronto Maple Leafs Hockey Club. Over the years, many writers have speculated about the reasons for the Leafs' downfall. Harold Ballard, in particular, receives considerable blame. But it was Punch Imlach's purge of key players over a two-year period that robbed the Maple Leafs of its heart and soul. The team missed the playoffs in 1968 after winning the Stanley Cup the previous season. Since then, the once proud Maple Leafs have descended into incompetence both on and off the ice.

Imlach hung on to Bob Pulford, but he deliberately didn't let him get too comfortable. That summer, Pulford's delight with a third Stanley Cup ring was tempered by the trade rumours that were circulating. Imlach's favourite adjective to describe Pulford, "irreplaceable," suddenly disappeared. The base of support for the NHLPA still lay in Toronto, but with so many players gone, Pulford was sure the organization would collapse if he were traded. By the end of the summer he was so worried about his future that he finally begged Baun, now Oakland Seals property, to take over as president of the association. "Bob, I'll never play hockey again if you don't," he pleaded.

"We didn't know which way to go," says Baun. "But we had to keep it [the association] going until we got all the regulations resolved and the documentation done." Just before training camp in the fall of '67, an NHLPA meeting was called in Toronto. Seals' coach and general manager Bert Olmstead gave Baun some advice. "He said if I came back as president [of the NHLPA] he was going to shoot me. The League and team owners put a lot of pressure on him: 'Now Baun's coming back from that meeting and you'd better have him onside.'"

Baun ignored him and returned from the meeting as interim president. Olmstead retaliated by telling him, "Unless you resign it's going to cost you $1000 a day." Baun countered by buying five plane tickets back to Toronto for himself and his family. Olmstead quickly backed off, but the Seals traded Baun to Detroit at the end of the season.

Though Pulford was no longer president and the NHLPA had the governors' nod of approval, Imlach still hoped to convince the Toronto players to withdraw. When training camp opened in September, he stepped up the pressure on Pulford. One day he held a meeting with the entire team—except Bob Pulford. "You go out there and fucking skate around until we're finished," he told him. For three-quarters of an hour, Pulford skated alone while Imlach shrieked and ranted about "this stupid fucking association thing."

Finally, sick of Imlach's raving, Tim Horton stood up without a word and joined Pulford. One by one they were joined by most of the other players. "In my opinion," says Pulford, "that was the turning point right there. I knew we were going to stand up to Imlach after that."

Neither Baun nor Pulford can remember exactly what Alan Eagleson was doing while they were being intimidated and harassed. But the players integral to the NHLPA clearly recall his partner, Jim Blaney, holding everything together and keeping everyone focused during the association's first six months. "He was the one who kept us all sane at that time," asserts Baun. "Jim wouldn't abuse anybody, and that's why we were able to pull through, because of Jim's very even plane and keeping everybody on a low level and low key."

While the players felt the ground shaking beneath them, Eagleson flourished. Though he quickly stopped bragging about how lucrative his hockey agency was, his clientele was increasing almost daily. By his own reckoning, he represented 250 minor-league and NHL players in the first post-expansion season. In essence, Alan Eagleson had cornered the market in hockey players.

For example, less than six months after the fabled meeting with the Bruins in Montreal, Eagleson, by his own account, was acting for seventeen of the twenty players drafted by the expansion Pittsburgh Penguins. Eagleson's 10-percent cut of his Pittsburgh clients' salaries, factoring in bonuses, was close to $50,000. That year, his gross, as a player agent, easily topped $500,000. But the real figure was undoubtedly much higher, since he represented many of the game's top stars.

Eagleson even managed to collect fees from players he

didn't represent. Just before training camp in 1967, Bert Olmstead asked him for an indication of the salaries the seven Toronto players he had acquired would want. At a quarter to eleven the next night, Eagleson called Billy Harris.

"Look, I just talked to Bobby Baun. Bobby wants to sign a two-year contract with Oakland. What are your thoughts?" Harris, who always negotiated his own contract, said he intended to request a two-year deal and asked Eagleson to recommend a salary. Eagleson suggested $25,000 a year, up from Harris's $18,000 the previous season. Eagleson didn't mention that Baun had told him that he intended to ask for a $70,000 annual contract (which he got). In comparison, Harris would have been worth at least $45,000.*

At the Seals' training camp Harris sat down with Olmstead to hammer out his contract details: they met three more times before coming to terms. Shortly afterwards, an astonished Harris received a $750 bill from Eagleson. Since that single phone conversation had lasted no more than three minutes, Harris estimates that Eagleson charged him $15,000 an hour.

When Oakland played in Toronto, Harris confronted Eagleson, who hastily backpedalled. "I had to send you the bill because there is Wally Boyer, Bobby Baun and about six other guys in the dressing room and I didn't want them getting this fee I submitted and you not getting anything. Just send me 150 bucks and forget the whole thing." Today, Harris is amused by Eagleson's brass. "He probably submitted a fee to the Oakland franchise for acting on their behalf. I would be surprised if he didn't do that." Baun also got a bill; he "sent it right back."

Until 1970, Alan Eagleson was the dominant player agent, but in the early years of that decade, aggressive

---

* The contract secrecy of the day was so great that neither player had any idea what the other finally received. Harris was clearly shocked in 1990 to learn of Baun's $70,000. "He got that?" Harris said, a shade too brightly, "Good for him." "Is that *all* Harris got?" commented an unbelieving Baun.

new entrants began picking off his disaffected clients and snatching up many young prospects before Eagleson had even heard of them. With the advent of the World Hockey Association in 1972, the number of pro players jumped from 250 to 400. An agent explosion followed close behind.*In 1969 there were eleven full- or part-time hockey agents in Canada. Four years later, there were forty-one. The poaching of clients from Eagleson temporarily declined as fierce battles took place in the amateur ranks across Canada, where agents elbowed each other viciously to claim kids as young as thirteen.*

By the time the puck dropped at the first WHA game, Alan Eagleson's Sports Management, though still by far hockey's largest agency, was in serious trouble. He retained the majority of big names, but he was being virtually shut out of the suddenly critical junior market.

Eagleson isn't a Machiavellian master planner. Though intelligent enough to develop a long-range view, he's neither patient enough nor organized enough to carry it out. What he has is a peerless sense—more biological than intellectual—of where opportunity is or is going to be; then he can slither into a position that gives him maximum advantage. He moves into a power vacuum and proceeds to fill up the space so utterly that no one remembers what it was like before.

In 1972, Alan Eagleson made the cleverest move of his career by turning himself into the kingpin of international hockey. To do so he had to displace John Francis "Bunny" Ahearne, a short, rotund, Irish hustler who had been controlling the International Ice Hockey Federation (IIHF) since the '30s and had served as president of the organization since 1954. Ahearne had stumbled upon international hockey in 1933 when his travel agency rented an office to the obscure British Ice Hockey Association. That year he became the BIHA's general secretary.

Ahearne quickly showed his affinity for the main

---

* Though midget and junior players could not legally sign contracts, they, or their parents, would verbally agree that a particular agent would represent them once they were drafted by the NHL or WHA.

chance and demonstrated his mastery of the back room. In 1935, he lured a number of British-born Canadian players from the Depression-stricken Prairies to play in the London & District League, for fifty dollars per week. He suited up eight of them to represent Britain in the 1936 Olympic Games. The bogus British team beat the Canadians and, thanks to a tidy bit of Ahearne conniving, won the gold medal. It was the first of Ahearne's many triumphs over Canada, and he made the country his whipping boy for nearly forty years.

Elected president of the IIHF in 1954, Ahearne remained firmly in place until 1975, even though a 1940 by-law change clearly stipulated that the presidency was to alternate between the North American division and the European division. Despite frequent and intense opposition from Canada, Ahearne hung on to power by wielding proxies from IIHF members like Kuwait, Saudi Arabia and South Korea. In return he always ensured that those countries got a disproportionate share of international profits. He kept the Eastern Bloc countries in his corner largely because it suited the Russians' purposes to keep Canada impotent internationally while they developed into a hockey power.

Ahearne used his skilful backroom dealing, coupled with a shrewd business sense, to transform international hockey into a money-making operation. He negotiated the first European television contracts and introduced the highly lucrative board advertising to hockey.

For years, IIHF officials, particularly the North American ones, suspected that it wasn't just international hockey's profits Ahearne was protecting. "A lot of us thought he was fiddling things for years," says Fred Page, former president of the North American division, "but you could never prove anything because no one saw the books, you only saw Bunny's version of the books. I think he probably had it in for me because I always asked him questions about the money. You could never pin him down. He'd say something was an absolute fact one minute and the next he'd be saying, 'I never said that at all!'"

Ahearne may have been capricious and unpredictable, but two things were certain as long as he ran international hockey: he knew exactly where every dollar came from, and if you didn't book through his travel agency, you didn't play international hockey. Teams who didn't use his agency found their permissions to attend international hockey tournaments revoked at the last minute. When a protest was made, no record of any request for a permit could ever be found at IIHF headquarters. Teams that booked through Ahearne's travel agency had no problems.

The Canadian amateur hockey officials were completely fed up with the wily and dictatorial Ahearne, but because international hockey politics was a constantly shifting morass of allegiances, they were never able to pin down sufficient supporters to challenge him. "You would get a phone call in the night from the Swiss guys," recalled former Canadian Amateur Hockey Association president Joe Kryscka, "and they would say, 'Hey, we heard on the grapevine that the Russians and the Czechs had a secret meeting with Bunny and you guys are going to get shafted at the meeting tomorrow.'"

Feuds, counter-feuds, power struggles and attempted coups were an everyday occurrence on the international scene. Within Canadian amateur hockey, things often weren't much better. The corps of volunteers who ran the largest sport organization in the country battled over endless regional and philosophical differences.

In 1967, the Western Canada Hockey League divorced itself from the CAHA and an outlaw junior league began in Ontario. The CAHA altered the structure of junior hockey and the WCHL came back into the fold. No sooner had it done so than the Ontario Hockey Association and the Quebec Major Junior Hockey League boycotted the annual championships. "We can't carry on like this," growled an aggravated Clarence Campbell. "It's nonsense." He threatened that the NHL would form its own player-development leagues if the CAHA didn't get its house in order.

In 1968, the federal government, prompted by a barrage

of complaints, commissioned a task force on amateur sport which focused primarily on hockey. Out of its recommendations Hockey Canada was created. A completely separate entity from the CAHA, it eventually took responsibility for the Canadian entry to international events like the World Championships, the Olympics and even the World Junior Championships, all previously the CAHA's sole preserve. Though Hockey Canada included several CAHA officials, its creation was bitterly resented by the amateur group—a resentment that remains to this day.

No sooner had Hockey Canada ordered its letterhead than it ran straight into Bunny Ahearne. Hockey Canada has never had a seat on the IIHF, and thus no official power on the international scene, but Ahearne suspected that the weak CAHA would be overwhelmed by "professionals" like Alan Eagleson, who made up the Hockey Canada board. In an attempt to shut out the new organization, Ahearne promised to support the CAHA in its bid to place nine NHL players on the Canadian team at the 1970 World Championships, to be held in Winnipeg.

At the eleventh hour, Ahearne, wearing a woeful face, withdrew his support, sadly explaining that Avery Brundage, International Olympic Committee head, had threatened to expel any country that played against the tainted team. In January 1970, the furious CAHA pulled Canada out of the World Championships and all international competition for the next two years.

Since the CAHA had nothing to lose, its officials stepped up their attempts to negotiate a one-to-one series with Russia, professional players included. "They had been bugging us about it since 1967," recalls Page. "We always said fine, but we want you to support us in having professionals play at the World Championships. They always said no and that was that."

When Joe Kryscka, an Alberta Supreme Court judge, was elected CAHA president in 1971, the Soviets appeared willing to compromise. Over the next fourteen months Kryscka spent weeks in Europe trying to come to terms. Finally, in April 1972, at the IIHF Congress in

Prague, the Soviets agreed to work out the final details. For days, Kryscka and Gordon Juckes, executive director of the CAHA, delicately picked over contentious issues, soothed fears, offered deals and promised concessions.

In the late afternoon of April 18, Fred Page sat in a Prague hotel lobby while Kryscka and Juckes were in one of the rooms putting the finishing touches to the agreement with the Soviets. As he gazed out the window into Prague's ever-present coal-dust haze, he saw a vaguely familiar figure walking towards the door. The man opened the door and a startled Page exclaimed, "Alan Eagleson! What the hell are you doing here?" With elaborate casualness Eagleson replied, "Oh, my wife and I just happened to be touring in Europe and we thought we'd drop by." Today Page snorts, "Just *happened* to be touring in Europe! What a crock!"

Eagleson asked offhandedly, "So, how's the meeting going anyway?" "Alan, it's a CAHA affair," chided Page. "It's between the CAHA and the Soviets." Eagleson then asked if Charlie Hay [Chairman of Hockey Canada] was in the meeting. "Alan, it's a CAHA affair," Page repeated. "Charlie's not in the meeting, he's in his room." Eagleson edged away toward the elevator. "Well then, I think I'll just go up and say hello to Charlie."

The same day, after a six-hour session, a one-and-a-half-page agreement was signed by Joe Kryscka and chief Soviet IIHF delegate Andrei Starevoitov, and approved by Fred Page and a reluctant Bunny Ahearne.* The next day, the papers trumpeted the historic breakthrough, and Alan Eagleson was quoted praising the deal. Within a week, virtually everyone had forgotten Joe Kryscka and the CAHA. Though neither Hay nor Eagleson were present at the critical meetings, and their names appear nowhere on the agreements, today they are ceded the pre-eminent roles. One version features Charlie Hay as the lead nego-tiator with the Russians. "They wouldn't even talk to

---

* Ahearne opposed the talks every step of the way, but by 1972 the Soviets were so adamant he approved the deal in return for their support of him as IIHF presi-dent for yet another term.

Charlie Hay," says an irritated Kryscka, in the tones of one who has made this correction many times. "He sat out in the hall. We reported to him how our negotiations went."

According to Aggie Kukulowicz, then Air Canada employee in Moscow, it was his close friend Alan Eagleson who negotiated with the Russians, starting way back in 1969. During those talks, Eagleson papered the room with "fuck," "shit," "bastard," and "cocksucker" and told the Soviets if they didn't talk with him "I can guarantee you will never play against the world's best." Then he turned to Kukulowicz who was translating. "You tell them every fucking word!"

In Kukulowicz's own words, "the whole thing took shape that day." Eagleson's own notes from the period, as quoted by Kukulowicz, read, "Our meeting went well and set the tone for what became, three years later, Canada versus Russia."

After the April meetings in Prague, Alan Eagleson's profile became larger day by day while the CAHA's role diminished, to the point where few now know the indispensable role the amateur body played. "There was supposed to be a committee composed of Hockey Canada, the CAHA and the NHL guys, which were supposed to be Eagleson and Campbell," recalled Kryscka in 1990. "Well, of course, Campbell couldn't have cared less. So basically it was Eagleson running everything. How do you stop a runaway freight train?" The normally loquacious Kryscka then stopped and sat in untypical silence for several minutes, his eyes drifted out to the panoramic view through his living-room windows over Calgary's Fish River valley. "It has bothered me for 20 years," he said very quietly.

Kryscka spoke with moving pride and pain about listening to "O Canada" at the first game in Montreal, and of watching Paul Henderson's winning goal at the last game in Moscow. Then his voice broke, his smile crumbled and, in tears, he stared at a twenty-year-old memory. "The credit—the credit doesn't really matter. I knew what I did. I was proud, *really* proud to be part of it."

Today, even most CAHA officials believe that Eagleson brought Canada back into hockey by single-handedly negotiating the 1972 series. "I think Alan Eagleson is very destructive for hockey at this stage of the game," states Pat Reid, CAHA vice-president of high performance. "He was good when we needed him. There is a price you pay for people to make change. We needed him at one time because we couldn't find our way out of the forest and he kind of got us back into international hockey in 1972."

At the time, Kryscka was less disturbed by the lack of credit than by the excesses of Eagleson and the entourage who accompanied him. "There were always swarms of people. It was disgusting, a regular gravy train."

Eagleson's international entourage, or "floaters," numbering between twenty-five and thirty superfluous doctors, dentists, lawyers, businessmen and friends, has been a continual source of friction between the CAHA, Hockey Canada and Eagleson. Each is togged out with a tailored blazer, tie and pants and provided with air fare, game tickets, food and accommodation—all at Hockey Canada's expense. Total annual cost for the "floaters" is an additional couple of hundred thousand dollars according to one highly placed Hockey Canada insider.

In the 1972 Canada-Russia series, the tab for the players, officials and Eagleson's entourage came to $1 million, leaving only about $700,000 to be split evenly between Hockey Canada and the NHL players' pension. It took the CAHA nearly eight years of haggling with Hockey Canada to get their $100,000 cut. Though Kryscka was a director of Hockey Canada, he maintained he tried unsuccessfully to get a financial statement or a copy of the audit for the series.

Alan Eagleson has never been paid a penny in salary for the thousands of hours he's put into international hockey since 1972. But the hundreds of thousands of dollars in office expenses, gifts and charge-backs for the use of his personnel has caused bitter infighting for nearly twenty years.

The Canada-Russia series made Alan Eagleson the most recognizable name in Canada, after Pierre Trudeau and Anne Murray. But his agency was still haemorrhaging clients. The man he brought in to stem the flow was Bill Watters. Originally hired by Eagleson to run the Orr-Walton Sports Camp in 1970, Watters moved up to agent in 1973. "Eagleson felt as a lawyer he couldn't solicit business," snorts Watters today. "And this is an oft-used phrase by lawyers—so I became the solicitor of business. In 1974, I started being the guy who went to the parents and said, 'Look, we have a company that will represent your son and we have a lawyer who is in charge, etc."

Watters had many advantages over his boss, the biggest being that he genuinely liked the players. Unlike Eagleson, the former professional football player was a real professional athlete and didn't need any hyperactive displays of macho to prove it. As a former high school teacher, he also knew how to communicate with teenagers and their families. Within two years, Watters knew no equal in prospecting the junior ranks.

Watters is a great huggy-bear of a man, but his tongue could cut a telephone book in half. Once Watters hangs a nickname on someone, they never get rid of it. He dubbed competitors Norm Caplan and Art Kaminsky "the Duke and Puke Twins," a moniker Kaminsky still isn't able to shake.

Watters used innate charm, skilful manoeuvering, a genuine love of the game and the priceless connection with Bobby Orr to quickly re-establish Eagleson's pre-eminence in the business. At first, he personally prospected the promising players, developed a relationship with their parents and then brought Eagleson in to close the deal. In later years, Rick Curran took charge of prospecting and Watters negotiated the contracts, with Eagleson brought in only for the big names.

Watters set up an unparalleled network of sub-agents: ex-players, amateur coaches, high school teachers and firemen in small towns across the country who scouted players and passed along valuable tips. In return, he dispensed the kind of favours that only someone sitting at

Eagleson's right hand had access to. "I might have tickets to some of the Players' Association functions and I would look after them," recalls Watters. "It was a nice position to be in."

International hockey kept Eagleson's name in the news, but without Bill Watters, it's unlikely that Eagleson's player agency would have benefited as much as it did. Between 1976 and 1979, Watters held positions with seven Canadian international teams as general manager, business manager or tournament co-ordinator. Rick Curran, whom Eagleson hired in 1974 to assist Watters, did everything from chauffeur IIHF officials at the 1976 Canada Cup to co-ordinate the Canadian entry into the 1977 World Junior Championships. "You have come a long way, from the front seat to the back seat," observed a Swedish delegate, who recognized that Curran had been his chauffeur the previous year.

What international hockey gave Watters and Curran was tremendous credibility and ready access to both amateur and pro players. Every player liked the two men, and Curran, in his early twenties, developed close ties with the juniors. When those players got around to thinking about an agent, Watters and Curran naturally were the first and last names they considered.

No one can match Eagleson when it comes to maximizing his resources, particularly people. Most of his employees and associates did double or triple duty with international hockey, the player agency, the NHLPA or Hockey Canada. "I do tax work and I help out with the association," says Marvin Goldblatt. "I've never been paid by the association over all the years I have been doing it."

Goldblatt may not have been paid for his NHLPA duties, but Eagleson scrupulously billed Hockey Canada for the work done by both Curran and Watters. Watters' salary as Eagleson's assistant was about $45,000 annually in 1977 and '78. But because Hockey Canada paid Watters $107,500 during those two years for his role in various international tournaments, Eagleson refused to pay him further for his regular job as a player agent. "The guy works for me, and if I can put him to work and make a million dollars, it's my million dollars, not his," Eagleson told *Sports Illustrated*. "If I pay my guy 30 [thousand] and rent him for 50 that makes me smart."

Watters and Curran continued their recruiting and negotiating while doubling up with international hockey duties. The fact that Eagleson was profiting from their services left rather a bad taste. "How would you like to be me sitting in meetings with Hockey Canada," grumps Bill Watters, if someone mentions his cushy job in international hockey, "and them looking at me and saying, 'Huh! We are paying him $20,000 to run the tournament. He is also running Eagleson's business. This guy is making tons of money.' I was on Hockey Canada's budget as getting $30,000, but when I went to get my full pay from Eagleson, the $30,000 was deducted."

As a young Thistletown lawyer, Eagleson had been the thriftiest partner in his law firm, and that didn't change once he became a millionaire. Though he was munificent at times, Eagleson never understood the value of paying his employees what they were worth. "He never liked to deal directly with me when talking money," points out Curran. "He would always put Marvin Goldblatt in that position. Every time I would try and talk to Alan, he would always try and skirt the issue."

During one salary negotiation, Goldblatt told Curran that Eagleson was prepared to pay him $22,000. A little upset, Curran said, "I think I'm worth a lot more than that." Goldblatt eyed him for a minute, then got up and closed the door. "You know," he began kindly, "Alan likes you. You've done a great job, but we brought you on here at considerable expense in order to provide you with an opportunity to work."

Curran reminded Goldblatt that as international co-ordinator he was responsible for getting all the international hockey contracts typed up. He knew that Hockey Canada was paying the Orr-Walton Sports Camp (Curran's employer of record) $25,000 for his services as co-ordinator. He also knew that Eagleson only paid him $15,000 annually for those same services. "I don't think I have cost Alan money," he countered. "I think he's made $10,000 on me. In addition to doing my work for Hockey Canada, I'm also doing extra work for Sports Management. I don't think I'm costing anybody any money. I think I'm making someone some money."

"Well, don't forget there are secretarial fees and your office space and all that," responded Goldblatt. Curran shook his head. "Marvin, I don't have a secretary."

Despite the irritations, the Watters-Curran, one-two combination continued to be a lucrative one for Eagleson. In 1977, for example, his agency represented nine of the seventeen first-round draft picks. There were always challengers, but no one topped Eagleson's Sports Management team.

Watters was far more than Eagleson's workhorse. He acted as his fixer, solving problems and patching up the rifts, which occurred more and more frequently. When an exasperated Eagleson told the temperamental and demanding Marcel Dionne to "go fuck yourself" and "get the fuck outta my office," it was Watters who coaxed him back, saving the agency hundreds of thousands in lost fees. It was also Watters who soothed players' increasing concerns over Eagleson's 10 percent commission when competitors were charging as low as 3 percent.

Watters wasn't the only long-time Eagleson associate having second thoughts about his relationship. Throughout the early '70s, Eagleson's old law partners had remained mesmerized by his persona and the opportunity to be part of his entourage on international junkets and at high-profile events. But the firm expanded rapidly, and the new lawyers lacked the blinkered loyalty Eagleson demanded. Nor did they have the same passion for hockey that had united the partners in the early days. They began questioning his billing and wondered if a reasonable percentage of the money Eagleson earned made its way back into the firm.

There also developed, among the senior partners, a well-suppressed rancour about old debts. In 1975 they were each drawing $50,000 annually from the firm—a good wage in those days, but peanuts compared to

Eagleson's take from his many interests. What rankled was the fact that they had played a vital part in setting him up, and Eagleson seemed to have forgotten that fact.

In June 1975, Eagleson left Blaney, Pasternak, Smela and Watson and formed Eagleson and Ungerman, in partnership with the twenty-seven-year son of Irving Ungerman. "I was forty-two," he told his biographer, "and I wanted to change my style. The reason for leaving the firm came when they asked me to run the Canada Cup without pay. I knew it was going to take two years and I wanted to do it . . . and I wanted to do it my way, without obligations to anyone."

Eagleson's partners all tell a slightly different story about the break-up. Publicly, they are still very supportive of him, but privately, off the record and anxiously urging "no attribution," they gingerly skate around the great bitterness and animosity they felt when he left, taking over half a million dollars' worth of work-in-progress with him. Eagleson's pocket book certainly didn't miss his law buddies. Less than three years later, he bragged that his various interests were grossing $14.5 million annually.

Bob Watson is the most candid of the ex-partners, most of whom vibrate like a tuning fork when the break-up is broached. As he talks about the old days with "Al," his face lights up and his pleasant, boyish features become elfin. But when Eagleson's departure is raised, he struggles unsuccessfully to hide his hurt. "[We] spent a lot of time making it happen when Al was going to meetings with the Players' Association" he told Eagleson's biographer in 1981, "there would be months when he wasn't doing much legal work, in fact, when he wanted to go somewhere we paid for it, so when he left he more or less took a debt with him. . . .

"[We] didn't know what each other was billing, no one really went into it, so we were very vulnerable. Whereas if we knew he was leaving we would have made sure we had continuing contact with his clients. There's where the hardship arose, because we felt we'd been very supportive in developing Alan Eagleson."

Trying to put his former partner into perspective, Watson now adds, "Al and I were very good friends, but we don't see a lot of each other. You find sometimes that you get a little hurt by it, you often say, 'Well, gee, some people don't know who their friends are.' But I think it goes with that position and ambition—I know I could phone Al and ask him anything. . . .

"I always say [to Eagleson's friends], 'Don't get hurt, Al is Al. You have to learn that.'"

Chapter 9

Merchants of Promise

Since Alan Eagleson negotiated Bobby Orr's contract in 1966, agents have been as integral to the game as the players, coaches and general managers. Their presence has changed how and when players negotiate contracts, retire, are traded or get "terminated." More important, agents provide a much-needed buffer between the player and the powers that be. In the past, few players would ever have had the nerve to renegotiate a contract without an agent, yet now it's a common occurrence. Agents are routinely able to coerce teams to trade out-of-favour players who would have rotted in the minors twenty years ago. And general managers think twice before levying the kind of arbitrary punishment that was once routine.

Today, the NHLPA lists ninety full-time agents, and there are probably the same number again of firemen, lawyers, high school teachers and hockey fathers representing one or two players. Then there are a dozen or so agents specializing in other sports who have picked up a handful of hockey clients. Despite these numbers, fewer than a dozen agents represent 75 percent of the 539 players currently in the NHL. Though, if you count up all the

226

players agents *claim* to represent, the League's active list would top 2,000.

When those involved in the game utter the word "agent"—even agents themselves—there is a tiny glottal inflection at the end of the word, as if the speaker were clearing his throat of some noxious substance. Few actually set out to become agents, or, more correctly, admit to doing so. Hockey agents throw up a bewildering array of pseudonyms—player representative, sports attorney, advisor, business manager—as camouflage. Art Breeze, an up-and-coming Calgary agent, pauses when asked what words most people would use to describe the men of his profession. "Wellll, there's a lot. Scum, sleaze, parasite, leech, weasel, bloodsucker—take your pick."

"I don't like the image and I like to identify myself as a sports lawyer because of it," confesses Ron Simon, a Minnesota lawyer with prominent clients in all the major sports.* "Really, it's all the same. I always try to euphemistically describe myself as an attorney who represents professional athletes or a sports lawyer or something like that. Really, I'm an agent."

Agents come by their ambivalence honestly. They've wiped more phlegm off their shoes, nursed more sore noses from doors slammed in their faces, pulled more daggers from their backs and heard more stories of abuse than any other people in the sport. They were despised by management when they started out in the '60s and early '70s, and twenty years later they find they're none too popular with their clients, either. "Listen, there's nothing most of your clients would like better than to be able to get along without you. And even the best of them hate you a little bit for needing you," emphasizes Brian Burke, now happily an ex-agent and vice-president and director of hockey operations for the Vancouver Canucks.

In the good old days, general managers rarely troubled to hide their contempt for the flesh-peddlers. Alan Eagleson recalls sliding notes under doors because GMs

---

* Simon's clients include baseball's Paul Molitor and Ken Hrbek.

wouldn't talk to him. Montreal agent Norm Caplan had his life threatened by a Prairie coach who told him to get out of town. Gus Badali was once banned, not from one rink, but from every junior hockey arena in Ontario.

In the early '70s, agents who phoned the generally hostile Punch Imlach were occasionally surprised by the warmth and friendliness of their reception. Imlach would consent to let them talk to their client, and once even offered his office for the conversation. In each case, the agent showed up at the agreed time and waited for hours before discovering that the player had been lent to a minor-league team and had left town that very morning.

Life for a hockey agent is strewn with unexpected hardships. One agent got into a heated exchange of unpleasantries—commonly called a "fuck-you contest"—with a general manager over a contract. When he pointed his finger for emphasis, the GM bit it so hard the nail fell off the next day.

Another agent, who begs to remain anonymous, got into an argument with a coach and a GM while the three of them stood at the urinals. The conversation took a nasty turn, when the two men wheeled around and hosed the agent down from waist to ankles. Such stories may have something to do with the fact that most agents now prefer to negotiate over the phone.

It doesn't help agents that standard practice in the profession is viewed as nauseating or reprehensible by outsiders. Some clients do just walk in the door, but by and large, building a clientele requires either wooing them from other agents—referred to in the trade as "poaching" or "stealing" if it's done to you and "rescuing" or "helping out" if you're doing it—or discovering them as prepubescent marvels, called "recruiting" or "prospecting." Notwithstanding their avowed love of hockey, cold rinks and teenagers, most agents privately feel recruiting is a degrading process.

When an agent loses a client (or has him stolen), two stories invariably circulate. The rejected agent sadly, or angrily, points to enticing, but false, promises made by his competitor. The competitor claims that the player came to him "broke" or "badly fucked up" by the previous agent. The successful agent scrupulously avoids naming his defeated rival but provides plenty of clues to his identity.

In 1975, Ron Salcer moved from the grit of New York, where he was working as a financial consultant, to the warmth and gloss of Marina del Rey, California. There he met L.A. Kings players like Dave Hutchison, Gary Sargent, Bert Wilson and Dave Taylor, who lived nearby. "In those years I heard all the horror stories about how they were disenchanted with their agents and how many of them were financially insecure."

Dave Taylor came to Salcer one day in 1980 and said, "Ronnie, I know you. I trust you. I feel comfortable with you, so I would like to have you represent me." Salcer then embarked on a year-long battle with Kings owner Jerry Buss that turned Taylor's then $140,000 annual salary into a seven-year contract for $6 million.*

Art Kaminsky, Taylor's former New York agent, who was on the losing end of this one, has a slightly different version of events. "Salcer came to me years ago. He was some kid in L.A. He had a scheme. He was talking to all our L.A. Kings players that he was going to pool money together, buy low-income housing for small down payments in places like Houston when the price of housing was going up rapidly. The players were going to make a lot of money."

"He stole Dave Taylor from us. He used that as a vehicle to simply get in to know the players, and he had come to us on the supposition that we would become business partners in this deal. I introduced him to all my players in the Kings and gave him carte blanche to talk to them. He just tried to steal them all."

Poaching has its roots back in the dawn of hockey agenting, when Alan Eagleson had virtually every player.

---

* According to Salcer, Wayne Gretzky came to him in 1984 and said, "I heard about the contract that you got for Dave Taylor." Salcer replied, "Wayne, I got that three years ago. I thought you knew?" Gretzky shook his head, "No." "Well," shrugged Salcer, "you make that much!" Again, Gretzky shook his head. "I don't make half of what Dave Taylor makes!"

If a new agent, or an established agent from another field, wanted clients, they had to take them from Eagleson. Poaching is a delicate art, especially when the lord of the manor is a guy like Eagleson. The favoured technique has been to make inroads in a club by treating one or two lesser lights royally, then using them to persuade their teammates to switch.

The direct approach was also popular. "I bet you got a good contract this year," an agent would say conversationally to a prospect. "Yeah, I did okay," the player might respond. "Well that's just great!" the agent would enthuse before beckoning the player closer. "Between you and me, I got Mike six figures and a one-way deal. But, hey, I'm sure you did much better. After all, *you've* got talent." Mike would inevitably be an inferior player. The prospect, once delighted with his $75,000 contract, would sink into gloom.

Equally effective was, "Al's a great guy. I've got nothing against Al, he's done a lot for hockey." Then a meaningful pause. "But you know, Al's got 250 clients. I wonder if he can really look after all you guys?" Then another pause, and a few polite questions about the last time the player had talked to Al, seen Al or got a letter from Al. The agent would depart, content in the knowledge that a seed had been planted, and that some day soon he'd likely receive a plaintive call in the middle of the night.

For years, agents paraded their successes at the annual NHL entry draft. "Who've you got?" and "How many've you got?" were the two most asked questions when they bumped into each other. But lately, more and more of them are avoiding the cattle call. Well before most other agents did, Ron Salcer realized that the frenzied seduction of midget and junior players was a heart-breaking and money-losing exercise, suitable only, in his words, for "pimps and whores."

Salcer's luxurious L.A. location, coupled with his techniques and success, has earned him the nickname "the Prince of the Poachers" among his colleagues. While other agents are hustling around in godforsaken prairie rinks at forty-below, Salcer basks in the Los Angeles sun, working out of his home in the pleasant family neighbourhood of Manhattan Beach, only a few miles from The Great Western Forum. He watches as many games as he wants via the satellite-dish in his backyard. When there's a game in town, he drives fifteen minutes to the Forum, sees his clients, has dinner before or a beer after and returns home to his wife and daughter.

Salcer's system is clever and effective. Best of all, it is inexpensive and relatively stress-free. The top agents often spend $75,000 annually on travel alone. Gus Badali, who once represented Mario Lemieux and Wayne Gretzky, says that before he scaled down his client list a few years ago, he would sometimes attend nine games in a single week. As teams often schedule lay-overs in Los Angeles, Salcer's biggest expense is taking clients out on the town. If, by happy coincidence, those clients bring along teammates or players from other teams who belong to other agents, that's fine too. And Salcer suffers none of the marriage-killing stress that constant trips from home impose.

Salcer's "recruits" are already making money; he doesn't face the financial and emotional uncertainty of carrying a junior player who might never make it to the NHL. If a Salcer recruit is still represented by another agent a settlement is reached: usually the player pays fifty to seventy-five cents on the dollar to the former agent for the remainder of the fee owing. Salcer may have to wait a year, or at the very worst two, for a return, but he knows that there *will* be money—something no agent can be sure of when he recruits a sixteen-year-old.

Recruiting from the juniors by agents has its roots in the 1972 formation of the WHA. With the addition of twelve professional teams, hockey players were suddenly a scarce commodity. Agents responded to the new market by fanning out across North America and signing up juniors in order to get a jump on their rivals.

Back then, competition for clients was so vicious that junior teams could strike very profitable deals to guarantee exclusive rights to their players. "The situation is so drastic now that in order to sign a junior player, you have to shell out all kinds of money," complained Montreal agent Sid Kronish in 1974. "I'm talking about payoffs to coaches, general managers and other people and even then you're not sure of getting the player."

Teenage players have an alarming tendency to sign with one agent on Friday and a different one on Monday. Kronish and his partners prospected western Canada regularly, returning to Montreal with agreements to represent several youngsters. Sometimes it was only a matter of days before they discovered that the players had switched to another agent, and that agent was invariably one who had a "deal" with the junior team.

Agents bought protection with small favours, like promising to help a junior team get the development fees they were entitled to when an NHL or WHA team drafted one of their players. Others went further. In return for cash or a percentage of a player's future NHL contract, junior teams would bar other agents from talking to the team and exert pressure on the players to sign with the designated agent. Agent Frank Milne, for example, agreed to pay the Victoria Cougars 6 percent of the contract whenever a Cougars player made it to the NHL. Victoria GM Pat Ginnell called the arrangement "natural and good business." Another agent got exclusive rights by providing a team bus.

If a player wouldn't go along with the deal, he might suddenly find himself benched, bumped from the specialty squads or playing on a low-scoring or ineffective line. Whispers might be passed to scouts that he was afraid to go into the corner—a cardinal sin.

The Swift Current Broncos were the private preserve of agents Dave Schatia and Dick Sorkin, the latter being an expert at working the juniors. But Dave (Tiger) Williams dug his heels in and chose his own agent. He asked Saskatoon lawyer Herb Pinder Jr. to represent him because he knew of Pinder's family, "and if anything went wrong, it wouldn't be such a long journey for me to go up to Saskatoon and throw bricks through the windows of his father's drug stores."

"[Sorkin] arrived in Swift Current in a three-piece suit, and he was full of big promises," recalls Williams of Dick Sorkin's recruiting trip. "He said he knew what hockey players wanted. They wanted money and cars and broads, not necessarily in that order, and he was the man to provide all these things. I was sickened.

"I walked out of the room and told the other guys to follow me. I could tell that a lot of them wanted to come out with me, but not one of them moved. You could see that they were scared of the situation."

On a road trip afterwards, Broncos coach Stan Dunn sat down beside Williams and made it clear that he should sign with Sorkin. Dunn told him the arrangement was good for the club and pointedly mentioned that the deal improved all the Swift Current players' chances of making the big leagues. Williams wouldn't budge.

"Well, the club applied the heaviest possible pressure. They didn't play me against Flin Flon in the first game, which we lost quite badly. After the game, I said to Dunn, 'You better play me tomorrow night. If you don't, I'm going to call every goddamned newspaper in Western Canada and tell them the whole story.' I played the following night; we won, and I didn't hear any more about who I should select as my agent."

Sorkin retired as an agent when he was convicted of fraud and theft involving his clients' accounts. "I became totally obsessed by greed," he testified. "I said, 'Holy shit, look where I am. If I can make money for these players, a year from now I can have the largest agency in the country—no, in the world!'" In 1973, Sorkin attempted to speed things along by investing his clients' money in the stock market. Within two years, the millions he handled had dwindled to $500,000. To recoup his losses, he threw the remainder into another sinkhole: gambling. "I never bet on hockey," Sorkin said virtuously. "That would be morally wrong."

Today, junior team general managers speak of the days of Sorkin as a distant memory, but they're not. The coercion and kickbacks are less obvious, but agents still have arrangements with teams. The main difference is that they are as likely to strike deals with midget clubs as with the juniors. "Some teams I can't get near," says Rollie Thompson. "The old coach in Lethbridge . . . his players only went to Bill Watters and nobody else. I remember one summer I called a player and about two hours later I get this phone call, 'What are you doing with my players?' That's the way it happens. Was it a payoff? I don't know. Or was it a friendship? In Ottawa, this guy, a coach from Ottawa, says, 'All agents are scum except Larry Kelly.'"

In 1976, recruiting took on a new dimension when Wayne Gretzky became Gus Badali's client. Badali had scouted, pursued and signed Gretzky as a fifteen-year-old midget player. Two years later, Gretzky signed a twenty-one-year contract with Nelson Skalbania, then owner of the WHA Edmonton Oilers. "I was considered not a very good person to be telling a boy at the age of seventeen to turn professional," says Badali, with a hint of pain in his face from all the slings and arrows that flew over his cradle-robbing. "This young man was so dominant that everybody on every other team, if they had any tough guys at all, were out there to practically kill him. As I say, he survived, but I don't think he would have survived the following year. . . . I felt it was much safer for this kid to go and play in a men's league."

Almost overnight, prospecting below the juniors intensified. Ironically, Gus Badali, who is often blamed for starting the stampede for midget players, bemoans the fact that agents now have to go after fourteen-year-olds, and even then the pickings are meagre. "I would like to have five or six new clients of quality. It's difficult for me to get the quality. I'd even be happy with three, but with the competition that's out there. . . . Now it's even your uncles and your aunts—doesn't matter who they are—they can all do the job. . . . There is always somebody already there promising them that somebody will look after them."

When the WHA merged with the NHL in 1979, an important negotiating lever evaporated as jobs vanished and salary increases flattened out. All this spelled heightened competition for the seventy-four men then calling themselves agents. But the event that irrevocably changed the course of many hockey agents' lives was the disintegration of the sport's most powerful agency—Alan Eagleson's Sports Management.

Bill Watters and Rick Curran, Eagleson's lieutenants, had adjusted nicely to the changes brought about by the WHA and Gus Badali. By the time the WHA folded, Curran was already the controlling force in the annual Ontario midget draft, where junior teams selected fifteen- and sixteen-year-olds in a mini-version of the NHL lottery. But striking a non-binding agreement to represent a fifteen-year-old is one thing; holding that player to it until he is drafted up to five years later is another.

In order to keep these teenage clients, agents must show they "care" by having long, searching conversations with parents, and by being on call twenty-four hours, ready to chat about a player's grades and girlfriends. Agents often become surrogate fathers for homesick boys playing in another town or in another province.* Those who don't like this part of the job call it "baby-sitting."

Alan Eagleson considered recruiting and the subsequent care-taking of teenage prospects an unprofitable waste of time. He particularly objected to Curran continuing contact with youngsters even when it was clear that they weren't going to make it past the minors. "He just didn't understand that I would have to spend some money to look after them, even though we would never get a return on the investment," laments Curran. "To me, you get returns in other ways—your reputation."

Friction over the baby-sitting issue was exacerbated by Eagleson's unwillingness to lower his fees. By 1978, his 10 percent slice stood out in sharp contrast to the rest of the industry, who were charging 7 percent or less. "It used to be enough to walk in and say 'I represent Alan Eagleson's firm' to get a client," Curran says. "But the

---

* The Western Hockey League junior teams are spread out over the four western provinces. Players are drafted from a list drawn up every year. The Quebec Major Junior Hockey League has a similar system.

guys that were competing against us, they were doing a pretty good job. People weren't all that enthralled with paying an extra percentage to get Alan Eagleson, when it was apparent that they weren't getting him anyway."

As the '70s progressed, rancour crept into the relationship between Eagleson and Watters. Eagleson resented his employee's popularity with the players and increasingly abused him in front of players and business associates. "He was forever trying to discredit him or shit on him," says Curran, "which was a silly business practice, because if you hire somebody to be your assistant and be your representative, don't shit on him, praise him. He needed Bill to do the work for him, but he would never acknowledge Bill's efforts. For years, people always thought that Alan Eagleson did the contracts, but it was Bill that was doing them."

As the irritations mounted, Watters and Curran came to see their boss in a new and less flattering light. Once they had joked affectionately about Eagleson's profanity, his behind-the-back ridicule of friends and his cheapness with his employees. Now, when either Watters or Curran wanted to indicate that the other had stepped out of line, he'd simply say "Thanks a lot, Al!" or "That's just the way Al would have done it!" the latter spoken with mock approval.

Eagleson's legendary Christmas parties, where he behaved like a reincarnated Lenny Bruce, humiliating the wives of employees, players and friends, became less funny. "Hey you, where the fuck are ya going?" Eagleson would shout as one of the women headed to the bathroom. "Ya going to take a piss? A crap? Hey, can I come with you?" And when they returned, "Hey, did you wash your hands? Wipe yourself?" all accompanied by raucous guffaws. The women loathed it, and over the years more and more of them refused to attend.

In 1977, Eagleson and Watters flew to Pittsburgh to visit their seven clients there. Adolph Donadeo, a friend of the team, arranged a cocktail party in the Pittsburgh Press Club, which he managed. Everyone drank heavily, and at one point Eagleson knocked over a lamp and broke it.

"If you can do that, watch this!" shouted Rick Kehoe as he picked up a plate and fired it like a frisbee at the newly painted English hunting dog mural on the wall. Watters, Syl Apps, Annie Apps and Dennis Owchar watched in amazement as other players joined in and plates ricocheted off walls, fixtures and anything else that looked like a target.

"Ha, Eagleson, you couldn't hit that goddamn light!" shouted Kehoe pointing at the ceiling. "Oh yeah?" Eagleson retorted as he scored a direct hit on the chandelier. Food was splattered everywhere and wine dripped like blood down the walls. At first, the waiters cowered in the corners, hiding behind their trays. "Don't worry!" Eagleson assured them. "We'll pay for the damage." The waiters obligingly brought more ammunition.

The next day, a disgusted Bobby Orr called Watters in Toronto. "What were you two guys doing last night?" A thick-headed Watters admitted, "We had a party." "Well, you sure as hell had a party, you better get a hold of the guys at the Pittsburgh Press Club because there is over $10,000 worth of damage." Eagleson paid the bill and Donadeo hurriedly met with the powerful Press Club board to suppress the story.

Watters's and Curran's disenchantment with Eagleson might have remained just that for many more years had it not been for Bobby Orr. After Blackhawks owner Bill Wirtz brought the injured Orr to Chicago as a favour to Eagleson, the relationship between the two "brothers" sagged. "Al would phone Bobby daily when he was on top. But once Bobby went to Chicago and things weren't going so good, Al wouldn't even return his phone calls," recalls one of Eagleson's associates sadly. "I remember being very shocked. It was like Al was saying, 'I don't need you any more.'"

Bobby Orr retired as a player in 1977 and refused to draw any more of the $1.3-million salary the Blackhawks were paying him. Over the next eighteen months, he slowly began to realize that he was far from the millionaire Eagleson had promised. Not only that, but the mighty corporation, Bobby Orr Enterprises, started eleven years earlier, had few assets and no future.

Orr was personally in debt and, worst of all, Eagleson, who had once said Orr was "fixed for life," now told him it was all his fault for spending too much and ignoring Eagleson's sound investment advice. Only three years earlier, Eagleson had boasted that the company generated $400,000 annually; now it suddenly couldn't pay its bills. Angry at the turn of events, nearly broken inside over the loss of his career and hurt by Eagleson's clear message that he had become a liability, Orr walked away from the man he had once called a brother.

A few months later, on April 1, 1980, Bill Watters, Rick Curran and accountant Dave Snowdon left Sports Management. A frantic Eagleson paid a bonus to accountant Tom Brown to stay but he, too, left a few months later. Their departure decimated Eagleson's agency. For example, twenty-nine of Snowdon's thirty-one clients went with him. Eagleson's hurt, disappointment and anger enveloped everyone around him. "There was a lot of noise and smoke in the 65 Queen Street office," remembers Brown ". . . and it wasn't even worthwhile asking a sympathetic question, 'How is it going, Marvin?' It would just be a sigh and a shake of the head and a 'Don't ask, it's not fun.'"

Overnight, Alan Eagleson, having lost at least 100 of his 160 clients, had become a minor player in the agent business. He wondered publicly, like a tormented Hamlet, how Watters, a man he'd done so much for, could betray him. "He's the only guy I ever trusted with my negotiation notes. Here's my book on every guy who's a general manager. I gave him the keys to the kingdom. He had one big problem. He didn't know that when he took The Eagle's money ($100,000 including expenses last year) that The Eagle was the boss. I must say though, I don't learn. I can't hold a grudge. Guys have lined up to pee on me and, even if it happens again, what the hell, I don't care. I've got a long memory but I'm not malicious."

"Oh yes, I was *earning* $100,000," Watters agrees, "but

I wasn't being paid it." In fact, his salary for 1980 was $55,000 a year, $30,000 of it paid by Hockey Canada. Watters *had* signed an agreement with Eagleson in 1977 which called for him to be paid $100,000, but not until 1985.

As for his claim that he didn't hold a grudge, Eagleson systematically cut Watters off from his entourage of doctors, dentists, lawyers, jewellers, photographers and journalists. "It was unbelievable, the transformation that took place overnight." Watters mused years later about being shunned by a close friend who had been part of that group. "It was almost like the guy had been threatened with his life." Eagleson also threatened, or filed, several lawsuits over the next few years. The first came over a clause in Watters's 1977 contract that prohibited him from setting up his own agency if he left Eagleson. Watters ignored the clause and Eagleson sued. They settled out of court.

Eagleson thereafter boasted about the monetary penalties he imposed on his former employee, but the settlement was only $100,000 and spread over ten years. In comparison, the NHL clients Eagleson lost cost him, at the very least, $350,000 in annual contractual fees alone, and about the same again in money-management fees and other services. His law firm, Eagleson and Ungerman, also lost, as many of these former clients had been giving the firm all their legal work.

Though there's been much unpleasantness over the years —legal action and threats of legal action, legal process-servers at the door at 3:00 A.M. and veiled digs sent via the media—there's a wistfulness about Watters and Curran that suggests the extent of the magic, the bewitchment, that Alan Eagleson casts on those he touches. Despite all the anger, there's a definite sense of loss in their voices when they talk of Eagleson. "Al's next to a genius," Curran said recently. "He could have done something special, but his ego got too big and he got too greedy."

The shattering of Sports Management flung open the doors, and a stampede of new hockey agents rushed through them. No longer was Alan Eagleson an omnipotent force vacuuming up the choice players and leaving the rest of the field to chew on scraps. Watters's new company, Branada Sports Management, quickly became the most powerful agency, though it never approached Eagleson's former dominance.

Over the next few years, various agents vied to challenge Branada as the biggest in the business. The most persistent challenger was Don Meehan who won a fierce competition to represent Pat LaFontaine, the New York Islanders' first choice in the 1983 draft. The victory gave Meehan a foothold, and he went on to snag the number-one picks in both 1985 and 1986. Over the next two years, Meehan and Watters, between them, had twenty-two of the top forty-two first-round draft picks.

By June 1988, Don Meehan was breathing fiercely down Watters's neck. That year, the two men had five of the top seven first-rounders and eight of the top twenty-one. "It's impossible to get a whole lot now because there are more people in the business," grumbled Watters, when asked about the inroads made by Meehan. "But Meehan and I are pretty much it. We grudgingly acknowledge each other's existence." Watters admitted to having eighty NHL clients and Meehan forty-six.

At that point, Bill Watters had decided to move on, fed up with the business. "It wasn't recruiting any more, it wasn't prospecting . . . it was baby-sitting, plain and simple," he says, disgust evident in his voice. "You have to baby-sit. Hold their hand. Go to the rink, watch them play, talk to them after the game, tell them how well they played or how poorly they played, ad nauseam."

In 1989, Bill Watters sold out the agent side of Branada to Rick Curran, keeping promotion and event-management for himself. Curran has since begun "downsizing" to cope with the pressures the agency business puts on a young family and the terrific stress of maintaining his position with a dozen other agents snapping at his heels. He has cut back his trademark midget and junior recruiting, pared his client list and has moved to Philadelphia to reduce travel costs.

At the June 1990 NHL entry draft in Vancouver, Curran,

for the first time in fourteen years, didn't have a single client taken in the first round. He attended anyway for "therapy" but spent almost all his time huddled miserably with another agent, also bereft of clients. "It was the worst day in my life," he later admitted. Curran is consoled somewhat by the knowledge that his pruned business is actually netting more money and allowing him to spend more time on the clients he has.

Today, the undisputed heavyweight champion agent is Don Meehan. At the 1990 amateur draft, while former powerhouse Curran looked on, Meehan ushered an unprecedented 10 first-round picks to the arena floor to shake a general manager's hand and pull on an NHL team jersey. Even more important, 4 of the top ten belonged to him. In 1991, he had 9 first rounders and 5 of the top 10. Meehan now represents at least 75 NHL players, and his total clientele, including juniors and minor-league players, hovers around 115.

Meehan leaves nothing to chance. At any major hockey event, he strategically places himself at the choke point. At the 1989 Ontario Hockey League midget draft in Toronto, while other agents were fidgeting in the stands, hoovering the crowd with their eyes, Meehan, at rink level, stood calmly just inside the only entrance onto the floor. It wasn't the best viewpoint, but everyone could see him, and he could shake the hand of each draft choice, client or not, as he entered to receive his team's jersey.

At the 1990 NHL entry draft, Meehan's clients all wore badges identifying themselves with Newport Sports, his agency. They sat in a row anchored by Meehan, and when their names were called, the camera picked out each delighted player, his parents, his siblings and his agent. In the end, Meehan's face occupied the cameras more than any individual player.

Meehan's clients, particularly the young ones, are amazingly successful in incorporating the phrase "my agent Don Meehan" into radio, TV and print interviews. He's created such a camaraderie that his players are proud to be in his stable, as if being Don Meehan's client sets them above the rest and guarantees a happy and prosperous future.

Since 1983, Meehan has hosted a party on the eve of each NHL draft. The gathering has grown until it is now an event second only to the draft itself. In June 1990, it was held in the Hotel Vancouver's Pacific Ballroom and cost at least $15,000. There were five free bars and four huge food tables groaning under the load of hors d'oeuvres and mammoth lard sculptures, depicting heroic scenes from the Classics.

Admittance is by embossed invitation only, but judging by the crowd of roughly three hundred, precious few haven't been invited. Each entrant is greeted by a brace of badged Newport secretaries, uniformly young and attractive. About half the coaches, a good number of minor pro and junior coaches, a majority of the NHL general managers, dozens of scouts and even a few owners drop by. About the only group conspicuously absent are other agents, who all happen to be *very* busy elsewhere that night.

Apart from everything else, Meehan's instincts are terrific. He arrives when the party is already in full swing and is never seen loitering with nothing to do. He works the crowd like a Kennedy, sliding effortlessly in and out of conversations but never descending into the door-to-door-salesman hype that frequently afflicts his colleagues.

His handshake is dry, cool, just long enough to register sincerity but not so long as to be grasping or desperate. Lingering, overlapping, two-handed shakes are reserved for a client's parents or someone really important. "He's all over you like a boa constrictor," observes one of the rare parents not totally charmed. If there was such a thing as a three-handed shake, Meehan would be a master.

Meehan's twelve first-rounders are all badged, brushed, laundered, pressed and well-prepped. For eighteen- and nineteen-year-old boys they make an impressive amount of eye contact when they speak, and about half use the patented Meehan two-handed grip when they shake hands. They listen attentively when spoken to, respond intelligently (if virtually identically), and not one of them is drinking anything but pop.

Alone among the new crop of hockey agents, Meehan has genuine charisma. He isn't a handsome man, but he is tall and lean, with a Lincolnesque quality to his plainness. From a distance, Meehan's interchanges are all flashing teeth and pressing palms. Even his receding hairline works to his advantage, making an already friendly face seem more open and appealing. Up close, the conversations are intimate and informed; Meehan seems to know each player's family history down to the fourth generation.

Meehan's draft parties aren't just ego-building extravaganzas. For one thing, the hockey executives present can't be somewhere else, talking to his competitors' clients. Also, in addition to the other luminaries, there are dozens of scouts, who rarely get invited to anything. Their presence is a perfect example of Meehan's shrewdness. Developing a rapport with these men might just mean a client is picked twelfth instead of twenty-first— a difference of $100,000 or more when the contract is negotiated.

What Meehan does isn't new or unique, he just does it bigger and better than anyone else around. The secret of his success is quite simple, and he'll impart it to anyone who wants to know. It's the only time his cultured bonhomie slips to reveal the granite beneath. "I work harder than everyone else. That's all there is to it."

Agents are accustomed to each other's exaggerated claims: fifty NHL clients translates into ten actually playing for a franchise, ten drafted but playing in the minors, ten drafted but playing in the juniors and ten more who have been to a draft or two and await their big chance. When an agent talks about a "huge" contract with "big, really big numbers," the other agents know it means he wangled his client a 10 percent raise with a lot of improbable bonuses. But no one disputes Meehan's claim that he puts in more hours than anyone else. "Meehan could sell snow to the Eskimos," observes Guelph agent Rollie Thompson. "He is not married. He has 150 percent commitment to the job. That is his life. To some extent, to be in this business, if you want to be part of it, to be successful, you have to live and die it." •

The other agents, even the most envious, genuinely like Meehan. The best they can do to bring him down a notch is to wrinkle their brows with heavy concern and utter some variation of, "Yeah, Donny's doing great, but I'm really worried about him. He's getting in way over his head. There's no way that he can service that many clients. He's gonna burn himself out. It's the Bill Watters syndrome, you know." There is truth in their comments, and no one knows that better than Watters. "Donny's getting it now just like I did. Every time you turn your back someone says, 'Don't go with him. He can't look after you.' And all of a sudden they're spreading rumours about how you don't return phone calls."

Contrary to popular belief, most hockey agents are decent, honest men with a passion for the game and a genuine fondness for the youngsters playing it. But even the most cheerful and optimistic suffer from bouts of the corrosive melancholy endemic to their profession.

Agents compete in a snake pit where the only rules anyone respects are Darwin's. Unlike other sports, in hockey there are no regulations, not even a code of ethics for agents. Their friendships with each other are wary and guarded. The most honourable know that the minute they turn around, some colleagues eagerly circulate stories about poaching, questionable recruiting tactics and even, in a few cases, their sexual preferences.

Agents are classic middlemen. By definition, they get it from both sides. And, if they're doing their job properly, there will be numerous people who hate them at any given moment.

The biggest problem in the agent profession is not management or one's colleagues, but the clients themselves. Though today's players typically are more educated than their predecessors of the '50s and '60s, their basic life skills are often lacking. They are not stupid, but they *are* systematically trained to be submissive and obliging, except on the ice. Few have university degrees, and many haven't even finished high school. As a result, even into their thirties, hockey players are often short of the basic tools one expects young adults to possess.

A surprising undercurrent of disdain for the players runs through the conversation of many agents. "We're not dealing with a series of Einsteins," Alan Eagleson commented in 1984. "You have to realize these hockey players aren't rocket scientists," agrees another agent. "Try to get them to read books! All they know about is 'Secret Storm' [a soap opera]." The instant the words slip out of his mouth, the agent shrieks, "Your tape recorder isn't on, is it? The interview hasn't started, has it? This isn't on the record, is it?"

It isn't uncommon for agents to get phone calls in the middle of the night from distraught players who have been benched, traded, had their marriages break up or received an unpleasant letter from the IRS or Revenue Canada. Barry Beck, formerly with the New York Rangers, once phoned his agent to find out how to change a tire on his car. Another player called his agent for instructions on how to write a cheque. A more ambitious eighteen-year-old wanted his agent to help him start his own bank.

Agents' duties frequently go far beyond contract negotiation and money management. Early one December 1989 evening in New York, an agent starts packing up to begin his long drive home. His weariness is accented by the knowledge that he's got three games to see that weekend and his wife is on the verge of mutiny. When the phone rings he grimaces, yanks his much-abused ear, gets up as if to go, then mutters, "Ah what the hell!" and snatches it from the cradle. "Ricky, Ricky, how ya doin'!" he bellows with hearty insincerity. A hysterical voice issues from the phone.

"I gave you the name of that pecker doctor, did you go see her? C'mon kid," he soothes, "go see her, she'll talk you out of it. No, I don't know how they do these things but you aren't sick, this is just marriage. It happens, trust me, to everyone. Okay, so don't go see the doc, but why don't you lay off the weights and stuff for a little while, you're so goddamn fit you'd scare the balls off

Schwarzenegger. Listen, you got so many muscles your pecker's shitting itself cause it can't compete, so it's just gone into hiding."

The sound of shouting, laced with expletives, coming from the phone is clearly audible fifteen feet away. "Okay, okay! Calm down," pacifies the agent, who can't quite keep a smirk off his face. "I'm not making fun of this, but it's good to laugh a bit, ya know? Okay, so don't laugh but go see the goddamn doctor, will ya?"

One of Dave Snowdon's clients phoned him early on a Sunday for bail money after he had been picked up on a drunk driving charge. Snowdon explained that the banks were closed on Sunday, and besides, the player didn't have sufficient cash in his account anyway. "Just get it for me," his client demanded, expecting Snowdon to post bail out of his own money. "Go ask your father," Snowdon advised, "or go to jail. It will be good for you." He adds that the player is no longer his client. "He was just about done anyway."

In Toronto, an agent's four lines ring constantly. "Give your client fifteen minutes, his parents ten, a GM five and everyone else thirty seconds," is his motto. He reaches over to grab the phone after eight insistent peals. "Yeah, hi!" he shouts, face instantly stretching into a bear-like grin. Realizing, after a few sentences, that it isn't the player he expected, his voice drops several octaves. "Oh, it's you," he says sadly.

The voice at the other end of the line is loud, truculent and aggrieved. "Well, I'll tell you," the agent interrupts in deadly soft tones, "if the information that I got from training camp yesterday is accurate, then I am extremely disappointed in you. And very, very upset with you. You should be with yourself. You've embarrassed your family. You've embarrassed your teammates. And," he adds with finality, "you've embarrassed me."

Then the agent makes a Laurence Olivier transition from disappointment to anger with a pause for an exaggerated wink in between. "You are 243 fucking pounds with a fucking body fat of 19 percent! You are 50 goddamn pounds overweight! My pregnant wife is skinny beside you. Whattya mean you are working hard? Pah!

"I am so goddamn furious with you and very upset and personally hurt I'm almost prepared to wash my hands of you. You are twenty-two years old and I'm your third agent. I'm sure as hell going to be the last if I don't get a goddamn iron-clad promise, and don't fuck me around, that you will get down to—what do they want you to play at, 210? You can't wait two and a half goddamn months to do it. They will send you back to the fucking minors!"

Another long pause, and the sounds of whimpering emanate from the phone. "Now listen," says the agent with a "watch this" gesture. "I will try to get them not to void your contract. To agree only to suspend you for a definite period of time. You have to give me a firm undertaking that those thirty-three pounds are going to go. Talk to the doctor first and call me back."

He hangs up the phone gently, shakes his head, sinks into his antique leather chair and props a scruffy loafer against one corner of his chrome-and-glass desk. "The goddamn owners were with him [the GM] yesterday when this blimp walked by to go on the ice. The owners said to the GM, 'You paid that son of a bitch? You paid that guy all this money?' Well, he was almost beside himself, he phones me up and says, 'I almost lost my goddamn job.'

"I know what I would do if I was the GM. I would send him back to the minors. I'd say 'You bastard, you rot there for the whole year. Learn, you little prick. Go ride the buses again scum-bucket!'" He shakes his head again for several minutes and stares into the corners of the room, as if trying to figure out why he's in the business anyway.

The moment of introspection passes and the agent smiles. "Well, that's one down. I was soft on him. I can talk a lot tougher than that!"

It is an axiom in hockey that agents are sleazy and callous. In truth, most of them are not, but it's a perception that's hard to shake. The stories that circulate invariably feature a rotten agent versus well-meaning management or a gullible youngster. No one seems to know or care about all the times when the victim is the agent, not the player.

Don Reynolds, a bulky, effervescent man, makes an excellent living in insurance, but he became a hockey agent as a sideline because his sons played the game. He does well enough to carry a $5,500 snakeskin briefcase. He has a respectable client list of twenty-three NHL players and, in 1989, had eight first-rounders in the midget draft. But financially, he would do far better putting in a little overtime selling insurance.

Reynolds is a mature man, not dependent on hockey to make a living or to define his ego. Yet, during a conversation, a single page flutters out of his fax machine. He quickly scans it and returns to the conversation as if nothing has happened. A tiny tear rimming his left eye is the only clue that a piece of Don Reynolds has just died.

The fax is a form letter from an Ottawa lawyer-agent informing him that an eighteen-year-old player who has been with Reynolds for three years is no longer his client. The timing is particularly cruel, coming on the eve of the NHL draft, when the player has an excellent chance of going in the first round and signing a healthy contract. Though practices vary, as a rule, agents don't sign contracts with players until they've negotiated their first pro contract. Some sign a non-binding letter of intention with underage players, and others rely totally on a verbal agreement. "You never *really* know who your clients are until the cheque's in the mail," Reynolds says with a sad shake of his head.

"I'll tell you," says Gus Badali, "it's not worth it, because it costs money to look after a kid for two or three years, and the return is not as great as you think. Also, the loyalty of some of the players is not there, and they will not pay you down the road sometimes."

Rick Curran's "death of a thousand cuts" comes each morning while waiting for the mail. A typical day begins at 8:00 A.M. as he scans the paper for the hockey scores. But his eyes don't see the words and he doesn't taste his coffee until the mail arrives. If it's even ten minutes late, his blood pressure climbs.

By craning his neck, Curran can look around the corner at Nancy, his secretary. "She opens up the mail," Curran says, as if describing an execution. "I can't see the letters, but I can see if it has a letterhead on it or not. If she opens up something that doesn't have letterhead on it, I start to worry."

One day, Curran's morning ritual took a particularly unpleasant turn. Nancy looked up and glanced at Curran, who quickly said, "Who is it?" "You are not going to believe it," she replied. "Who is it?" Curran insisted. "You won't believe it," she repeated, handing him a single sheet. The letter was from a player who had been taken in the sixth round, and two years later his career was over when nobody wanted him. Curran called in favours and got him a contract with an NHL team. The next year he pulled in more favours and got the player traded to a different club, where the coach comes from the young man's home town.

The letter is professionally typed and brutally free of the slightest nicety. It's what Art Kaminsky calls "a KOgram"—a kiss-off-gram. "Dear Rick, After careful consideration of my best interests, I have decided to have someone else handle my affairs. As of this date forward, please know that you no longer represent me and please do not suggest that you do."

"I'm looking at it and going 'Holy shit!' It hurt! You just don't spend that much time going through the highs and lows of life with them to have something like this . . . you feel like saying, 'It's not worth it. The business isn't worth it.' It's nothing to do with the money."

"We all get those," says Rollie Thompson, "and it's awful. You kind of live and die with these kids. Ninety-two agents out there—probably a hundred now—you can't be everywhere. Some guy comes along and he snows them with another line. He's successful. Bang! They're gone."

Everyone loses clients, more than even the most honest and open care to admit. Several well-known players have switched agents four times during their careers.

One agent snidely calls them "repeaters." It isn't uncommon for the new agent to renegotiate the current contract and for the player to refuse to pay the old agent the remainder of his fee. Most agents just let it go, or settle for fifty cents on the dollar, figuring that a lawsuit will cause more damage to their reputations than the money is worth.

Losing clients under any circumstances is galling, but both Bill Watters and Gene McBurney have flown in to conduct negotiations with a general manager only to receive the news that someone else had just done the deal for their client. One agent recently received a form-letter dismissal from a player whose new agent told him to copy it out in his own handwriting. "But the stupid fuck filled in the blanks of the form letter and just put my name in the Dear (Agent) blank."

First-rounders, according to one agent, are often the worst. "I met this kid before he was drafted. It was all 'yes sir, no sir, thank you very much sir,'" says Art Breeze. "Then he gets picked in the first. Donny Meehan represents him and probably gets him a decent contract. A few months ago I get a call. He starts whining at me, 'This goddamn fuckin' Meehan won't return my phone calls. He's playing around with me. I should be brought up, this stupid coach sat me out a whole fuckin' game. It's a joke here, Meehan's a joke!'"

So Breeze told him to phone Meehan, and in the meantime filled his ear with a few "home truths." "It was a hell of a short trip from 'yes sir, no sir' to 'the world owes me a living.' I told that kid, 'Don't you ever think you are ever going anywhere with that attitude, you jerk!' The more I got involved trying to get this message across to this prima donna, spoiled, little pampered brat, the madder I got. My poor secretary had to close the door."

The two biggest problems agents face with young clients, next to over-inflated egos, are money management and parents—not necessarily in that order. Twenty years ago, many agents offered complete service packages for athletes, including bill-paying, budgeting and tax-filing. But the complexities of handling a player's financial affairs proved too troublesome and risky, and most dropped that part of the service or turned it over to accountants like Dave Snowdon. "I had two players who I would suggest have paid to their parents in excess of $150,000—gifts, trucks, cars, houses—and they haven't got any cash. Of course the complaint is, 'You haven't done much of a job for me, I don't have any cash.' Of course you don't have any cash, you gave your parents $150,000—after tax—which means you have to make $300,000 in order to have $150,000. So why don't you go to your parents and get it?"

At the 1989 entry draft in Minneapolis, two eighteen-year-olds from the Toronto area, both touted to go in the first round, sat beside each other and dreamed aloud about their riches to be. "Dad's got this big loan and he keeps saying we have to move. When I sign my contract I'm gonna pay it off and maybe deliver the news by helicopter. Not bad, eh?"

Snowdon says it is a touching but frequently disastrous story. "You have to protect the players against the parents. It's almost like the parents expect it. I've been in situations at the draft, the player gets drafted and it's almost like the parents say, 'Now we can get paid back for everything we have done for the kid.' When I got a CA degree my parents didn't come to me and say, 'Now you have a degree that will guarantee us a good living forever.' It's funny the way hockey parents are."

But not all agents agree that full service is risky, low-return and frustrating. "It's a cop-out on their part," Art Breeze states vehemently. "They don't get burned. It's an absolute, colossal cop-out when they say that . . . it's a colossal indication of their non-professionalism and becomes more and more oriented towards the parasitical greed type of thing." Breeze argues that young players need financial planning advice even more than they need their contracts negotiated. "Generally speaking, your longevity in the NHL from a peak earning period is four years, and getting shortened each year. It behooves an individual to make sure that his short- and long-term interests are protected, and it is very difficult to put an old head on young shoulders."

The board of directors of Breeze's Pro-Rep Entertainment Consulting Group Inc. includes a chartered accountant, two lawyers, a psychologist, a plastic surgeon and a senior executive for a motion-picture company. Together, the group offers everything from stress-management to the handling of endorsements. Breeze, like most of his peers, charges 3 percent for contract negotiation and 5 percent for his whole package. Having started in 1985, and concentrating solely in western Canada, Breeze currently represents 186 players, 66 of whom have professional contracts with the NHL or minor pro teams.

"Mostly garbage from the late rounds," sneers one agent. But before long, the late-rounders may mostly be first-rounders, and Art Breeze the next super-agent. In the past two years alone, 40 of the 77 western players drafted by the NHL—including 3 first-rounders—have been represented by Breeze.

An agent might survive hours on the phone, soul-numbing travel and the demands, hopes and fears of parents and players, but he still won't be successful unless he knows how to handle general managers. GMs treat agents with the kind of aggravated tolerance a pregnant woman does hemorrhoids. While most are prepared to admit that Alan Eagleson has "done an awful lot for hockey," few will concede that agents in general do anything for players but make them greedy, needy and spoiled.

Agents, on the other hand, view general managers as intriguing or irritating obstacles to be "jerked off," "massaged," "stroked" and "finessed." A lot of them like this part of the game more than any other. There are only six GMs that the majority of agents will agree are "gentlemen" or "real class acts." Despite that, every agent works hard to develop a friendly relationship with all of them, playing the malleable ones off against the ball-busters.

When it comes to contract negotiations, agents are like banks, and their currency is promises, favours or concessions. When an agent is having difficulty closing a contract, he reaches into the vault, hauls out a deal and reminds the GM how he "saved his ass" or didn't "push him into a corner on bonuses" or didn't "break his nuts over the option clause."

The best hockey agents know that it makes no difference how *they* look coming out of a deal, it's how the other guy *feels*. "It doesn't matter if he walks away from the deal figuring he's screwed you," Rick Curran says. "That's good because he's going to be more than eager to talk business the next time. Let him save face, that's what you've got to do. Build that into every deal and you've got it made."

Good agents are careful to include triumphs for the other guy in every contract. Sometimes that involves proposing a $25,000, fifty-goal bonus for a rookie defenseman who hasn't ever been near the opposing net. Deletable clauses like these make everyone feel good. The GM gets to red-line it after fierce argument from the agent. And the player can feel good that his agent had enough faith in him to include the clause in the first place.

Hockey agents have to drive the best bargain for every client, and they have more ruses than Houdini to achieve that. One particular agent, knowing that three friends have been drafted from the same junior team, uses that fact to jack up the salary of his own client, who was selected considerably later than the other two. "On the junior salaries, what we have to do is make sure we balance them all out," he confides to the general manager. "We gotta make 'em all exactly alike. These little peckers are going to stand around and talk to each other, and we don't need dissension among them."

The GM murmurs in agreement as the agent slides in for consideration his lowest-drafted client. "Signing bonus? Even on the bottom guy? You're not going to make the signing bonus on the bottom guy?" he repeats in mock amazement and gratitude. "You don't have to, but I know you want to be fair."

Minutes later the same agent is talking to the general manager of another team. The situation is similar, but this time his client is the higher choice. "Yes! Yes! Don't give me any shit about how they're going to feel about each other. That's your problem. My guy gets the higher contract and that's the bottom line."

Since the salary explosion following Bruce McNall's signing of Wayne Gretzky, the $7-million Brett Hull contract and the NHLPA decision to make salaries public, a great many relationships between agents and GMs have been badly eroded. The cause is an increasing number of agents who are lobbying to have deals renegotiated.

Renegotiating can produce big bonanzas for players who suddenly come into their own a year into a three-year contract, or who discover that a low-scoring teammate is earning $75,000 more than they are. "I've got this guy, he's worth a million dollars and making $515,000, which a year ago was absolutely great fucking money, but today it is not," pointed out one agent in the summer of 1990.

"Now here's my problem, I have always been dead against walking in and asking for a contract to be renegotiated. As far as I am concerned, if I do a deal, I have to live up to it. If the deal turns sour, if I busted my fucking leg—I'm not going to ask the team if I can give the money back—I want the fucking money.

"But I work for this player. I tried to convince him that is not necessarily the way to do it. But if I don't do it, he will hire someone else. So, I say 'fine,' I have to do it. Now I'm faced with having to do it with the GM but do it in such a fashion as to get him to understand that it could be a win-win for him."

The agent pauses and adds hopefully, "Maybe he is smart. Maybe he is thinking of redoing this too."

Using every wile and artifice in his repertoire, the agent attempts to cajole a new deal out of the general manager. He fails. The player turns in a dismal 1990-91 performance. The team finishes near the cellar. The player is traded. The agent loses a client and the general manager is fired. Otherwise, they all live happily ever after.

Chapter 10

No Pain No Gain

Despite the crisis over the departure of Bobby Orr, Bill Watters and Rick Curran, Alan Eagleson's career blazed on into the '80s. Every day he seemed to strike a deal, make an announcement or shift an alliance that made him richer, more respected and more powerful. "His shadow eclipses those of both John A. Ziegler Jr., 50, president of the NHL, and Dr. Gunther Sabetzki, 69, of West Germany, president of the International Ice Hockey Federation, not to mention the NHL's club owners," *Sports Illustrated* concluded in 1984. "Almost every deal and dollar transaction between any two or more of the many groups that make up hockey—individual players, the NHLPA, individual NHL clubs, the league as a whole, the bodies controlling the sport in the Soviet Union, Sweden and other countries, the sponsors and advertisers worldwide—must pass, one way or another, through Eagleson."

Not only was Alan Eagleson hockey's pre-eminent figure, but he had also become a business and political heavyweight, with the Prime Minister's ear, easy access to some of North America's largest corporations and a personal wealth some estimate has reached $50 million.

Unfortunately, the National Hockey League Players' Association, under Eagleson's direction has not experienced the same good fortune.

It is a hockey truism accepted by friend and foe alike that Alan Eagleson's hard-nosed bargaining emancipated and enriched hockey players. But the simple fact is that the National Hockey League Players' Association, as a labour organization and negotiating entity, has been largely ineffective since the day it was formed in 1967. There have been gains, ranging from the abolition of the detested "training table"* to pension increases and the creation of a total disability plan, but these advances are paltry compared to what the players have given up in return.

Key advances, like salary improvements and the 1974 elimination of the reserve clause,† were not negotiated by the NHLPA but forced on the League by outside events like expansion, the formation of the WHA, threats of anti-trust suits and, lately, Wayne Gretzky's 1988 eight year contract for $20 million with the Los Angeles Kings. Even pension improvements, long thought of as shining examples of the NHLPA's bargaining prowess, have turned out to be one-sided compromises and giveaways made by the NHLPA when the stakes were far higher than the players realized.

Hockey owners have always been as flint-edged and parsimonious a group as exists in professional sport. Their basic nature wasn't instantly transformed the minute Alan Eagleson and the NHLPA appeared on the scene. They continued business as usual, dealing out the scraps and keeping the meat for themselves. Over the past twenty-five years, Eagleson and the NHLPA have won only what the owners have been willing to give up,

---

* On road trips, players would be fed as a group with a single meal organized in advance by the teams. Players hated it, because choices were limited or non-existent.

† The reserve clause had changed very little since Jim Norris's day. Once a player signed an NHL contract, he was bound to that team until he was traded, even after retirement.

and in some cases, not even that.

The tone of NHLPA bargaining was set on June 8, 1967, the second day of the association's existence, when Eagleson and NHL secretary Charles Mulcahy announced the fruits of the first owner-player negotiation session. The players won just two points: payment for exhibition games played in NHL cities between NHL teams, and a 50 percent increase—from $10 to $15—in the per diem rate for meals and sundry expenses on road trips. Eagleson hinted at "certain other matters" discussed but wouldn't reveal them.

The next day, the NHL unilaterally increased the League's minimum wage to $10,000, an apparently generous sum compared to baseball's $8,000. Clarence Campbell didn't mention the NHLPA, but nobody doubted that the credit belonged to Eagleson.

Jubilant players hailed the concessions as major victories for their fledgling association, but the facts suggest otherwise. Though they didn't seem to know it, the players had never been in a stronger position. A major selling point, made by the NHL owners to the new expansion teams, and repeatedly stressed during private negotiations, was the docility of hockey players. Any threat of a labour disruption might have jeopardized the expansion and the $12 million in franchise fees payable to the six original teams.

The owner most likely to balk at the sign of any player problems was the cantankerous Jack Kent Cooke. The Los Angeles Lakers basketball team owner wanted to fill empty dates in his Coliseum with a hockey franchise, but he was incensed by the inequity of the expansion draft and the number of players the original six would be protecting. Few doubted that Cooke would walk away if he were pushed too far. With him would go the long sought-after $3.6-million national television contract, which depended on a franchise going to Los Angeles.

Any concession wrung from the NHL owners was cause to celebrate, but, in light of the players' real leverage, the advances were pathetic. The much-touted increased minimum wage must have had the owners snorting into their whiskies. According to Clarence Campbell himself, only one player was earning less than $10,000 anyway. The new minimum wage was made even more farcical because, in that same year, the number of regular-season games increased from seventy to seventy-four. The League also added another playoff round with no additional remuneration for players, despite the fact that the playoffs are far more lucrative for the owners than regular-season games. In essence, the new minimum wage represented a net decrease for the players.

The concessions Alan Eagleson won for the players that first year were worth less than $100,000.* In contrast, the owners gained $18.5 million in expansion fees, broadcast revenue and additional income. The players didn't even win the basic right to have copies of their own contracts.

These first critical NHLPA negotiations were startlingly similar to those Alan Eagleson had had with Eddie Shore a few months earlier. Much was at stake but little was achieved. Small advances were ballyhooed as earthshaking, and the players went away happy with a pittance. It was a pattern that would be repeated many times in the future.

The owners remained as obdurate as ever about dispensing even a sliver of the real money. In September 1967 the League demonstrated this unequivocally. Eddie Shack made a beer commercial for the Carling brewery which Clarence Campbell promptly outlawed, citing the NHL's rule forbidding players from endorsing either cigarettes or alcohol. Somehow, it never bothered the League that Molsons, owner of the Montreal Canadiens, made most of their money in beer and advertised the product on hockey broadcasts.

The first four expansion years were excellent ones for

---

* The per diem cost the franchises $3,500 per team, for a League total of $42,000. On the surface, remuneration for exhibition games was a considerable advance, but only half of those games were against other NHL teams, and even fewer were in NHL cities. The rest were against minor-league teams, and the players received nothing for them.

the NHL owners, as the new NBC television contract and increased attendance zoomed League revenue from $892,000 per team to over $2.2 million. Incredibly, despite the natural inflationary pressures of expansion and the advent of the NHLPA, the players' percentage of the take actually *declined* by 1.4 percent. The League increased its gross revenue by 15.6 percent from 1969-70 to 1970-71, while players' salaries and benefits increased by only 9 percent. It was a situation Clarence Campbell called "gratifying" in his 1971 annual confidential report to the board of governors.

The true state of affairs may have been much worse. The U.S. Department of Justice, Anti-Trust Division, calculated that gross revenue from American teams alone in 1971 was $40 million, almost twice as much as the NHL admitted.

Part of the reason the National Hockey League Players' Association lost ground during this period was that their executive director, Alan Eagleson, was simultaneously pursuing at least four other highly demanding careers. He was part-time executive director, devoting, by his own estimate, between 20 and 50 percent of his work week to the job. In addition to his NHLPA duties, Eagleson operated the largest player agency in the sport. His private businesses included the burgeoning Bobby Orr Enterprises and a host of other new companies he either owned or controlled. He was also still a partner in a rapidly growing law firm and deeply immersed in politics as president of the Ontario Progressive Conservative Association, a job he took on the year after the NHLPA formed. "He's one person doing the job of five people," says a proud and awe-struck Marvin Goldblatt, his longtime associate.

Not only did Alan Eagleson do the work of five, but he was also the consummate family man for his children, Allen, then nine, and Jill, six. "My family is very important to me," he told George Gross, associate sports editor of the Toronto *Telegram*, in 1971. "But they realize that from Monday till Thursday I'm a very busy man. . . . But on Friday I pick up the family at 4 p.m. and off we go to the country. In the winter it's skiing near the home we bought on Georgian Bay, and in the summer it's swimming, fishing and water skiing. In addition every year I take a four week vacation."

A part-time executive director, particularly one as capable as Eagleson, might have been effective if the NHLPA had built up suitable staff and administrative back-up. But between 1967 and 1972, without even a part-time secretary, Eagleson was responsible for all the filing, phoning, arranging, organizing of meetings, banking and, of course, the essential jobs of researching and negotiating. No one could have done it all, let alone on a part-time basis.

When Mike Cannon was hired as NHLPA office manager in 1971, he found a chaotic mess. "There was a lot of—what's a good word?" he says, delicately searching for the least damning phraseology. "Flying by the seat of your pants type of thing. They had nobody working fulltime. Didn't have an office type of thing. It was out of Al's office—his law firm at Blaney, Pasternak on Bay Street. It was fine from a superficial—that's the wrong word—but from a loose way of doing things. It was fine, but there was no administration at all."

An argument can be made that the association didn't initially have the money to hire additional staff. But in 1971, Eagleson negotiated a $100,000 annual fee from the Licensing Corporation of America, which sold the NHLPA logo to various corporations for advertising and endorsements. That money was ear marked for the players' pension plan, but he could have easily devoted a portion of it to staff.*

The NHLPA remains a barebones operation to this day, despite a 1990 budget of more than $3 million, because that's the way Alan Eagleson wants it. "The other sports associations have payrolls that run into millions each

---

* The Licensing Corporation of America's deal with the NHLPA amounted to about "1.5 million over ten years," according to Eagleson. NHL Pension Society documents show that no money has been contributed by the NHLPA to the pension fund.

year. Our payroll consists of 2.6 persons," he wrote to NHLPA members in March 1989. "I am very cost conscious and our 22-year history shows that we manage reasonably well on a tight budget. I have been a part-time executive director because the NHLPA decided 60% of my time was sufficient. The facts prove that the decision was correct."

But the facts actually suggest otherwise. Because the players have been consistently unprepared to negotiate with the owners, the pennies saved on staff have cost the players millions.

Alan Eagleson can fly by the seat of his pants better than any man alive, making decisions on the run and amid confusion and pressure that would wilt lesser mortals. But no one could handle all of his various jobs *and* create a foundation on which to build a strong players' association. During the NHLPA's critical early years, Eagleson should have been devoting his time to educating the membership, developing negotiating strategies, outlining long-term goals and building a strike fund. Even more important, he should have been systematically attacking the NHL's many practices that were in clear violation of anti-trust laws.

When Marvin Miller became head of the Major League Baseball Players' Association in 1966, the owner-player relationship was similar to that in hockey. "If it weren't so tragic, it would be a comedy, because most of the time, their time was taken up with trivia. The big complaint was there was no water fountain in the bull pen. And some of the benches in the various bull pens needed sanding because you would get splinters sitting there."

Miller travelled endlessly around the league educating the players about their rights and designing an association structure to support their long-term aspirations. He made the players realize that, though they were playing a game, they were also working for a living and working in a "damned profitable" industry. He taught them what unionism means and how essential it was to remain united. He strengthened the office structure, bringing in

bright young talent from other fields, and began building
consensus on future action. Most important, he initiated a
strike fund and, though he didn't advocate striking, he
assiduously prepared the players mentally and financially
for that possibility.

A strike is any labour organization's ultimate weapon.
Without the potential to stage one, labour is impotent.
The NHLPA has never set aside a strike fund, nor have
the players ever been psychologically prepared to strike.
Today, hockey players still believe, as their baseball
brethren did twenty-five years ago, that a strike will kill
the game. The owners know this and exploit it unmerci-
fully at every opportunity.

From the beginning, players were concerned about the
multiplicity of Eagleson's roles and the amount of time
he devoted to the job of organizing the NHLPA. Glenn
Hall remembers Eagleson visiting St. Louis in 1968 and
telling the team he needed more money to run the association. Several players told him, "We are prepared to
give you more money, if you drop being an agent."
Eagleson assured them, "Okay, if I get that extra money,
I'll drop it." Hall scoffs. "Well, he didn't drop it. When it
was brought up to him he says, 'Oh no, what I said was
that I would not solicit people.' He didn't say that. Once
again, you lose a little bit of respect for him, because *I*
heard what he said."

If a player pressed too hard with questions or criticisms, Eagleson beat him into submission, not with his
fists but with his tongue. Resilient and combative as
hockey players are in their element, they have never
been a match for Alan Eagleson, who has a Freudian
knack, like old-time general managers, for unerringly
penetrating a player's deepest insecurities.

Eagleson's verbal object lessons are typically directed
at journeyman players who are naturally most concerned
about working conditions. Because their careers are short
and salaries low, even minor improvements in fringe
benefits can make a big difference to their future standard of living. "As soon as I questioned him," recalls
North Stars tough guy Basil McRae, "it was like he

jumped right on me. I started stuttering. He actually did intimidate me in front of my teammates and in front of his colleagues.

"Guys are scared, and they don't want to sound stupid. He talks at such a high level, he's almost got to communicate to hockey players at the hockey player's level. I'm not saying hockey players are stupid, but we definitely cannot talk or communicate at a lawyer's level, his lingo. So we are paying him to represent us. He's actually working for us, but he makes it feel like we are his labourers and he's the president of some big company. It's like we are scared of him."

The stories of how Alan Eagleson humiliated players like Basil McRae were passed around the League, ensuring that any prospective challenger would rethink his position.

Eagleson was never shy about taking on the superstars, either. "He embarrassed me," former NHLPA president Phil Esposito once admitted reluctantly. "If I asked a question he'd say, 'For christ sakes don't be so stupid!' in front of everybody. Al's smart. He knows if he does that to me or to a Bobby Clarke, the other guys are going to say, 'Holy shit, I'm not opening *my* mouth.'"

In the early NHLPA years, the players were so grateful to have an association it didn't occur to them to question its effectiveness. But the other agents who were quickly moving into hockey had no qualms about criticizing the NHLPA or Alan Eagleson.

In 1970, Pro Sports Inc., a reputable Manhattan-based agency already established in baseball and basketball, represented a solid core of NHL players, including Brad Park, Walt Tkaczuk, Vic Hadfield and Jean Ratelle of the Rangers and Murray Oliver of the Minnesota North Stars. To the surprise and disgust of the two partners, Marty Blackman and Steve Arnold, both the Rangers and the North Stars categorically refused to talk to them when their clients' contracts came up for negotiation. Arnold appealed to the NHLPA for help, and Eagleson told him he was on his own. "It was as if the Players' Association didn't even exist," stresses Blackman today.

Arnold advised his clients not to attend training camp until the clubs agreed to negotiate. When the Rangers proposed that Eagleson and Clarence Campbell be appointed as arbitrators, Arnold was flabbergasted. "How can Eagleson arbitrate when he's a competitor of ours? For example, he can come back next year and tell a player like Park that he could have done better for Park on a contract if Brad had gone to him and not to us." Arnold's partner Marty Blackman added, "Our objection to Campbell is obvious. As for Eagleson, the good of the group—that is the NHL Players' Association—does not coincide with the good of the individual. He represents both the association and individuals."

Bob Woolf, another agent already active in other sports, had similar problems representing Derek Sanderson and Gerry Cheevers of the Bruins. The experience of these and other agents fuelled the first groundswell of public criticism of Eagleson and the NHLPA.

Eagleson responded to the growing criticism on January 17, 1971, by abruptly resigning as head of the Players' Association. In his place, he appointed Mike Cannon, the office manager, a twenty-four-year-old recent university graduate in French Literature. Cannon had been filing, writing letters and organizing meetings for the NHLPA for less than two months at that point. "My decision was made some time ago," said Eagleson about stepping down. "And I have quietly interviewed about fifteen people for the position." Cannon had no experience in labour, hockey or law, but Eagleson promised to be available for consultation.

Less than two weeks later, Eagleson was back on the job, claiming it had all been a misunderstanding, even though at least three highly respected reporters had independently announced his resignation. George Gross had even written a lengthy feature article extolling the virtues of the departing executive director.

It was the first time Eagleson unveiled this tactic for dealing with dissent. Between 1970 and 1990 he publicly threatened to resign from the NHLPA at least eight times. Each time he subsequently explained that the NHLPA had begged him to remain. "I've offered to resign a dozen times just to get rid of the job." He usually mentioned that his "standing letter of resignation" was on file at the NHLPA offices.

In 1972, dogged by criticism of his comportment at the Russia-Canada series and of his attitude toward the newly formed World Hockey Association, Eagleson brought up the subject of retirement once again. "There's not enough in it for me," he told the Toronto *Star*. "I can make $75,000 a year handling Orr's accounts without half the trouble some of the others give to me. The players are after me all the time and some of the requests are really unreal. This job is really getting to be too much. It's getting to be too big a job. I think I'm going to quit. The players don't need me any more. They're all set. Besides, Marvin Miller, the head of the baseball players association, gets something like $85,000 a year. How can you compare that with my [$20,000] salary."

This second bout of resignation talk was punctuated by disconcerting rumours that Alan Eagleson was going to become the next president of the NHL. "For openers, I'm just not interested," he stated categorically in March 1972. "Secondly, I couldn't afford to take the job. They'd never pay me what I'd ask. And thirdly, they'd never give me authority I want." Later that month he softened his unequivocal stance dramatically when Bill Brennan, of the Detroit *News*, asked if he wanted Clarence Campbell's job. "Not as president. If they were to make me commissioner, yes. But not as president."

The "Alan Eagleson for president" rumours, coupled with the "I'm resigning" fan dance, kept NHLPA members offbalance. Always lurking beneath the surface was the unsettling possibility that they could lose their key man at any time, or worse, that he might decamp to the opposition.

Amid the confused leadership and administrative chaos of those early years, the NHLPA formulated a negotiating strategy that cost the players dearly. Essentially, the Players' Association elected to trade freedom of movement, equitable grievance procedures, arbitration reform, a cut of broadcast revenue and an improvement in the playoff split—all advances made by other sports associations—for meagre improvements in the pension plan and medical benefits.

This strategy is riven by two basic flaws. The first is that the players do not control or even have any input into the pension plan. The pension is run by the owners, who feel no obligation to disclose any more than the most basic information to the players.

Twenty years after the formation of the NHLPA, hockey players still had no idea what was in the pension fund, what the investments were or even what the return was. At collective-bargaining meetings in February 1986, Larry Latto, legal counsel for the NHLPA, tried to press NHL president John Ziegler for "the co-operation of the NHL to supply the necessary information that NHLPA is entitled to under law." Ziegler blandly responded that he didn't have to tell the NHLPA anything. ". . . the present pension fund is fully funded and it is audited each year which is the extent of the NHL's obligation to the NHLPA."

What has happened to the NHL pension fund is the biggest sucker-play in the history of professional sport. Five times—in 1971, 1975, 1979, 1982 and 1986—the NHLPA gave up the chance for freer movement of players in exchange for enhancements to pension benefits. Even then, the players' gains came, not from the owners, but from the surplus in the pension fund, which resulted from the players' own deposits in the '50s and the '60s.

Since 1957, when the fund had a $1.5-million surplus, the League has been dipping into it and taking money out in the form of "dividends," "disbursements" and "contribution holidays." The surplus was large enough to allow the owners to fund virtually all the pension increases the players have won in their twenty-four-year history of collective bargaining. After 1972 what the pension surplus didn't pay for the players' own contributions from international hockey did.

Until 1969, the owners were supposed to be matching the players' contributions to the pension plan. That year, the owners agreed to pay for the plan entirely. But the players didn't realize that the pension surplus already amounted to at least $2 million. According to the pension agreement, that money belonged to the players. But the owners used at least a portion of the surplus to fund this gain. In 1986, Eagleson negotiated a $250,000 retirement bonus to be paid at age fifty-five to players with 400 or more games to their credit.* Again, the owners simply allocated a percentage of the surplus already in the fund to pay for it. Not a penny came from new money and not a whisper of protest came from the NHLPA.

The second major flaw in the NHLPA's pension negotiations is the apparent failure to understand the present value of money; essentially, a dollar paid today is far more valuable than a dollar paid twenty years from now. The players and their executive director, Alan Eagleson, didn't seem to realize that the huge pension improvements they negotiated in 1979 and 1986—reportedly worth $8 million and $12 million respectively—would be worth rather less than their face value when paid thirty years down the road.

In 1972, the annual amount of pension paid per year played increased from $350 to $500. To begin with, this increase was funded, not out of the owners' profits, but out of the players' own efforts in international hockey. Even worse, its current cost was tiny. In order to pay for that $150 increase at age forty-five, only $27 per player had to be deposited from the supposedly vast international revenues.†

In order to pay for the 1986 $250,000 retirement bonus, only $16,871 per eligible player had to be set aside in 1986. If 20 percent of the players then in the NHL were to make the magic 400-game mark, the League

---

* It only applied to players active from that year onward.

† The series was constantly extolled as a great money-maker for hockey and the first time the game, as a whole, earned anything significant from television. But confusion over the figures remains rampant. Some CAHA and Hockey Canada officials insist that Hockey Canada netted as little as $40,000 from the vast TV revenues, while Eagleson claims $1.1 million was turned back to the organization. In fact, financial statements indicate that only $414,889 was actually turned over to Hockey Canada.

would have had to set aside only $1.36 million to cover the commitment when the first players claimed their bonus in approximately thirty years time.*

Even Eagleson himself admitted that the owners bene-fited more from these various pension "improvements" than the players. "The agreement [in 1972] we made gave the owners a free ride for 1-1/4 years," he said, referring to the fact that the owners were using international hockey profits to lower, and in some years eliminate, their contributions to the pension plan.

Despite a potent public image, the NHLPA has been a flaccid entity throughout its history. The starkest example of its weakness is found in the birth, seven-year exis-tence and death of the World Hockey Association. During the WHA's brief, tumultuous life, from 1972 to 1979, hockey players, for the first time, increased their salaries in proportion to the owners' revenues. In the WHA's first year of operation, competition between the two leagues jumped NHL average salaries from $28,500 to $44,000.

By 1977, the average NHL salary had rocketed to $96,000, despite several years of sagging attendance, lack of interest from corporate advertising and the League's complete failure to boost American interest in the game or make any inroads in the big television markets.† The tripling of player salaries during the WHA years clearly demonstrated what even limited free agency could yield.

Though there were numerous golden opportunities to strike deals with the owners that would benefit players for decades, salaries, driven exclusively by market condi-tions, were the only major advances.

The WHA was the greatest boon to player well-being since the invention of the protective aluminum cup, yet Alan Eagleson was curiously ambivalent towards it, one moment giving it his full support and the next appearing

---

*   The NHL allocated $12 million of the accrued surplus to fund this benefit. But be-cause the benefit will cost about one-quarter of that amount, there appears to be a strategy to set the money aside to build future surpluses.

†   In comparison, the NFL's average salary was $55,000, baseball's $76,000 and basketball's $143,000.

ready to cut it off at the knees.

"The WHA appears to have a solid foundation which will make it the greatest thing ever to happen to the hockey player," he said late in 1971, after meeting with WHA officials. Two months later he'd reversed his opinion. "I'm not as bullish on the WHA as I was three months ago. I'm not as convinced as before that the WHA will get off the ground in the twelve cities that they have named. Only five or six are sufficiently solid to offer contracts."

By March 1973, everything was rosy again. "The best thing that happened to the players was the competition the NHL is getting from the World Hockey Association," he proclaimed. "We have to pray that the WHA continues." Eighteen months later, however, he was reading the WHA's last rites. "I'm reluctant to even talk contract with most franchises and rest assured the only contracts I will allow clients to sign will have to be personal services deals that tie the owner to fulfilling the deal." The WHA lasted for four more years.

The emergence of the rival league gave the NHLPA the perfect opportunity to tackle the NHL owners' total control over the players. The linchpin of this control was the repressive reserve clause, which dated back to the formation of the NHL in 1917. Since 1969, Alan Eagleson had complained regularly about it, but he had never launched legal action even though other sports had successfully challenged their own versions of the clause in court.

Then, in 1972, the WHA swept in and totally ignored the reserve clause, stripping players willy-nilly from every NHL franchise. Technically, those players were in violation of their contracts and thus barred from competing in professional hockey—according to the NHL. A welter of back-and-forth lawsuits erupted which quickly tilted in the WHA's favour when a powerful ally intervened—the United States Department of Justice.

The department's anti-trust division had been monitoring hockey since 1968, when the backers of a Baltimore expansion bid had complained about restraint of trade because the NHL had awarded a franchise to St. Louis instead, "a bald and concerted act by the NHL to 'bail out' [Jim] Norris and [Arthur] Wirtz from their $4 million investment in the antiquated St. Louis arena," the investigating officer summarized.

Interestingly, the Americans were not the only ones concerned about the NHL's monopolistic practices. "Canadian authorities have been urging us (informally) to look into this for some time," Richard McLaren, the U.S. assistant attorney general wrote to his superior.

In 1971, the Department of Justice launched a full-scale investigation into hockey.* After a little more than one year of investigation, the Department of Justice concluded that virtually everything upon which the NHL was based—from the draft through to the joint-affiliation agreement with minor-league teams—constituted a violation of one or more sections of the powerful Sherman Anti-Trust Act. "Entry by a new league and by a new team without approval by the NHL seems virtually impossible. Furthermore, as a result of this domination, hockey players are severely restricted in negotiating with or shifting teams or leagues. By breaking the ties which bind all hockey to the dominant NHL, it is hoped that players will be able to negotiate more freely permitting the formation of new teams and leagues."

Campbell sandbagged the Justice investigators at every turn. Even so, by September 1972 he had run out of arguments, and anti-trust officers visited League offices in New York and Montreal. Before they arrived, Campbell instructed NHL lawyers to comb the files and remove key documents from 1965 and 1972—the expansion and WHA formation years—which contained the most evidence of restraint of trade. The furious investigators assured Campbell they would be back for those papers.

As the Department of Justice prepared its case, the

---

* Clarence Campbell always maintained that hockey was not subject to American anti-trust laws because it was a Canadian game headquartered in a Canadian city (Montreal). The anti-trust division decided that because 458 of the NHL's 546 games per season were played in the United States, the department could launch action against the League.

WHA launched its own private anti-trust action in August 1973, bringing the number of major and minor lawsuits between the two leagues to twenty-three. In November, the Department of Justice filed a brief in support of the WHA, and suddenly things looked very bad for the NHL. Then Judge Higginbottom of Pennsylvania issued a temporary injunction, forbidding the NHL to enforce the reserve clause. At that moment, the players, at least in the U.S., were completely free and theoretically could sign with any team or any league. If either one of the lawsuits were successful, the very fabric of the NHL would disintegrate.

In a bid to fend off the government action, the NHL sued for peace, offering to settle with the WHA. In August 1974, the League agreed to pay $1.7 million in restraint-of-trade damages to the WHA and promised to institute fifteen inter-league exhibition games. Both leagues dropped all outstanding lawsuits against each other, and the NHL agreed to stop interfering with or penalizing minor-league teams that negotiated with the WHA. Finally, to placate the Department of Justice, Clarence Campbell unilaterally announced the abolition of the reserve clause. It was replaced by an only slightly less punitive option clause.

Instead of binding a player to a team for life, the new arrangement called for an option year to be tagged on to the end of each contract. Contracts typically ran for two to three years. At the end of that option year, if the player were not signed by his team he would become a free agent.

Any team signing him, however, would have to compensate the former team according to an agreed-upon formula. The costs of signing these "free" agents proved so high that hardly any club took advantage of it. Between 1976 and 1980, 137 players declared their intention to move to another club, but only 23 actually did so. In essence, the players were as restricted as they had been under the reserve clause.

Congressman Peter W. Rodino, Jr., chairman of the Committee on the Judiciary, called the settlement a "sham," stating that the agreement between the two leagues was itself a violation of anti-trust laws. But the Department of Justice disagreed and closed its case.

The WHA hardly took a breath before resuming its request to force a merger. Within a few months of the settlement, the WHA signed 116 more NHL players, including several superstars like Frank Mahovlich. Overnight, the merger question took on new urgency. WHA/NHL merger talks had been a well-publicized secret since the spring of 1973, when Bill Jennings, president of the New York Rangers, first promoted the idea. The talks fell apart quickly but opened again after the 1974 settlement.

A big part of the reason for the on again, off again merger talks lay with the leaderless NHL board of governors. Clarence Campbell, though a loyal employee, simply didn't have the skills to build consensus among the divided owners. "Bill Wirtz [Chicago], and Ed Snider [Philadelphia] at one time were absolute antagonists," recalls John Ziegler, then Bruce Norris's right-hand man. "Bruce Norris was more to Bill Wirtz's side, but more towards the middle. Ed believed that there was going to be a conspiracy of Bill Jennings, Bill Wirtz and Bruce Norris running the League for purposes of their own interests."

The disagreements, especially over the WHA, involved not only the owners, but League and franchise staff as well. "I thought Gil Stein was hired by Ed Snider to legally examine everything and come in and question everything that went on," says John Ziegler. "Gil Stein and I had some fantastic fights. . . . Between 1973 and 1977-78, there wasn't a board meeting where somebody didn't say, 'Where the hell is the light at the end of the tunnel?' Somebody [else] would say, 'I see it. It's a train coming at us.'"

The fractious owners leapt in and out of each other's camps until it got to the point where nobody was in full support of anybody else. Ed Snider and the Rangers' governor Bill Jennings favoured a businesslike merger, with everybody getting back to making money as soon as possible. The Harold Ballard faction maintained "You'll never make peace with the enemy." The Jack Kent Cooke faction advocated limited concessions. The powerful Bill Wirtz faction promoted a "wait until they collapse" approach. Throughout it all, the WHA remained. "They kept hanging around like lint on a suit," laughs Ziegler. "Worse than that, they were right in your pocket!"

Complicating matters was the escalating enmity between the Canadian teams and the American teams over sharing broadcast revenues. The suspicion north of the 49th that the U.S. was trying to take control of the game fanned these flames. There was also tremendous friction between the expansion clubs and the original teams. Many of the new franchises blamed their rapidly deteriorating economic conditions on the harsh 1967 expansion terms and the inferior players they were forced to draft.* The various groups met behind each other's backs, and at least three sets of negotiations with the WHA were being carried on without Clarence Campbell's knowledge or the sanction of the other owners.

The NHL players had been in an excellent position in the early '70s, while the rival league was at its peak, to negotiate their first and long-overdue collective-bargaining agreement with the NHL. Curiously, serious talks didn't begin until 1975—the best time for the owners and the worst time for the players. By then, much of the players' leverage had evaporated. The Department of Justice and the WHA had just dropped their anti-trust action, and both leagues, hurting financially, were beginning to cut back on expenses, including player salaries.

The ailing seventy-year-old Clarence Campbell may have been unequal to solving the labyrinth of troubles facing the NHL, but he still knew his hockey players better than any man alive. There was little doubt in his mind

---

* Many pointed to the rapid rise to respectability of the Buffalo franchise and, to a lesser degree, the early success of the Vancouver Canucks. Both teams, which began operating for the '70-'71 season, had unfettered access to the best junior talent, something the original six expansion teams didn't enjoy for their first five years.

that, when faced with even the faintest threat to the stability of the League, the players would accede to virtually anything the owners wanted.

To soften up the players prior to negotiating, the League wheeled out its most effective weapon, the claim that the players would kill the game if they pressed their demands, any demands. And just before serious bargaining started, hitherto secret financial information about the weak franchises and the League's declining profitability mysteriously began finding its way into the papers.

The negotiation of the NHLPA's first collective-bargaining agreement should have been a monumental event. Marvin Miller recalls that baseball's first agreement required a year and a half of intense preparation and the perusal of "truckloads" of documents, legal cases and other background material.

Between June 1975 and February 1976, while the owners were dickering with the NHLPA, Alan Eagleson was once again caught up in a frenzy of outside events and activities. He had just withdrawn from his law firm and was setting up his own practice with Howie Ungerman, the son of his longtime friend Irving Ungerman. In 1975, the Canadian government named him official negotiator for Hockey Canada, and he immediately threw himself into organizing the 1976 Canada Cup, an undertaking that required protracted absences from Canada.

At the same time, Eagleson's sports agency, with Bill Watters and Rick Curran, was at its zenith. Eagleson was also still deeply involved in Canadian politics, campaigning and raising money all through 1975 and early 1976 for Brian Mulroney's first and unsuccessful bid for the Conservative Party's leadership.

In the end, the 1975 collective-bargaining agreement was not so much an agreement as a rubber-stamping of what the League had been forced to concede by the WHA and the U.S. Department of Justice in 1974. The NHLPA meekly embraced the restrictive option clause, with its onerous compensation provisions, and would spend the next sixteen years unsuccessfully trying to eliminate it. The only glimmer of light was an increase in the pension from $500 to $750 per year of service, but the increase was to be paid out of international hockey profits. In essence, the players, once again, funded their own gain.

When the collective-bargaining agreement was signed in February 1976, the League's financial crises were worsening. In the 1976-77 season, eleven of the eighteen clubs didn't have a single sell-out. Crowds in Detroit were down by almost 50 percent for some games. Boston enjoyed 117 consecutive sell-outs in the early '70s but only one in 1976-77. Cleveland (formerly the Oakland Seals) and Colorado (formerly the Kansas City Scouts) played to half-empty houses, and Atlanta, added in 1972, couldn't give tickets away.

Atlanta and the New York Islanders, also added in 1972, had fallen far behind in payments on their $6-million franchise fees, and when the Kansas City team moved to Denver in 1976, the NHL forgave $3.5 million of the club's $6-million fee, prompting an indignant outcry from the other expansion teams.

Though the League offices were in disarray, hockey's competitiveness at its lowest ebb, the owners at each other's throats and the League with no prospect of a national television contract, Clarence Campbell characteristically blamed the players. "Affluence has taken over, and now many players don't have that spark to do their best," he groused. "The best incentive for a hockey player is hunger, and we've removed that. We've created a fat cat syndrome, and now we've got to end it—or else."

Campbell claimed that players' salaries had increased by 533 percent since 1967, and now took up 50 percent of the League's gross revenues—and no one challenged him. Campbell had only included gate receipts—which the NHL habitually underestimates—in the revenue figures, conveniently leaving out money earned from local broadcasting, promotions, concessions, licensing and expansion.

While all this was going on, a harried Alan Eagleson was publicly and privately describing his NHLPA duties as "onerous." Coincidentally, an old rumour reappeared—

Alan Eagleson for NHL president. "There is one man qualified to move right into Campbell's seat without much training," hailed Jim Vipond, the well-connected sports editor of the *Globe and Mail*. "He has been involved in the legal intricacies of professional sport, mainly at the player level for many years, but with an executive touch."

The NHL struck a five-man selection committee to find a replacement for Clarence Campbell and in late 1976 made an offer to Eagleson. "They've tried to draft me, but I've told them over and over again that I'm not interested in becoming president. I'm devoting all of my energy to the players and that's it." But ten months later Eagleson admitted that not only had he been negotiating with the League but he was willing to become president under certain conditions. "I suggested to a few of the governors that I would take a year off and work with anybody they appointed—preferably [Montreal Canadiens Manager] Sam Pollock—if they gave us absolute control for a year," he told the *Toronto Star*. "I felt Sam and I might get some sense into this whole situation."

Clarence Campbell was firmly in Eagleson's corner. "I shudder to think of what would have happened to the NHL if we had a Marvin Miller (baseball) or Ed Garvey (football) as head of our players' association," Campbell told the Minneapolis *Star*. "They have been militantly hostile to management. Eagleson hasn't been a tooth fairy. But when the chips have been down, he has acted like one. . . . He would have to change some of his ways, but he has all the qualifications to become president."

No doubt a grateful Campbell was referring to Eagleson's bailout of the NHL's fibrillating Cleveland Barons; a few months earlier, on February 24, 1977, Eagleson had loaned the team $600,000 of NHLPA funds.* "Quite frankly, I wasn't sure of the authority I had, but a

---

* The Oakland Seals, formerly the California Seals, transferred to Cleveland in 1976. Kansas City moved to Denver that year and became the Colorado Rockies.

decision had to be made and quickly," Eagleson told George Hanson of the Montreal *Star*. "Before I went back [into the New York meeting room] it worked out to a half dozen. Bobby Clarke (NHLPA president) was the key one and he said go ahead."

Bob Gainey of the Montreal Canadiens was one of the eighteen NHLPA player reps not consulted in advance about the loan. "I have to believe anything Alan did was in our best interests. If we are being asked to play one extra game to pay off the loan, I don't think that's too much to ask. It means a guy is being asked to give out 60 extra minutes for the good of the league."

It was a bizarre gesture, unreasoned and hastily done. Just fourteen months earlier, Eagleson had adamantly opposed propping up weak franchises and recommended that failing clubs merge with each other. Insiders had long maintained that Cleveland, owned by Mel Swig and Gordon Gund, was a lost cause, no matter how much cash they got. The NHL itself couldn't even come up with a penny to save one of its own. All the League did was to advance, by a few months, the $350,000 in franchise fees from the '70, '72 and '74 expansions that were owed to the club anyway. Nearly half the Barons, nine of nineteen on the roster, were Alan Eagleson's clients. The next year, Cleveland merged with Minnesota.

A few months later, Eagleson regretted his action. "We did it once, but we'll never do it again. The minute there's a pay day missed we'll challenge the authority of the contract and declare the collapse of the team. When that happens, the players recognize that only the strong will survive."

Campbell's health deteriorated seriously in 1977. The bowel and stomach problems that plagued him made it difficult for him to stand for any period of time. At one press conference in New York, he was forced to retreat to his hotel after only five minutes. The grey pallor of his skin was alarming to his friends, and the board began hearing stories about a tangle of long-overdue work piling up in the Montreal office.

Though Campbell occasionally said he wanted to retire,

particularly when discussing Eagleson as a possible successor, no one who knew him believed it. "I don't think Clarence ever wanted to go," observes John Ziegler. "It was his life. He loved the game. He was very proud of what he had done. Proud of his connection with the game, as he should have been. I think he felt that he brought and helped keep a Canadian presence significantly to the game, which he patriotically believed was important for Canada."

In desperation, the governors settled on three names for a new NHL president: James Cullen, Bob Sedgewick and John Ziegler, all lawyers for various League clubs. Eagleson scoffed at the list, declaring there wasn't a tough guy in the bunch: "They need a benevolent dictator like we have in the players' association."

Before the player-owner meetings in June 1977, the selection committee, which included Bruce Norris tried to ramrod Ziegler into the president's chair, insisting he was the only feasible candidate. There was tremendous division among the owners, and several were angry at the selection committee's tactics. "We did not appreciate that move in any way, shape or form," one of the expansion team governors fumed anonymously. "That committee has been working on screening possible successors to Mr. Campbell for two years and all it was able to produce was one name!"

But the most powerful owners—Bruce Norris and Bill Wirtz—were behind John Ziegler, and on September 4, 1977, he became president of the National Hockey League. Ziegler's mandate was clear: rid the NHL of its ruinous war with the WHA, hold players gains to a minimum, get a national TV contract and do something to force the Canadian owners to share their broadcast revenues.

Ziegler also had his own agenda, to move the NHL headquarters to New York and sort out the inefficient way the Montreal office had conducted its affairs for three decades. "There was a little different work pace there than I had been used to in the practice of law," recalls Ziegler about his visits to the League office in

Montreal's ornately beautiful Sun Life building.

For years, governors had been arriving at meetings with no background material on the issues they were to discuss. Often, agendas were put together the night before. "Hilda [NHL secretary] and Clarence ran the NHL," says Ziegler shaking his head at the memory. "Clarence would read everything that came across his desk. He answered every letter. He read every pleading. They would work until ten o'clock at night. Of course, you couldn't get things done at night. Clarence would not delegate. Hilda would not delegate. I don't think she would let him delegate. She ran the shop."

When Ziegler suggested altering procedure concerning press releases, conference notes, by-law amendments or compilation of statistics, Hilda primly and forcefully informed him, "We don't do it like that."

As Ziegler tried to free the bottleneck in Montreal, he also rekindled merger talks. The two leagues came close to an agreement in 1978, and by January 1979 every hockey fan in North America knew that some kind of accommodation was imminent. "I'm not totally optimistic," Eagleson told reporters in May, striking exactly the right negotiating chord. "If we work together on this we could come up with something, but I will be telling the player reps if we don't we will be placed in the position to instruct our counsel to initiate an anti-trust action, terminate the collective bargaining agreement and strike."

Just before the pivotal meeting between owners and players in Nassau to hammer out what the players would and wouldn't accept in the merger, Eagleson successfully walked the fine line between toughness and flexibility. "The owners are calling the merger expansion, but we know very well what it is, and under those conditions, we want to do away with the compensation clause or come up with a new formula that permits mobility for the free agent. . . . All they have to do when they come down to Nassau is to tell us they won't insist on compensation any more or, at least, under its present formula—then fine! We've got a deal. It's not going to be easy!"

It's important to realize that Alan Eagleson's demands

for free agency were not a call for unfettered movement between teams after a player's contract had expired. The NHLPA wanted only a slight easing in the option clause which was, to all practical intents, just as restrictive as the reserve clause.

Eagleson repeatedly stated that the players wanted at least half of the $24 million that was to be paid to the NHL by the four merged WHA teams: Edmonton, Quebec, Hartford and Winnipeg.

In the twelve years that had passed since the formation of the NHLPA, Eagleson's growing distance from the players had become obvious. "I hardly saw him at all," says former client Dennis Owchar. "I'm not sure he even read my contract. I don't think he did anything for me really. Bill [Watters] did all the work." Eagleson still made his annual visits to every team, but the visits were often rushed and perfunctory. On top of it all were the problems surrounding Bobby Orr's retirement and Eagleson's increasing friction with Bill Watters, his key employee.

As had been the case at every other pivotal point in the NHLPA's history, Eagleson was deeply immersed in innumerable other projects. International hockey, in particular, had become a behemoth. Soviet and other international teams were playing against the NHL regularly, and Eagleson was the key figure in all of it. As the WHA/NHL merger talks heated up, he was preoccupied with negotiating and arranging the 1978 Challenge Cup and the 1979 Super Series.* "Since January 1975, I've had time for very little else but Hockey Canada business," he said in early 1978.

Still, Eagleson was able to find the time to provide a notable service to the NHL. One of John Ziegler's priorities when he became president was to end the Ed Snider–Bill Wirtz feud. "Alan Eagleson and I felt that from

---

* The 1978 Challenge Cup, consisting of three games between the Soviet national team and NHL All-Stars, was so profitable it set advertising records in Canada. Advertisers paid $30,000 per minute, the highest ever paid for any programming. The rights for the event were purchased jointly by Canadian Sports Network and Harcom Consultants Ltd., run by Eagleson's friend Arthur Harnett.

the players' standpoint and the ownership standpoint, two important people like Bill Wirtz and Ed Snider, being so estranged was going to be continually damaging to the League," Ziegler revealed in 1990. "So Alan and I worked very hard bringing the two together. And Alan played a very important part. Alan could do some things that I couldn't do. Alan could curse them and call them names and he was a very significant factor."

Just what the head of the NHLPA was doing sorting out his bargaining adversaries' problems is far from clear.

Throughout the first half of 1978, Eagleson was lending a hand to the NHL in other ways, the most astonishing of which was his agreement to help John Ziegler get rid of the no-cut clause some players had written into their contracts.* "Thanks to the National Hockey League Players' Association and Alan Eagleson's leadership, however," a grateful Ziegler said, "there was a realization by the players that they were responsible for the product on the ice. Now they've agreed to eliminate the no-cut contracts. In essence, they're giving up their security and saying 'we'll go back to relying on our talent.'"

While Alan Eagleson was helping out the NHL, an undercurrent of player concern was starting to become visible. Players who had been privately worried about their lack of preparedness for previous negotiations were advocating inclusion of outside experts like their own agents. "Eagle is no longer your basic guru," one of the player reps said. "Why shouldn't some of the lawyers who represent us have a say? Eagleson doesn't represent all of us you know."

Among the agents wanting input into the merger agreement were Larry Rauch and the Art Kaminsky–Norm Caplan team, who together represented more than a hundred NHL players. But Eagleson wouldn't have anything to do with them. "Norman Caplan has more or less told me that he represents eight players reps and he would be in Nassau keeping an eye on things," Eagleson

---

* The clause simply meant that once a player signed with a team, that team could not terminate or trade him until the contract expired.

sneered on the eve of the 1979 meetings. "Well, he can be around all he likes but he isn't getting into the meetings."

All the cards were stacked in the NHLPA's favour as the Nassau meetings drew closer. Both the NHL and WHA had set June 15, 1979, as the deadline for signing a merger/expansion agreement. The NHL teams were counting on the huge influx of cash from the merged clubs and the return of key players pilfered by the rival league.

Adding urgency to the need for the players' blessing of the merger was the U.S. Department of Justice, which had kept hockey under a microscope, hoping for an opportunity to reactivate anti-trust action. In their view, a merger would clearly violate the Sherman Act, and judgments made in both hockey and basketball indicated that the players would win easily if they challenged it in court. The only way for the NHL to head off a catastrophic anti-trust ruling was to get the players' approval.

The NHLPA even had a blueprint for legal action provided by the NBA/ABA merger in 1976. The basketball players had emerged victorious in virtually identical circumstances. As in hockey, basketball team owners claimed to have been suffering financial setbacks since the early '70s. Even so, in exchange for not blocking the merger, the players were able to negotiate huge concessions that did not destroy the sport as the owners had predicted.

In return for dropping its anti-trust action against the NBA in 1976, the players got a new collective-bargaining agreement, which entirely abolished compensation payments for free agents, starting in the 1980-81 season. The agreement also did away with the old draft system whereby a team could draft a player and hold on to his rights for an unlimited time without signing him to a contract. The new arrangement provided a one-year period for signing, after which the player could be drafted by any team. If that team didn't sign the player within one year, he became a free agent. The agreement turned the players from supplicants into partners and laid the groundwork for their historic revenue-sharing agreements in the 1980s.

The hockey players had never been in a position of such strength. Everything was on their side—the courts, the ground-breaking experience of the basketball players and, most especially, the anxious owners, who desperately needed the merger. "In principal the [merger] deal was set; it was going to be made either way," Glen Sather later told *Sports Illustrated*, to put the power of the players' position in perspective. "Essentially . . . whatever the players wanted they could have gotten."

But, paradoxically, Alan Eagleson's early resolve inexplicably weakened when he got to Nassau. His tough talk evaporated, and he privately warned the players that the NHL might not be able to withstand an anti-trust suit, let alone a strike—the key weapons in their arsenal. "He presented, as an executive director, what was in front of us," recalls Brad Park, then a player rep for the Boston Bruins and vice-president of the NHLPA. "He told us that hockey is nothing like as strong as the other sports and could not withstand a strike, and he made that clear."

The players were surprised and confused by the passivity of their normally forceful and bombastic leader. "I wanted to find out what the players thought," Eagleson later explained. "I studiously sat back and avoided [taking part in] any discussion." Many players asked themselves if this was the same man who, two years earlier, had lent $600,000 dollars of their money to bail out the Cleveland Barons without a by-your-leave.

The sudden absence of Alan Eagleson's formidable leadership left a vacuum in the negotiations, one that the owners were only too happy to fill. Unopposed, they trundled out their heavy artillery, claiming that they'd lost as much as $80 million during the ruinous war with the WHA. Under these circumstances, they contended, any move to establish any form of free agency without compensation would destroy the game. Several owners buttonholed players and warned them that they were ready to "walk away from their team" if the NHLPA caused any problems over the merger.

The "We're going broke—your demands are going to kill us" line is a familiar one in sport. In 1972, the NBA/ABA owners claimed that they had to merge because the competition had cost them $13.5 million the previous year alone and had brought both leagues to the verge of ruin.

It was an argument that Senator Sam Ervin, who later headed up the Watergate hearings, gave short shrift to during Senate anti-trust investigations into the NBA/ABA merger. "The only way you can pass on the validity of this claim that the basketball teams are losing money is to have the owners produce not only the income tax returns of the clubs, but also their individual income tax returns, because in most cases they are allowed under the tax laws to deduct them on the individual tax returns. Furthermore, the owners own franchises for concessions, which are organized by separate corporations. In some cases they own the stadium in which the teams are placed under separate corporations.

"Yet when I called upon these owners to produce their income tax returns, which are the only real evidence of the truth of their claim that they are losing money, they threw up their hands in horror as if I had laid foul hands on the Ark of the Covenant."

The Senate Anti-Trust Committee hired economists Dr. Roger Noll and Dr. Ben Okner from the prestigious Brookings Institution to examine the financial statements provided by the NBA and ABA. They used other, equally recognized accounting techniques on the basketball owners' data and transformed the same $13.5 million loss into a $4.5 million profit.

Not only were the arguments made by the NHL owners in Nassau the same, but the circumstances were virtually identical, with at least three-quarters of NHL teams also owning their own arenas. The hockey players, however, had no experts from the Brookings Institute to combat the owners' arguments. With an executive director who was "sitting back and listening," they were easy prey. At a key point in the discussions, Eagleson made an "impassioned plea" to NHLPA president Phil Esposito, who had been asking some penetrating questions about the deal, to "search your soul" and "do the right thing for all the players." "I was like his puppet, I admit that," Esposito says ruefully.

In retrospect, these crucial negotiations most closely resembled a unilateral disarmament of the Players' Association. At the players' first private meeting on June 3, their legal counsel, Larry Latto and Wendy White of Shea and Gardner in Washington D.C. reported that "they felt our position was sound and that there was a high degree of success in the event an anti-trust suit was necessary." Even though the confident lawyers predicted that a suit would only take between eighteen months and three years to settle and would cost less than $200,000, the NHLPA voted to discard this powerful weapon.

The next day, the NHLPA conducted the one and only strike vote in their history. The voters were the player reps, most of whom were under the owners' extreme and continued pressure. "It was decided among the players on Tuesday that it would not be in the best interest of the Association to have a strike on this issue," Alan Eagleson later explained to NHLPA members. "When the matter was discussed on a team-by-team basis it appeared that only one team was convinced that its players would strike. The other sixteen teams in the league indicated that their players would not support a strike."

No one has ever asked why the NHLPA wasn't prepared to strike, even though merger talks had been going on for six years.

The owners played the NHLPA beautifully, sticking to hardball declarations when, in reality, they were in a very weak position. Reading through the minutes of those meetings, it's difficult not to avoid the conclusion that someone was informing them in advance of the players' discussions. On Wednesday morning, after the players decided they couldn't mount a strike, the owners maintained that they were going ahead, with or without their agreement, strike or no strike. "They were prepared to pursue the merger and pursue our position through the courts," explained Eagleson.

On June 7, 1979, the NHLPA ratified the merger, diplomatically called "an expansion." In return, the League promised improvements in meal allowances and reasonable moving expenses for a traded player. They agreed to *allow* the players to continue to "profit" from international hockey. The owners also increased pension payments from $750 per year played to $1,000 at age forty-five, and doubled the group life insurance payment from $50,000 to $100,000. The changes were so minor that a new collective-bargaining agreement was not deemed necessary; the old one was merely extended until 1981. No change occurred in player movement, and the biggest thorn of all, compensation, remained firmly in place.

The players reportedly got a $7.25-million injection of cash into their pension fund—or so they thought. But if the benefits even remotely approached that amount, it was in *future* benefits, payable years down the road, when the players were eligible for their pensions. What the players really got, according to NHLPA documents, was as little as $200,000 annually. The NHL owners did increase their contributions to the pension fund in 1979 from $125,000 annually to $250,000 annually, but three years later they quietly began withdrawing hundreds of thousands from the accumulated surplus in the form of dividends and contribution holidays.

What little the owners did pay to get the merger, they were more than compensated for by reductions in salaries. "The elimination of the WHA could cost a first round pick as much as $250,000," Bill Watters fumed after the agreement was signed. "The most lucrative contract negotiated for the first round pick last year was about $750,000. I would be surprised if anyone could get more than a four or five year $500,000 deal now."

In contrast, the owners came away from Nassau with a $24-million injection from the four merged teams. And the existing franchises faced the happy prospect of unloading between $5 and $6 million of inflated contracts on the new clubs, which had already agreed to draft their new roster from players made available by the NHL. The

WHA also promised to wipe the litigation slate clean and indemnify the NHL against any suits launched by former WHA teams.

Most important, the NHL owners tightened their hammer lock on the players, something they haven't relinquished to this day. In virtually every respect, it was a disastrous deal. Based on salary figures alone, the players, without any ability to market their services to the highest bidder, rapidly lost ground to other professional sports. Though the '80s were a decade of unprecedented prosperity for the NHL owners, the players fell from second among all professional sports in average salary to last. By 1988, the average hockey salary was $179,000, compared to $240,000 for football, $450,000 for baseball and $500,000 for basketball.*

To add insult to injury, the NHL's bonuses at playoff time—when owners can double their total revenue—rapidly became the laughing-stock of professional sport. In 1991, players on the victorious Stanley Cup team were paid only $25,000 in league bonus money for playing twenty-four punishing playoff games. In contrast, baseball's 1990 World Series winners were each paid $130,000 in playoff bonus money, for a maximum of fourteen games.

Once again, though playing for huge stakes and holding most of the cards, the players came away with little. They'd traded away their best chance for free agency and reform of the grievance procedure, and got almost nothing in return.

---

* Using basketball as a comparative benchmark, the figures are even more damning. In 1977, hockey players made 67 percent of what basketball players did. Even allowing for the fact that basketball's popularity would keep it ahead, hockey should have stayed within that same range, especially since it was entering its most profitable years ever. By 1988, the average hockey salary had fallen to 38 percent of the average basketball salary.

Chapter 11

Resignation No Longer on File

The first concerted attempt by players to overthrow Alan Eagleson rose directly out of their anger over the 1979 merger terms. Though many players were confused about the terms of the agreement and others resented the pressure put on them, only Mike Milbury of the Boston Bruins actually voted against it. "I think the association took a total retreat," he said angrily the next day. "It is my view that we should have forced the issue with the owners on equalization and earned much greater freedom of movement. They threatened to cancel the expansion of the NHL if we didn't reach an agreement. But I feel they would have bulled away anyway, no matter what happened with the agreement."

It wasn't just the players who were angry. "What they settled for in Nassau was totally appalling," fumed New York agent Larry Rauch. "Certain owners said they would walk away from their franchises if the players didn't go along with them on the compensation question. That was a fake out. The players were poor poker players."

Eagleson refused to accept any blame. "It was a process of collective bargaining. It's very easy to say what should be done. . . . The fellows around the table were satisfied that it was the best deal available."

But more and more of the "fellows" were questioning the deal. At a follow-up meeting in August, Denis Potvin of the Islanders demanded to know "why the NHLPA hadn't negotiated a total free agency with owners in Nassau." Other players questioned Eagleson's closeness to several owners, and especially League president John Ziegler. Mike Milbury and Brad Park proposed to put an end to the issue, which erupted regularly like a boil, by offering Eagleson a full-time NHLPA job at $200,000 a year.

Eagleson, far from grateful, heatedly told them he would resign rather than work full-time for the association. But he did commit to finding a successor and gave 1982 as his retirement date.

Hockey players rely far more heavily on their association's executive director than do other professional athletes. They turn pro younger, and most are gone from the sport before they are more than a few years into manhood. NHLPA player reps have a difficult job. The association provides no education for new reps, a good percentage of whom are parachuted in as replacements for those who are traded or retire. Between February 1985 and February 1986, in the middle of the collective-bargaining agreement negotiations, there was a 50 percent turnover in player reps. "By the time everybody gets intelligent enough to make a business-like decision they are no longer there," states Brad Park.

To make matters worse, the NHLPA provides very little background information. "You go in cold—no briefing," confirms Dave Barr, the 1990 Detroit player rep. Jim Fox, Los Angeles rep for six years, adds, "I never saw a constitution. And there was never anyone taking minutes."

Even when players disagree with NHLPA decisions, few dare criticize. Mike Milbury was different. Seeing no progress in Eagleson's promise to name a successor, he mounted a campaign, first among the Bruins, and then League-wide, to demand that Eagleson devote more time to the NHLPA. Hockey's situation was similar to basketball's, where an agent, Larry Fleischer, was part-time director of the players' association. But Fleischer was being paid $50,000 annually for his part-time job, while Eagleson was getting $150,000.

"The last thing I want is this resolution misinterpreted as the first step in kicking Al out," Milbury carefully pointed out. But, since Eagleson had steadfastly refused to do the job on anything but a part-time basis, kicking him out was the only possible conclusion.

One thing that Eagleson does better than anyone is react quickly, and usually definitively, to unfolding events. "I think he really *likes* putting out fires," acknowledges his wife Nancy, with a sigh. By the time the Milbury rebellion had made it into the papers, Eagleson had already announced publicly that he was going to quit anyway, and he repeated the statement numerous times between November 1979 and January 1980.

Milbury, Brad Park and the Bruins also wanted a beefed-up administrative structure; the NHLPA was still limping along with a part-time executive director, one secretary and one operations manager. They also wanted a copy of the NHLPA constitution and by-laws (something most reps had never even seen) sent to every player, a brief history of past association decisions, clarification of voting procedures, a stenographer to record minutes and an agenda mailed to player reps before association meetings. "There was no agenda for those meetings," recalls Bobby Orr, an association vice-president in the '70s. "Mr. Eagleson ran everything."

Milbury and Park also wanted each player on every team to vote on important issues, particularly those concerning the collective-bargaining agreement or amendments to it. Unlike the other professional sports associations, no member-wide vote had ever taken place on any issue in the NHLPA.

When he heard of Milbury's demands, Eagleson let fly his opposition-eating grin, winked and spoke of the Bruins' defenseman as if he had taken one too many pucks in the head. "His heart's in the right place," he told reporters with heavy sincerity, "but Milbury doesn't understand how the Players' Association works."

The Bruins pressed on and retained Price-Waterhouse to administer and count a confidence vote. By the time the press picked up the news, the balloting was already underway. "I didn't want Al to hear about it and then tell people not to vote on it," Milbury said, explaining the secrecy.

"I'm always ready for a fight," the supremely confident Eagleson retorted. "I'm not going to let these guys scare me away." But, just to make sure, he declared that *only* player reps could dethrone him, and that, in any case, the vote violated the NHLPA's constitution.* "What constitution?" queried Milbury.

Of the 154 players responding, 101 voted for a fulltime director. Eagleson declared that the survey had been "flubbed" and was invalid.

A few days later, on the eve of the February 5, 1980, All-Star game in Detroit, Eagleson counter-attacked. He called an NHLPA meeting; fifty players attended, including twenty player reps, the NHLPA executive committee and a phalanx of Eagleson sympathizers. The extra twenty players attending were All-Stars, many of whom were Eagleson clients attending or playing in the game. After five sweaty hours closeted in a Detroit Plaza Hotel meeting room, they voted on whether to retain Eagleson or not.

Reversing his unequivocal position of only a few weeks earlier that only player reps could vote on such a motion, Eagleson allowed all votes to stand. He claimed "a total 100 percent endorsement," though Brad Park and Pittsburgh goalie Greg Millen voted against, and Milbury abstained. "The only people whom I have to respond to are the player representatives," Eagleson jubilantly proclaimed. "I can't care if 400 other guys in the league think I'm a jerk."†

---

* There is a brief NHLPA constitution, and nowhere is the regulation mentioned.

† As a concession, Eagleson did promise to hire an assistant, and a search committee was formed. But nine months later, the whole thing fizzled and no assistant or replacement materialized.

The oddest aspect of this series of events is the sudden about-face Eagleson did regarding the 1979 WHA merger agreement. In the space of only nine months, it went from being "the best deal possible" to a seriously flawed and forced compromise. "We had to make a quick decision last June that many of us were somewhat uncomfortable with, but we really had no choice in the matter because we weren't in a position of having called a strike vote."*

But the players did *not* have to endorse the merger—something they never seemed to realize. If it had gone ahead without their approval, it would have constituted a violation of their 1975 collective-bargaining agreement, not to mention the U.S. anti-trust laws, a fact their own legal counsel had made abundantly clear.

Despite many threats the NHLPA has been strangely reluctant to use legal action as a bargaining tool. In 1979, the players didn't file an anti-trust suit, even though their own law firm recommended it and assured them that it would cost no more than $200,000 and take less than three years to settle.

Baseball players, in contrast, have sued early and often. In 1990, for instance, they won $102.5 million in compensation for the owners' conspiracy against free agents in the 1987 and 1988 seasons. "There will be much more to come when the remaining damages are determined, including lost salary for 1989 and 1990, and other damages," assured association head Don Fehr. "Protest as they will, the owners can no longer downplay either the significance or the effect of their intentionally wrongful conduct." Basketball players have also made enormous gains by using their legal rights as a bargaining tool.

In 1981, the NHL and the Players' Association began

---

* In September 1979, Eagleson did advise the player reps to poll their teammates informally regarding support for a strike. But the merger was already history and, in any case, training camp is the worst time for players to be asked such a question. Most of them had yet to sign contracts for the new season, and the level of uncertainty runs high as many wonder if they will be playing for the franchise or in the minors.

discussing a new collective-bargaining agreement.* In February, Eagleson said the players would not press too hard on the issue of the option clause and compensation for free agents. Five months later, he said the compensation formula was unworkable and must be changed or the players would strike. The next February he changed his mind again. "I've emphasized to the players that we have to consider the financial situation in the league. We are asking for total free agency but what good would that be if there are only 10 teams left. Eleven teams might lose money this year." In July 1982, Eagleson once again threatened strike.

In the end, the agreement worked out in 1982 between the owners and the players was little changed from the previous one. The high-priced stars (earning over $200,000) *could* change teams when they became free agents. But their new teams still had to compensate the old ones with two first-round draft choices, or a first-rounder and any player they wanted from the other teams roster, excluding a protected list of two.

The new compensation system was so restrictive that not a single free agent switched teams between 1982 and 1986.

"Sure it's a great contract," chortled Harold Ballard, "for us." General managers around the League privately told agents that the players "got screwed" or, more frequently, "screwed themselves."

In effect, the 1975 collective-bargaining agreement was allowed to stand until its expiration in September 1984. When that date rolled around, Eagleson agreed to extend the expiration date, first to 1985 and then to 1986. By that time, many of the malcontents of 1980 had either retired or were in the last year or two of their careers.

Hockey agents have been griping about Eagleson and the NHLPA almost as long as hockey players. They trade stories of inaction and neglect the way kids do hockey cards. At the St Louis Blues' training camp in 1983, Herb

---

* The 1975 collective-bargaining agreement renewed in 1979, expired in 1984, but the players could legally give notice to terminate it as early as September 1982.

Pinder's client Blair Chapman, who still had eighteen months left on his contract, arrived one morning to a nasty surprise. "They told me basically to hit the road. They would pay me a third of my remaining contract."

Chapman immediately called Pinder, who quickly contacted Eagleson.

"It's a dispute, and all disputes must go to the League president," Eagleson told him. "We are going to have this dispute with the League President?" Pinder exclaimed. "Sure," Eagleson blandly replied. "John Ziegler has been absolutely fair in every one of these kinds of things."

Chapman then tried to talk to Eagleson but couldn't get him on the phone. "I figured the Players' Association would stand behind me but Sam Simpson told me I was on my own. They didn't help me one bit," he adds bitterly.

Ten long months after submitting the matter to arbitration, John Ziegler did indeed rule in favour of Chapman, but added a slick addendum to the settlement that snatched away any real victory. Because Chapman had submitted the matter to arbitration, Ziegler ruled that he had terminated his own contract, and therefore St. Louis was liable only to pay him up to that point, not to the end of his contract.

It was a classic catch-22: if Chapman hadn't filed a grievance, he wouldn't have gotten any money, but *because* he filed the grievance, he didn't get all of it.

To make matters worse, Chapman had also filed for disability insurance after injuring his back and having surgery before the Blues terminated him. "The Players' Association didn't help me out with that either. I never got a penny."

After it was all over Chapman received a letter from Eagleson, who wrote, "If I can be of any more help please give me a call."

"It was just an awful, awful thing to happen," says Pinder, still anguished seven years later. "After that last letter from Eagle—he has to get the last word—I remember sitting in my office. I will always remember saying, 'Okay, now what do I do? Do I rip him right back?' What good does it do? I just closed the file and put it away. How do you beat the system when the guy has the control?"

In 1985, just before the June draft, Boston agent Brian Burke, with the support of twelve other agents, drafted a volcanic proposal, really a manifesto, to reform the NHLPA. In a section ominously titled "Sanctions," he wrote: "Mr. Eagleson's position is that the union is his own personal fiefdom, and that the role people like us play is superfluous to the bargaining procedure. . . . I am going to recommend that each player/agent present (and any others who wished to attend but could not) instruct each and every player he represents to abstain from joining the NHLPA until such time as Mr. Eagleson either adopts a program in line with ours or resigns."

The agents were excited, angry and infused with the sense of invincibility that usually precedes slaughter. They were also more than a little afraid. "There are more squealing, welshing little bastards than you can ever believe!" says a scornful Bill Watters. "Guys you think are completely anti-Eagle will pick up the phone and tell him word for word what you've just said."

Burke softened the next draft and removed some red-flag words like "sanctions." But he left in demands for audited NHLPA financial statements and an agent association that would "serve in an advisory role to the NHLPA." Not surprisingly, the agents loved the idea of advising the Players' Association. "That way we could best influence the process and interestingly later dispense with the present Executive Director," Pinder bluntly wrote to Burke in December.

But nobody wanted to bell the cat. Finally, Brian Burke, Gus Badali and Montreal agent Pierre Lacroix were deputized to present their concerns and suggestions to Alan Eagleson. On Tuesday, January 7, 1986, a cordial, jovial Eagleson ushered the three men into his antique-strewn boardroom. Gus Badali showed up in a multi-coloured ski suit and looked like he was ready to leave at the first opportunity. Pierre Lacroix, with a distinct tremor in his voice and body, agreed with everything

Eagleson said, and Brian Burke could have given all three a shower with his sweat.

To their surprise and relief, Eagleson was all conviviality and concern. He agreed with many of their points, amended some others and only objected outright to one or two. "Their presentation was reasonable, sensible and positive," Eagleson said after the meeting. "I might as well have written their proposal. These were the basic things I've been talking to the owners about over the years."

The delighted agents congratulated themselves on Eagleson's response, but no one stepped forward to carry their initiative to completion. It was as if Eagleson, by *not* opposing them, had taken the wind out of their sails.

Feeling everything slipping away, Pinder appealed to Wayne Gretzky for support. "I think most would agree that your influence with both fellow players and the owners could be considerable in what is an extremely important round of negotiations that will effect the well-being of players for the next three to five years. . . . Our group has not been informed nor asked for its views through the process which is consistent with Eagle's approach in the past."

Pinder's entreaty came too late. Gretzky never replied, and the cause was dead. Not surprisingly, the agents' recommendations never made it to the bargaining table. "We were a bunch of whipped assholes," admitted Burke years later.

The 1986 collective-bargaining agreement turned out to be a reprise of every previous negotiation since 1967, but with a nasty twist. A few hours before talks with the owners were to begin in Toronto, Alan Eagleson walked into the room where the players were gathered. "My contract is up. I'm going to leave the room and I want you to discuss it," he told the dumbfounded group. "Until I get a new contract it won't be possible for me to represent you." He then walked out. The players spent the next few minutes frantically discussing the rumours then circulating that the NHL owners had once again offered Eagleson John Ziegler's job. They quickly caved in and set up a committee to structure a new contract.

"We should have called the owners and asked for two or three days' delay while we discussed it," Jim Fox says today. "We made a rash decision and signed him up for several more years. It was the surprise and the fear. You're going into a meeting with owners and you have no leader! I will take part of the blame. We had the whole summer, we should have gone for a postponement."

"Why wasn't he ever that tough with the owners?" asks another former player wistfully.

The next day, a satisfied Eagleson told reporters, "I am committed to the players. Now they don't have to worry about getting a new deal on Sept. 1, then getting up on Oct. 1 and finding me as president of the NHL."

Alan Eagleson kicked off negotiations by once again stating that free agency was the number one issue, and quoting examples of top stars who had tried, unsuccessfully, to change teams under the current compensation system. "If you don't indicate that you are going to be responsible and take a reasonable course of action. . . ." he warned the governors, "We will likely be on strike during the training camp in 1986."

In turn, the owners trotted out their perennial "your demands are going to kill the game" arguments. "Mr. Bill Wirtz, the Chicago owner, stated categorically that total free agency would destroy his franchise," read the NHLPA minutes. "He reported that over the past four years his operating costs had increased from $6.6 million to $10 million per year." John Pickett, owner of the New York Islanders, added that "total free agency would bankrupt the weaker clubs."

John Ziegler presented reams of inflated statistics proving that the players had never been better off, with salary increases of 17.4 percent in 1984-85 and 18.5 percent in 1985-86. He also told them that the League could not survive the 50 percent wage hike that any type of free agency would bring.

As usual, the NHLPA had no experts, no studies and no financial analysis to challenge the owners' claims. "I don't believe in wasting the players' money," Eagleson had explained a few years earlier. "It would be very easy for me to have a 10 or 12 man operation at the Players Association and have a budget of half a million dollars as some of the other associations do. It is more convenient for the Association to hire outside help when necessary. . . . I'm the liaison of the Association with the greatest lawyers in the U.S. and Canada who help me solve the problems. It's worked out well in the past; we've committed ourselves to some major projects with relation to pension and to the collective-bargaining agreement involving experts in the field."

In 1986, the NHLPA's "experts in the field" were "special consultant" Tony Esposito, a fine, retired NHL goaltender and former NHLPA president, with no known labour, business or legal expertise, and Sam Simpson, the NHLPA's office manager. The association did, however, have Larry Latto and Wendy White of the Washington, D.C. law firm Shea and Gardner, whose anti-trust advice the NHLPA had totally ignored in 1979.

The deal was settled when the owners placed the offer of a staggering $15 million (Canadian) pension "security" package on the table, in exchange for the NHLPA dropping their demands for total, or even limited, free agency. The plan would give players active in 1986 who went on to play 400 games by retirement, a $250,000 lump-sum payment at age 55.*

Eagleson emerged from the meetings hailing the agreement as a great victory, but, unfortunately, it was just one more con job pulled on the players by the owners. The owners didn't give them nearly as much money as they'd claimed, and in any case the money they contributed came from a $25-million surplus in the players' own pension fund.

---

* Two games were added to the first playoff round, and the compensation system was altered slightly so that future draft choices, instead of active players, would be used to compensate teams losing free agents. The revised system was still so restrictive that the first player to switch teams as a free agent was Scott Stevens in 1990.

During their private meetings, the players had discussed the $25-million surplus.* Several players advocated taking action to claim the money. Eagleson told them that a related court case was underway over the issue of pension surpluses, and the players could not take a stand until it was resolved.

According to Jim Fox, and others who attended every meeting, Eagleson supported the owners' contention that "they had the complete right to decide how the remainder of the refund would be used. . . . The NHLPA accepted this premise and sought to negotiate for as much of this money as possible for the Security Package."

Fox and other players don't remember Eagleson explaining that the Pension Society's own documents from 1967 to 1981 explicitly state that all surpluses must be allocated to provide "additional pension benefits" to the players only, according to their years of service. Nor does he recall Eagleson informing the players that the NHL had unilaterally changed that clause in 1983 to allow the surplus to be allocated by the NHL clubs to "reduce Member Club contributions to the Club Pension Plan . . ."

Fox falls silent when he considers these facts. "I don't believe the players had *any* information on the pension, and none of the documents. I never saw those documents. If the NHL changed that clause in 1983 I never heard about it. There's no way I would have let it [the security package] go by if I had known."

Adding a final insult to the whole deal was Eagleson's later admission that the owners' so-called concessions to the players amounted to only $9.4 million, not the $15 million claimed at the time.

In essence, it didn't cost the owners a penny of their

---

* On July 25, 1985, ManuLife, the insurance company with which the pension was invested, refunded $25 million to the NHL. The League unilaterally decided that $16.5 million of the total was "attributable to annuities purchased with contributions made by the clubs." $4.4 million was allotted to retired players—which is the focal point of the retired players' suit filed on April 30, 1991. $2.5 million went back to the minor leagues, and only $1.2 million, attributable to contributions made by the Players' Association, was thrown back into the pot as part of the security package.

new money to fund the much-ballyhooed security package. But the story doesn't end there. Fewer than 8 percent of all NHL players make that 400-game mark annually. In 1986, there were 186 players currently in the League who had played 400 or more games. The League had to set aside just $3 million that year to pay for the bonus when those players turned fifty-five. And, since an average of only 41 players each season reach the 400-game mark, it costs the League less than $600,000 annually to pay for their bonus. That is a far cry from the $9.4 million the owners supposedly put into the fund.

The next anti-Eagleson insurrection was part vendetta, part holy crusade and part Don Quixote-like search for justice. It all started innocently enough when Ron Salcer met Rich Winter, a twenty-eight-year-old lawyer and little-known agent from Edmonton who dabbled in a bit of everything, from law to entertainment. At various times his clients have included goalies Ron Hextall and Grant Fuhr and Oilers forward Esa Tikkanen.

Tall, slender, long-faced and appealingly sad-eyed, Winter has a youthful, unlawyerly demeanour that is a definite plus among his clients. In the jaded, seen-all, heard-all, done-all world of hockey agents, Winter wears his emotions like an ill-fitting overcoat. Hurts and insults stick with him like acne scars, and the least provocation can send him off on an impassioned rant. "The guy's nuts," one general manager said bluntly. "I mean, we're talking about bonus points and all of a sudden it's like I'm about to trash the holy grail or something. I'm saying no to a lousy five-grand bonus and he wants a Royal Commission on the subject, a lynching or something."

Winter has heard those comments since the early '80s, when he negotiated his first contract with Glen Sather. He fidgets, shakes his head and says he doesn't care, but his face tells a different story. "I really love these people that I represent because they are good people. For the most part, I have very good clients who put their pants on one leg at a time, who have kids, who have colicky kids, have all the same problems that we have. The fans see this guy as a superstar. I see him as a guy who has a chance over four years to make enough money to help his kids to college. That's it!"

Then, as it usually does when he talks owners versus players, his face contorts a little. "I want these guys to get what they deserve. I don't want Peter Pocklington . . . I don't want that man taking $6 million home a year when a superstar client here is getting $300,000. That's not right!"

The Winter-Salcer combination seems the most unlikely of alliances. Salcer, slight and balding with the earnest manner of a Methodist preacher, looks like the last person to be involved in a crusade. He's sanguine, calm and outwardly self-assured—everything that Winter isn't. With an established clientele of twenty-five to thirty NHL players and an extremely comfortable California way of life, Salcer had the least to gain and the most to lose by rattling the NHLPA chains.

But Winter and Salcer had their fingers on a changing pulse. Anger and animosity about Eagleson and the NHLPA had surged since the 1986 collective-bargaining agreement. The players saw salaries in other sports taking off while theirs stagnated. Crowds in the NHL rinks were increasing steadily, and in 1987 the League signed a three-year $51-million television contract with Sports Channel America, by far the largest in NHL history. At the same time, the players saw their careers steadily eroding, slipping from an average of more than six years in 1980 to only four and a half by 1986.

When oily rags sitting neglected by a furnace suddenly burst into flames, it's impossible to pinpoint the precise moment when combustion became inevitable. So it was with the coup of 1989. Winter and Salcer's talk of ousting Eagleson escalated, and sometime in 1988 they found themselves committed to a showdown. But if the two men were to take on Alan Eagleson, they needed a paladin—someone outside the game. He had to be a wily scrapper, impervious, and someone Eagleson couldn't intimidate. Not only that, but he had to be willing to work for free.

First they approached Marvin Miller, retired head of baseball's Major League Players' Association. But Miller knew Eagleson well and understood, despite his endless threats to resign, that he would fight like a cornered wolverine to keep his job. He politely declined.

Next they turned to Ed Garvey, former head of the National Football League Players' Association. Winter had reservations about enlisting the highly controversial Garvey. "I didn't like Ed Garvey. I didn't like what he had done. I thought he was a socialist," he says, a little amused at his early impressions.

Ed Garvey *is* one of the most controversial men in sport. Depending on who you talk to, he either ruined or saved the NFL Players' Association, and he either vaulted football into the modern era or sent it back to the dark ages. Garvey, however, was the perfect choice for the job. Completely self-assured, with a rhino-like hide and an omnivorous sense of humour, he thoroughly enjoyed the idea of attempting to sack hockey's entrenched quarterback.

Garvey loves a battle—the bloodier the better—particularly if it suits his sense of mission. Round-faced and slightly plump, Garvey looks more like an armchair athlete than a warrior. But when he fixes his granite gaze on you, his mouth flattens out and twitches against a suppressed volatility, as if he's fighting the urge to bite.

Garvey has a basic cynicism about all sport owners, and he's none too fond of agents, either. "Management loves agents," he sneers. "They get them in the back room one-on-one, and then they make their cosy little deals and arrangements." He was dubious about Winter and Salcer's motivations, and also doubted that they fully understood what they were up against. He knew that Eagleson's wealth, power and status depended on his ability to deliver the players—at collective-bargaining time, over contracts, for endorsements and for international hockey. He also knew that Eagleson had an ally in the management of the National Hockey League; if anyone challenged him, they would be facing two opponents, not one.

"I told them I'd be interested in getting involved in trying to clean up the Players' Association," says Garvey of his conversations with Winter and Salcer. "I felt the association was a disgrace for a long time. But I told them I would only do it if the players wanted me." Garvey demanded that Winter and Salcer ask the players for $100 each in "earnest money" to demonstrate their support and defray expenses.

Herb Pinder played a critical but unheralded role in the uprising. Supportive, but carefully out of the direct line of fire, he buttressed Winter, Salcer and Garvey in times of weakness and criticized them when he thought they were advocating a scorched-earth policy. Using the lessons he'd learned from the agents' failure in 1986, he continually pressed for full involvement of the players. Pinder laughs when he compares what the three men did with the agents' attempt to influence Eagleson in 1986. "Here are all we agents getting together and intellectually defining issues and sending them to Eagle. These guys went right to the players. The source of the power. Simple and brilliant."

Ron Salcer made the first move in Los Angeles when the Hartford Whalers came to town on November 3, 1988. He had no clients on the team, but one of the players agreed to set up a meeting. Salcer walked into the dressing room, more nervous than he had been negotiating his first contract. To his surprise, the entire team was present.

Salcer started haltingly by suggesting that "perhaps they weren't getting the best representation from the NHLPA." Before he had uttered more than a few sentences, a growled "cocksucker" reverberated from the back of the room. Salcer blanched, and then relaxed when he realized the player wasn't referring to him. "I'm sick of this, the way he operates," another player exclaimed, waving his fist in the air.

One after another, players shouted out stories of humiliations or inequities suffered at the hands of Alan Eagleson. The discussion, billed as a brief introduction, turned into a ninety-minute catharsis that more closely resembled a religious revival than an information meeting. The only thing missing was a chorus of amens. It was an eerie reprise of 1966, when the Springfield Indians had complained about their oppression at the hands of Eddie Shore. But the object of the players' rancour in 1988 wasn't Eddie Shore, but the emancipator himself, Alan Eagleson.

Salcer emerged from his next meeting with the North Stars with a crawling feeling in his belly. "I remember having real remorse after doing it. I called up Ed Garvey and I said, 'Ed, am I doing the right thing? Am I opening up a can of worms? This is my livelihood.'"

Over the next four months, Salcer, Garvey and Winter met with players from sixteen of twenty-one franchises. There quickly evolved a core of supporters—outspoken, tough-minded players like Jim Korn, then with the New Jersey Devils. Korn, a journeyman defenseman, was a veteran of four NHL teams. In 1988, Korn had had the temerity to stand up at an NHLPA meeting and ask why the association headquarters in Toronto had been moved, and who owned the new building.*

"Who the hell are you to bring that up Jim Korn, you cocksucker?" derided Eagleson. "You never even joined the NHLPA or paid your dues until three or four years ago." Under Eagleson's invective-laden assault, the six-foot, three-inch Korn steadily lost stature as bits and pieces of his hide were flayed off.

"We all started thinking, Yeah, you cocksucker. What the fuck are you doing asking questions?" recalls Dave Barr, the Detroit player rep. "It wasn't until a few days later that I realized that a perfectly good question didn't get answered."

At every gathering and in hundreds of phone calls, the three men and their supporters told players they intended to make a presentation at the June 1989 NHLPA meetings in Florida and press for a vote of confidence in Eagleson's leadership. Most teams welcomed them as

---

* One of Eagleson's companies did.

occupied Kuwait did the Coalition liberators. "I was really surprised, I got the [$100] cheques in immediately," said Barr, shortly after Rich Winter talked to the Detroit players in Edmonton. "Finally we had a vehicle to go after him, but we didn't have to do it ourselves."

Ed Olczyk, then playing for Toronto, was very specific about the players' need for a buffer. "Nobody's willing to put their balls on the line. Guys are just afraid, you're only in this League for so long. You don't want to piss the wrong guy off. I'm kind of glad I'm not a rep. I'm the kind of guy who says what he feels. I've got kids coming and I'd like to stick around a lot longer. You don't want anyone looking at you any different."

At first, the NHL clubs treated the Winter-Salcer-Garvey efforts with benign neglect, even allowing meetings on sacrosanct game days. A few teams provided players' addresses and telephone numbers, rarely given out under any circumstances. "If they burn Al's ass a little, why should I give a shit?" a general manager of an eastern U.S. franchise said, with poorly disguised relish.

A remarkably sanguine Eagleson dismissed the whole thing as just one more power struggle. "Every four or five years someone takes a run at me," he scoffed. Winter and Salcer, he said, were just trying to get more clients at his expense.

Not even the distribution in November 1988 of a badly typed and misspelled but highly inflammatory list of charges disturbed Eagleson's equanimity. The document accused him of receiving indirect payments from "various sources" in return for favouring certain corporations with the NHLPA account.

The paper also slammed the existing collective-bargaining agreement as the most restrictive in professional sport, despite the NHL's record profitability. Eagleson was accused of personally profiting from players' problems: "When [injured player] Glen Sharpley asked the NHLPA to assist him collect his disability pension Eagleson agreed to assist him. He charged Sharpley $14,250 to collect his NHLPA disability pension."

Eagleson's strategy of ignoring the insurrection worked

perfectly, at first. Many hockey players who read the charges were initially shocked but lost their outrage as time passed. "Yeah, I wondered a bit," admitted Edmonton Oilers star Mark Messier. "[But] I figured look, if there was any truth to any of this Eagleson would have been up there screaming at these guys to fuck off and get off his back. That's the way he is, he doesn't lie down for anyone."

The opposition finally flushed Eagleson out from under cover with the devastatingly effective *Player's Voice* newsletter, authored by Ed Garvey. The first issue—four plain, typed pages folded together—hammered away at points and used examples that even the most unsophisticated hockey player could understand. Many, for example, didn't know that Eagleson's part-time 1989 salary of $200,000 was paid in U.S. dollars, though the association had always been based in Canada. This was a particularly sore point with Canadian players who were paid in Canadian dollars.

Eagleson, and most other hockey agents, were scathing in their criticism of the newsletter. "If I had a son in sixth grade and had written that paper, I wouldn't let him hand it in to the teacher," said New York agent Larry Rauch. "I thought it was completely inadequate. I felt it was sloppy work and I thought it disqualified the people from any serious consideration on my part."

In fact, *The Player's Voice* was an immensely subtle piece of work aimed, like a laser, at the players themselves. Carefully crafted to be authoritative but not glossy and slick, the newsletter radiated sincerity and common sense. The first issue was dedicated to "those who have asked questions and been put down, those who have been hurt because they couldn't go to court or have the NHLPA process a grievance, to Gordie Howe who played for 26 years and gets a pension of $875 (Canadian) a month compared to Alan Eagleson's $50,000 (US) per year upon retirement."

A chorus of "oh yeah" and "fuckin' right" rippled throughout the twenty-one NHL cities.

The second issue contained a cartoon portraying a

winged John Ziegler wearing an Alan Eagleson mask, holding a hockey player in his talons. "Is it an Eagleson, is it a Ziegler? No it's a Z-eagle!" ran the caption. Within days, the cartoon began appearing on locker room doors and team bulletin boards.

Again and again, the newsletter accused Eagleson of conflict of interest, double-dealing and fraternization with the NHL owners and League president John Ziegler. Each issue provided details of the Florida meeting and urged players to attend, to "change the direction of the NHLPA as well as the National Hockey League."

By mid-March, 175 players had sent in their $100. Several teams, like the Calgary Flames, had total support for the rebels, and even in clubs like the Canadiens and the Islanders, where Eagleson had powerful loyalists like Bobby Smith and NHLPA president Bryan Trottier, the number of players contributing $100 kept climbing.

On March 13, 1989, Alan Eagleson finally counter-attacked the "half-truths and untruths," "lies" and "absolute lies" with a bulging packet of information sent to each NHL player. That Eagleson was deeply worried and a little overwhelmed by what he was facing is evident in the hastily assembled, self-serving document, which actually confirmed some of Garvey's most damaging claims.

A February 1989 *Newsday* article, which he included in the package, presumably to buttress his position, was far more damning than supportive. Eagleson claimed that the piece "exonerated him," but the story comes under the "with friends like this who needs enemies" category. "He seems to win every faceoff when it comes to enriching himself, making several million dollars and a bundle of enemies along the way," ran the article, which reiterated the *Player's Voice* charges that Eagleson was close friends with the NHL brass and that he'd indirectly profited from the international hockey events he'd organized.

Much of the sparring between Eagleson and the Garvey group swirled around numbers. Eagleson claimed the players earned 46 percent of gross revenues; the other side claimed 20 percent. Eagleson maintained players earned $130 million in wages; the usurpers scoffed, saying he must have added in minor-league salaries, and lowered the figure to $80 million. Eagleson said League revenues were $300 million; his opponents, quoting Cliff Fletcher, the highly respected Calgary Flames general manager, upped it to $425 million. And so it went.

The question of who was right had little to do with the main point: the players had never read these figures before, coming from anyone. And they were beginning to wonder—about Eagleson, about international hockey, about the pension, about their collective-bargaining agreement and about their futures.

Some of Eagleson's strongest backers were in the NHL itself. "We're concerned," Steve Ryan, NHL vice-president of marketing and public relations, admitted. "Of course we're concerned when a handful of people with a handful of clients start attacking the man who has done a lot for the good of the game. Of course we're concerned."

At NHL committee meetings, governors fretted about losing their "tame union" and discussed strategies to pressure the players into backing away from Winter, Salcer and Garvey. "They were so terrified," confirms Bruce McNall, then the League's newest owner. "What is going to happen to Alan? They are terrified to this day."

The owners' support might have warmed Eagleson's heart, but it was a tactical blunder in that it reinforced many players' concerns that Eagleson was far too close to management. "The President and Eagleson shouldn't be buddy-buddy. It just doesn't look right," stated Toronto centre Ed Olczyk. "I wonder where that friendship goes. A favour here, a favour there. Each issue should be dealt with separately. Not on the basis of favours."

In the *Player's Voice*, Ed Garvey jumped on the issue of John Ziegler's protection of Eagleson: "With the lowest average salary in team sports, lowest minimum wage, lowest percentage of gross revenues going to players, worst collective-bargaining agreement, he should like Alan."

An exquisite irony flitted past unnoticed. In 1975, Ed Garvey had faced ferocious criticism from two NFL teams in his capacity as executive director of the players' association. "If anyone in hockey ever talks about me the way some of the players have talked about Garvey in some of their public statements," Alan Eagleson said at the time, "I'd just blast whoever it was and say get yourself another boy . . . if anything like what's happened to Garvey ever came up with hockey players, I'd be gone in a minute. I don't need a job that badly."

But, as momentum grew in the "oust Eagleson" campaign, so did his determination to hang on to the job he didn't need.

Eight weeks before the Florida meetings, Winter, Salcer and Garvey suddenly began finding it a lot more difficult to talk to the players. In Buffalo, for example, the team cancelled practice on the day scheduled for a meeting, and dressing rooms across North America were suddenly closed to them. In both Philadelphia and Edmonton, Rich Winter's clients were told point-blank that if they got rid of him, the clubs would renegotiate their contracts.

Publicly, Eagleson projected a slightly martyred but calm façade. Behind the scenes, however, he was feverishly manning the barricades. In May, player rep Dave Barr called NHLPA office manager Sam Simpson with a question, and right in the middle of his conversation up popped Eagleson. "Hey Dave, how the fuck ya doin'!" Barr shakes his head in wonderment. "I could never talk to him directly before. All of a sudden he's on the phone right away. Right away!"

Agents who hadn't heard from Eagleson in years also got fulsome phone calls. Herb Pinder smiled when he heard the high-pitched, rapid-fire voice at the other end of the line. "Herb, this guy Rich Winter—can you imagine him doing this? He's the guy who just stole Ron Hextall from me."

Pinder, enjoying himself thoroughly, commiserated: "I have no use for that kind of activity." Then he added, "But why are you castigating Rich Winter? Don't you remember when you stole Brian Propp from me?"

Eagleson's breath hissed tightly over the line: "I never did that."

"Alan, . . ." Pinder chided sadly.

"I don't remember that," Eagleson insisted.

"You may not remember, but I assure you that I remember that, Alan."

Most of the top player agents' feelings about Alan Eagleson range from passive dislike to intense loathing. But it was a measure of Eagleson's immense power that nearly all of them toed his line. They repudiated Garvey as "that guy who fucked up football" and dismissed Winter and Salcer as client-hungry. As for the specific attacks regarding pensions, the grievance procedure, the playoff split and free agency, most limply shrugged, "Well, you know. Al's done a lot for hockey."

Interestingly, those agents who did support the investigation into Eagleson and the NHLPA were concerned, not so much about what Al did or didn't do for the players, but about the perennial too-many-hats issue. "What other labour management relationship do you know of where the head of the union is rumoured to be the next president of the corporation?" scoffs Toronto lawyer and agent Gene McBurney. "The labour bar is very clear. I act for unions, I don't act tomorrow for management. I don't have some management clients and some labour clients. . . . He acted for a corporate law firm. He is a partner in a major corporate law firm. He has always been a management guy. His background is blue suit, blue Tory Machine."

McBurney doesn't believe that Eagleson's interest in hockey is, or ever was, grounded in any interest in labour. "Al probably got into this for the same reason that everybody else did. It's jock sniffing of the worst kind. It really is. Any lawyer who tells you that it's not is lying to you."

For hockey's eighty-nine player agents, choosing sides was a difficult matter. Even Herb Pinder, independently wealthy and thus relatively immune from any counterattack by Eagleson, found himself staring down the barrel of his future. "Everybody was afraid of getting on the wrong side," he admitted at the time. "The agents were, sort of, finding excuses, 'It's not my idea, therefore, I'm not going to let Winter—people didn't like Winter—I'm not going to let Winter lead me. I'm not going to support it if it is his idea.

"Boy did I have to do some soul searching! A lot of it was if I came out against Eagleson and he wins—he always has in the past—then where am I? Are you serving the players if you fight the system and lose? What if you lose and your players are disadvantaged?"

Two of the NHL's top agents were notably absent from Eagleson's telephone list. He rectified that at the March 30, 1989, press conference to announce which NHL players had been invited to play for Team Canada at the World Championships in Sweden. Completing his speech, Eagleson hurried over and attached himself like a leech to Bill Watters and Rick Curran. After nearly ten years of being shunned, the two men were surprised by his approach, which they described as "unctuous" and "grovelling." They vaguely agreed to keep "an open mind" about the issue and in Curran's words, quickly left to take "a long shower." (One observer noted with amusement that Eagleson was so bent over he could have tied himself into a knot.)

The instant Watters and Curran left the press conference, Eagleson addressed a clutch of waiting reporters. "It seems every five years someone tries to take a run at me," he said, speaking with his usual expansiveness. "This time it's Salcer and Winter. But they are two agents out of eighty-nine in the League. The scenes that took place today should tell you something." Eagleson then pointed to where he and Watters and Curran had been standing.

Later that same morning, at his Maitland Street offices, an entirely different Eagleson was on the thin edge of hysteria. Normally hyperactive anyway, he now walked and talked like an auctioneer on speed. Every few seconds, he glanced out into the corridor as if afraid a lynch mob might suddenly materialize.

One moment he claimed full control of the situation. "*Sports Illustrated* spent 750,000 bucks to try to nail me. They weren't successful. How do Winter and Salcer think

they're going to be [successful]?" The next moment he
screeched into the phone. "Do you know what those
fucking assholes have done now?" His vocabulary, always long on obscenity and high on volume, grew even
more so.

"They say fuck me?" he bellowed in someone else's
ear. "I'll fuck you if you try to steal my clients. And that's
one fuck those assholes will never forget."

That same night, yet another Eagleson was on show at
the fundraising reception for the 1990 Commonwealth
Games.* This Eagleson was the essence of power, a
rooster strutting in a chicken coop. Moving through the
wealthy, well-connected, dignified crowd, he dispensed
back slaps, arm squeezes and bon mots.

"You old fucker!" Eagleson shouted to the president of
a multinational corporation walking in the door. "You
son of a bitch!" he yelled at a provincial cabinet minister.
Those who were abused preened and smiled with pleasure.

After the toasts and speeches, Eagleson lifted one hand
and flicked a summoning wrist at a prominent sports
columnist. In under thirty seconds, a bevy of the thirteen
media people present had clustered tightly around him.
Bowing and guffawing hugely, they reacted like a single
organism to his scatological references to his current
"troubles".

That night, Alan Eagleson was unassailable, untouch-
able, utterly invulnerable. There was no way a couple of
jumped-up agents were going to topple this man.

One of the few perks of being a player rep in hockey is
attending the NHLPA annual meetings, usually scheduled
for some salubrious place like Nassau or Florida. After
months of travelling to places like Pittsburgh, Winnipeg,
Hartford, Edmonton and St. Louis—often at night or at
the crack of dawn, and mostly in the dead of winter—the
reps looked forward to these get-togethers. Eagleson

---

* Eagleson was co-chairman of the National Campaign Committee, the 1990
Commonwealth Games' fundraising arm.

once described the meetings as "something of a holiday. We'd meet in the morning, do a little business, and then go out and play golf or swim the rest of the day."

But beaches and golf links were a long way from the players' minds when eighty of them came together in Palm Beach, Florida, on June 2, 1989. The pro-Eagleson supporters, the association reps and the executive committee holed up at the fabled Breakers Hotel. The hotel atmosphere thrummed with tension as the responsibility of the next few days draped itself like a blanket over the players' shoulders. "I was there doing what I thought was best for the players," says veteran Bobby Smith, then a Canadien, "which was seeing that Eagleson's leadership remained intact."

The rabid anti-Eagleson faction, the doubters and the fence-sitters checked into the shopworn Hilton, a mile away. There, too, the air crackled with stress, but underlying it was a barely suppressed excitement, the half-dread, half-thrill that grips soldiers going into a battle they have a fifty-fifty chance of winning.

The bars in and around the two hotels resembled the anterooms of a major political convention as players, agents, lawyers and the inevitable floaters formed and re-formed into groups, like pools of oil in a fast-running tide. Support was tallied, then tallied again, and the good persuaders, ex-roommates and former teammates on both sides were dispatched to convince the doubters and the fence-sitters.

Many players slept poorly on June 3, the night before Ed Garvey was scheduled to speak, and quite a few didn't sleep at all. They lived with fear; it was as much a part of their profession as the equipment they wore. But this was fear of a different sort. "They were afraid if he [Eagleson] was not in control, our benefits would immediately disappear, which is totally ridiculous," says Mark Johnson of the New Jersey Devils. "Secondly, that we would be going on strike. Those were two things that they were barking about. The players were told, 'Your benefits and your dues are going to go up. Your benefits are good right now, why do you want to change things?'

People got intimidated and scared."

At 8:30 A.M. on June 4, the Starlight A room in the Breakers Hotel began to fill up. At one end, the NHLPA executive, Eagleson and his lawyer, Ed Sexton, sat at a long table. Players, some of them very careful about who they sat next to, found chairs throughout the room. The agents jockeyed for position, looking for the best sight-lines without giving any hint of whom they were supporting.

Centred part way down the room stood a podium with a mike, which the pro-Eagleson group had unwisely left unprotected. Ed Garvey slid quickly into place behind it and managed to stay anchored there for most of the day.

The air resonated with shuffling feet and a low, tense murmur. NHLPA president Bryan Trottier called the meeting to order and introduced Bill Sutton, owner of William J. Sutton & Co., Ltd., the company that carries the players' insurance policies. Sutton had been holding forth on the subject of insurance for a few minutes when L.A. Kings defenseman Dean Kennedy interrupted.

"Look, Ed Garvey has come all this way and has done this study. Let's hear him first." Kennedy then proposed this motion and the players voted to give Garvey the floor.

Until that moment, many of the rebels privately wondered if Ed Garvey could really stand up to Alan Eagleson. Neither players nor agents had ever seen anyone match Eagleson's verbal barrages, his ability to think on his feet and his uncanny knack of going right for the soft underbelly of his opponent. They had seen many sides of Ed Garvey in the previous eight months; a clear sense of what issues would win them the most support, an inclination to use his elbows and knees and a trade-unionist militancy. But would he be equal to Alan Eagleson?

Early in the proceedings, Garvey turned slowly and fastened his gaze on Eagleson's Toronto lawyer. "Now, Mr. Sexton, let me ask you a question. Who are you representing?" "Mr. Eagleson," came the firm reply. "In what capacity?" Garvey queried softly. "Well, Rich Winter has threatened to sue him." Garvey matter-of-factly explained that while Winter had indeed threatened to sue the NHLPA, no writ had ever been issued and no lawsuit was pending.

"Now what are you doing in Florida?" Garvey rapped out. "This threat of an action was commenced in Edmonton on someone in Toronto. But this never happened. Why did you have to be here, and at whose expense?"

Sexton set his mouth, raised his chin a little higher and said nothing. Later he tried to even the score. "And who are you here representing, Mr. Garvey?" he demanded. Instantly, fifty hands shot up, many of them clenched. Alan Eagleson's ghostly pale face twisted as if he'd been slapped.

Throughout the whole day, Eagleson sat, subdued, like a man who faces the rope and has run out of hope. At one point he stood up to talk. "Speak up Al!" bellowed a player from the back. Eagleson blinked, smiled weakly and, barely above a whisper, said, "Can you imagine anyone telling Al Eagleson to speak up?" A cascade of unsympathetic laughter filled the room.

What the players remember most about the Florida meeting was the transformation of Alan Eagleson. Overnight he had become a husk. Gone was the obscene and jocular repartee, gone was the confident strut, gone were the vicious put-downs, and the ego that had surrounded him like a permanent halo had shrivelled. "He was like a beaten puppy," recalls an amazed Dave Barr.

Eagleson began one explanation about NHLPA finances, and Jim Korn leapt out of his chair as if propelled. "No! No, you didn't say that, Al. I heard you. I was there in the room and this is what you said." Eagleson meekly sat down.

An hour and a half later after the meeting began, Rangers goalie John Vanbiesbrouck arrived, a hollowed-eyed, unshaven spectre. He had flown in late the previous night from Vancouver and spent a little too much time washing the dryness of the flight from his throat. The next morning, no one could wake him up, and they'd left for the Breakers without him. When he finally appeared, Vanbiesbrouck wasted little time, wading in with a volley of questions about the pension, sounding, comically, like an outraged husband grilling an unfaithful spouse.

There is always a certain amount of luck inherent in war, and always a surprise or two. In the corridor outside the meeting room Ed Garvey overheard an unguarded remark about Eagleson and mortgage funds. It was just a tantalizing hint, but Garvey swooped in and used the information to pummel Sam Simpson, eventually eliciting an admission that since 1982 more than $3 million of NHLPA funds had been lent to clients of Eagleson's law firm.

The loans involved Eagleson's law partner Howie Ungerman, his old friend Irving Ungerman and, indirectly, his daughter, Jill Eagleson as a co-lender. Eagleson defended the loans as "blue chip investments," but an independent lawyer examining the portfolio later called them "high-risk investment vehicles." The lawyer concluded that "the use of funds over the course of the years for private mortgages does not appear to have been a particularly successful investment strategy as interest paid on these funds has not garnered a more significant (nor a more secured) return than one might have obtained from guaranteed investment certificates."

Eagleson virtuously stated that "no commissions or fees have been charged to the NHLPA with respect to any of these mortgages." He neglected to mention that his law firm, Eagleson and Ungerman, had charged some of the borrowers thousands of dollars in fees "for legal services performed in the purchase of the property."

The players and the agents were transfixed by what they heard. "It caught up to him," says Herb Pinder. "Eagleson was so sloppy—the things that were found. He wasn't even being smart or careful, just blatant 'these are my 450 chickens for plucking here.'"

The next day, blood pressures soared as the player reps banished everyone from the room, including Eagleson, while they debated the fate of their leader.

Darryl Sittler, retired since 1982 and one of Eagleson's closest allies, shuttled in and out of the conference room, often disappearing in the general direction of Sam Simpson's suite. Then one of the agents challenged, "Sitt! What are *you* doing in there?" A white-faced Sittler scurried away.

Everyone knew it would be a very close vote. During the lunch break, two of Wayne Gretzky's closest friends—Kevin Lowe, an Eagleson supporter, and Marty McSorley, an insurrectionist—took turns on the telephone, trying to win his decisive vote for their side.

Herb Pinder tracked down Eagleson in Sam Simpson's room and suggested they meet. "I'll be right down," Eagleson responded quickly. He greeted Pinder and steered him out a side door so the two would not be seen together. As they set off down a long, tree-lined path, Pinder said gently, "I'd like to see a happy ending here. Is there anything I can do to help the discussion between the parties?" Eagleson eagerly agreed that any help would improve things. "You are going to have to resign," Pinder told him bluntly. "No! I will not do that. I will not resign! I have to go back to Toronto as head of the association."

Pinder then suggested that Eagleson propose a successor be hired, and that he stay on in a consulting role to the end of his contract. "Like in international hockey?" queried Eagleson hopefully. "Yes, something like that, where you have the background and you are good at it. You are not going to carry on anyway, you have been at it for twenty years." Eagleson nodded. "Yes, they are not going to have any tag days for me. I've done pretty well in business."

A tide of relief swept over Eagleson's face; he looked like a man trapped in a fire who has finally found an open door. He interrupted Pinder in mid-sentence. "Herb, we are back at one o'clock. I'd better hurry! I'll go talk to my advisors." With that, he wheeled around and bolted back to the hotel at a dead run, leaving Pinder standing alone. "If you could believe all the times over the years where he has dicked me around, . . ." says

Pinder today. "But I didn't feel vindicated. I felt sorry for the guy. Here was the Lone Ranger *running* back to his advisors. My emotions surprised me."

The NHLPA executive and player reps voted on whether to fire Eagleson outright or to retain him on terms to be dictated by the players. When the ballots were tallied, sixteen players had voted to keep him, twelve voted against. On the surface, it was a monumental victory for the man long touted as hockey's czar. But Eagleson lost that day just as surely as if the vote had been reversed. Seven of the twenty-eight votes were cast by the NHLPA executive committee, giving some teams two votes. Had there been one team, one vote, Eagleson would have been gone.

Even though he technically won the vote, the conditions he agreed to violated every aspect of Eagleson's personal and business code. He acquiesced to the formation of a search committee to hire an assistant to eventually replace him, agreed to have his income tax return inspected, promised to have NHLPA finances audited and assured the players there would be a July meeting in Toronto to discuss how these terms would be carried out.

At the last moment, Eagleson cancelled the July meeting and rescheduled it for August. Coincidentally, a large number of his opponents had unbreakable commitments that month—to hockey camps, wives, sponsors—as a result there was a small turnout, the majority of them by far Eagleson loyalists.

Compared to the Florida gathering, this meeting was skilfully orchestrated. NHLPA president Bryan Trottier allowed only player reps in the room, and the agenda was strictly controlled. Among the many conditions Eagleson had agreed to in June was that he would cease being a player agent. In Toronto, he waffled, claiming that he couldn't very well drop his clients unless he was sure the players wanted him. Another vote was taken. This time a much larger majority voted in his favour.

A few hours afterwards, a concerned John Ziegler called Aggie Kukulowicz in his Air Canada office to inquire about the results of the meeting. They sounded like family members commiserating about the health of a loved one. "It didn't go too badly," Kukulowicz told him. "Alan feels optimistic. At the end, even those like Marty McSorley were coming over to his side. It started like Florida but it turned around at the end. . . . Yeah, he's tired, John, but he looks good. It's all coming together for him."

Alan Eagleson's victory that August day in Toronto may have helped his morale, but the real victors were the players. In trying to unseat Eagleson, or at least hold him accountable, they underwent a subtle, psychological transformation. Never again would they, as a group, be terrorized by their executive director.

In Florida, Ed Garvey had humiliated, belittled and mocked him in front of everyone. And Eagleson, the former heavyweight intimidator of the NHL, had, in hockey's parlance, "turtled."

Chapter 12

Bucks, Pucks and the Million Dollar Kid

It is a given in hockey wisdom that Alan Eagleson has been the most powerful man in the sport for the last twenty-five years. Many assume that John Ziegler is controlled by Eagleson, or at least under his influence. Since 1977, the League president and the Players' Association executive director have developed a relationship that is unprecedented in recent labour history. "Ziggy and Iggy as they are sometimes called," wrote columnist Al Strachan in 1989, "travel to the Soviet Union together. They attended Wayne Gretzky's wedding together. When Gretzky was traded Ziegler was sought out for comment and he was found sharing a [golf] cart with Eagleson."

Typically, Ziegler has been portrayed as Alan Eagleson's dupe or his whipping boy. But John Ziegler has been content to let Eagleson generate the headlines while he transformed him, the man Clarence Campbell once called the NHL's "tooth fairy" into a veritable fairy godmother.

Ziegler has assiduously nurtured the friendship with Alan Eagleson, defending him, supporting him and subtly reinforcing his power over the players. In return, Ziegler has won for the NHL the complete passivity of the players bargaining agent, the NHLPA.

While all other sports have experienced skyrocketing player salaries, NHL player salaries have actually decreased in relation to the League's profitability. Keeping your employees' salaries low during a time of spiralling inflation in other sports is a significant business achievement, but doing it without making any particular concessions of your own is an astounding feat. When the NBA owners convinced players to back down from their demands for total free agency and agree to team salary caps, they were forced to introduce revenue sharing with the players. The NHL under John Ziegler has made no such concessions.

Even Alan Eagleson agrees that the NHLPA has generally done the giving and the NHL the taking. "The NHLPA was always willing to listen and renegotiate when the NHL presented their problems," he complained during 1986 collective-bargaining talks. "But when the NHLPA presented their requests, we were advised that we would have to wait until the present agreement expired."

While the League has profited from its relationship with Alan Eagleson, Ziegler's public image has not. No president of any sports league has ever been mocked and vilified like fifty-seven-year-old John Ziegler, Jr. His reign as NHL president began in 1977 with Harold Ballard publicly belittling him as an "office clerk" and "know-nothing shrimp"—privately, Ballard was less terse and more scatological. From the first, Ziegler was compared unfavourably to his predecessor, Clarence Campbell. Ziegler, it was said, didn't like hockey and neither looked nor acted the part of president. The public always assumed that Clarence Campbell was a man with clout and authority. In contrast, John Ziegler seemed small and inconsequential, especially compared to powerful figures like Eagleson and Bill Wirtz, owner of the Chicago Blackhawks and chairman of the board of governors since 1978.

Ziegler's unfortunate public persona was at its worst

during the great doughnut fiasco of May 1988. After a Friday evening playoff game between the New Jersey Devils and the Boston Bruins, Devils' coach, Jim Schoenfeld, ambushed referee Don Koharski as he left the ice and lambasted him with abuse. "Have another doughnut, you fat pig!" was Schoenfeld's most coherent and least offensive statement.

The NHL promptly suspended Schoenfeld without a hearing, but New Jersey filed for, and got, a court injunction against the decision just before the puck was dropped at the next game. In protest, the referees refused to take the ice, and the game was hilariously refereed by well-meaning amateur volunteers in yellow sweatshirts and hockey shorts, whose skating skills weren't quite up to par.

The event was turned into a catastrophe by the absence of John Ziegler who didn't attend the Friday game and, in spite of an intensive manhunt, couldn't be found until Monday. Lesser NHL officials scrambled madly to field increasingly belligerent questions and make eleventh-hour decisions. When he finally surfaced on Monday, Ziegler faced a hostile media—a situation that brings out the worst in him.

"'Where were you?' the reporters asked the president of the National Hockey league in 78 different ways. 'Why weren't you on the job?' 'I was on a personal errand,' he replied again and again. 'I don't have to explain my personal life to the public.' . . . John Ziegler was ridiculous," the Boston *Globe* reported, noting that the League seemed amazed at the public reaction. "Strangers are saying, 'Have a doughnut, you fat pig,' to other strangers, and everyone was laughing. Not with the NHL. At the NHL."

Recently, however, under the tutelage of Fraser Kelly and Bill Wilkerson, of Toronto public relations firm Fraser Kelly CorpWorld, Ziegler has metamorphosed. He has become more accessible to selected reporters and has appeared frequently on television looking more at ease and more statesmanlike. No matter what the subject, Ziegler manages to work in amusing stories about his own college hockey days, or shrewd analyses of a recent game he's watched.

Writers intending to deal with "touchy" subjects spend endless hours being briefed by Wilkerson on how to couch questions that the president might get "emotional" about. "Avoid pejorative words like 'Americanization' and 'violence,'" he advised one writer firmly. "He's better with initial interviews once you've got his intellectual facilities engaged, not his emotional," Wilkerson assured another writer.

Despite this "personality transplant," as *Globe* columnist Al Strachan acidly called it, if Ziegler is not well-briefed in advance or uncomfortable with the setting, he still puts his charm in his pocket. When cornered, his small, round and slightly rheumy eyes register ineffable boredom.

Late in 1989, a writer waylaid Ziegler as he waited for a reception hosted by the mayor of Toronto to begin. The writer politely explained that she hoped to schedule an interview soon and casually mentioned she'd made the first request eight months earlier, accompanied by all the requisite bona fides. "Well, I don't know about that," he said vacantly. "I just do what I'm told." And he darted off.

It would be easy to dismiss John Ziegler, but it would be a big mistake. The simple fact is that he—not Bill Wirtz or Alan Eagleson—is the single most powerful person in professional hockey, and has been for years. His gift of managing people in small groups, coupled with his ability to build movable coalitions when contentious issues are involved, has provided the League with nearly a decade of relative stability and profitability.

There are few people alive more spellbinding in a small group than Ziegler—when he has his heart in it. Those writers fortunate enough to get a lengthy interview are deluged with wonderful anecdotes and penetrating analysis. Sitting in the nook of his magnificent Fifth Avenue office in New York, resplendent with antiques and oil paintings, Ziegler is as accommodating as a long-time friend. His wry humour, which he uses to establish a comfortable intimacy, has a self-deprecating twist. He welcomes the most contentious topics, sliding around and through them with tolerant reasoning, easily transforming the NHL's many gaffes and blunders into either well-thought-out ventures with an as yet unseen "upside" or uncontrollable "acts of God."

Even before he took power in 1977, Ziegler sent a clear message that he had no intention of being a figurehead like Clarence Campbell. He bargained hard with the NHL governors, gaining considerably enhanced autonomy plus a $220,000 (US) salary, more than twice that of his predecessor.

Most assume that John Ziegler is and has been the creature of Bill Wirtz. "Wirtz pulls Ziegler's string and he jumps like a puppet," asserts Patrick Ducharme, who, as Detroit player Bob Probert's Windsor, Ontario lawyer, has had considerable dealings with the League. If anything, the relationship is a symbiotic one in which Ziegler has used his political skills to bolster Wirtz, while trading on the influence the older man has as owner of one of the original six franchises. Certainly in his running of the Chicago franchise, Wirtz has shown none of the skills attributed to him as the NHL's chairman of the board. During the forty-seven years that his family have been all or part owners of the Blackhawks, the team has managed only one Stanley Cup. Other owners privately sneer at the antiquated Chicago Stadium and the club's outmoded and haphazard marketing techniques.

Even Ziegler's critics applaud his mastery at keeping internal battles to a minimum. Though there have been two serious coup attempts by owners in recent years, the insurgents were quickly neutered by Ziegler's supporters and branded as marginal members of the League with petty grievances. Ziegler has held his opponents at bay by building carefully balanced compacts within the board of governors and using the strengths or power of one group to offset the weaknesses or animosity of another. "There are only four or five teams that support John 100 percent," observes an eastern U.S. owner. "So far that's been enough."

Perhaps the best example of Ziegler's skill is the sweetheart deal he arranged that gave the Gund brothers the expansion San Jose Sharks franchise without inciting a riot of discontent among the other owners.

It wasn't the first time Ziegler had rescued the Gunds. As chairman of the NHL board, he negotiated the NHLPA's bailout of the Gunds' Cleveland Barons in 1977. By persuading Alan Eagleson to offer up Players' Association funds, Ziegler avoided a storm of protest while keeping the enormously wealthy Gunds in hockey and grateful to him personally. When the Barons merged with Minnesota shortly afterward, the NHL quietly paid back the NHLPA.

Since then, the Gunds have been close to the seat of power in the NHL. They have demonstrated little aptitude for marketing hockey or managing a franchise, as evidenced by their handling of the Minnesota North Stars, a team that lost millions between 1982 and 1989, despite its enviable location in the heart of America's hockey country. Still, the Gunds are members of the NHL's powerful marketing committee. After years of whining about the city not supporting them and threatening to close down or move the club, the Gunds dumped Minnesota at the first opportunity. When Norm Green, formerly one of the Calgary Flames owners, took over the team, the North Stars went straight to the Stanley Cup and turned a tidy profit for the first time in ten years.

The Gunds were given the San Jose Sharks, the plum expansion franchise. Starting a full season before the new Ottawa and Tampa clubs, the Sharks will have a better selection of juniors to pick from while being bolstered by good young players brought over from Minnesota. After the dust and deals have settled, the cost of the Sharks franchise is only about $12 million, compared to $50 million for the other expansion teams.

Many governors balked at the special treatment accorded the Gunds and complained that such obvious preferential treatment made the League look unprofessional. Others suspected they knew only half of the deal. But Ziegler, stressing that the deal meant a stronger start to expansion, convinced the majority that keeping the Gunds in hockey was a priority for the game.

Ziegler's cultivation of L.A. Kings owner Bruce McNall is another example of his subtlety. As the newest owner, and the one furthest removed from traditional hockey centres *and* traditional hockey wisdom, McNall could have caused a lot of trouble. He's not afraid to throw convention out the window, and he's never been shy about protesting inequitites or trying to change something that doesn't work.

"I was kind of prepared to have battle with him [Ziegler]," McNall admits. "Early on, when we wanted to change divisions, I couldn't understand why would we be playing this all-Canadian division where I can't even get a plane flight directly to the city where I'm going. It was ridiculous. Why are we doing this? It doesn't help the sport. It's stupid." McNall appealed to Toronto to switch divisions. He lobbied other governors and made public statements, but got no sympathy or support.

Then Ziegler put McNall—to his and everyone else's surprise—on the powerful expansion committee. It was a brilliant move. Once part of the inner circle, McNall agreed to put his own agenda temporarily on the shelf until the latest expansion was complete.

Unenlightened self-interest is undoubtedly the biggest hurdle that John Ziegler vaults day after day. Individual teams' well-being in the other major professional sports is far more closely tied to the league's overall health. It isn't that the other pro sports owners are more benevolent than their hockey counterparts, but agreements, decisions and strategic plans—forced on them in part by strong players' unions—have required the owners to structure profits as a joint venture. They must co-operate for maximum individual gain. Hockey alone among the professional team sports doesn't have a major revenue-sharing agreement. "Hockey is very conservative," points out L.A.'s Jerry Buss, who has owned teams in both the NHL and the NBA. "It is much slower moving in terms of changes."

Jim Lites, executive vice-president of the Detroit Red Wings and owner Mike Ilitch's son-in-law, agrees that self-interest, to the point of suicide, is the biggest problem hockey faces. "In order to creep along, you are going to have twenty-one different approaches, all of whom pay lip service to 'Let's do it right for the League.' . . . They are being deceitful if they say they have the League's interest at heart. To a degree they do, but they are really worried about their own ass first. We are no different in that regard. We have the League's interest first—after our own!"

Self-interest in the League is nowhere more prevalent than in the area of broadcast rights. A source of vicious infighting since the early '60s, broadcast revenues have, more than any other issue, polarized the NHL. In large part, the anti-Canadian sentiment now prevalent in the League was created and inflamed by the battle over television.

In the early days, the American owners blamed the lack of a U.S. network contract on the Canadian owners, who were complacent with their own lucrative broadcast deals. Even as recently as the early 1980s, the fourteen American teams split approximately $3 million annually in broadcast revenue. In Canada, the Maple Leafs alone earned that much.

Molson Breweries was at the centre of the storm over television. The company had been a co-sponsor of hockey broadcasts in Canada since the early '60s and over the years used its advertising position and ownership of the Canadiens to dictate NHL policies regarding broadcast revenues. In 1971 Molson took over as major sponsor of "Hockey Night in Canada." By buying TV rights from all NHL teams, American and Canadian, Molson then gained control over the lion's share of broadcast revenues.

John Ziegler vowed to rectify this situation when he became president. "He promised to break Molson," states one television executive. "By 1984 when that hadn't

happened a lot of people weren't happy with him."*
Ironically, the whole issue was brought to a head, not by
the American owners, but by a stocky little Québecois
potentate by the name of Marcel Aubut, president of the
Quebec Nordiques. "I have been made for power," he
said solemnly shortly after the underdog Nordiques made
an improbable appearance in the 1981-82 Wales
Conference championships.

The NHL has a remarkable ability to send its own into
battle with their legs tied. As a condition of entry into the
League during the 1979 merger, the Nordiques had to
surrender claim to national TV revenues for five years.
With only local television exposure, a large debt and the
League's smallest market, it should have been a crippling
blow.

But the Nordiques survived, and after the five-year
penalty, Aubut didn't slide gratefully into the fold and
sell his broadcast rights to Molson, as did the other three
ex-WHA franchises. Instead, Aubut was instrumental in
helping the League put together an American television
package that competed directly with Molson. In the three
year deal, signed in 1984, the 14 American teams sold
home game rights to Carling O'Keefe, Molson's number
one competitor in the beer market. Molson had owned
those rights previously but the agreement had expired
that year

Ziegler, seeing the opportunity to loosen Molson's
hammer lock on television and win the gratitude of the
American owners, quietly supported Aubut. "It's open
warfare now," warned Molson Breweries' Roger Samson,
as lawsuits flew.

At first, Molson executives drew up various scenarios
to oust Ziegler, but in the end they chose a less con-
frontational route. They simply blocked CTV's efforts to
broadcast U.S. games back into Canada by cutting private

---

* It wasn't just the Molson monopoly that bothered the Americans. In 1983, a thirty-
second television spot during an NFL game cost advertisers $300,000. A thirty-
second spot in the NHL playoffs went for $20,000. Even accounting for the
relative popularity of the two sports, many considered the gap far too wide.

deals with major local stations to carry only CBC games. As a result, CTV broadcast some games but hardly anyone saw them. If CTV had been able to carry games on days when Canadian teams didn't play, the deal would have worked nicely. But the Canadian teams ensured they played on the same days as the U.S. teams so television stations were contractually obligated to carry the Canadian games. "It was," admits a television executive of the time, "dirty pool." In 1986, CTV walked away from their unprofitable $30-million deal. Molson made sure there would be no repeat of the situation by buying Carling O'Keefe in 1989.

So the NHL was back in virtually the same situation, the only difference being that Ziegler had forced Molson to give up their rights to the playoff games, allowing him to control the rights and share the revenue with the entire League. Many American owners still weren't happy, and their discontent increased with Ziegler's 1988 cable-TV deal. In 1985, ESPN had signed a three-year contract to carry NHL games. When the upstart SportsChannel America outbid ESPN in 1988 with a $51-million, three-year offer to the League, the sound of back-patting echoed throughout NHL corridors.

As has been the case since the 1950s, the NHL paid bitterly in the end for choosing the quick buck. The $51 million placated the anti-Ziegler faction in the short term, but it quickly became apparent that SportsChannel couldn't deliver the 27 million homes it had promised. Desperately in need of exposure, especially just before expansion, the NHL suddenly found itself with access to only 9 million homes, less than a quarter of the American viewers it had with ESPN.

Though they will stoutly deny it, many within the League secretly believe that hockey can never hope to compete with baseball, basketball or football in the all-important American market. And, though they may dream of it, League executives don't really contemplate the day when the Stanley Cup playoffs will prompt viewers in Topeka, Houston or New York to change channels in the middle of early-season baseball games. In their hearts, more than a few owners don't even believe that hockey will ever again get an American network television contract.

A 1990 American survey placed hockey forty-ninth in a list of favourite spectator sports, behind bowling and water-skiing. Even in Canada, hockey is losing ground. According to a national survey conducted by the University of Lethbridge, 26 percent of respondents named the Toronto Blue Jays as their favourite sports team. The Toronto Maple Leafs garnered only 9 percent and the 1990 Stanley Cup Edmonton Oilers, who had won five cups in seven years, received only 6 percent.

Interestingly, the Montreal Canadiens, considered the most skilled marketers in hockey, received 21 percent of the vote, even in the midst of rising anti-francophone feelings. This result suggests that attaining the stature of a major-league sport is possible if the NHL is able to utilize its assets. And that means marketing.

Just comparing the League's pathetically thin retail sales catalogue with those of other sports speaks volumes. The trinkets and other knick-knacks it contains generate sales of only $80 million a year. Retail sales in major League baseball topped $300 million for 1990, and renting out the league's logo brought in a further $750 million. Again, the hockey figures are low, even accounting for the relative popularity of the two sports.

For over a decade, members of the NHL's board of governors have agreed that marketing should be a priority. "We really haven't pushed it as much as we should have. I think that's starting to happen," says Arthur Griffiths, Vancouver Canucks vice-chairman and governor, a bit hopefully. "I'm sure you'll see much more emphasis on that in the future."

The League's official marketing plan, "NHL Marketing —A Vision for the 90's," prepared by Steve Ryan, president of NHL Services Inc., is a brief and fatuous document. Its four pages, including the cover page, are strewn with platitudes and generalizations. "Net, Net!" ends the epistle. "'Vision for the 90's' is a global marketing driven business with continued focus on excellence and growth."

John McMullen, owner of the new Jersey Devils and also of baseball's Houston Astros, is far more scathing about the League's attempts to market itself and, more importantly, its star players. "I'm not satisfied," he states tersely, emphasizing that hockey actually has a wider and larger audience geographically than the other three big American sports, and implying that it has taken hockey executives far too long to wake up to the potential of the worldwide audience.*

But the issue is not so much how many puck-shaped ashtrays the NHL sells but the cohesion within the League's board of governors and the motivation to push hockey into taking maximum advantage of its potential. The board of governors is still a fractious bunch, undermined by internecine squabbles. The fact that most of these fights don't see the light of day is a tribute to John Ziegler's leadership.

Still, a growing number of owners are again complaining about Ziegler's failure in the areas of television and marketing. They also feel completely isolated from the League's powerful core group. "I'd like to see a rotation basis of all committees and so forth," says McMullen, who battled against terms for his Devils (first the Kansas City Scouts, then the Colorado Rockies) that were so punitive many predicted his team would not last the 1982-83 season, its first in New Jersey. "I would like to see *different* people involved—that is where you get the best results. That's not done in hockey. They [the committees] tend to be much more stable. I think that the different committees should be changed and rotated, and the abilities of the people better utilized."

Red Wings owner Mike Ilitch, the Little Caesar's pizza franchise king, dragged a money-losing team out of the basement, wooed back the fans and, using a promotion-first philosophy, pulled Detroit out of the red and back

---

* John McMullen has a keen feel for hockey's appeal outside North America. His was the first NHL team to court Eastern Bloc players and successfully bring them into the League.

into the black in just five years. Yet Ilitch and his senior staff are among the most under-utilized in the League.

"We have always felt a little slighted here in Detroit," admits Jim Lites, "and I don't think the League has taken good advantage of our strengths. [It's] disappointing that teams that couldn't market their way out of a paper bag are being utilized. The same people get selected to these committees that have real authority and can really make changes in the system. . . . I think it's an inbred situation."

A large part of the NHL's problem is inept marketing, but an even bigger part is confusion about exactly what is being marketed. Because the NHL has never understood that the players are its biggest asset, the sport has consistently failed to live up to its potential. John Ziegler's dextrous handling of the players had led to the League's prosperity throughout the eighties, but it is the kind of double-edged sword on which the NHL has always gored itself.

Professional hockey is entertainment—nothing more, nothing less. Part of the allure of recording and film stars like Madonna, Arnold Schwarzenegger and Eddie Murphy is that they are billed, treated, promoted and most importantly, paid like deities. But the NHL views high salaries and player freedom as the ruination of hockey. Others have a different view. "People are saying, 'Eddie Murphy, how can he possibly be paid $12 million a movie?" observes Bruce McNall. "It's easy when he's generating $300 million a movie. It's very simple."

McNall has proved that what works in the movies also works in hockey. The NHL fraternity drew a sharp, hissing breath when he bid $18 million (US), just $2 million less than he paid to buy the entire franchise, to get Gretzky from Edmonton to Los Angeles. Hockey seers inhaled again when McNall voluntarily renegotiated the $1.25 million (US) annual contract Gretzky had with the Oilers.

"I said, 'Wayne, I have to be honest with you,' McNall recalls. 'I know basically what most players in this League should be making, but I have no idea in your case. I have no idea.' He said, 'Well, I don't either.' So I threw out a number to him [$3 million a year]. I said, 'How does this sound?' He goes, 'No, no, that's way too much. How about this amount [$1 million]. I said, 'I don't think that is consistent with what will happen in the near future. We don't want to have to redo this every two minutes.'

"So we were negotiating in reverse. He was at one price lower and I was trying to pull him up. He was trying to keep it down. That was before we ever sold a ticket. That was before we ever knew his value to the franchise. He could have said '$10 million a year is what I want.'"

Gretzky has always been an advocate of the Gordie Howe school of negotiating—"Pay me what you think I'm worth." When he finally happened on an owner who did just that, a whispered revelation rippled through the League's four hundred players: "Wayne has been holding us back for a decade."

In the end, Gretzky and McNall settled on $2.5 million (US).

Though a hockey neophyte, McNall knew a drawing card like Gretzky could make or break a team. He understood the value of an honest-to-goodness star, and he didn't mind paying to get him. "My first thought, prior to the Gretzky deal, [was] I felt I was buying an undervalued asset at a cheap price. . . ."*

Based on the money he has generated for the Los Angeles team, McNall estimates that Gretzky was worth $50 million the day he walked into the Forum in Inglewood, California.

Jerry Buss, who owned the Kings until 1988, is one of

_____

* Not only did McNall pay an unheard-of sum for Gretzky, but with one stroke he dismissed one of hockey's most dearly beloved tenets—the importance of building a team through draft choices—by including three first-round draft choices in the deal, in addition to players Jimmy Carson and Martin Gelinas. "I've never viewed the draft picks as being worth a lot. I don't to this day. I did a lot of research on that prior to the deal. It's like my horse business. When you buy a yearling at yearling sales, you are buying pedigree only. You have no clue as to whether this horse has any heart or an ability to run or anything else. In many ways it's the same with a very young hockey player."

the sharpest sports entrepreneurs in the world, yet he couldn't even get the Kings on local radio. He negotiated a TV contract, but only because he owned the cable network. To get people to watch the Kings he forced Lakers fans to buy package deals that included Kings tickets.

Year after year, the crowds at hockey games hovered around 10,000 per game. The year before Gretzky went to Los Angeles, the Kings brought in about $4 million at the gate. Receipts jumped to $13 million in the 1989-90 season, his second year with the team. McNall also believes Gretzky is directly responsible for a further $15 million annually in advertising revenues. After amortizing his contract, and adding in additional costs like insurance, Gretzky has improved the Kings' cash flow by $7 to $10 million a year, minimum.

Moreover, the franchise McNall paid $20 million for three years ago is now worth in the neighbourhood of $100 million. He has been offered more than $30 million in cash just to relocate his team in another arena. "I underestimated Gretzky's enormous response here," McNall admits happily. "I knew in Canada it was huge, but I misread that myself. Thank God! Had I read it well, I probably would have paid Peter [Pocklington] more money!"

In the sixteen months following Gretzky's signing, a record eleven high-profile players had negotiated or renegotiated contracts for large increases, including Mario Lemieux's $2-million annual deal. "There's no question the Gretzky contract catapulted the NHL salary structure," stated Bob Goodenow, then still an agent. "There is an ability to pay that has been unlocked." And it wasn't just the stars who profited. "In the last six months the salary structure has changed dramatically," confided New York agent Jay Grossman. "It's not acceptable to offer a first-year player $105,000 anymore. Now they're getting $135,000 to $145,000."

In the summer of 1990, the St. Louis Blues, long one of the NHL's weakest teams, got into the act. First they paid seventy-two-goal-scorer Brett Hull $7.3 million over three years. He had made $125,000 the previous year. Then, taking a page out of the Bruce McNall book, they signed free-agent defenseman Scott Stevens, then with the Washington Capitals. In return, the Blues willingly gave up two first-round draft picks as required compensation to the Capitals.* Stevens is a good player but hardly a superstar. Still, the Blues raised his $300,000 annual salary to $5.1 million over four years.

Other NHL teams howled that the Blues were going to ruin themselves in particular and hockey in general. But the St. Louis management jumped ticket prices more than $5 a seat and filled the arena for the first time in a decade. Spending $2.25 million annually in salary on two players turned out to be a pretty good business deal when the club grossed an additional $6 million in 1990-91.

The '90s are filled with uncertainty for the NHL: the next television contract, the success of the new expansion teams, the effect of rising salaries, the possibility of at least one rival league and the ramifications of the retired players' lawsuit over the pension surplus. But the most dangerous uncertainty of all is the future of the NHL's profitable relationship with the Players' Association. Since Eagleson's wings were clipped by the players at the 1989 confrontation in Florida, no one has been sure who is running the NHLPA or, more important, who will make the real decisions in the 1991 collective-bargaining talks.

Though Eagleson intends to remain until the new collective-bargaining agreement is negotiated, there are signs that his control in hockey has slipped significantly. In May 1991, several players invited to play for Team Canada at the Helsinki World championships declined. Eagleson was also having difficulty putting together a team for the September 1991 Canada Cup. Some players openly objected to Team Canada coach and longtime Eagleson client Mike Keenan, whose player relations techniques make marine corps drill sargeants seem like softies. Others privately explained they didn't "have to

---

* Washington received $100,000 and two first-round draft picks in the top seven in 1990 and 1991. If the Blues don't have a top-seven pick, Washington receives three first-round choices through 1995.

put up with abuse from Alan Eagleson any more." Many of those who did agree to play in the Canada Cup did so only because Wayne Gretzky had committed himself to act as a "buffer."

It was a surprising state of affairs for the man who had recently signalled his interest in becoming president of the International Ice Hockey Federation. Though most in pro hockey have long assumed the job was his for the taking, the thought provokes gagging, laughter or both from the CAHA *and* Hockey Canada officials. Gord Renwick, an IIHF council member since 1979 and a candidate for the position, pauses to consider the question. "There's not a chance," he states quietly and firmly. "First of all, he's seen as being head of the union. The IIHF sees itself as an amateur organization, he's a full-time person. The other thing is, he would be seen as so dominant for the NHL, and all of a sudden Canada would be way too strong."

In 1989, the internationally respected Renwick was Canada's best chance to break the traditional European lock on the position of IIHF president. But dedication and proven competence were not sufficient to alter events at the highly political hockey federation Congress in Bern, Switzerland that year. Renwick, recovering from a devastating car accident which nearly killed him and his wife, also had to fight a nasty rumour campaign. Word circulated that the accident had left him with irreparable brain damage.

Many involved in the sport complain that altering the course of the IIHF is a ponderously slow task. President Gunther Sabetzki, supported by Eagleson, was re-elected that year. Still, there are strong indications that change is not far off in the international organization. Eagleson's hockey power outside of Canada is a little like an inverted pyramid balancing on a very fine point. He does not, and never has had, the domination in international hockey he's been credited with.

Eagleson's international power came directly out of his ability to deliver NHL players cheaply to a series of enormously profitable international events. But if he doesn't have the players, he doesn't have the clout. Additionally, those events, primarily the Canada Cups, aren't nearly as important as they used to be.

In recent years, the IIHF's kitchen-table operation has changed dramatically. Not long ago, the federation had to beg countries to host the various world junior tournaments because funding was so meagre. Today, major sponsors line up, and finding a host is never a problem. With far more sophisticated marketing, the IIHF now makes more than twice as much money from a World Championship as a Canada Cup event.

Within Canada, hockey officials are increasingly less willing to put up with Eagleson's international image. During the 1987 World Junior Championships in Prague, Czechoslovakia, Eagleson organized a dinner party for himself at a restaurant. At one point, the restaurant owner brought out a cake and went through a little ceremony in honour of Eagleson. Before he was finished, Eagleson looked up and snapped, "Look, okay, thanks for the cake. Now fuck off, we are trying to have our dinner."

"The guy just looked at him," Pat Reid recalls, still amazed. "He just crushed the guy and everybody said, 'What an ignorant son of a bitch!' The guy kind of turned and left. . . . He was going through this whole elaborate thing because he was so proud of Canada and hockey and Alan as the leader. That reflects on everybody. Everybody is then viewed as being a belligerent asshole."

The other point of contention in Canada is Eagleson's entourage, which accompanies him to international events. One CAHA official estimates that these "floaters" cost Hockey Canada as much as $200,000 per tournament. "I see their clothing contracts, which I'm privy to. Hockey Canada would take four or five doctors, people who wouldn't even have a role to play! They outfit fifty or sixty people. So you are talking twenty players and eight staff, which is not even thirty, and then there is another twenty or thirty for the floaters—at least. . . . We collectively pay, the hockey fraternity pays, for him to maintain his entourage."

Hockey people in Canada don't believe Eagleson has the support to win Gunther Sabetzki's job. But they are very worried that Sabetzki will create an executive directorship for the IIHF and unilaterally hire Eagleson for the job.

While those on the international scene are very clear about where Alan Eagleson fits in, there is less certainty about his position with the Players' Association.

Bob Goodenow, NHLPA assistant executive director since 1989, looks like an Irish barroom brawler with coarse, heavy-set features.* Yet, there is an inscrutability about the man, a sense that he's making many small and subtle moves that will pay off far in the future.

Goodenow was deeply involved in the 1986 agent uprising against Eagleson, but his name is conspicuously absent from the most inflammatory documents and correspondence. And in the months prior to the 1989 Florida vote on Eagleson's future, Goodenow positioned himself so well that both factions came away convinced he was sympathetic to their side. Even though several of Goodenow's clients were among the prime insurgents, nobody can remember exactly what he was doing or where he was sitting during the two-day showdown.

Goodenow has needed all of his inscrutability since moving in to await Eagleson's departure when he will take over as executive director. Over the past year he has absorbed dozens of large and small slights. At the 1990

---

* As a Detroit lawyer and player agent, Goodenow slowly built up a formidable client list, capped by the August 1990 signing of Brett Hull to the St. Louis Blues. But his contract with the NHLPA called for him to drop all his clients by 1991.

World Championships in Switzerland he asked Eagleson for accreditation to watch the games but was told, "You are an American, go ask the American team for accreditation."

Still Goodenow is methodically taking control of all the little levers of power. He has met with agents many times, individually and in groups. He has begun to streamline the NHLPA administration, and has worked to repair the association's relationship with hundreds of disenchanted players and agents. "It's refreshing. We had a meeting, we had speakers, we even got information we didn't ask for. And, if you can believe it, Bob actually asked for our opinions!" marveled player agent Herb Pinder after a 1990 conference with Goodenow.

As they did in 1979, the players now hold the future of the NHL in their hands. If they and Bob Goodenow recognize this, they may be able to rectify years of terrible deals, one-sided concessions and blatant inequities that previous bargaining has built into their relationship with the owners. They might also be able to force the League to see them, for the first time, as the NHL's primary asset. Harry Ornest, former owner of the St. Louis Blues, sums up the prevailing attitude: "The players are like actors. You have to have them or you don't have anything, but there is an endless supply of them."

No one really believes that there is an endless supply of talented players. The trick, as far as the NHL owners is concerned, is to keep them—particularly the stars—thinking that they are as replaceable as tissue paper.

The NHL's sins of the past may catch up to it in the form of centre Eric Lindros. The League has to come up with a more equitable deal for the players, especially in freedom of movement, because the new breed of players aren't likely to buy the old "for the good of the game" argument. Lindros could be the one to ram that message home.

Clearly the prototypical NHL star of the 1990s, Lindros has one glaring failing, at least as far as the owners are concerned: he doesn't know his place. He is the first rookie of his calibre who refuses to approach hockey on bended knee and ransom his future for his love of the game. At eighteen, Lindros knows what he's worth, and, more to the point, he knows exactly how his team and the entire League will profit from his presence.

As talented as Mario Lemieux, with Wayne Gretzky's drive and determination, Lindros is the most coveted player to come along in generations. First choice at the 1991 NHL draft, he could actually have played in the League as a sixteen-year-old. When all the secret deals are made and codicils written, he will be the first NHL rookie to make $1 million annually, and that's not counting a $1-million signing bonus.

Physically, Lindros is matchless. At six feet, five inches and 220 pounds, even as a teenager he's one of the largest players in hockey. Though he lacks a man's full muscularity, he's already conquered the large-player gangliness that often plagues oversize players into their twenties. He skates with the compactness, speed and power of a smaller man.

People can't help but notice the big things that Lindros does, but it is the subtle ones—the polish and the small, but incredibly difficult moves that he turns into everyday occurrences—that make him distinctive. He can take the puck off his skates without losing momentum, use the boards to carom deadly accurate passes to teammates and handle the stick as if it were an extension of his body.

A frustratingly common scene in front of the net is an unattended puck sitting while attacking players sail helplessly past or scramble in the vicinity, unable to stop and get a shot on net. Lindros routinely stops, pivots and snaps a precise shot in a single motion. It is a combination of skills only a handful of players have ever been able to master.

When he has time alone on the ice, he'll practise, as most players do, firing pucks at the net. But Lindros doesn't stand thirty feet out and blast away. He will stand slightly to one side, give himself a small shooting margin and whip one after another into the top corner. He'll also practise shifting his stick from side to side and shooting with one hand, the other hand, or both. A sensible thing for a centre to practise, but it's rarely done.

For all Eric Lindros's speed and finesse, it is his mastery of the primal side of the game that electrifies the hockey fraternity. He likes that aspect, even seeks it out—a characteristic rarer than one might think among hockey players. At the 1990 World Junior Evaluation camp in Saskatoon, Eric was one of the youngest of the top forty-five juniors, sixteen of them already first-round draft choices, in the country. Observers marvelled as older, more experienced players hit him, bounced and went down hard, with surprising regularity.

Though Lindros checks well and usually cleanly, even managing to keep his stick down while he's at it, there's a tantalizing hint of dirty play surrounding him that never fails to excite hockey people. In Saskatoon a group of scouts—the Don Quixotes of sport—sat together extolling his virtues. Lindros scored a pretty goal out of one scramble, but the scouts didn't care. "Did you see that knee! Did you see that knee!" one of them squealed. "He almost got him right in the fucking stones!" "Yah, he can hardly fucking walk," happily chorused a second as the victim of the Lindros knee dragged himself back to the bench.

Another scout merely nodded and smiled serenely, like the Dalai Lama. Alone among those present, his team had a shot at finishing last in the NHL and drafting the prodigy.

There is a fine line players must find and not stray from in order to win the approval of both their fellow players and management. They must be tough and determined on the ice, yet biddable and easygoing off. They must be "team players" and selfless when it comes to the good of the club, yet individuals with self-direction and ambition at the same time. It is a confusing combination, which Lindros has sorted out in his own way. And already that's bothering the hockey world.

As a marketing commodity, Eric Lindros is an irresistible package. Hockey players with gapped teeth, sidewinder noses and chainsaw scars are the least physically appealing of professional athletes. Lindros, with the darkly brooding intensity of a young Rudolph Valentino, plus sharply etched features and full, sculpted lips, could be Hollywood beefcake.

And when he opens his mouth, he's refreshingly un-hockeylike. His words are articulate, clear and obviously intelligent, with none of the droning monotone larded with clichés that makes interviewing athletes such a tough job. Refreshingly, when a TV interviewer asks a particularly dumb question, Lindros lets him know it with a slight irritation in his voice, a hard quarter-second stare or an overly patient answer.

There's also a wholesome niceness to Lindros that many admire but still scrutinize suspiciously for signs of insidious weakness. Unlike many of the other highly touted juniors at the Saskatchewan camp, Eric endeared himself to the equipment managers by not bitching about his equipment.

"When we were over in Finland last year," recalls Pat Reid, "I walked back into the arena to pick up my bag. We had this little Finnish guy who was helping us carry sticks and pucks. There was Eric down in the net with the milk crate, picking up the pucks for the guy and putting them in. . . . He didn't see me and nobody was in the arena . . . he didn't do it because he was trying to im-press the scouts in the stands or anybody. He just did it because that is the kind of kid he is."

When Eric agreed to let the CAHA use his picture to promote the 1990 World Junior Championships in Saskatchewan, he did so only on the condition that he be accompanied by teammates. "I don't like to be promoted in front of the players," he emphasizes. "I won't do them [promotions] in front of other players. When someone goes up to me and asks me for an autograph, I go, 'This is so-and-so next to me,' too. I'm trying to plug my team-mates because I realize that when they get attention, I get attention too. It's a two way street. When jealousy arises, it makes it a little tough to play. No one needs that."

Like their son, Bonnie and Carl Lindros are nice peo-ple, solid people, the sort of people you'd like to have as neighbours. But if they have to, they'll straight-arm any-one who tries to tell them what to do. Carl's size six-foot five and self-assurance would make him a formidable foe, but he's really the family "good cop." Bonnie is the "bad cop" and bullshit-detector. "I get a lot of mom jokes at the rink," Eric admits. When there's a problem to sort out, it's Bonnie who exhorts and bullies through to a solution. It's a thankless role, and she has become a lightning rod for the animosity and controversy surround-ing Eric in recent years. But it does take the pressure off her son.

When Eric was only ten, and it became clear to the Lindroses that he could be an NHL prospect, they began planning. Carl, a chartered accountant, was once scouted by the Chicago Blackhawks and had a first-hand grasp of the realities of professional hockey. "I could skate rea-sonably well, but I had cement hands. The only reason I was a starter in Junior A was because I was thumping people. I was told to go and pound the piss out of some-body and for a couple of weeks I did it. Then I finally said, 'If this is what I have to do to be on the team, who needs it?'"

Eric's parents initially registered him in a non-competi-tive league, a "church league type of environment." His passion for hockey soon overshadowed everything, and despite his lack of competitive experience, his parents soon noticed he did things a little differently than his teammates, like using the boards to make passes, and an-ticipating the play.

The Lindroses don't do things by halves, and they all waded in and became involved in his evolving career. Their enthusiastic participation wasn't and isn't, without its dark moments. Today, Carl admits that for a while he became a demanding, obsessive "hockey jerk parent." It wasn't long before Eric, and his younger brother Brett, began wishing someone else would drive them home. "He was so overwhelmed with wanting me to succeed and my brother to succeed that after a game around the peewee level, we would be coming home and, even though I had a good game, he would still be trying to tell me what to do and how to improve," says Lindros. One day, Bonnie insisted they take two cars to the rink. Carl took the hint.

Carl and Bonnie did all the regular things that parents of superstars like Bobby Orr and Wayne Gretzky did. They constructed the requisite backyard rinks, even filling in a swimming pool to make one, paid for additional early morning rink time and took a very active role in Eric's coaching. "I'm a firm believer in practising skills," says Carl. "Basically, it forces them to do the things they don't do well, taking a pass out of their skates, using their backhands." They had no difficulty persuading their intense son to spend time at drills.

None of that is unusual in the life of a hockey family. But the Lindroses went one step further—they looked into the future and decided to put Eric on the path to controlling his own destiny. "We weren't saying Eric was going to be a superstar. But once he demonstrated an interest in it, we researched it, talked to as many people as we could . . . came up with a game plan."

The game plan involved writing to Wayne Gretzky's parents, Bobby Orr's parents and agents Bill Watters and Rick Curran. They even investigated athlete stress and burnout with a coach from the University of Western Ontario. And they contacted Paul Beeston, the vice-president of the Toronto Blue Jays, to discuss professional sport in general. The result was that, unlike most players his age, Eric had a strong sense of his own worth and the importance of putting his personal priorities before those of others who might want to manipulate him for their own interests.

It was at the 1989 Ontario Hockey Midget Priority Selection Draft on May 29, 1989, that Eric, then sixteen, sent his first message to the NHL brass about the kind of player they would be dealing with in two years' time. And it was there that Lindros learned his first real lesson about the business of hockey.

The midget draft is an abomination in a sport that specializes in practices ranging from the merely cruel to the blatantly illegal. Anyone who thinks that minor hockey in

Canada is about fun, character-building and recreation need only attend the annual OHL draft. At least in the NHL entry draft, the chosen eighteen-, nineteen- and twenty-year-olds are nearing adulthood. At the midget draft—a harsh, face-first slam against reality—it is fifteen- and sixteen-year-olds who are having their future careers launched or ended.

It is a system that makes no allowance for disparities in maturation rate, physical or psychological, and forces parents, coaches and players to stress immediate performance over development. Since junior hockey teams are businesses whose survival depends, in part, on income they receive for sending players to NHL teams, even the most noble of coaches, general managers and owners have difficulty justifying gambling on a player for the sake of his development years down the road.

In May 1989, two thousand friends, teammates and parents packed the North York Centennial Centre, on the outskirts of Toronto. Tension reverberated through the stands. People squirmed in their seats, eyes darted, hands fidgeted. Hardly anyone could sit still, but, for all the movement, an eerie silence prevailed.

The players congregated uncomfortably at one end, near the entrance. There was a huge line-up at the washroom, where the searing smell of vomit, mixed with sweat and urine, seeped out into the foyer. Inside, players were gingerly moving around the slick floor as if they were on skates, and one desperately tried to scrub off the results of errant urination with a paper towel.*

None of the people present knew that the real drama of the draft was being played out between two men in the cramped quarters of an anteroom next to the ticket both. At issue was Eric Lindros, who had done something

---

* Many were weary from the night before, when dozens of little dramas were enacted in various hotel rooms. Until 3:00 A.M. clusters of agents, sometimes with players and parents in tow, scurried from room to room making last-minute deals. Expectations were hyped or subtly lowered. Teams and agents bargained furiously. GMs struck deals with agents over players worth drafting for their trading value. Parents fussed and worried over letting their sons leave home for a sensitive coach or insisting they stay nearby and suffer under a martinet.

unpardonable. He had refused to report to the Sault Ste. Marie Greyhounds, the team with the first draft choice if the club picked him.*

Eric's parents, along with his agent, Rick Curran, had patiently explained to the Greyhounds and owner Phil Esposito that Eric would not play in Sault Ste. Marie under any circumstances. The Lindros family liked the Sault Ste. Marie team and Eric did want to play in the OHL, but the combination of the distance from home and lack of educational opportunities in the Soo was simply not acceptable to the close-knit family. Carl Lindros met with the Greyhounds twice and politely but firmly told them Eric wouldn't report. The family's preference was Oshawa, but they gave the OHL a short list of three teams he would report to if drafted.

Junior hockey is amateur in name only. Situations like this have occurred many times in the past, but usually they are smoothed over with a signing "bonus"—a car, or some other favour. But Curran and the Lindroses were adamantly opposed to such "bribes." They knew how friction can develop on a team when word leaks out that one player is set so far above the rest. And those things never remain secret for long.

Curran had spent a long night calling team and league officials and was disheartened by what he heard. Essentially, they'd rather teach Eric Lindros a lesson than accommodate him and allow everyone to profit. "I told those sons of bitches—you know I've fucking manipulated the draft so that a first draft goes tenth and that some years I've had the first ten choices," he said with exasperation the day of the draft. "So if I tell them Lindros isn't going to report, there's no fucking way he's going to report!"

Phil Esposito has a flambuoyant manner, articulation and sartorial style. Even in celebrity-weary Manhattan, while general manager of the Rangers, he cut a broad swath.

---

* Under OHL rules at the time, players picked in the first round could not be traded to any other team. A first-round choice who didn't report could not play for any other Ontario Junior A team.

At a 1989 lunch in a Manhattan hotel to honour Esposito and Mickey Mantle, legendary centre fielder of the New York Yankees, crowds lined the corridors surrounding the dining room. Autograph hounds jostled each other to get near the media lounge, where a sweating Mantle was pinned against the bar by a horde of reporters. Esposito, already an hour late, was nowhere to be seen. Mantle shook hands, posed for promotional shots, signed autographs and looked like he'd rather be at the dentist.

Just as lunch was announced, a tall figure in a dark, double-breasted suit strode into view. An entourage surried, dipped and circled around him. Quiet reigned briefly before virtually everyone abandoned Mantle and rushed out to be enveloped in Esposito's magnetic aura.

Phil Esposito is a nice guy, and for an ex-superstar professional athlete he's even thoughtful, but emotion races through him, and when it escapes, commonsense and kindness can evaporate. The day of the draft, Esposito's state was explosive. His beloved New York had turned against him. Just days before, he had been humiliatingly fired as Rangers GM and publicly savaged by the New York press.

In the North York arena ticket booth, Rick Curran faced Esposito. Short, slight, greying and dressed in a dapper but conservative three-piece suit, Curran's lack of height and boyish demeanour are deceptive. His steel was honed on the whetstone of Alan Eagleson, and he was more than a match for the angry 220-pound Esposito.

On the surface, the confrontation between Esposito and Curran was the classic struggle between owner and player buffered by an agent, but as with most things in hockey, many wheels spun beneath the surface. Both men had a lot to lose. Though they obviously relied on him, the Lindroses had made no formal commitment to Curran. A dozen competitors were snapping at his heels. In order to properly look after Lindros as well as his existing clients, Curran had taken the risk of reducing his client load. He had stopped recruiting with his former gusto and had actually turned away clients. If he should lose the young star, it could spell disaster.

Esposito's potential loss was more subtle, but equally painful. Most star players treasure their public image. Phil Esposito was born in Sault Ste. Marie and is a hometown hero, with a park named after him. When he headed a group of businessmen who bought the local team in 1986, he was hailed as a saviour. Yet, unknown to the Soo townspeople and officials, Phil Esposito and his group had been secretly negotiating for several months to sell the franchise to an American computer company, which intended to move it. If Esposito lost Lindros, he'd face the town's wrath and the collapse of the deal. If Lindros did report and Esposito sold the team, the tarnishing of his good-guy image would be more than offset by the profit he would make.

The interchange in the anteroom was brutal. The two men stood so close they could feel the force of each other's breath. Except for the requisite "fucks," "assholes" and "bullshits" thrown in for emphasis, Curran spoke in the controlled, assuring manner one assumes when talking to an irrational child. Curran tried to impress on Esposito the damage he might be doing to a sixteen-year-old boy and his family. "There's no fucking way that little fuck is going to fuck me around," Esposito huffed. The conversation ended in an angry stand-off. Esposito left abruptly, brushing against Curran, almost flattening him as he went.

Back in the stands, Curran said Esposito was "bluffing," but there was more hope than conviction in his statement.

The first choice was announced and, as the crowd expected, the name called was Eric Lindros. For a few seconds the collective nervousness was released in a crescendo of applause. But no one appeared to put on the Greyhounds sweater, pose for the seven cameras and make a short, stilted speech thanking Mom and Pop and perhaps his coach and teammates for making everything possible.

The young man in question, the merciless crusher of

other young players' bodies, his huge frame curled up like a pretzel, was sitting morosely in the back seat of the family's car. "I thought my life was over," he said later. "There were a lot of lessons in that. Hockey is the business world now. I realize that more than anything. It's bucks. It's flash. It's go, go, go. Phil Esposito didn't really care about where a sixteen-year-old kid was going to end up playing hockey. Didn't really care about his life. That is the way it goes." Then he added after a pause, "And what goes around comes around."

Carl and Bonnie Lindros were simultaneously amazed and infuriated by the Greyhounds. "I couldn't have been more clear with those people. I still can't believe they picked him. We thought the people we were dealing with were well-intentioned people and were putting Eric first."

After the draft, the well-worn "for the good of the game" rationale was invoked to explain everything. "We had no choice; you have to do what's right for the organization," Esposito intoned virtuously. "It's too bad, but as long as teams like us stick to our guns, and the OHL supports you, sooner or later people will know 'hey man,' if you're going to go this route [OHL] you'll be drafted by whatever team and you've got to report or you won't play."

"No one person is bigger than the league," harrumphed Dave Branch, OHL commissioner, "and we've got to do what's in the best interests of our league, and actually that was done today. I'd be less than honest to say it wouldn't hurt us. To what degree I don't know, but I think the person it may ultimately hurt the most is Eric."

The Soo citizens worked themselves into a frenzy. "If Sault Ste. Marie was good enough for Wayne Gretzky it's good enough for Eric Lindros," the townfolk howled. Teachers reported that boys *and* girls were gathering in the schoolyards and discussing, like miniature mercenaries, ways to "kill Lindros," "rip his face off" or "bomb his car."

But the citizens of the Soo had one more hockey lesson to learn. On June 20, 1989, the Algoma Group and

Phil Esposito sold the Greyhounds to Compuware Corp., a slick, Michigan software firm that wanted an OHL franchise, wanted to move it to Detroit and, above all, wanted Eric Lindros.

When Compuware and Esposito first started talking numbers before the draft, they discussed a price of $800,000 for the team. "There's no question Lindros boosted the price by a couple of hundred thousand," says Jim Rutherford, Compuware's director of hockey operations. At the time, most junior teams in the OHL were selling between $450,000 and $550,000 with the Greyhounds definitely on the lower end. Esposito had paid $550,000 for the club three years earlier. Shortly after the draft, Esposito and Compuware met in New York. After a few hours of dancing around, an aggravated Rutherford said, "Look, I'll give you $1 million. Just shut the fuck up and sell the team."

The price seemed insane, especially without Eric Lindros. But Compuware intended to move the team to Detroit, at which point Lindros would change his mind and, amid heavy publicity, report to the club, guaranteeing full houses. The additional revenue would more than pay off the premium that Compuware paid for the team.

From there it would be an easy step to using Lindros as the centrepiece for a franchise in a rival professional league. (At the time, two were in the works.) At the very worst, the new league would fail, but Compuware, knowing the NHL's vulnerability to anti-trust charges, felt they could force a merger in which they would keep Lindros.

In essence, Compuware pegged sixteen-year-old Eric Lindros' worth at half a million dollars.

Back in the Soo, all hell broke loose as the entire town rose up in condemnation. "He hung us up to dry," says Sault *Star* hockey writer Bill Montague of the former favourite son. "He said he bought the team because his father was the man who kept the club going for years. Selling it was like holding a gun to your head."

Compuware knew that the Soo had the right of refusal and thirty days to match any offer, but they never dreamt that a city of 85,000 could come up with $1 million in just a month. The ferocity of the town's support for the team surprised everyone. The previous year, the Greyhounds had sold a paltry 800 season tickets. After a "Save the Greyhounds" campaign, 1,600 three-year season tickets had been spoken for, enough to enable the town to buy the team.

When the 1989-90 hockey season started, Eric Lindros slipped across the border to Detroit and joined Compuware's Eastern American B League Tier II junior team. The Ontario junior owners were confident that Lindros would relent, but they hadn't reckoned on the unwavering resolve (more than a few called it objectionable, bullheaded interference) of Bonnie and Carl.

The Lindroses saw things differently: they felt they were acting as parents concerned about their child's welfare. And they had good reason to be concerned. After being vilified by the Sault Ste. Marie populace and a large cross-section of the junior hockey world, Eric began to receive hate mail. For a while, he slept with a knife under his pillow. When his Detroit team played in an Ontario junior tournament, some fans and players were openly hostile and several of the parents patently murderous. "If people are calling us pushy hockey parents or whatever, well, that's their opinion. But let's face it, hockey is a hell of a way to make a living," snorts Carl.

And yet, as forceful parents, the Lindroses are pikers, far from being eligible for junior hockey's Pushy Hall of Fame. "Parents," groans one agent. "If I could send at least half of them to Siberia the hockey world would be a far better place, I can guarantee you that."

Carl and Bonnie are willing to be loathed for a few years. They know that even the best junior teams have neither the personnel nor the time to worry over a boy's psychological health let alone concern themselves with a player's future. They also know that junior hockey is a business with very young employees, and, a single self-serving owner or GM could turn their son's life into a nightmare.

The Lindros saga didn't end when he crossed the border. Behind the scenes, Rick Curran played a brilliant hand. He fed stories to selected reporters about how well Lindros was performing in Detroit and earnestly discussed with them the unfairness and stupidity of the OHL's position. At the same time, Curran also probed for loopholes in the NHL rules. He discussed with Toronto putting Lindros on an American Hockey League contract, which would allow him to play for the Leafs until age eighteen, when he would be released for the draft. But Toronto shrank in the face of anticipated NHL backlash and declined.

Curran then approached the Philadelphia Flyers, traditionally run by mavericks and coincidentally a team sinking rapidly into mediocrity. "I had to go to somebody who had the balls to challenge the whole thing. I thought the Flyers would be somebody that would do that. They would have, but at the end [Flyers governor] Jay Snider decided it wouldn't be worth the risk." Snider regretfully told Curran, "You really can't do that to your business partners," indicating that he thought it was a rather good idea, if only he could get away with it.

Meanwhile, back at the OHL, the Greyhounds weren't the only ones suffering from Lindros's exile. Without the drawing power of his name, the entire league lost thousands at the gate. Worse, league officials and teams were constantly reminded that only a simple rule stood between them and Eric Lindros. Throughout the fall of 1989, his name and accomplishments appeared irritatingly often in the press. *Sports Illustrated* interviewed him for a feature story, a singular occurrence in the magazine's history.

Curran craftily built the publicity about Lindros to a crescendo in a very short time. In October 1989, when it became clear that Lindros intended to stay in Detroit, the OHL bowed to the unrelenting pressure and created a rule allowing first-round choices to be traded. The OHL's terse press release didn't mention any particular player, but the ruling was immediately dubbed "the Eric Lindros rule." Soo hockey fans were outraged and gathered three thousand names on a petition urging the Greyhounds' manager not to trade Lindros but let him rot in the United States.

A wheeling and dealing free-for-all ensued, with rumours flying about exorbitant offers. Newspapers reported that the Hamilton Dukes offered Lindros 2 percent of the gate, and one general manager dryly remarked that some team owners were ready to put their wives and children on the block too. The same men who had been willing to let Lindros freeze in the dark six months before, now gleefully leapt into the bidding orgy. By the time the dust had settled, eight teams had tendered offers to Greyhounds GM Sherry Bassin.

The Oshawa Generals won the auction, paying $80,000 cash and three front-line players as well as its second-round picks for 1990 and 1991. "Blockbuster Deal," the headlines shrieked as many club owners shook their heads. But, like Bruce McNall's purchase of Wayne Gretzky, the Generals' bid for Lindros was cheap at the price.

When Eric arrived, Oshawa lay in fifth place, some distance away from making the playoffs, which are far more lucrative for the club than regular-season play. The Generals won fourteen of the next nineteen games. All but one of their home games were standing room only. In May 1990, Oshawa took home the Memorial Cup for the first time in forty-six years. In the second half of the 1989-90 season alone, Lindros generated between $75,000 and $120,000 for the team in gate receipts and promotional revenues.

Throughout all the hype, excessive predictions and media feeding-frenzy, the Lindroses, except for one slip, kept to the high road. In March 1990, Eric participated in a Kelly Promotions Inc. hockey card autographing session. He received a $1,000 appearance fee and fans got a free Lindros autograph as part of the $4 admission. Additional signatures cost $3.

When the terms were revealed, junior team officials reacted with righteous indignation. "As far as I'm concerned, no athlete should be charging for his signature," scolded Sherry Bassin who had just made $80,000 selling

Eric Lindros. "I've always believed we owe something to the community. If people think they have to pay for an autograph they might stop asking. And if people stop asking for autographs they might stop watching players play."

"For him to be selling autographs to young kids at his age is not good for Eric Lindros or the Ontario Hockey League," pontificated Wayne Maxner, general manager of the London Knights. "If he was mine, I'd bring him aside and say that this kind of stuff would be okay down the road when he's a professional. But not now."

The sounds of dry retching in reaction to these pious statements could be heard throughout the length and breadth of professional hockey. At the core of the problem was the fact that a junior player was getting uppity. No one criticized the Oshawa team for raking in $60,000 selling their own trading cards, T-shirts and other merchandise featuring Eric Lindros, without sharing the profits with him or any of the other players.

As Eric's second season with Oshawa got under way, the Lindroses became increasingly concerned that the unpleasantness of the 1989 OHL draft would be repeated at the June 1991 NHL junior entry draft. They knew that there was no way to dictate terms but they wanted to be in a position of strength. So Curran set about solidifying their bargaining position. His first priority was to guarantee Lindros an income, no matter where he played.

In his last year as a junior Lindros signed an impressive array of "quality" deals, netting roughly $100,000 annually. Stick manufacturer Jofa-Titan Equipment paid him $30,000, making him the first junior to have a stick-endorsement contract. Another $30,000 was added when Score Cards included him as a bonus in a rookie *baseball* card package. In April 1991 HarperCollins Canada won an auction to publish Eric Lindros's autobiography with a $40,000-plus profit-sharing deal. Some questioned whether an eighteen-year-old should be writing his autobiography, but two different writers were already marketing Eric Lindros books. At least this way he would get the money and be in control.

In the last few seasons, the NHL's two or three top drafts pick have signed contracts for around $150,000 annually with an equivalent signing bonus. In November 1990 suggestions began appearing in newspapers that a $1 million signing bonus wouldn't be out of order for Lindros, and by January 1991 it was an established, if totally unattributed fact that he would be demanding $1 million up front and a $1 million annual salary.

To put more aces in Lindros's hand, Curran began investigating alternatives to the NHL. He didn't have to work too hard. The North American Hockey League which has since folded, eagerly offered Eric Lindros a totally guaranteed $1 million signing bonus with a $1 million annual salary for three years. Another new league, the Continental Hockey Association came up with a bid of $6 million over three years a few weeks before the draft.

Dave King, head of the Canadian national team, drooled at the prospect of Lindros anchoring Canada's bid for a 1992 Olympic gold medal. Insiders predicted that, even playing for the amateur national team, Lindros could earn $500,000 in endorsements. Several European teams jumped in and offered record sums for him.

But money wasn't the only worry. Ideally Eric would play in an eastern American team that would be close to home and offer him the maximum endorsement prospects. For a time it looked as if the New Jersey Devils, which had the Toronto Maple Leafs' first draft choice, would get Lindros. But the Quebec Nordiques beat Toronto in the NHL's last place derby and won the right to choose Eric Lindros.

Quebec isn't any more appealing to Lindros than Sault Ste. Marie. He doesn't speak French and the city is isolated from the mainstream of hockey, limiting endorsement and other marketing possibilities. The Nordiques' fans also have a history of intolerance toward highly touted players, particularly Anglos, who don't quickly measure up to expectations. The annals of hockey are repleat with depressing sagas about top young players who collapse under the stress of unrealistic demands.

A few months before the draft Bill Watters, Rick Curran's former partner and close friend, just happened to let slip, during an interview, that Lindros would "never" report to Quebec. That got the hockey world's attention.

In May 1991, Nordiques owner Marcel Aubut denounced a flurry of rumours that he would trade his first pick as "bull." Sounding remarkably like Phil Esposito two years earlier, he stated unequivocally that Eric Lindros would play for Quebec, for around $200,000 annually, "whether he likes it or not." Just hours before selecting Lindros as the first 1991 draft choice, a Nordiques' official said the club was prepared to let the young star "sweat it out."

Eric Lindros absorbs such threats with equanimity. "I won't be dictated to," he says firmly. Marcel Aubut may not have learned any lessons about hockey from the 1989 OHL draft, but Eric Lindros did. "Hockey is a game and it's also a business. . . . Hopefully, I'll be a trend-setter in the salary structure for the NHL too. That's my goal, that's everyone's goal. I mean, if I get more, then everybody else is going to get more. Don't go off on some belief that I'd play the game for nothing, because I wouldn't."

There is much throat-clearing and tut-tutting in NHL circles and among hockey fans about the way Rick Curran is positioning Lindros and the way the eighteen-year-old is putting himself in front of the game. But Eric Lindros is one of the few hockey players ever to understand that when the NHL does something for *the good of the game* it really means for *the good of the owners*. And he's determined to turn that understanding to his advantage.

As if to prove Eric Lindros's point the NHL filed notice of a defamation suit against Bobby Orr on April 30, 1991 for holding the League up to "hatred, contempt and ridicule."* Within the next few weeks, suits were filed

---

* The suit related to an article appearing in *The National*, a now defunct American sports daily, about the NHL pension plan. Also named in the suit were Frank Deford, the paper's publisher, and former player David Forbes.

against Gordie Howe, Bobby Hull and Carl Brewer, among others.

Imagine, for a moment, the National Basketball Association suing Wilt Chamberlain or John Havlicek, major league baseball going after Mickey Mantle and Willie Mays or the National Football League filing suit against O.J. Simpson and Don Meredith.

John Ziegler, who earlier couldn't fit the retired players into his busy schedule, found time to write an ominous letter to all current and retired players. He was forced into action, he claimed, "because of the attack upon the integrity of the NHL, the NHL Pension Society and the NHL Member Clubs."

"The NHL has traditionally practised restraint in dealing with public criticism so as not to divert the fans' attention from the game—especially during a time such as now, when the Stanley Cup playoffs are under way. However, the untrue accusation that the NHL is failing to honour its obligations to retired players cannot go unanswered. . ."

As it has many times in the past, the NHL faces two diverging paths. By taking the well-trodden route, the League will continue to place its need for control over the players, its insatiable desire for short-term profits and the owners' self-interest ahead of hockey's future. By taking the other and unfamiliar route, the NHL can put itself into partnership with the players, both past and present, to ensure that, for the first time, the good of the game really will come first.

Afterword

"A Vision of the '90s"?

Not since Jim Norris rescued the NHL during the Depression has professional hockey been besieged on so many fronts. On April 1, 1992, less than two weeks before the start of the Stanley Cup playoffs, 564 players walked away from the game. The first strike in NHL history threatened the League's most important source of revenue—the playoffs, which represent hundreds of millions in gate receipts, broadcast revenue and merchandising income.*

To many the strike was cataclysmic, the ruination of hockey as we know it. But in the end, it turned out to be merely the long overdue loss of virginity for thousands of amateur, semi-pro, pro and retired players. For the NHL owners, it was a large dose of reality as they faced an organized and no longer subservient labour force. Hockey has been founded upon the dependable naivety and

---

* Privately, League officials were deeply concerned that local stations and the Canadian Broadcasting Corporation could successfully reclaim broadcast fees that the NHL had already received and spent. An even bigger fear was the prospect that the two new expansion franchises, already in financial ill-health, would fold if the '92/'93 season didn't commence on schedule. Were that to happen the two newest would-be hockey owners could have sued the League for the return of $100 million in franchise fees.

fealty of its primary assets. But its continuance as a business, human relations, entertainment and sporting dinosaur has relied on a bedrock of outmoded regulations, attitudes and assumptions. In the spring of 1992, all of those were under attack.

American and Canadian lawsuits over the pension surplus promised costs ranging from $50 to $75 million, should the League lose. Eric Lindros, the player of the future, began eyeing anti-trust action after a season of being forced to play on the fringes of pro hockey. The League's entire disability and insurance structure, plus its partnership with the NHLPA in international hockey, lay under the FBI's microscope.

The board of governors, once grouped into fairly reliable rival factions, clawed at each other in confusion over the League's disintegrating leadership. Moreover, the complacency of wealthy teams was shattered as small-market clubs finally began to press the issue of revenue sharing. Fans, taken for granted throughout the eighties, complained in increasing numbers about every aspect of the game. And one by one the paying customers, particularly the key younger families, turned their backs on hockey, sickened by the uncontrolled violence, stick fouls and inconsistent refereeing that marred the game's inherent skill and beauty.

As further evidence of hockey's deterioration, the NHL's tenuous foothold on the American television market slipped again when the League actually had to *pay* NBC to broadcast the 1992/93 All Star Game.

Personalities are vital in understanding how hockey, dubbed "The Albania" of professional sports by journalist Tom Alderman, has withstood the advance of time and the infiltration of progressive ideas. The League's three most powerful men since 1977, president John Ziegler, chairman of the board Bill Wirtz and Alan Eagleson, are men of domains—private, guarded and exclusive. The three of them ran the League like a hobby farm with all the zeal, passions and possessiveness that favourite pastimes engender.

As managers and leaders they have been exceedingly

nimble at grabbing the fast buck but utterly lacking in long-term entrepreneurial vision. Bill Wirtz, who inherited his wealth along with the Chicago Blackhawks, is a shadowy figure within hockey. In many ways he's like the emperor who paraded around minus his clothes. He has been called the most powerful man in hockey for so long no one has really bothered to question whether it is true or not. Even those who realize that his importance is based on his connections, not on his hockey or business acumen, have loyally perpetuated the assumption.

John Ziegler's advice helped Bruce Norris turn the Detroit Red Wings, his father's flagship, into a ruin. Using the Detroit experience as a stepping stone, and aided by the support of Bill Wirtz and Bruce Norris, Ziegler vaulted into the League presidency in 1977. His favourite expression and overriding philosophy is, "If it ain't broke don't fix it."

To be fair to John Ziegler, his hold on power was so tenuous—based on the solid support of only four or five teams—that he expended a great deal of his energy simply preserving the status quo. If he had any vision for the future he wouldn't have the time or energy to pursue it.

The Ziegler maxim, coupled with Alan Eagleson's help in keeping players' salaries relatively low, worked perfectly for years. Throughout most of the eighties, for example, salaries declined almost every year relative to revenue Ziegler, Wirtz, Eagleson and their supporters have ensured that the game remains very profitable over time, but the byproduct of their actions produced a management structure peerless in its incompetence. Every aspect of the game, from the draft to television, marketing, expansion, legal planning and public relations, has stagnated.

Ironically the only aspect of the game that remains strong is the actual calibre of the play, but that is being slowly debilitated by the NHL's unwillingness to crack down on gratuitous violence. By the second round of the 1992 Stanley Cup playoffs, four of hockey's great stars—the men fans pay to see—Ray Bourque, Mark Messier, Mario Lemieux and Wayne Gretzky, had been either eliminated or hampered by flagrantly deliberate attempts to injure. Other factors affecting the quality of play include the League's unwillingness to legislate larger, Olympic size rinks, despite the fact that nearly 90% of the franchises are building, planning or thinking about new arenas. Today's larger, faster players make the game appear increasingly cramped, chippy and less appealing to television viewers who have difficulty seeing the puck for the mass of bodies. The NHL has also been reluctant to enhance the offensive—crowd pleasing—side of the game. In comparison, the NBA has worked hard to make its sport more exciting with the three-point basket, twenty-four-second clock and the barring of zone defences.

When the League decided, in 1989, to add seven new franchises during the 1990s, the opportunity was there to shed the prevailing image that hockey was run by greedy and short-sighted quick-buck artists. Men who, as Jim Lites, vice-president of the Detroit Red Wings, says "put the League's interest first—after their own." This time expansion was to be an integral part of the League's "strategic business plan" which the hockey bosses proudly called "A Vision of the Nineties". Supposedly grounded in solid business principles, this expansion would lay to rest the NHL's history of cosy sweetheart deals and seat-of-the-pants scrambling for franchise fees.

But the NHL, in a move reminiscent of the 1967 expansion, showed its "vision" by choosing the two weakest applicants from a field of ten. By coincidence, they were the only two applicants willing to guarantee, unconditionally, all of the highly inflated $50 million franchise fee.

After their acceptance the Tampa Bay Lightning and the Ottawa Senators violated at least half of the iron-clad criteria set down by the League. Both missed payment deadlines. Neither city had suitable arenas and both immediately fell into wrangles with the citizenry over costs associated with housing an NHL team.

Ottawa was shaky but Tampa was seismic. The franchise, which had changed ownership just three days before being welcomed into the NHL, changed ownership once again after months of uncertainty. Three Japanese corporations, Nippon Meat Packers Inc., Tokyo Tower Developments and Kikusai Green Co., Ltd., a golf course operator, were given the barest, cursory once over by the League, before purchasing majority interest.* Rounding out the Tampa Bay board of directors were George Steinbrenner's son, Hank, and Phil Esposito, the club's general manager and lone hockey expert. Smooth and friendly Esposito may be, but no one has ever suggested that he is a hockey management genius.

"The question now is, what's left to salvage," moaned New York *Newsday*, after the Rangers fired Esposito as coach and general manager in 1990. "Phil Esposito leaves behind a legacy of chaos and bankruptcy in the Rangers' organization . . . He traded away the club's future in forty-three deals he made, and his disastrous pursuit and dismissal of Michel Bergeron was only one example of his appalling lack of judgement. Surrounding himself as he did with yes-men advisors who owed him their jobs may have boosted his ego, but it did nothing to bring the Stanley Cup closer."

Few were surprised when, three months before the 1992/93 season started, the Tampa Bay Lightning had sold only 2,000 season tickets.

While at least one expansion franchise seemed to be self-destructing, the pension surplus issue rapidly evolved from a minor irritant into a fissure that threatened to cleave the game financially and psychologically. The retired players filed two separate lawsuits, in Toronto and Philadelphia. The American action was particularly worrying to the League, since U.S. laws are much more unequivocal about pension surpluses and representation of employees on pension plan boards.

---

* In marked contrast to hockey's frantic grab for dollars, no matter what the source, is baseball's careful consideration of the purchase of the Seattle Mariners by Hiroshi Yamauchi, chairman of Nintendo Co. Ltd. of Kyoto. The deal, first proposed on January 23, 1992, was subjected to nearly five months of review and considerable amendment before the sport agreed to the takeover of a franchise by offshore interests.

The players were only contesting pension operation during the 1980s. Still, the eventual cost of both suits, including lawyers, court fees, damages and interest, could easily top $100 million. If the players reached back to 1957, when the owners started dipping into the pension by dispersing a $1.7 million surplus to themselves, the NHL could face havoc. "I'm coming around to the idea that the *real* money is to be found in the '50s, '60s and '70s," Carl Brewer, who spearheaded the current action by the players, says ominously.

No other sport would treat its great stars, the idols of millions, with such cavalier disregard, but hockey owners have never understood that the players are the only thing of value they have to sell: the game is no more and no less than the players themselves.

Virtually forgotten among all the other catastrophes facing professional hockey was another example of the League not realizing where its assets lay—Eric Lindros. Lindros was unimportant as a single player confronting the NHL. But as an idea he was vital. He represented everything that was wrong with the system so many players were beginning to chafe against.

L'affaire Lindros, as it came to be called, disintegrated into a stand-off between the Nordiques and a young man and his family. The Nordiques were tacitly supported by the approval of the entire League and the vast majority of the establishment press, Lindros by only a handful of players, fans, ex-players and journalists.

The pressure on the Lindros family was immense. The prime minister even suggested that, as a gesture for national unity, Eric report to Quebec. Two separate psychological profiles appeared in newspapers, as if the Lindroses were a family of mass murderers. In one town, Brett, Eric's sixteen-year-old brother drafted second in the 1992 OHL draft, was hung in effigy.* Death threats and promises to rape Lindros' sister became routine. Some teams deliberately went after him and, too often to be

---

* Brett, partly in response to the treatment of his brother, quickly announced that he would be heading south to play U.S. college hockey.

coincidence, referees looked the wrong way.

All this because an eighteen-year-old boy didn't want to go where a bunch of rich men tried to send him.

The Lindroses' greatest weakness has been their steadfast belief that common sense would prevail—that Marcel Aubut would do what was best for his team, not only to maximize profits, but to create the best mix of players with the resources he had available. What they didn't fully realize was the extent of Aubut's lust to be a folk hero in Quebec. Being pushed around by a young anglophone would not get Aubut to the throne of Quebec City any faster. Nor would a quick trade endear him to his colleagues, who would not thank him for setting such a precedent with recalcitrant first-rounders.

Between June and September 1991, rumours of offers and counter-offers became as common as a flock of agents at the OHL draft. Lindros reportedly turned his nose up at tens of millions, a new Ferrari every year for life, a Zermatt ski chalet and a private jet to take him between games to lessen travel fatigue. In fact, it wasn't until September that Aubut advanced any tangible offer. To most it was a stunning, even obscene deal—a ten-year, $55 million contract. If it was money the Lindroses were after, Eric would have scrawled his name within minutes.

At the beginning of September Eric Lindros was wedged in a no-man's land—chronologically a boy, contractually an amateur, yet really a professional without a team. Still, some benefited from his awkward status. The Canadian national team was thrilled at the prospect of capturing Lindros for the Olympics, if he decided to play another year with the Oshawa Generals. The top hockey colleges in the United States were willing to sell their football teams to get Lindros, who was about to become the first North American amateur player to compete in the Canada Cup alongside Wayne Gretzky and his hero Mark Messier. It looked to be a full year, with or without the Quebec Nordiques. The only uncertainty was how long the Lindros family could bear the strain of indecision and the weight of general condemnation for the choices they had made.

Far from the ice, other contracts and deals were being considered and constantly re-evaluated in light of what the various players in the Lindros stakes might or might not do. Chief among the Eric watchers was the Upper Deck sports card company. Upper Deck had been dogging Lindros for years, desperate to get his face on one of its cards.

Shortly before the 1991 Canada Cup began, thirty-five players congregated in and around Marvin Goldblatt's office, also headquarters of the NHLPA. Per diems were dispensed, the travel arrangements, uniforms and equipment checked. Amid the fuss and confusion each player received a paper and Goldblatt directed them to sign, acknowledging what they had received. Buried within the verbiage were a few lines relinquishing the players' licensing rights to the Canada Cup Committee. The few players, including Lindros, who queried it, were hastily told it simply protected them from anyone taking commercial advantage of them.

They all signed. Upper Deck, which had purchased the Canada Cup rights in the summer, could now issue a card with Eric Lindros' face on it. The deal, negotiated through Licensing Corporation of America, had been approved at the Canada Cup end by Alan Eagleson. Score Cards was furious and Rick Curran apoplectic. "Upper Deck had been trying and trying and trying to get Eric," says a still disgusted Curran. "We already had the Score deal. Eric had an exclusive agreement and everyone knew. He's not a carpetbagger. He's not going to turn around and screw Score."

Curran vehemently protested the clever end run, claiming it violated the standard NHLPA practice of notifying players before making any group licensing agreement, to avoid individual conflict. Marvin Goldblatt feigned innocence about Lindros' well-publicized deal with Score. "The thing that pisses me off was the response I got back when I complained," says Curran. 'We're not the NHLPA. We're not obliged to give notification.' Well, it's Alan Eagleson, it's Marvin Goldblatt who is the fucking NHLPA accountant and it was all done in the NHLPA office!"

While Marcel Aubut continued in his role as the jilted lover, Eric Lindros played junior, world junior, Canada Cup and Olympic hockey, everything but the NHL. Despite at least two $20 million plus offers for him, and a handful of All Star players thrown in, Aubut righteously refused to trade him. Finally, in desperation, Lindros upped the ante, raising the grim spectre of anti-trust action against the NHL. "You'd hate to have come to a situation where you'd have to sue the league," Lindros, told Steve Dryden, editor of the *Hockey News*, on May 29, 1992, three weeks before the NHL entry draft. "Then again, you'd hate to have a situation where you sit around."

Just in case the possibility of having the hockey draft declared illegal wasn't enough, Lindros took the League through some compelling mathematics, pointing out that triple damages are a component of U.S. anti-trust legislation. "It seems to me I was offered $5.5 million a year [by the Nordiques]. We're talking about a 16.5 figure if you win outright." Predictably, the NHL's legal department pooh-poohed any suggestion that an anti-trust decision might go against the League. But Lindros's lawyer, Gordon Kirke of Toronto, a specialist in sports law, had a different point of view. "Most professors I've talked to call it a slam dunk as far as proving the draft is oppressive or restraint of trade."

To get the message across to the obdurate Marcel Aubut, the Lindroses began telling people that if Eric was not traded by the end of June 1992, he would not play the next season in the NHL—under any circumstances. By voluntarily sitting out one more year, Lindros would be eligible to be re-drafted in 1993. Overnight his value to Quebec would drop to zero. It may have been a bluff, but the Nordiques' posturing ended and serious trade talks began instantly.

Ironically the Lindros trade, when it finally came, completely eclipsed the NHL's showpiece entry draft and the expansion draft for the two new teams. On June 20, 1992, a year after he'd been initially selected by the Nordiques, the Eric Lindros saga ended—predictably it turned into another international public relations fiasco for the NHL.

With all pretence of high moral principle jettisoned, Marcel Aubut danced a wildly abandoned jig to greed. First he traded Lindros to the Philadelphia Flyers for $15 million plus players and then, when offered $5 million more, retraded him to the New York Rangers. Enraged, both teams appealed to the befuddled NHL, which quickly shuffled the explosive matter off to an arbitrator. By the time the arbitrator awarded him to Philadelphia ten days later, even the most ardent Eric Lindros haters were starting to wonder if he hadn't been right all along.

In truth, this debacle should have been known, from start to finish, as the L'affaire Aubut.

The fallout from Lindros, expansion and the pension were serious enough. But overshadowing them all was the transformation of the NHL's previously tame labour force. Alan Eagleson's co-operation with the NHL owners had been so absolute that it earned John Ziegler kudos from influential *BusinessWeek* magazine for his "spectacular" work at keeping "hockey a relatively low-paid professional sport free of the bidding wars that bedevil other sports."

Eagleson's modus operandi of entering negotiations unprepared and weaponless, with few staff, few experts, no research, no consensus among members, no strike fund and no strike vote, was discarded with breathtaking speed once Bob Goodenow unpacked his briefcase in Toronto in the summer of 1990.

Eagleson's contract negotiations had habitually commenced at the end of the season and culminated in late summer or fall prior to training camp, when the players are most vulnerable and most anxious to get their first pay cheque after a summer hiatus. Conversely, the owners would bargain with the playoff receipts and season ticket money tucked safely in their pockets.

Though Bob Goodenow had been hired to replace Alan Eagleson, most assumed that little would change until after the next collective bargaining agreement, due to expire on September 15, 1991. "My understanding is that Alan Eagleson is the executive director and will be in that position through the bargaining this year," John Ziegler stated flatly in June 1990.

"A lot of us figured that Al would be there pulling strings right through to the end of the new collective bargaining agreement," confirmed the governor of an eastern U.S. franchise. "We all thought, 'Hell, no problem. We can talk to Bob but it'll be Al setting the agenda. That way, we know where we're at and where we're going."

For his part, Alan Eagleson clearly intended to hang around to "help" with the CBA negotiations, but events dictated otherwise. In September 1991, American journalist Russ Conway wrote a devastating series of articles which appeared in the Lawrence, Massachusetts newspaper, the *Eagle Tribune*. In graphic and unequivocal detail Conway laid out what had only been whispered about—Eagleson's financial dealings, his handling of disability benefits and insurance claims, his real estate acquisitions and his management of both international hockey affairs and the NHLPA escrow account. Eagleson dismissed the articles as more of "the same old rubbish", but that rubbish narrowly missed winning a Pulitzer Prize for Conway.

Shortly thereafter CBC television reporter Bruce Dowbiggin aired a flawlessly documented series which revealed, among other things, that Eagleson, despite repeated protestations to the contrary, had supported the NHL's efforts to keep the players he represented off the pension board.

Then Eagleson, in one stroke, did as much damage to his own credibility as any of his opponents, with the publication of his autobiography, *Power Play*. Even his biggest media sycophants had difficulty finding anything good to say about it. At best they limply called it "a fun read". But most were embarrassed by the book's many misrepresentations and its self-serving and pathetically defensive tone. In particular Eagleson's unwarranted attacks on his old friend, Bobby Orr, seemed out of place and pitiful.

Spurred by continuing revelations about Eagleson's handling of the NHLPA and his representation of players, first the U.S. Federal Bureau of Investigation and then, belatedly, the Royal Canadian Mounted Police, launched investigations into the Players' Association and its executive director. "I got back [from a trip to Switzerland] and read about another list of accusations, some of them twelve years old," an eerily soft-spoken Eagleson told reporters at his January 6, 1992 retirement dinner. "I thought all of those accusations were answered by an independent audit [of the union's finances] in 1989. I can't comment because of the legal issues involved."*

By the spring of 1992, the FBI had gathered enough evidence to warrant convening a grand jury in Boston. Those testifying included Eagleson's closest associates as well as a who's who of hockey. Interestingly, the NHL repeatedly denied persistent rumours that the FBI probe also targeted League operations, though the Bureau hauled away carloads of documents from the NHL offices.

Concurrently, the Law Society of Upper Canada began its own investigation of Eagleson, prompted by a complaint from Edmonton lawyer and player agent Rich Winter. It was far less serious than his other problems, but it cut right to the core of Alan Eagleson's identity. Law had set him apart from a hundred other working-class kids in New Toronto, had given him stature, clout with the players and a lifetime of valuable business and political contacts.

Long before the results of the welter of investigations were known, Eagleson's influence with the players had evaporated. Former reliable apologists like Bryan Trottier and Kevin Lowe, both long-term NHLPA executive members, worked hard to avoid any discussion of the Association's past history, or Alan Eagleson. It was a startlingly quick transition from the man the game couldn't do without, to the man no one in the game wanted to talk about.

---

* Though Eagleson wouldn't answer the charges of serious misconduct related to his twenty-five years of NHLPA stewardship, he could find time to repeatedly publicly claim, without substantiation, that he had information that CBC television reporter Bruce Dowbiggin, his most dogged Canadian Inquisitor, had beaten his wife.

Bob Goodenow had only two choices as time ran out on the collective bargaining agreement. He could make a new, short-term deal and save his energy for sorting out the horrific mess in the Players' Association office. The breathing space would also give him a chance to educate the woefully ignorant players, create a strike fund, investigate and ready his legal options and line up his strategies for the future. Or, he could wade in and fight for the players' first real CBA. Daringly, Goodenow chose to do both.

A few owners, notably those who'd actually negotiated with Goodenow, felt that Ziegler was badly "overmatched" but most were unconcerned. They felt that any hint of radical action could be cauterized by the trusty "your demands will kill the game" arguments. But those who closely followed the course of Goodenow's negotiations with St. Louis over Brett Hull's four-year $7 million contract in 1990 weren't so sure. "That was an education in negotiation," grudgingly concedes a well-known agent. "He could have settled for five or six hundred thousand a year but he didn't. He hung on, he used all the levers and he used them well. He's a *very* ballsy guy."

Those who were unconcerned about Bob Goodenow should have listened more carefully when he was hired in February 1990 as NHLPA deputy executive director. Amid all the careful platitudes about how much Alan Eagleson had done for hockey and how closely he intended to work with him, was a clear and ominous message. "The association has been a very responsible partner in the past to accommodate the League," Goodenow told David Shoalts of the *Globe and Mail*. "At this point, however, in light of reports and comments from John Ziegler, the League is enjoying unparalleled prosperity. It's time for the owners to share some of that with the players who work so hard."

When Goodenow arrived in the NHLPA headquarters, a building owned by Eagleson, he was given a closet-sized office. The place was in chaos; files were missing, or had never existed, Eagleson was alternately frenetically boisterous or wretchedly depressed and some staff were openly hostile. But Goodenow, with the sublime patience of a heron stalking fish, persevered as he waited for Eagleson's official departure from the NHLPA, scheduled for January '92. In the meantime, he made his important phone calls and held his important meetings outside the premises. (The NHLPA moved out of Eagleson's office on February 15, 1992.)

Throughout the NHLPA's history the League has never been seriously threatened by any of labour's ultimate weapons: strike and legal action. Some owners, concerned about their vulnerability to a strike just before the playoffs, advocated locking the players out in September, and then again in January. But the majority, reassured by Wirtz and Ziegler, were confident that the players would never strike under any circumstances.

Goodenow realized that the owners' stinginess had led the League into a grievous strategic error. Because their playoff share was so low—the winning team' players in 1991 made only $25,000 for twenty-four games—the players had relatively little to lose financially if they decided to strike prior to the playoffs.[*]

Goodenow was determined that for once the players would set the agenda. If the owners wanted to conduct reasonable negotiations in the summer that would be fine with him, but he would be happy to wait. The perfect time to negotiate would be in the final few months of the season. In the interim, he set about building an organization and communicating with the players as never before. He knew that the biggest impediment to reaching a good deal with the owners would be the players themselves. He used video tapes of Bruce Dowbiggin's CBC series and copies of Russ Conway's revelations, bulletins, hundreds of phone calls, and he hastily assembled a strike fund of close to $20 million. He also corralled a team of gunslingers with real expertise. Ominously, the lawyers he retained were heavy-weights in the area of anti-trust.

---

[*] The players' total payment for the 1991 Stanley Cup playoffs was $2.8 million. In contrast, the owners' net revenue ranged between $50 and $75 million.

The first player-owner skirmishes occurred in the summer of 1991.

By September 15, 1991, negotiations were at a stalemate. The owners had made an offer in August which they re-tendered in September, with a few cosmetic changes, in a document entitled "*The Best Proposal on the Essential Issues*". The main gain for the players was a minuscule reduction in the restrictive free agency provisions. Ten-year veterans earning less than the League's average salary would become free agents. But, since only a small percentage of players ever reach the ten-year mark, and well over half of those earn more than the average salary, it seemed like a rather small step forward.

The owners, still rooted in the Eagleson era of negotiation, brought out faithful pension carrot that had enticed the players so many times before. They offered the "average career player" the expectation of being able to draw a pension of $400,000 a year, for the rest of his life, starting at age sixty-two. They had used exactly the same ploy in 1979 to seal the WHA merger agreement and again in 1986—promise huge benefits far in the future and pay for them in vastly deflated dollars.

"I think the owners really believed that we'd all jump at the pension offer," mused NHLPA vice president Ryan Walter. "Probably some of us did but we're smarter now and not quite so grateful." It also helped that Goodenow had a team of lawyers and accountants present who could explain the implications of the owners' offers.

To add insult to injury, the money to pay for the enhanced pension benefits would once more come out of the pension surplus. This was the same surplus that was the focus of a law suit from the retired players. It was also the surplus earmarked to pay for the pension benefits negotiated in the 1986 CBA.

As negotiations started to get serious in early March 1992, a sense of solidarity grew within the players' ranks. The owners, on the other hand, were confused and angry when faced with an opponent who didn't fold when they huffed and puffed about the fragility of the game. "Those guys were so fucking scared," one player agent observes, not without a small amount of pleasure. "They didn't know where Goodenow was coming from."

A veteran player put it more succinctly. "They didn't know what to do with themselves when they didn't have Al winking across the table at them."

Nervous shivers raced down the spine of management when the NHLPA set Monday, March 30 as a strike deadline. The players primarily wanted a reduction in the age when a player became a free agent without compensation from thirty-one to twenty-eight, an easing of the punitive compensation formula for other free agents and a reduction in the number of draft rounds from twelve to six. They gave ground in every area. A deal seemed imminent. During a marathon negotiating session in Toronto in early March, insiders agreed that both sides were close.

Conspicuously absent from the key negotiations was Bill Wirtz.

Then the bargaining moved to Chicago. With the same inexplicable force that turns a barking dog into a biting one and a crowd into a mob, the owners whipped themselves into a frenzy of distrust. Hard-liners like Bill Wirtz were convinced that Goodenow intended to strike a deal and, after consultation with the players, return to the relieved owners and squeeze "our balls" for extras. Stone-faced and unreadable, Goodenow was as much a cypher to the League governors as Eagleson had been a well-known and easily understood entity.

Even though they supported Goodenow many players couldn't really believe they were on the verge of a strike against the National Hockey League. Nor could many agents. Three of them, with laudable, but misplaced, concern for the good of the game, decided to intervene. They started a phone campaign urging their clients to pressure Goodenow into settling, anything to keep the season rolling.

The owners misread the agents' intentions to mean that the players were turning against Goodenow. Privately and publicly they triumphantly announced that the NHLPA boss did not have the support of the membership. Goodenow countered by delaying the strike date by two days, from March 30 to April 1, to allow a League-wide secret ballot of players.

Overnight, the owners' priority changed from making a deal to breaking the union. John Ziegler was the point man as the League launched a vicious public relations battle to sway the players. Even the moderates within the NHL became infected by the attitude. When asked about the possibility of a strike, Bruce McNall sneered, "Make my day!"

The owners zeroed in, like a pack of hysterical hounds, on salaries which they claimed would soar out of control if free agency were granted. They successfully managed to convince the public that the players were after "total free agency", though it doesn't exist in any other major professional sport. Interestingly, long after the players had already met the owners on the issue of freedom of movement, the owners kept up their obsession with free agency and skyrocketing salaries.

A compelling theme hammered home was the threat to Canadian and small-market teams. "We're not going to sign our own death warrant," Pat Quinn said repeatedly to the media. "This is a situation where a lot of clubs, not just Vancouver, are going to lose money this year. . . . I'm disappointed for the people who have paid the price to come to this rink and for the Griffiths [the owners], who have picked up the differences in the losses. It [the strike] has the potential for a disastrous effect for hockey in Vancouver and for hockey in Canada. I know the numbers. Hockey in Canada is in danger of being extinct as we know it."

No one asked Quinn why the Canucks or the Griffiths family had a right to make a profit after fifteen consecutive years of bungling and mismanagement during which the team had never had a winning season.* For that mat-

---

* The Vancouver Canucks have had only three winning seasons in their woeful twenty-two-year history; 1974-75, 1975-76, and 1991-92. The team did reach the Stanley Cup final in 1981-82 and lost in four straight games. Even the diehard Vancouver fans admit that only a chain of fortuitous misadventures suffered by the leading contenders got them there in the first place.

ter, no one asked why the players should sacrifice when the NHL is the only major professional sport without any real form of revenue sharing.

But the owners' hysterical rhetoric frightened the fans. In many cities they willingly took up the cudgel and bludgeoned the selfish players who drive Porsches and earn more in a year than many honest men do in a lifetime. The players, though expecting little support from the fans, were nonetheless taken aback by the angry attacks. (Many observers and some of the Canuck players believe that Vancouver's sluggish play in the early games of the first round of the playoffs was a direct result of the vehemence and personal nature of the attack on them by their own management.)

The NHL's owners scored many direct hits in the media battle with the players, but it was John Ziegler who had his finest hour. The hundreds of hours of laborious work with his media guru Bill Wilkerson finally paid off. In interview after interview, using ridiculously inflated figures, Ziegler portrayed the players as selfish, ungrateful and callous. He claimed that the players' demands meant the League would lose $150 million in the next three years.

"Ownership can't stand that," Ziegler intoned sorrowfully. "You are asking people who back this game to start losing substantial personal fortunes if they are going to sustain it. And rather than lose their personal fortunes, they certainly will have no choice but to lock up the shop."

A particularly effective ploy in the NHL owners' repertoire was the constant repetition of the fact that the NHL player's average annual salary was $379,000. After the strike League general counsel, Gil Stein, admitted that the real figure was $233,900.

As Ziegler pilloried the players for being greedy and ungrateful he metamorphosed into the game's number one fan. Three times on national television he wept over the plight of the game and the players' cruelty to the fans. "I don't know if . . our fans will ever forgive us," he uttered between sniffles. "I have difficulty understanding why the players want to ruin or irrevocably scar this great season."

Somehow, in his enthusiasm for blaming the players for the fragile state of the game, John Ziegler forgot to mention that the League had been highly profitable throughout the 1980s and had netted over $150 million in the previous three years—a fact he had often crowed about in public. The additional $150 million in expansion fees, $50 million of which the owners had pocketed three months before, slipped his mind. Also overlooked was a record marketing deal, already negotiated, that the League was keeping under wraps until negotiations were over.

Ziegler scored point after point in the media battle with the somewhat wooden Bob Goodenow, but the NHL had once again chosen the path of short-term gain. No one at League headquarters stopped to think how relentlessly portraying the game as on the brink of economic disaster would affect prospects of selling four more franchises during the 1990s. Moreover, the owners' tactics radicalized and united the players in a way that Bob Goodenow could never have hoped to do by himself. If Goodenow had a hidden agenda, as many owners claimed, this was it: to push the owners to the point where they'd strike back and unite his union.

On April 1, 1992, the players voted 560 to 4 to strike. They walked out the next day with 27 games remaining in the regular schedule.

Goodenow, while losing the public relations battle, stuck carefully to his strategy and successfully unnerved the owners. But once again, the players themselves almost undid him. As the negotiations were heating up, a cabal of agents and some players, including Wayne Gretzky, appeared. Gretzky, who flew to New York on April 11 at a key point in the negotiations, was credited with plans to start a new League, unseat Goodenow and negotiate a contract with the NHL single-handedly. The agents and Gretzky, driven by the long-held belief in the fragility of the game, were motivated by the best of intentions.

Goodenow weathered the interference. At just the right moment a group of owners belatedly realized that Ziegler and Wirtz's scorched earth policies would be far more damaging than any strike. It occurred to them that pushing the players into a strike would cost the NHL more than just $50 to $75 million in playoff income. The CBC alone stood to lose a staggering $75 million in broadcast revenues if the strike ended the season. The CBC's lawyers were already examining ways to recover the money from the NHL. Then there was the very real possibility of anti-trust action.

On April 12, 1992 the NHLPA and the NHL cut a deal. In the end it wasn't a huge gain, as far as the players were concerned, but it was the first time they'd sat down with the owners and come away with anything.

The players returned to finish the regular season and the playoffs which culminated in the brilliant and entertaining Pittsburgh Penguins winning a second consecutive Stanley Cup. But the damage had been done. As much because of the League's anti-player rhetoric, as the strike itself, the fans stayed away from the games in droves. The financially weak Hartford Whalers, for instance, drew only 5,700 fans to a home playoff game against the immensely popular Montreal Canadiens. Television ratings for Hockey Night in Canada were disastrously low in the early playoff rounds, and even during the Stanley Cup finals, the ratings were down an average of 200,000 viewers a game from the previous year.

The only ray of hope for the future of hockey among its considerable litany of woes lay in the dismantling of hockey's triumvirate of Alan Eagleson, John Ziegler and Bill Wirtz. Armed with his overwhelming mandate from the players and bolstered by the outcome of contract negotiations, Bob Goodenow travelled to the World Championships in Prague to lay down the law in international hockey. His message: Alan Eagleson was out and Bob Goodenow and the NHLPA were in—or else.

After fifteen years as the world's most successful contortionist, John Ziegler had a majority of the owners mad at him—at the same time. Some were convinced he hadn't been tough enough during negotiations while others thought he'd been too tough. Still others, like Detroit's Mike Ilitch and John McMullen of New Jersey, had been angry and appalled for years about the constant stream of gaffs and catastrophes brewed up in the League's New York offices. The strike was simply the last straw.

As well, a growing number within the League were coming around to the idea that it hadn't exactly been smart business to publicly denigrate the players during the strike. By diminishing the only asset they had to sell, the owners successfully convinced a percentage of fans that a greedy bunch of bandits weren't worth watching. To make matters worse, after one very short year the owners would be facing a hostile, smarter, more politicized, better educated and better financed group of players to negotiate a new contract with all over again.

Finally, in private offices and backrooms in many NHL cities, a handful of key owners worried about the progress of the FBI investigation of Alan Eagleson and the NHLPA, an investigation that John Ziegler kept assuring them had nothing to do with the NHL.

On June 12, 1992, after a frenzied battle to hang on, John Ziegler resigned "for the good of the game". (To ease his departure, the governors granted him a US $2 million golden handshake plus a $250,000 annual pension starting in 1996.) At his side during this final battle, and the only person to speak supportively, was Ziegler's loyal old pal, Alan Eagleson. "He settled the strike, and they were playing hockey. If they had taken a vote then, he would have been given the Order of Lenin," Eagleson lamented. "Six weeks later, the owners are saying we have to sign players and it's John's fault. They needed a scapegoat and he was it."

Bill Wirtz, the NHL's chairman of the board, quickly discovered that once severed from Eagleson and Ziegler, his former clout evaporated. He announced his resignation as chairman, then dithered and reneged, but by that time it was clear to all that his era had ended. On

Monday, June 22, 1992, Bruce McNall was unanimously voted in as the new chairman of the NHL board.

Many options lay open to McNall and the NHL. Chief among them was the possibility of creating the independent position of commissioner and filling it with a person from outside the League. With a little luck, and support from both the owners and the players, the right person could return the glorious sport of hockey to its previous eminence by dragging, kicking or cajoling it into the 1990s. Unlikely as it may seem, given its record, the NHL has given itself one last chance to make good on its favourite maxim; for the good of the game.

Acknowledgements

After two and a half years, four filing cabinets of documents, nineteen research trips and over four hundred interviews, it is difficult to spend a page or two thanking the many people who were so helpful to us in the writing of this book. The following are our best efforts to acknowledge those who were indispensable.

The late Linda Waddell was a good friend and helped us through uncertain times as rookie writers. She was a fine person and her death came far too soon.

Jack Cruise, our biggest fan. Once again, we couldn't have done it without you. We miss you.

Pat and Peter Griffiths were pillars of strength during our family crisis and helped the book along in many large and small ways. Having you near made all the difference.

Special thanks to Quinn and Claudia Cruise for bravery, patience and fortitude above and beyond the call of duty.

Fiona Griffiths tirelessly clipped the Toronto newspapers and cheerfully provided accommodation, transportation and support. Marlene Webber, Natalie MacLean, Dave Greber and Ann Hall put us up in Calgary,

Edmonton and Toronto.

Special thanks to dear friends, George and Marguerite Duck.

So many friends were supportive, calling at the right intervals and asking if we were finished yet. In particular Sid and Jennifer Tafler, Craig Piprell, Tom Henry, Jennifer Nicholson, Wayne Melvin, Loni Gallagher, Peter Newman and many of our students at the University of Victoria Creative Writing Department.

Jane Widerman was a true friend who kept Alison reasonably sane and reasonably fit. Similarly, Dave Owen helped with David's fitness and provided comic relief, even buying coffee occasionally. Nancy Bourey and Patricia Walsh guided us through some very difficult times.

David Colbert, our former agent, suggested the idea for the book in the first place.

Cynthia Good, Morton Mint, Iris Skeoch and the rest of the gang at Penguin stood by us unflinchingly. David Kilgour's deft touch and unflappable manner—phoney of course—contributed immeasurably to the final product. Catherine Marjoribanks did a superb job of copy editing. Charlotte Coddington did excellent transcribing for us.

Many librarians and officials of various government departments were also extremely helpful. Our deep thanks to Amanda Valpy of the *Globe and Mail*, Pat Zacharias, supervisor, reference section, Detroit *News*, Linda Hughes and Pat Garneau of *The Edmonton Journal*, Agnes McFarlane of the Montreal *Gazette*, Joe Romain of the Hockey Hall of Fame, Shirley Mooney of the Vancouver *Sun*, the staff at the National Archives, Archives of Ontario, who let us stay past closing, the Chicago Board of Trade, the U.S. Department of Justice, Nancy LaGuerra of the New York State Senate, John Halligan, former guardian of the New York Rangers historical material, the St. Catharines Archives, the staff of the New York Public Library's special reference section and the British Ice Hockey Federation.

The Minnesota North Stars, the Detroit Red Wings, the Vancouver Canucks, the Los Angeles Kings and the New

York Rangers were particularly generous with their files. We also appreciate Dean Lombardi of the Minnesota North Stars for sharing and copying his collection of material. Lincoln Cavalieri and Bill Brennan loaned us both books and documents.

Al Strachan, Trent Frayne, Jim Proudfoot, Stan Fischler, Eric Duhatschek and many other sports scribes gave us information, leads and opinions. Bill Montague of the Sault *Star* was very generous and copied many stories for us. Also, Mike Royko gave us valuable insight and information.

We are particularly grateful to Senator Hartland Molson for making his previously restricted private papers available. We also owe special thanks to Marguerite Norris for allowing us into her home and sharing priceless memories of her extraordinary family with us. Marvin Miller, James Dworkin and Milton Mound gave us insights that shed new light on hockey's history.

Steve Brunt temporarily parted with his treasured copy of Barney Nagler's wonderful book, *Jim Norris and the Decline of Boxing*. Jim Kearney, for his advice and encouragement, and likewise to Jim Taylor, for opening up his considerable sport library to us. Mike Squire of Sportsland in Victoria for lending us valuable books. Allan Turowetz for generously providing transcripts of interviews from his fine book. Don Fehr, head of the Major League Baseball Players Association, and Dave Mondress of the National Basketball Players Association gave us valuable insight, information and statistics.

Many individuals at the NHL offices in Toronto, Montreal and New York provided information and documents. Bill Wilkerson was particularly helpful.

Thank you to all the current and former players, owners, general managers, coaches and agents who shared their recollections of the game with us. Though most of you didn't end up being quoted, your stories, insight and corroboration were critical to the development of this book. We have deliberately not thanked most of you by name because, as Ed Olczyk put it, "You don't want to piss the wrong guy off, you don't want anyone looking at you any different."

And finally, to Libby, Molly and Sherry for a delightful evening of education about the servicing of professional athletes.

Notes on Sources

Unfortunately, there are very few archives or libraries with hockey collections. Still, we were fortunate to come across a handful of excellent resources. The following were extremely useful, particularly in the preparation of the historical chapters:

The Smythe Papers—Ontario Provincial Archives, Toronto

The Molson Papers—National Archives of Canada, Ottawa

New York Rangers Collection—This material goes back to the formation of the NHL and was painstakingly collected and indexed by various New York Rangers staff.

Additionally, the Hockey Hall of Fame has hundreds of files with material clipped from all over Canada. The staff there are also working on a computer index of *The Hockey News*, making it the first major hockey publication to be so referenced.

We used material from dozens of different newspapers but the following were particularly useful:

The New York *Times*   The Toronto *Star*
The Boston *Globe*   The Montreal *Gazette*
The Detroit *News*   The Edmonton *Journal*
The Minneapolis *Star*   The Vancouver *Sun*
The *Globe and Mail*

We also consulted dozens of different magazines and found the following to contain some of the best and most thoughtful information about hockey:

The Hockey News   *Sport Inc.*
The Sporting News   *Sports Illustrated*
Sport   *Newsday*

Hundreds of hockey books have been written over the past seventy-five years. We consulted a large cross-section of them and found the following to have reference material that is unique or particularly helpful in understanding the background of the sport. Many others not listed here are cited fully in the endnotes.

Brenner, Teddy, as told to Barney Nagler. *Only The Ring Was Square*. New Jersey: Prentice-Hall Inc., 1981

Coleman, Charles I. *The Trail of the Stanley Cup* (Vols. 1, 2 & 3). Though not in general circulation, these three massive volumes (published by the National Hockey League) are a gold mine of statistics and other information.

Davidson, Gary, with Bill Libby. *Breaking the Game Wide Open*. New York: Atheneum, 1974.

Dworkin, James B. *Owners Versus Players: Baseball and Collective Bargaining*. Boston: Auburn House Publishing, 1981.

Fischler, Stan. *Fischler's Ice Hockey Encyclopedia*. New York: Thomas Y Crowell Company, 1979.

Frayne, Trent. *The Mad Men of Hockey*. New York: Dodd, Mead & Company, 1974.

Gallner, Sheldon M. *Pro Sports: The Contract Game*. New York: Scribner's Sons, 1974.

Goyens, Chris, and Allan Turowetz. *Lions in Winter* Toronto: Penguin Books Canada, 1981

Heinz, Rick. *Many Are Called Few Are Signed: The Hard Realities of Professional Hockey*. Toronto: Heinz Publishing, 1988.

Houston, William. *Ballard: A Portrait Of Canada's Most Controversial Sports Figure*. Toronto: Seal Books, 1985.

Houston, William. *Maple Leaf Blues—Harold Ballard and the Life and Times of the Toronto Maple Leafs*. Toronto: McClelland & Stewart Inc., 1990.

Nagler, Barney *James Norris and the Decline of Boxing*. New York: The Bobbs-Merrill Company Inc., 1964.

Patterson, Gerry. *Behind the Superstars: The Business Side of Sports*. Toronto: Prentice-Hall of Canada Ltd., 1978.

The Study Committee on Hockey of the National Advisory Council on Fitness and Amateur Sport. *Report on Amateur Hockey in Canada*. Ottawa: Government of Canada, 1967

Young, Scott. *The Boys of Saturday Night* Toronto: Macmillan of Canada, 1990.

All quotes not referenced in the endnotes come from personal interviews.

Endnotes

Chapter One:
For the Good of the Game

P. 8: *"I'd always had an agreement"*: Colleen and Gordie Howe and Charles Wilkins, *After the Applause* (Toronto: McClelland & Stewart, 1989), p. 195.

P. 9: *"I hope that makes Colleen happy"*: *After the Applause*, p. 196.

P 12: *"I've always wondered where"*: Frank Orr, "Phil Esposito: 'I wouldn't want to do it again,'" Toronto *Star*, September 2, 1982.

P 12: *"The current collective agreement indicates"*: Mark Zigler to Carl Brewer, *Preliminary Report—National Hockey League Club Pension Plan*, September 27, 1990.

P 13: *"All-Star game proceeds"*: Ken Sawyer to Mark Zigler, October 23, 1990.

P 15: *"While playing hockey the players"*: Gerald Eskenazi, *A Thinking Man's Guide to Pro Hockey*, (New York: E.P. Dutton & Co. Inc., 1972), p. 163.

P 18: *"the financial statements of the NHLPA"*: R. Alan Eagleson, "Memo to: All Retired Players of the NHL," December 10, 1990.

P 18: *"Dave! Forbsie! Hey, what's this"*: David Forbes to Carl Brewer, December 14, 1990. Includes entire interchange.

P 21: *"Gordie Howe has told me"*: "Alumni players suing NHL over pension plan," Vancouver *Sun*, January 21, 1991

P 22: *"No matter who we have gone to"*: David S. Forbes to John A. Ziegler, Jr., January 21, 1991

P 22: *"You have joined your colleague Mr Brewer"*: John A. Ziegler, Jr. to David S. Forbes, January 22, 1991

P. 25: *"In round figures"*: Jack Saunders, "NHL pensioners sue for millions," Toronto *Sun*, May 1, 1991.

Chapter Two:
One Man Rule

P. 31: *"Don't get us wrong, Elmer"*: Brian McFarlane, *The Story of the National Hockey League* (New York: Charles Scribner's Sons, 1973), p. 26.

P. 32: *"put another team in Chicago"*: "Clash of Rich Men's Wills Lies Behind Red Wings Rise to Hockey Leadership," Detroit *Free Press*, January 29, 1933.

P. 34: *"He seldom speaks to his players"*: "Clash of Rich Men's Wills Lies Behind Red Wings Rise to Hockey Leadership."

P. 37: *"You own Schmeling"*: "Jim Norris' Common Sense Aids Title Fight Impasse," New York *Times*, August 23, 1936.

P. 37: *"You're a disgrace!"*: "Norris Sr. and Stewart Aftermath Due at Meeting," Chicago *Tribune*, December 5, 1939.

P. 41: *"Operating on his own"*: Conn Smythe with Scott Young, *Conn Smythe: If You Can't Beat 'Em in the Alley* (Toronto: McClelland & Stewart, 1982), p. 192.

P. 42: *"National Hockey League chief executives"*: *Sports Illustrated*, October 28, 1957.

P. 43: *"was to call his father"*: "The New 'Mr. Big' of Boxing," Marshall Smith, *Life*, October 15, 1951.

P. 45: *"a tall, slender, bespectacled man"*: Barney Nagler, *James Norris and the Decline of Boxing* (New York: Bobbs-Merrill Co. Inc., 1964), p. 64.

P. 46: *"his personable giant of a son"*: "Clash of Rich Men's Wills Lies Behind Red Wings Rise to Hockey Leadership."

P. 48: *"Mr Norris pretty quickly realized"*: Chicago *Sun-Times*, July 7, 1983.

P. 49: *"Each time I made a match"*: Teddy Brenner with Barney Nagler, *Only the Ring was Square* (New Jersey: Prentice Hall Inc., 1981), pp. 36-37.

P. 50: *"more control over boxing than"*: Marshall Smith, "The New 'Mr. Big' of Boxing," October 15, 1951.

P. 50: *"It's rather like the diplomatic service"*: "Shy Head Directs Boxing's 'Octopus,'" *Associated Press*, April 11, 1954.

P. 51: *"I'd rather win a Stanley Cup"*: New York *Times*, February 12, 1964.

Chapter Three:
The Good Old Days

P. 54: *"on probation"*: Henry Roxborough, *The Stanley Cup Story* (Toronto: The Ryerson Press, 1964), p. 151.

P. 56: *"contracts of guaranteed figures"*: Detroit *Free Press*, October 11, 1938.

P. 57: *"Jack Adams was, in the parlance"*: Ed Fitkin, "Jack Adams, A Great Guy," *Maple Leaf Gardens Official Programme and Sports Magazine*, February 9, 1966.

P. 58: *"sportswriters were very low paid"*: Conn Smythe with Scott Young, *Conn Smythe: If You Can't Beat 'Em in the Alley* (Toronto: McClelland & Stewart, 1982), p. 115.

P. 58: *"I mean . . . you're not giving our men money"*: *Conn Smythe: If You Can't Beat 'Em in the Alley*, p. 116.

P. 58: *"I thought there was no nicer guy"*: *Conn Smythe: If You Can't Beat 'Em in the Alley*, p. 137.

P. 60: *"a blood-red flash"*: *Look*, February 26, 1952.

P. 60: *"carried out on a board"*: *Look*, February 26, 1952.

P. 61: *"Hockey's most spectacular bloodlettings"*: *Look*, February 26, 1952.

P. 62: *"She wasn't just a*

landlady": Detroit *News*, October 17, 1966.

P. 63: *"He said to me one day"*: "Jack Adams, A Great Guy."

P. 64: *"When I signed Gordie Howe the other day"*: Scott Young, "Detroit GM Sees Barry Cullen as Possible Asset," *The Hockey News*, September, 1959.

P. 64: *"We had four children to support"*: Colleen and Gordie Howe and Charles Wilkins, *After the Applause* (Toronto: McClelland & Stewart, 1989), p. 195.

P. 65: *"I do not know who owns the club"*: *Globe and Mail*, February 21, 1951.

P. 66: *"The reference to the ownership"*: Clarence Campbell to Conn Smythe, February 23, 1951, Smythe Papers.

P. 66: *"I have several times asked you"*: Conn Smythe to Clarence Campbell, February 26, 1951, Smythe Papers.

P. 66: *"in the best interests of the NHL"*: Ian S. Johnston to Clarence Campbell, June 26, 1951, Smythe Papers.

P. 67: *"make a proper investigation"*: Conn Smythe to Clarence Campbell, April 10, 1951, Smythe Papers.

P. 67: *"Up to the present it has been"*: Conn Smythe to Clarence Campbell, August 2, 1951, Smythe Papers.

P. 67: *"I do not know what prompted"*: Clarence Campbell to Conn Smythe, August 7, 1951, Smythe Papers.

P. 68: *"The handsome young Amazon"*: "Gold Mine in Red Wings' New President Margie," Detroit *News*, December 16, 1952.

P. 68: *"When I kept calling her"*: "Gold Mine in Red Wings' New President Margie."

P. 69: *"I'm a dishwater blond"*: "Margie Norris on Her Way," Chicago *Tribune*, December 15, 1952.

P. 70: *"I didn't know Jim was"*: "Hockey Shock: Olympia's Future," Detroit *News*, April 6, 1953.

P 71: *"I was forced to divorce myself"*: "Hockey Shock: Olympia's Future."

P 71: *"Someone had to come up with"*: "Hockey Shock: Olympia's Future."

P 71: *"It is not necessarily"*: "Marge 'Considers' Sole Wing Control," Chicago *Sun-Times*, April 16, 1953.

P 75: *"I think he's so much in love"* Look, February 26, 1952.

P 75: *"Gordie's awfully nice"*: "Big Date Saturday," Detroit *News*, April 30, 1952.

P 77 *"Shifting the responsibility"*: John Walter, "Lindsay out as Captain," Detroit *News*, September 9, 1956.

Chapter Four:
Lindsay's Dream

P 78: *"football, baseball, softball, hockey"*: National Hockey League Standard Player's Contract, 1957

P 79: *"in any and all promotional activities"*: National Hockey League Standard Player's Contract, 1957

P 79: *"without the written consent"*: National Hockey League Standard Player's Contract, 1957

P 80: *"at a period not more than"*: National Hockey League Standard Player's Contract, 1957

P 80: *"If he can fuckin walk"*: Trent Frayne, *The Mad Men of Hockey* (New York: Dodd, Mead and Company, 1974), p. 19.

P 88: *"Even businessmen's clubs in Florida"*: James A. Bouchard, "Ice TV Brings Problems," November 1, 1957

P 89: *"Boy! When they gang up"*: Tom Fox, "New Orleans to See Tin Can Hockey Boom," Toronto *Star*, January 7, 1957

P 89: *"If we begin operating a union"*: James B. Dworkin, *Owners versus Players: Baseball and Collective Bargaining* (Boston: Auburn House Publishing Company, 1981), p. 28.

P. 92: *"The association will be news"*: "NHL Players' Association Formed, Wings' Ted Lindsay Is President," New York *Times*, February 12, 1957.

P. 93: *"I'm completely surprised"*: "NHL Players' Association Formed, Wings' Ted Lindsay Is President," New York *Times*, February 12, 1957.

P. 94: *"Lindsay has averaged"*: John Walter, "Lindsay on the Block—Adams," Detroit *News*, April 21, 1957.

P. 95: *"The truth is I never"*: Conn Smythe with Scott Young, *Conn Smythe: If You Can't Beat 'Em in the Alley*, (Toronto: McClelland & Stewart, 1982) p. 12.

P. 95: *"utterly charming man"*: *The Mad Men of Hockey*, p. 151.

P. 95: *"What to you want to be paid"*: *Conn Smythe: If You Can't Beat 'Em in the Alley*, p. 101

P. 96: *"We cannot tell you"*: Maple Leaf Gardens prospectus 1931, Smythe Papers.

P. 97: *"They'll be sorry if"*: "Player Suit May Extend Into AHL," New York *Mirror*, March 11, 1957.

P. 97: *"As I told you before"*: Clarence Campbell to Jack Adams, November 22, 1957, Smythe Papers.

P. 98: *"I find it very difficult"*: Transcript, Conn Smythe Press Conference, Commodore Hotel, New York, Mar 17, 1957, Smythe Papers.

P. 98: *"Whoever signs my men"*: Transcript, Conn Smythe Press Conference, Commodore Hotel, New York, Mar 17, 1957, Smythe Papers.

P. 99: *"My legs have just"*: Conn Smythe: If You Can't Beat 'Em in the Alley, p. 202.

P. 99: *"As far as I was concerned"*: Conn Smythe: If You Can't Beat 'Em in the Alley, p. 202.

P. 99: *"I think they should be"*: Rex MacLeod, "Players' Association As Bargaining Agent Hinges on Balloting," *Globe and Mail*, November 5, 1957.

P. 99: *"Any resemblance between"*: Conn Smythe to Milton Mound, April 8, 1957, Smythe Papers.

P. 99: *"Let Mound talk and say"*: Ian S. Johnston to Conn Smythe, May 31, 1957, Smythe Papers.

P. 99: *"Rank impertinence"*: Ian S. Johnston to Conn Smythe, May 31, 1957, Smythe Papers.

P. 100: *"to call your attention"*: Ted Lindsay to CBC and CBS, September 30, 1957, Smythe Papers.

P. 101: *"I wanted to close my"*: John Walter, "Lindsay 'Disloyal' Adams Snaps Back," Detroit *News*, July 25, 1957.

P 102: *"There is no place"*: "Lindsay 'Disloyal' Adams Snaps Back."

P 102: *"I didn't want anyone telling us"*: Conn Smythe: If You Can't Beat 'Em in the Alley, p. 208.

P 104: *"It may come as a surprise"*: Toronto Star, September 13, 1952.

P 104: *"the good of the sport and the benefit"*: Ted Lindsay to Clarence Campbell, March 4, 1957, Smythe Papers.

P 105: *"a smokescreen to enable"*: Transcript, Conn Smythe Press Conference, September 25, 1957, Smythe Papers.

P 105: *"I cannot believe that"*: Transcript, Conn Smythe Press Conference.

P 105: *"monopolized and obtained complete"*: "Group Sues NHL," Globe and Mail, October 11, 1957

P 107: *"certify that we the"*: "Leafs Blanked in First Joust With Player Association," Toronto Daily Star, Nov 6, 1957

P 108: *"I see you finally made"*: Lewis H. Walter, "Why Lindsay Was Traded," New York Times, November 8, 1957

P 110: *"I understand that [Jimmy]"*: Ian S. Johnston to Conn Smythe, January 16, 1958.

P 111 *"In fairness to our owners"*: "Hockey Group Survives," Boston Globe, February 6, 1958.

P 111 *"They told us they weren't"*: Leonard Schecter, New York Post, February 6, 1958.

Chapter Five:
The Lost Years

P 114: *"It must be obvious"*: William Leggett, "In New York, hockey's house is not a home," Sports Illustrated, March 8, 1965.

P 115: *"like a man who has"*: "In New York, hockey's house is not a home."

P 115: *"Weston has been at me"*: Stafford Smythe to Conn Smythe, February, 1965, Smythe Papers.

P 119: *"A very amicable discussion"*: NHL Owner-Player Council Minutes, October 4, 1958.

P 119: *"that the President of the League"*: NHL Owner-Player Council Minutes, October 4, 1963.

P 121: *"either start playing the game"*: Hartland de M. Molson to Walter A. Brown, March 23, 1963, Molson Papers.

P 122: *"That's the way hockey should"*: Globe and Mail, April 4, 1964.

P 122: *"Our goal is a national"*: "NHL Image Building Chore Means Assault on All Media,"

Detroit *News*, December 20, 1964.

P 122: *"Hockey has been looked on"*: "NHL Image Building Chore Means Assault on All Media," Detroit *News*, December 20, 1964.

P 123: *"I intend to stay"*: Jesse Abramson, "Norris 'Won't Quit Boxing,'" Detroit *News*, June 25, 1957

P 123: *"I'm sorry I ever"*: "Norris Ends His Boxing Connection," Chicago *Tribune*, September 28, 1960.

P 123: *"I like boxing"*: Red Smith, "Norris Tells His Side of Ring Story," New York *Herald Tribune*, September 26, 1966.

P 124: *"There was a great charm about"*: Doc Greene, "Press Box," New York *Post*, September 29, 1950.

P 127: *"It's a black day"*: Jim Hunt, "The triumphant return of truculent Ted Lindsay," *Canadian Weekly*, January 14, 1965.

P 128: *"The little SOB beat us"*: Jack Batten, "The Return of Hockey's Proudest Warrior," *Maclean's*, January 23, 1965.

P 133: *"Right now we're a pretty"*: Marvin Moss, "Cities aren't ready: Big Season Forecast by Campbell, *Canadian Press*, March 6, 1963.

P 133: *"Increasing the league*

doesn't": Jack Olsen, "Private Game: No Admittance!" *Sports Illustrated*, February 11, 1965.

P 133: *"You can't schedule Montreal"*: "Private Game: No Admittance!"

P 134: *"No definite time limit"*: "NHL Moves to Expand to Second Six-Team Division," London *Free Press*, March 12, 1965.

P 135: *"They'd have to do it with"*: Larry Fox, "The West Coast Is Getting Ready For Big League Hockey," *Hockey Illustrated*.

P 136: *"I haven't met with"*: Dink Carroll, "NHL Expansion Discussed," Montreal *Gazette*, March 12, 1965.

P 136: *"We don't want any"*: Red MacLeod, "L.A. and St. Louis Acceptable to NHL," *Globe and Mail*, March 3, 1966.

P 137: *"The formula has not been"*: Red MacLeod, "L.A. and St. Louis Acceptable to NHL," *Globe and Mail*, March 3, 1966.

P 137: *"I'm not a policy-maker"*: "Five and dime heirs make bold NHL franchise bid," New York *Post*, February 8, 1966.

P 137: *"The governors feel each"*: Red Burnett, "Expansion key is 'When'?" Toronto *Daily Star*, June 10, 1965.

P 138: *"unlikely the franchise was"*: Al Laney, "NHL: Adding

Six-Team Division for '67," New York *Herald Tribune*, February 10, 1966.

P. 139: *"St. Louis is an attractive"*: "Five and dime heirs make bold NHL franchise bid."

P. 139: *"There was no real head"*: Elmer Ferguson, "Only U.S. Can Support Expanded NHL," February 19, 1966.

P. 140: *"The new teams will be weaker"*: Dink Carroll, "The NHL's Expansion," Montreal *Gazette*, December 15, 1966.

P. 140: *"We have our own interests"*: "NHL operators show reluctance, call expansion draft 'forced sale,'" New York *Post*, June 4, 1966.

P. 140: *"What we really need"*: Dick Beddoes, "Governors or NHL tight-lipped about distribution of players," May, 1966.

Chapter Six:
The Young Lions

P. 142: *"I sat up in my private box"*: Conn Smythe with Scott Young, *Conn Smythe: If You Can't Beat 'Em in the Alley* (Toronto: McClelland & Stewart, 1982), p. 211.

P. 144: *"one of the young Leaf players"*: Billy Harris, *The Glory Years: Memories of a Decade, 1955-1965* (Toronto: Prentice-Hall Canada, 1989), p. 54.

P. 146: *"In the space of two*

seconds": Scott Young, in *The Leafs: The First 50 Years*, ed. Stan Obodiac (Toronto: McClelland and Stewart, 1977), p. 65.

P. 146: *"an emotional high strung"*: George Imlach with Scott Young, *Hockey Is A Battle* (Toronto: Macmillan of Canada, 1969), p. 119.

P. 152: *"When I grow up"*: John Papanek and Bill Brubaker, "The Man who Rules Hockey," *Sports Illustrated*, July 2, 1984.

P. 153: *"He was just like"*: Deidra Clayton, *Eagle: The Life and Times of R. Alan Eagleson* (Toronto: Lester & Orpen Dennys, 1982), p. 24.

P. 153: *"Lawyers around New Toronto"*: "Alan Eagleson," *Today*, March 7, 1981

P 153: *"Don't try that again"*: "Alan Eagleson."

P 154: *"If the rest of his class"*: *Eagle: The Life and Times of R. Alan Eagleson*, p. 26.

P 154: *"He was a regular little"*: *Eagle: The Life and Times of R. Alan Eagleson*, p. 28.

P 154: *"When I got to U of T"*: "Alan Eagleson."

P 164: *"My relations with Mr Campbell"*: Leo Monahan, "Legal Eagle Eagleson Helping Hockey Players Win Pay Hikes," *Sporting News*, November 2, 1967

P 165: *"Any one of those moves"*:

Ron Base, "Yes, but could Canada stand a prime mover as Prime Minister," The *Sunday Sun*, August 17, 1975.

Chapter Seven: Slaying the Dragon

P 166: *"It's nice to know that"*: John Lardner, "One Quick Boo for Shore," *Newsweek*, Nov 13, 1939.

P 169: *"What kind of anaesthetic"*: Red Smith, "Eddie Shore—the toughest of them all," *News & Chronicle*, December 23, 1965.

P 169: *"A fanatic, almost psychopathic"*: Ed Fitzgerald, "Eddie Shore: 'Old Blood and Guts' of Hockey," *Sport*, February, 1950.

P 170: *"My memories of Shore"*: Jimmy Powers, "The Powerhouse," New York *Daily News*, February 7, 1962.

P 170: *"Bailey went down hard"*: "Eddie Shore: 'Old Blood and Guts' of Hockey "

P 171 *"That's the style of hockey"*: "Eddie Shore: 'Old Blood and Guts' of Hockey "

P 171 *"He never missed an opportunity"*: "Eddie Shore: 'Old Blood and Guts' of Hockey "

P 173: *"You see, here is the way"*: Ken McConnell, "Eddie Shore Is Holdout, Demands $2,500 More Pay; Is Suspended by N.H.L.," Edmonton *Journal*, November 3, 1933.

P 174: *"Where do the Bruins"*: "Eddie Shore: 'Old Blood and Guts' of Hockey "

P 175: *"Shore has a heavy"*: "Eddie Shore: 'Old Blood and Guts' of Hockey "

P 175: *"He shone more brightly"*: Al Silverman, "Old Blood and Guts," *Sport*, February, 1959.

P 178: *"the richest man to come"*: James W Bagley, "Shore Gains Ice Riches," Boston *Record*, March 25, 1947

P 180: *"If you fell down"*: Brian Smith, "The iron hand of the legendary Eddie Shore," *Canadian Oldtimers' Hockey Association Journal*, November/December, 1984.

P 181 *"Mr Schinkel   Please return"*: Don Cherry with Stan Fischler, *Grapes: A Vintage View of Hockey* (Toronto: Prentice-Hall Canada, Inc., 1983), p. 110.

P 182: *"Gee Barclay, is that right"*: *Grapes: A Vintage View of Hockey*, p. 117-118.

P 183: *"The club is not doing"*: *Grapes: A Vintage View of Hockey*, p. 118.

P 184: *"When I left Springfield"*: David Dunbar, "The Farm Boy Who Became 'Old Blood and Guts,'" *Hockey*, January, 1979.

P 185: *"Mister Smith, come down to the rink"*: "The iron hand of the legendary Eddie Shore."

P. 187: *"When I first arrived in Springfield"*, *Sports Illustrated*, October 17, 1977

P 187: *"When you hear one Shore story"*: Trent Frayne, *The Mad Men of Hockey* (New York: Dodd, Mead and Company, 1974), p. 186.

P 188: *"They weren't on strike yet"*: Deidra Clayton, *Eagle: The Life and Times of R. Alan Eagleson* (Toronto: Lester & Orpen Dennys, 1982), p. 60.

P. 191: *"It's incredible"*: Stan Fischler, "Shore Inspired Hatred and Devotion," *The Sporting News*, March 21, 1970.

P 191: *"I ended up negotiating"*: *Eagle: The Life and Times of R. Alan Eagleson*, p. 62.

Chapter Eight:
The Young Lions

P. 193: *"There were players in the NHL"*: Bobby Orr with Mark Mulvoy, *Bobby Orr: My Game* (Boston: Little, Brown and Company, 1974), p. 24.

P. 194: *"We wouldn't trade Bobby Orr"*: Bobby Orr with Mark Mulvoy, *Bobby Orr: My Game* (Boston: Little, Brown and Company, 1974), p. 31

P 195: *"For a moment I thought"*: Bobby Orr with Mark Mulvoy, *Bobby Orr: My Game* (Boston: Little, Brown and Company, 1974), p. 34.

P 196: *"Six naked hockey players walked"*: Rick Heinz, *Many Are Called   Few Are Signed: The Hard Realities of Professional Hockey* (Toronto: Heinz Publishing, 1988), p. 100.

P 197: *"the greatest player ever"*: *Sports Illustrated*, March 30, 1971

P 198: *"the best pension plan"*: Anita Latner, "Eagleson: He wheels and deals in pine, too," Toronto *Star*, December 6, 1976.

P. 199: *"I obviously have a lot"*: Deidra Clayton, "The Eagle: He's uncompromising and maybe guilty of arrogance but his connections open any door," *Financial Times*, May 15, 1978.

P 200: *"Orr lives very well"*: Ron Base, "Yes, but could Canada stand a prime mover as Prime Minister?" The *Sunday Sun*, August 17, 1975.

P. 202: *"Bobby Orr Enterprises was worth"*: Wayne Parrish, "'Bobby Orr Owes me an Apology,'" Toronto *Sun*, September 9, 1990.

P. 202: *"I suppose either of us"*: Tim Burke, 'Scarred but victorious from hockey wars, Eagleson out to harness 'player power,'" Montreal *Gazette*, January 6, 1973.

P 206: *"Eagleson   is in the forefront"*: "Hockey Players' Best Friend Is Attorney," Boston *Globe*, March 5, 1967

P 206: *"The players need an association"*: "Hockey Players' Best Friend Is Attorney "

P 207: *"I don't like unions"*: Deidra Clayton, *Eagle: The Life and Times of R. Alan Eagleson* (Toronto: Lester & Orpen Dennys, 1982), p. 63.

P. 208: *"I have been directed to tell you"*: Dick Beddoes, "NHL bears union label," Toronto *Star*, June 8, 1967

P 208: *"There was no ultimatum"*: Bill Brennan, "NHL Recognizes Player Organization," Detroit *News*, June 8, 1967

P. 215: *"We can't carry on"*: "NHL not happy with CAHA's problems," Toronto *Star*, October 31, 1970.

P. 221: *"The guy works for me"*: "The Man Who Rules Hockey," *Sports Illustrated*, July 2, 1984.

P. 224: *"I was forty-two"*: *Eagle: The Life and Times of R. Alan Eagleson*, p. 162-163.

Chapter Nine:
Merchants of Promise

P. 231: *"The situation is so drastic"*: Montreal *Gazette*, June 2, 1974.

P. 232: *"natural and good business"*: Don Ramsay, "Hockey agents ante up to represent players," Toronto *Sun*, June 3, 1975.

P. 232: *"and if anything went*

wrong": Tiger Williams with James Lawton, *Tiger: A Hockey Story* (Toronto: Seal Books, 1984), p. 68.

P 233: *"[Sorkin] arrived in Swift Current"*: *Tiger: A Hockey Story*, p. 67-68.

P 233: *"I became totally obsessed"*: Stan Fischler, *Off Side: Hockey From the Inside* (Agincourt, Ontario: Methuen, 1985), p. 187

P 233: *"I never bet on hockey"*: *Off Side: Hockey From the Inside*, p. 186.

P 238: *"He's the only guy I ever"*: Kevin Boland, "It's thorny in The Eagle's Nest," The Sunday *Star*, May 11, 1980.

P. 239: *"It was unbelievable"*: William Houston, "The czar of hockey," *Globe and Mail*, February 7, 1987

P 240: *"It's impossible to get"*: "2 Agents Split Draft Bounty," *Sports Inc.*, June 20, 1988.

Chapter Ten:
No Pain No Gain

P 255: *"His shadow eclipses those"*: John Papanek and Bill Brubaker, "The Man Who Rules Hockey," *Sports Illustrated*, July 2, 1984.

P 257: *"certain other matters"*: NHLPA press release, Hockey Hall of Fame, June 8, 1967

P 259: *"My family is very*

important": George Gross, "Alan Eagleson steps down as voice for the players," Toronto *Telegram*, January 18, 1971.

P. 260: *"The other sports associations"*: R. Alan Eagleson, "Memo to All Members of the N.H.L.P.A." March 13, 1989.

P. 263: *"He embarrassed me"*: "The Man Who Rules Hockey."

P. 264: *"How can Eagleson arbitrate"*: Stan Fischler, "Eagleson as an NHL salary arbiter? Never, vows a competitor," Toronto *Star*, September 16, 1970.

P. 264: *"My decision was made"*: Toronto *Star*, January 17, 1971.

P. 265: *"I've offered to resign"*: Red Fisher, "NHL Needs United Front," Montreal *Gazette*, September 20, 1975.

P. 266: *"There's not enough in it"*: "Working for Bobby Orr enough for Alan Eagleson: Other players not needed," Toronto *Star*, October 6, 1972.

P. 265: *"For openers, I'm just not"*: Jim Kearney, Vancouver *Sun*, March 1972.

P. 265: *"Not as president"*: Bill Brennan, "Soviet Series a New Plum for the Eagle," Detroit *News*, March 17, 1972.

P. 266: *"the co-operation of the"*: Minutes of NHLPA Player and Player/Owner All Star Meeting, February 3 & 4, 1986.

P. 269: *"I'm not as bullish"*: Dan Stoneking, "Eagleson Taking Dim View of WHA Future," *Sporting News*, February 12, 1972.

P. 269: *"The best thing that happened"*: Globe and Mail, March 7, 1973.

P. 269: *"I'm reluctant to even talk"*: Globe and Mail, November 7, 1975.

P. 270: *"a bald and concerted act"*: Herbert G. Schoepke to Charles L Whittinghill, U.S. Department of Justice memo, July 20, 1968.

P. 270: *"Canadian authorities have been"*: Robert McLaren, U.S. Department of Justice memo, January 17, 1972.

P. 270: *"Entry by a new league"*: Norman H. Seidler, U.S. Department of Justice, Anti-trust Division memo, October 22, 1971.

P. 275: *"Affluence has taken over"*: Peter Gammons, "A Matter Of Dollars And Sense," *Sports Illustrated*, December 12, 1976.

P. 276: *"There is one man"*: Jim Vipond, "Let's hear it for The Eagle," *Globe and Mail*, January 20, 1976.

P. 276: *"They've tried to draft me"*: "NHL post not for Eagleson," Vancouver *Sun*, January 8, 1977

P. 276: *"I shudder to think"*: Bob

Fowler, "Campbell endorses Eagleson," Minneapolis *Star*, May 10, 1977.

P. 276: "*Quite frankly, I wasn't*": "He wasn't sure of his authority, but . . . Moved on Barons quickly," Montreal *Gazette*, February 25, 1977.

P. 277: "*I have to believe*": "He wasn't sure of his authority, but Moved on Barons quickly."

P. 277: "*We did it once*": James Christie, "NHL players won't bail out troubled team again," *Globe and Mail*, June 3, 1977

P. 278: "*They need a benevolent*": James Christie, *Globe and Mail*, June 2, 1977.

P. 278: "*We did not appreciate*": "Foul Cry Hockey Bosses," *Globe and Mail*, June 4, 1977

P 279: "*I'm not totally optimistic*": "Eagleson threatens strike," Vancouver *Sun*, May 10, 1979.

P. 279: "*The owners are calling the merger*": Detroit *Free Press*, May 30, 1979.

P. 280: "*Since January 1975, I've had*": James Christie, "Tired of the woes, Eagleson quits Hockey Canada post," *Globe and Mail*, January 27, 1978.

P. 281: "*Thanks to the National Hockey League*": "Eagleson tosses in towel, quitting Hockey Canada," Vancouver *Sun*, January 27, 1978.

P. 281: "*Norman Caplan has more or less*": Donald Ramsay, "NHL merger," *Globe and Mail*, June 2, 1979.

P. 283: "*In principle the [merger] deal*": John Papanek and Bill Brubaker, "The Man Who Rules Hockey," *Sports Illustrated*, July 2, 1984.

P 283: "*I wanted to find out*": "The Man Who Rules Hockey."

P. 284: "*The only way you can pass on*": Sheldon M. Gallner, *Pro Sports: the Contract Game*" (New York: Charles Scribner's Sons, 1974), p. 154.

P 285: "*I was like his puppet*": "The Man Who Rules Hockey "

P 285: "*they felt our position was sound*": R. Alan Eagleson, "Memo to All N.H.L. Players Association Members," July 20, 1979.

P 285: "*It was decided among*": R. Alan Eagleson, "Memo to All N.H.L. Players Association Members," July 20, 1979.

P 285: "*They were prepared to pursue*": R. Alan Eagleson, "Memo to All N.H.L. Players Association Members," July 20, 1979.

P 286: "*The elimination of the WHA*": Dan Stoneking, "Will WHA's end burn contract bridges?" Toronto *Star*, August 17, 1979.

Chapter Eleven:
Resignation No Longer On File

P. 288: "*I think the association*": *Globe and Mail*, June 7, 1979.

P. 288: "*What they settled for*": "Eagleson's Settlement Draws Fire From Players," Vancouver *Sun*, July 7, 1979.

P. 288: "*It was a process of*": Vancouver *Sun*, July 3, 1979.

P. 289: "*why the NHLPA hadn't negotiated*": Players/Owner Meetings, Minutes, August 6 & 7, 1979.

P. 290: "*The last thing I want*": "Bruins agree on move to replace Eagle," *Globe and Mail*, November 8, 1979.

P. 291: "*I didn't want Al to*": "Bruins want to dump Eagleson," Toronto *Star*, January 8, 1980.

P. 291: "*I'm always ready for a fight*": "Eagle to follow players' will," *Globe and Mail*, Jan. 9, 1980.

P. 291: "*What constitution?*": "Bruins ballot bothers Eagleson," Vancouver *Sun*, January 18, 1979.

P 291: "*a total 100 percent endorsement*": "Despite poll, NHL association retains Eagleson as its head," Chicago *Tribune*, February 5, 1980.

P. 291: "*The only people whom I have*": "Despite poll, NHL association retains Eagleson as its head."

P. 292: "*We had to make a quick decision*": Vartan Kupelian, "Eagleson supported, sees players strike," Detroit *News*, February 5, 1980.

P. 292: "*There will be much more*": "Owners must play $10.5 million," Associated Press, Sept. 18, 1990.

P. 293: "*I've emphasized to the players*": "NHL strike is 'unlikely' when contract expires," Vancouver *Sun*, February 12, 1982.

P. 293: "*Sure it's a great contract*": "The Man Who Rules Hockey."

P. 295: "*Mr. Eagleson's position is that*": Draft Proposal, May 1985, p. 8-9.

P. 295: "*That way we could best*": Herb Pinder, Jr., to Brian Burke, December 2, 1985.

P. 296: "*Their presentation was reasonable*": Al Strachan, "Eagleson: NHL strike threat growing," *Globe and Mail*, January 22, 1986.

P. 296: "*I think most would agree*": Memo to Wayne Gretzky from Herb Pinder, Jr., Re: New collective-bargaining agreement, July 11, 1986.

P. 297: "*I am committed to the players*": Al Strachan, "NHLPA locks up Eagleson as executive director," *Globe and Mail*,

Wednesday, June 11, 1986.

P. 297: *"If you don't indicate that you"*: Al Strachan, *Globe and Mail*, Feb. 13, 1985.

P. 297: *"Mr. Bill Wirtz, the Chicago owner"*: Executive Player/Owner Meetings, Minutes, June 9-12, 1986.

P 297: *"I don't believe in"*: *The Hockey News*, December 5, 1980.

P. 299: *"they had the complete right"*: R. Alan Eagleson, "Memo to All Retired Players of the NHL," December 10, 1990.

P. 299: *"additional pension benefits"*: National Hockey League Club Pension Plan And Trust, February 20, 1967

P 299: *"reduce Member Club contributions"*: First Amendment to the National Hockey League Club Pension Plan and Trust, December 9, 1983.

P 305: *"Every four or five years"*: Lance Hornby, "Eagle fires salvo in agent wars," Edmonton *Sun*, March 31, 1989.

P 305: *"When [injured player] Glen Sharpley"*: Ron Salcer and Rich Winter, ARPA NHLPA Position Paper, November 11, 1988.

P 306: *"those who have asked"* *Player's Voice*, Vol. 1, No. 1

P 307: *"change the direction of the NHLPA"*: *Player's Voice*, Vol. 1, No. 2.

P. 307: *"half-truths and untruths"*: R. Alan Eagleson, "Memo to All Members of the NHLPA and NHLPA Executive Committee," March 13, 1989.

P. 307: *"He seems to win every faceoff"*: Jim Smith, "Eye on The Eagle," *Newsday*, February 7, 1989.

P. 308: *"With the lowest average salary"*: *Player's Voice*, Vol. 1, 1989.

P. 309: *"If anyone in hockey ever"*: Red Fisher, "NHL Needs United Front," Montreal *Gazette*, Sept. 20, 1975.

P. 311: *"It seems every five years"*: Lance Hornby, "Eagle fires salvo in agent wars," Edmonton *Sun*, March 31, 1989.

P 313: *"something of a holiday"*: Detroit *News*, May 30, 1979.

P 316: *"the use of funds over"* William P Dermody, "Preliminary Review of Certain Legal and Operational Aspects of the National Hockey League Players' Association," June 1, 1989.

P 316: *"no commissions or fees have been charged"*: *Goals*, Vol. 1, No. 1, 1989.

P 316: *"for legal services performed"* William P Dermody to Ed Garvey, August 10, 1989.

Chapter Twelve:
Bucks, Pucks and the Million Dollar Boy

P. 320: "*Ziggy and Iggy as they are sometimes called*": Al Strachan, "Ziegler's golf-cart buddy should get president's job," July 12, 1989.

P. 321: "*The NHLPA was always willing*": NHLPA Player and Player/Owner All-Star Meeting, Minutes, February 3 & 4, 1986.

P. 323: "*personality transplant*": Al Strachan, "President's presence is requested for Stanley Cup playoffs," *Globe and Mail*, April 28, 1990.

P 328: "*I have been made for power*" "*Quebec Nordiques: The team that Marcel built,*" Montreal *Gazette*, May 1, 1982.

P 328: "*It's open warfare now*" "Advantage shifting in hockey," Montreal *Gazette*, March 17, 1984.

P 330: "*Net, Net!   Vision for the 90's*": Steve Ryan, President NHL Services, Inc., "NHL Marketing—A Vision for the 90's."

P 334: "*There's no question*" "NHL salaries soaring since Gretzky trade," Toronto *Star*, December 24, 1989.

P 334: "*In the last six months*" "NHL salaries soaring thanks to Gretzky deal," Toronto *Star*, December 23, 1989.

P. 349: "*We had no choice*": Bill Montague, "Hounds get burned at OHL priority draft; Lindros not reporting," Sault *Star*, May 29, 1989.

P 349: "*No one person is bigger*": "Hounds get burned at OHL priority draft; Lindros not reporting."

P 353: "*As far as I'm concerned*": Neil Campbell, "Lindros hype reaches worry stage," *Globe and Mail*, March 7, 1990.

P 354: "*For him to be selling*": "Lindros hype reaches worry stage."

P 356: "*whether he likes it or not*": James Christie, "Aubut lays down the Lindros law," *Globe and Mail*, May 11, 1991

P 356: "*Hockey is a game*": Alan Adams, "A season of divine hype and statistics for Lindros" and "The business side of a junior star," Victoria *Times Colonist*, April 21, 1991

P 356: "*hatred, contempt and ridicule*": Al Strachan, "Litigation strictly minor-league during playoffs," *Globe and Mail*, May 16, 1991

P 357: "*because of the attack*" "NHL sues newspaper, Orr," *Globe and Mail*, May 14, 1991

Afterword:
"A Vision of the '90s"?

P 362: "*A Vision of the Nineties*":

"NHL Sets Goal To Seek Expansion To 28 Teams By The End Of The Century," National Hockey League News Release, December 9, 1989.

P. 363: *"The question now is"*: Helene Elliott, "Dealer's Choice," New York *Newsday*, May 25, 1989.

P. 367: *"You'd hate to have"*: Steve Dryden, "Lindros Ponders Anti-Trust Suits," *The Hockey News*, May 29, 1992.

P. 368: *"influential* BusinessWeek": "John Ziegler's Spectacular Save: The NHL," *BusinessWeek*, May 18, 1987.

P. 369: *"My understanding"*: David Shoalts, "Hull's $7-million Contract Rocks NHL Pay Structure", *Globe and Mail*, June 21, 1990.

P. 369: *"off the pension board"*: Alan Eagleson to Murray J. Elston, Chairman of Management Board of Cabinet, Ontario Ministry of Financial Institutions, August 1, 1989.

P. 370: *"I got back"*: David Shoalts, "Eagleson Goes out with a Whimper: FBI Investigation Looming over Head of Outgoing NHLPA Strongman," *Globe and Mail*, January 7, 1992.

P. 371: *"The association has been"*: David Shoalts, "Goodenow Brings New Style to NHL Job," *Globe and Mail*, February 3, 1990.

P. 375: *"We're not going to sign"*: Grant Kerr, "Quinn Bristles as Canucks Shaken from Dream Season," The Canadian Press, *Times-Colonist*, April 2, 1992.

P. 376: *"Ownership can't stand"*: "Hopes Fading as High Noon Deadline Near," The Canadian Press, *Times-Colonist*, April 1, 1992.

P. 377: *"I don't know"*: Damien Cox, "Leafs Vote to Strike," Toronto *Star*, April 1, 1992.

P. 379: *"They needed a scapegoat"*: "No Fanfare as Ziegler Era Ends with Statement Today," The Canadian Press, June 12, 1992.

Index